The Life Of George Mason, 1725-1792, Volume 2...

Kate Mason Rowland

THE
LIFE OF GEORGE MASON

1725-1792

BY

KATE MASON ROWLAND

INCLUDING HIS SPEECHES, PUBLIC PAPERS, AND CORRE-
SPONDENCE; WITH AN INTRODUCTION BY
GENERAL FITZHUGH LEE

VOLUME II

Thus show once more George Mason's iron face
(That friend to liberty ; to license, foe),
A man who *then* our coming fate did trace ;
Saw States diminish, central power grow—
But, happy, died before the crowning woe.

F. E. A.

G. P. PUTNAM'S SONS
NEW YORK   LONDON
27 WEST TWENTY-THIRD STREET   24 BEDFORD STREET, STRAND

The Knickerbocker Press
1892

Electrotyped, Printed, and Bound by
The Knickerbocker Press, New York
G. P. Putnam's Sons

CONTENTS OF VOL. II.

LIFE AND CORRESPONDENCE OF GEORGE MASON, OF VIRGINIA.

CHAPTER I.

IN PRIVATE LIFE.

1780–1782.

George Mason did not attend the fall session of the Assembly in 1780, as had been his design, and his temporary retirement from public life, which took place at this time, occurred, therefore, a little earlier than he had at first contemplated. In the letters of Joseph Jones, who was then in the Assembly, letters which have been recently published, there are several allusions to Colonel Mason. Jones wrote to Madison in October that he had been applied to both by Colonel Mason and Colonel Meade relative to the consulship for Spain, which they desired should be given to Mr. Harrison, George Mason's merchant friend in Martinique. It is satisfactory to know that this gentleman did get the appointment, some years later, after the adoption of the new Constitution. Joseph Jones wrote to Madison the 2d of December:

"Mr. Mason has not yet appeared, and I do not expect he will this session, as he has the remains upon him of a severe attack of the gout." [1]

[1] "Letters of Joseph Jones," p. 59. Department of State, 1889.

The project of the land cession had therefore to be carried through the Assembly without George Mason's personal assistance, and on the 2d of January, 1781, the act for this purpose was passed. But as two of its eight conditions were not satisfactory to Congress, the matter was not fully settled until some time later. Colonel Clark was in Virginia during this winter, and no doubt he visited his friend at "Gunston Hall" before leaving the State. Arnold's raid took place at this time, and Colonel Clark assisted in the defence of the James River. In the spring the Assembly, which met in March, was disturbed by the British and forced to adjourn from place to place. Colonel Mason, in his retirement at " Gunston," was keenly alive to the critical situation of the country, and though no longer in the councils of his State, he was revolving at home projects for the public good. And the fruit of some of his reflections appears in the following letter to the Virginia delegates in Congress:

*Letter to the Honorable the Virginia Delegates in Congress at Phila-
delphia, April 3, 1781.*

GENTLEMEN :

Permit me to recommend to your consideration a subject which I think merits the attention of Congress. The enemy is now professedly carrying on a predatory war against the United States contrary to the custom of civilized nations. A board of Refugees has been some time sitting in New York upon the subject of depredation and consulting upon the most effectual methods of plundering the defenceless part of the inhabitants of the American States in which they are avowedly authorized and supported by the British king and his generals. Several private people have lately been robbed, their houses burned and their estates ruined by the crews of British ships. Arnold is at this time preparing a great number of flat-bottomed boats at Portsmouth notoriously for the purpose of plundering the tobacco warehouses and the inhabitants upon the rivers and creeks in Virginia and Maryland. How practicable a plan of this sort is I need hardly mention to gentlemen acquainted with the situation of this country. What may be the fatal consequences not only of disabling many thousands from paying their taxes and contributing to the support of the common cause, but of throwing them also as a dead weight on the rest of the community, or how few of them may have public virtue enough to withstand the terrors of poverty and ruin are topics which, however disagreeable, deserve the most serious reflections that if possible the evil may be averted. Whether the king and his ministry encouraged by their success in Carolina expect by such means to make an easier conquest of the Southern States, or whether expecting the interference of the great powers of Europe to compel them to relinquish their claim to the American States, they are now acting upon the principles of revenge determined to desolate what they despair of recovering—be this as it may—it is surely the duty of the Great Council of America to endeavor if possible to prevent the mischief and save from ruin such numbers of their citizens. Whoever considers the importance of the trade of these States to Great Britain, and her expectations of great part of it returning into British channels, upon a peace, may readily conceive that she will be alarmed at any measures which must affect it hereafter by imposing such burdens upon it as will give a lasting preference to other nations. If therefore Congress were to recommend to the Legislatures of the different States immediately to enact laws, declaring that all private property which has been or shall be plundered or destroyed by the British troops or others acting under the authority of the King of Great Britain, beyond high-water mark, from a certain day shall be hereafter reimbursed and made good to the individual sufferers and their heirs by dutys to be imposed upon all imports from Great Britain into the respective States, after a peace and to be continued until full reparation shall be accordingly made, and for this purpose directing valuations upon oath to be made of all private property so plundered or destroyed, to be returned with the names and places of abode of the owners to some certain public office in each State and there duly registered, it is more than probable it would produce good effects. The fund is adequate to the purpose and the measure without conquest could not be counteracted. There is hardly a merchant or manufacturer in Great Britain who would not feel himself affected by it; if anything can restrain them this probably would. Their commanders here would immediately represent it to the ministry and inquire their further instructions and the nation would be cautious of repeating mischiefs which must one day reverberate upon themselves. If it had not this effect it at least would be a piece of justice to the injured to whom the community owes justice, if it cannot afford them protection. The only objection that occurs to me is the common maxim "that all dutys ultimately fall upon the consumer," and consequently that this would be a tax upon ourselves. If this were true I think it no good objection, because it would only be reimbursing by a voluntary tax one part of the community what they had suffered from their local circumstances more than the other without any fault of their own. But the maxim is not true with respect to dutys upon the imports of any particular country, while we are not confined to their market, but have an open trade with all the world, and therefore this charge would fall either upon the aggressing nation, or upon those who, disaffected to the American cause, were desirous of giving Great Britain an impolitic and undue preference. It would fall partly upon both. I got a bill passed a year or two ago in the Virginia House of Delegates but it was rejected in the Senate for no other reason that I could learn but that it was ruin for Virginia to make such a law unless similar measures were adopted by the other States. Should these hints be approved there is not a moment to be lost, and such a measure should not be intended merely *in terrorem*, but carried into the strictest execution.

There is another subject which deserves the public attention. I have always endeavored to make myself well acquainted with the sentiments of the bulk of the people, conscious that in governments like ours, upon this in a great measure must depend the success of the present contest. I live in a part of the country remarkable for its Whigism and attachment to the cause of liberty, and it is with much concern I find a general opinion prevailing that our allies are spinning out the war in order to weaken America as well as Great Britain and thereby leave us at the end of it as dependent as possible on themselves. However unjust this opinion may be, it is natural enough to planters and farmers burdened with heavy taxes and frequently dragged from their families by military duty in the continual alarms occasioned by the superiority of the British navy. They see their property daily exposed to destruction ; they see with what facility the British troops are removed from one part of the continent to another, and with what infinite charge and fatigue ours are too late obliged to follow. If our allies had a superior fleet here I should have very little doubt of a favorable issue to the war, but without it I fear we are deceiving both them and ourselves in expecting we shall be able to keep our people much longer firm in so unequal an opposition to Great Britain. Would it not be wise and honest to lay this matter candidly before them, and with decent firmness explain how much our mutual interest requires a fleet upon the American coast superior to that of our common enemy.

I have mentioned to you my thoughts upon these very interesting subjects, trusting that the motives upon which I act (the good of our country) will induce you to pardon such a liberty in a private gentleman and render any further apology unnecessary. Ill health hindering my attendance at Richmond upon the last session of the Assembly prevents my knowing which of the Virginia delegates are now in Congress, otherwise I should only have wrote to one or two of the members, instead of addressing myself to the delegates in a letter which from the superscription may appear to have the air of an official one.

I have the honor to be with the greatest respect, gentlemen,

Your most obedient servant,

G. MASON.

April 20.—P. S. Since the above letter was wrote, several of the enemy's ships have been within two or three miles of Alexandria ; they have burned and plundered several houses and carried off a great many slaves ; though I have hitherto been fortunate enough to lose no part of my property.[1]

The members of the Ohio Company proposed at this time to make another effort with the Virginia Assembly to secure their lands. Robert Carter of "Nomini" wrote to a friend, on this subject, April 14th :

"It is said that the House of Delegates rejected the Company's claim because their works of survey were returned by a surveyor

[1] Madison MSS., State Department.

[Hancock Lee] not legally appointed. Nevertheless that session established some officers' claims whose works of survey were returned by surveyors acting under no better authority than the surveyor appointed by the Ohio Company. It is expected that these cases will be relied on as precedents and the claims of the Ohio Company will be revived. This matter is of a joint concern, therefore the parties must join in presenting a petition which I apprehend should be done this approaching session, and I purpose to make some movement therein."

He accordingly wrote to Colonel Mason on the 11th of May, suggesting such action, and he adds. " If this idea should be approved on and a petition shall be prepared and presented, pray have my name inserted therein for two fortieth parts, I having purchased two shares of the late Mr. Augustine Washington and Mr. Gawin Corbin, members of the Ohio Company." [1]

The American troops, under Lafayette, Steuben, and Wayne, were in Virginia, in the spring of 1781, for the purpose of repelling the invasion of the enemy ; and an act of the Assembly, authorizing the seizure of cattle for the use of the army, to supply them with provisions, was put in operation, causing some dissatisfaction. George Mason thought that the commissioners were carrying out this law in a manner that would inflict needless injury on the people and alienate them from the cause of patriotism, and he wrote to Jefferson, then governor of the State, calling his attention to the matter.

FAIRFAX COUNTY, GUNSTON HALL,
May 14th, 1781.

SIR,

The order for seizing live cattle for the supply of the army is like to produce much confusion and oppression in this part of the country from the vague, and (as I apprehend) illegal instructions of Mr. Brown to his deputies, who are acting very differently in the different counties, according to each man's interpretation of instructions which no man understands. This, if not timely

[1] Carter Letter-Books.

prevented by clear and precise orders from the executive, will in many instances occasion lawsuits, and in some, most probably, violence. The instructions I have seen from Mr. Brown direct his deputies to take *a tenth part of every man's stock.* The true construction of this I take to be a tenth part of every man's stock, *in quantity and quality.* But it would be a wanton waste of cattle. In some counties they estimate the value of a man's whole stock, and take the tenth part *of that value*, in beef cattle. In other counties (particularly in this) the deputy commissary thinks himself authorized to take in *beef cattle* the tenth part of the *number* of each man's stock, which would generally be near *half of the value* of the whole. And as, upon the common average of stocks, there is not a tenth part of them beef cattle, if the measure was to be executed throughout the State in this manner, every family would be left without beef, tallow, or leather for the ensuing year; the quantity of cattle immediately taken would be enormous, not less, upon a moderate computation, I conceive than forty or fifty thousand beeves, and there would not be a beef left to supply the army another campaign. The only laws I know of upon which this power of seizure is founded are the two acts passed in the last May session, one " for procuring a supply of provisions and other necessaries for the army," empowering the governor and council to appoint commissioners for seizing certain enumerated articles at fixed prices, and the other " an act for giving further powers to the Governor and Council," extending the powers given by the former act to the obtaining so many live cattle as may be wanted for supplying the militia or other troops, to be valued and appraised by two disinterested persons upon oath &c; provided always that not more than *one half* of the bullocks and barren cows belonging to any person, fit for slaughter, shall be subject to such seizure. These two acts are continued by a subsequent session, with only an augmentation of the prices enumerated in the first act, occasioned by the depreciation of money in the meantime. But I think nothing is therein said about the price of live cattle, it being unnecessary as the price had not been ascertained by the former acts, and the cattle were to be appraised at the time of seizure. The words *fit for slaughter* can hardly be literally conformed to at this season of the year, and may reasonably be extended to such cattle as are fit to fatten for slaughter. But certainly the power is limited to the half of such cattle belonging to any such person, and any commissary presuming to exceed it will act contrary to law, and distress the people unnecessarily, as the one half of such cattle will afford more than an ample supply. There are also doubts with respect to draught oxen, which I am sure it was not the intention of the legislature to seize for beef, nor do they come within the description of the law. The people might as well have their waggon or plough horses taken from them as their draught oxen.

Another subject of dispute is the price of cattle. By a vote of both houses in November last the executive is empowered to pursue such measures as to them appear practicable and effectual for the laying in such quantity of beef and salt as shall be necessary for supplying the army, allowing for grass beef 24/ per pound and for salt £70 per bushel. And although from the whole tenor and style of the said vote, it is evident that it relates only to the supply of the army during the then slaughter season, and not at all to the powers, prices or valuations described in the before mentioned acts, yet some of the deputy commissaries apply it to the present seizure of live cattle, and instead of appraisement, the weight is judged by two men upon oath, and certificates given at 24/ per pound, for which they say they have late instructions. In some counties the judges fix this at what they think the nett weight of the cattle in their present poor condition; in other counties at what they think would be the nett weight if the cattle were fat and fit for slaughter, or what they would weigh in the slaughter season next fall, as in the mean time they would not cost their owners a penny. A grass bullock which would have weighed 400 last November, will not at this time weigh 200 pounds, so that in some counties the people will get less that half what their neighbors receive, or of the real value of their cattle, besides the loss by depreciation since last November. The commissary in this and some other counties is, by these difficulties, prevented from proceeding, whereupon I promised to lay the matter before your Excellency and the council, and to communicate to them the result. Sensible of the important objects in which the time of the executive is now taken up, I should not have troubled them with this, if I did not foresee that the purposes of the law will be in a great measure defeated, and great confusion ensue, unless prevented by speedy and precise instructions to the deputy-commissaries so as to put their business upon a just and equal footing.

The people in this part of Virginia are well disposed to do everything in their power to support the war, but the same principles which attach them to the American cause will incline them to resist injustice or oppression. I would further beg leave to suggest that it might be better to take now only such a number of cattle as are wanted for immediate use, and suffer the others to remain longer on their own pastures, where at this season of the year they will thrive faster, upon grass alone, than fed with corn, collected in numbers in strange pastures, and a great expense be saved to the public. It will be necessary also to order that the cattle be collected in places out of the reach of the enemy, when the situation of the county will admit it. I am led to mention this last circumstance from my knowing that the place pitched upon in this county is so near the river that a party from a single vessel might carry off the cattle in two or three hours, although a considerable part of the county is out of the reach of the enemy, except in great force.

I beg the favor of an answer by the first post, or other safe conveyance, and remain with the greatest respect, Sir, your most obedient humble servant,

G. MASON.

His Excellency, Thomas Jefferson, Esq. :
    Governor of Virginia.[1]

The raids of the enemy along all the navigable waters of Virginia were constant at this period, and the residents on the Potomac, among the rest of this exposed class of the population, were in a continual state of alarm. Col. Henry Lee, father of Henry Lee, the young lieutenant-colonel of cavalry, was the county lieutenant of Prince William, and in a letter to Governor Jefferson of the 9th of April, he tells of a small schooner which a few days before had gone up to Alexandria, the raiders stealing negroes and burning houses

[1] MS. Letter published in *American Historical Record*, p. 231. Edited by B. J. Lossing.

on their way, and he adds: "If the enemy had succeeded at Alexandria they intended, one of the prisoners says, to have burnt General Washington's houses, plundered Colonel Mason and myself, and endeavored to have made me a prisoner." [1]

On the 12th, Alexandria was in much confusion at the approach of the enemy's fleet. Six armed vessels went up the river, and the counties of Stafford, Prince William, and Fairfax were the "scene of war." [2] Colonel Fitzgerald, however, made such a bold show that the British did not land, and so "Gunston" was not molested. Under the apprehension of the enemy's approach, George Mason prepared to move into Maryland, farther from the river, and he sent his valuables, with the following letter, to his friend, Pearson Chapman, of Charles County.

GUNSTON HALL, Thursday Afternoon,
May 31st, 1781.

DEAR SIR :—The rapid march of the enemy obliges me to send as many of my effects, as I can readily remove, to Maryland, and I expect to follow immediately with Mrs. Mason and my daughters. I must therefore beg the favour of you to permit all the things I send to be put into your dwelling house, for safety, until I can carry them up to my son William's house at the head of Mattawoman, which I shall do with all possible expedition. I expect Mrs. Mason and the girls will be over early to-morrow.

Part of the Virginia Light Horse crossed at Fredericks[burg ?] on Tuesday night ; the Marquis' Troops (who are not strong enough for an action) were expected there last night, unless prevented by the enemy. Lord Cornwallis with the main body of the British army was at Hanover Court House (scarce fifty miles from Fredericksburg) on Tuesday morning, their object, no doubt, to defeat the Marquis' Troops before General Waine came up, or to prevent the junction : this intelligence comes from an officer sent express to General Waine and may be relied on. I think if the winds permit we may expect their fleet up this river in a very

[1] "Virginia Calendar Papers," vol. ii., p. 21.
[2] *Ibid.*, p. 39.

ew days. Our situation in Virginia is truly critical and dangerous; a very few weeks, unless the enemy can be checked, will
place Maryland in the same predicament. Nothing can speedily
extricate the two States but the arrival of a strong French fleet
which there is reason to expect every day. I have given you the
earliest information in my power, that you may endeavour to
secure your moveables by carrying them a few miles from the
river, where I think they will be safe for some time.

I beg the favour of you to let your people and cart assist my
people in carrying up the things from the landing to the house,
that the boat may return as quick as possible; and am dear sir

Your most obedient servant

GEORGE MASON.

If Mr. Chapman is from home, Mrs. Chapman will be pleased
to open this letter.

Mr. Pearson Chapman
Charles County
Maryland[1]

The Chapmans lived almost immediately opposite "Gunston" on the Maryland side of the Potomac, and the old
Eilbeck place, "Mattawoman," was three miles farther off
at the head of Mattawoman Creek. The mother of Pearson
Chapman, Mrs. Constance Chapman, was an intimate friend
of George Mason's first wife, and drawing up her will, in
1768, she makes therein the following bequest: "I give and
bequeath unto my friend Mrs. Ann Mason a mourning ring,
the stone to be set round with diamond sparks, the said ring
to be the value of three guineas and a half, and be inscribed
with my age and the time of my death." Mrs. Chapman,
however, survived Mrs. Mason many years, dying in Fairfax
County, in 1798. A great-grandson of Pearson Chapman is
living now at the old place in Maryland, which is called
"Vue de l'Eau."

Colonel Mason wrote two letters early in June to his son
George in France.

[1] A copy from the original in possession of Mr. Pearson Chapman, April 30,
1860, made by the late Mr. Joseph Horner, of Warrenton, Va.

VIRGINIA, GUNSTON HALL,
June 3d, 1781.

DEAR GEORGE :

A gentleman now here, on his way to the Northern States, and from thence to the West Indies, affords me a better opportunity of writing to you than I have had for a long time past ; and as I shall write duplicates, and direct them to be sent by different vessels, some of them will probably reach you : they will be enclosed in covers to Messrs. Schweighauser and Dobree, Merchants in Nantes. I find from some of your letters, that most, if not all of our letters to you have miscarried, and consequently that you are unacquainted with everything which has happened here in your absence. Your grandmother, Mrs. Eilbeck died last December and has willed her estate, in the manner she always intended ; some legacies in slaves and money to her granddaughters, a negro boy to John and Tom, and the bulk of her fortune to your brother William. Your estate here is at present in good order, and a promising harvest coming on, if we are able to reap it. There was a pretty good crop of corn made on it last year, and about 10,000 lbs. of pork sold at a high nominal price (£200 per hundred) but before the money could be invested in tobacco the rapid depreciation reduced it exceedingly. Part has been invested in tobacco, some in the usual way of Inspector's notes ; the remainder I have advised your brother Thomson to endeavor to invest in tobacco in the hands of substantial people, upon tobacco bonds, rather than having it in the public warehouses, where it is not safe a week from the enemy, who have within these two months burned more than ten thousand hogsheads of tobacco in Virginia, and still continue to destroy all they can get at. I observe what you say of our tobacco at Bordeaux being unsold in March. I hope it still remains so, as the quantity destroyed here must raise the price in Europe, beyond anything known within the memory of man. I will write to Messrs Delaps upon the subject. This family has not yet lost any tobacco, slaves or other property, by the enemy, although their ships have been as high as Alexandria, but we are in daily expectation of sharing the same fate with our neighbors upon this and the other rivers, where many families have been suddenly reduced from opulence to indigence, particularly upon James river, the enemy taking all the slaves, horses, cattle, furniture and other property they can lay their hands on ; and what they can't carry away they wantonly destroy. We have removed our furniture, backwards and forwards two or three times, upon different alarms, by which it is very much damaged : great part of it was packed up last week and sent to Maryland, where your brother Thomson and your sisters now are.

The schooner *Isabella* was drove on shore, on the coast of North Carolina, and the vessel lost ; some part of the cargo was saved, but upon the average settlement of the proceeds, our proportion in the present depreciated money was hardly worth the trouble of receiving. Mine was about £3,000 and yours £366, including Mrs. Eilbeck's, Dr. Brown's and the whole consignment to your brother Thomson. The letters, bills of lading, and invoyces all came safe to hand, but yours were so irregular, some packages mentioned in the invoyce not being inserted in the bills of lading, and some of the contents not particularized nor extended in the invoyce, so that if the goods had arrived safe we should hardly have been able to ascertain them properly, much less was it practicable to fix the real value upon the general average. You have probably been a loser by this, though very deservedly ; if ever you send any more goods, pray be more methodical and exact. The ship *General Washington* is fitted out as a privateer, and I believe is now upon a cruise. She arrived from Amsterdam in a New England port, where her cargo produced less than half the value here. I had better than £200 sterling cost of goods in her upon my own private account, which still remain in New England, from whence I am not likely to get them soon, if ever : by these disappointments the family are in great want of necessaries. Our bay and rivers are entirely in the possession of the enemy, our little trade totally at an end, and almost all the Virginia vessels taken.

The family, I thank God, are all well, except myself, who am but just recovering from a fit of the gout. No remarkable changes have happened among your acquaintance. Pray let me know if my order on Penet Da Costa and Company was duly paid. Let me know also where Mr. William Lee is, and in what circumstances, and way of life, &c., and give me the best information you can respecting your expences, and manner of life, health, &c. I am sorry to hear you make so slow progress in the

French language ; it is owing to your conversing too much among your own countrymen, and to your not accustoming yourself to write French. I hope, however, you will not be discouraged, but will still endeavor to make yourself master of it.

I have not yet received the surveys of my back lands ; when I do (if it is in time) I will transmit you copies of them, and particularize the terms by which I purpose to settle them. I can now only mention the outlines. I will on no consideration risk the importing, or maintaining people, at my charge. But if settlers can be engaged to come in, at their own charge, I will grant them long leases, at very low rents ; vizt., for three lives, or twenty-one years, paying the first three years, only the taxes of the quantity of land leased and afterwards the annual rent of about thirty shillings sterling per hundred acres, and the taxes ; with covenants to plant orchards and make the usual improvements of buildings (which you know in this country are not great) within four or five years after the end of the present war ; the lessee to have sub-tenants, if he pleases, preserving one third part of the quantity leased uncut and uncultivated, to supply the premises with wood and timber. Considering the conveniencies of game, fish, wild-fowl, and the navigation (my lands being below the Falls of the Ohio) and the extreme richness and fertility of the soil, the fineness of the climate, and the levelness of the land, these terms are very reasonable, and I should think would induce men of substance to take quantities and bring in settlers. I presume this will find you in Paris, or, as I rather hope, in the south of France. I cannot but think you judged extremely ill, in spending so much time in Nantes, where you could expect no great improvement, either in health, knowledge or manners. I think it will also be very imprudent in you to return to America, without trying the effect of one summer, either in the south of France, Italy or Spain, as the best physicians in Paris may advise you : the recovery of health should be considered as your primary object, for without that you will have incurred much expence and loss of time to little purpose.

I would recommend it to you to embark for America about next May, so as to have a warm weather voyage, and be some time again in your native climate, before the return of winter, and to endeavor to get your passage in a ship of war. If any are coming to America about the time, and you make proper use of your letters and credentials, I should think you might by means of Doctor Franklin, Colonel Lawrence, or some men of interest, procure an order from the court for a passage in one of them.

Mrs. Mason desires to be kindly remembered to you and joins in wishing you a restoration to health, and a safe return to your country and friends, with

Dear George,
Your affectionate father,
G. MASON.

P. S.—Under the same cover you will have a letter upon public affairs.[1]

VIRGINIA, GUNSTON HALL, June 3d, 1781.

DEAR GEORGE :—Your brother William writes you by this opportunity. He returned some time ago from South Carolina, where he commanded a company of volunteers (75 fine young fellows from this county). He had a rough campaign of it, and has acquired the reputation of a vigilant and good officer ; and I think is greatly improved by the expedition. Your brother Thomson has lately returned from a tour of militia-duty upon James River. He commanded a platoon, in a pretty close action at Williamsburg, and behaved with proper coolness and intrepidity. He is now from home or would have wrote you.

I have written you very fully lately upon domestic subjects ; but I am not able to give you any agreeable public news. Our affairs have been, for some time, growing from bad to worse. The enemy's fleet commands our rivers, and puts it in their power to remove their troops, from place to place, when and where they please without opposition ; so that we no sooner collect a force sufficient to counteract them in one part of the country, but they shift to another, ravaging, plundering, and destroying everything before them. Our militia turn out with great spirit, and have in several late actions, behaved bravely ; but they are badly armed and appointed. General Green, with about 1,200 regular troops and some militia, is in South Carolina ; where he has taken all the enemy's posts, except Charlestown. The enemy's capital object, at this time, seems to be Virginia. General Philips died lately in Petersburg ; upon which the command of the British troops there devolved upon Arnold ; but Ld.

[1] MS. Letter.

Cornwallis, quitting North Carolina, has since joined Arnold, with about 1,200 infantry and 300 cavalry, and taken the chief command of their army in Virginia, now consisting of about 5,000 men : They have crossed James River, and by the latest accounts were at Westover ; their light horse having advanced as far as Hanover Court House ; They have burned Page's warehouses, where the greatest part of the York River tobacco was collected ; they had before burned most of the tobacco upon James River, and have plundered great part of the adjacent county. The Marquis De La Fayette is about twenty miles below Fredericksburg with about 1,200 regulars and 3,000 militia, waiting the arrival of General Waine, with about 1,500 regular troops of the Pennsylvania line.

We have had various accounts of the sailing of a French fleet, with a body of land forces, for America ; should they really arrive it would quickly change the face of our affairs, and infuse fresh spirits and confidence ; but it has been so long expected in vain, that little credit is now given to reports concerning it.

You know from your own acquaintance in this part of Virginia that the bulk of the people here are staunch Whigs, strongly attached to the American cause and well affected to the French alliance ; yet they grow uneasy and restless, and begin to think that our allies are spinning out the war, in order to weaken America as well as Great Britain, and thereby leave us at the end of it, as dependent as possible upon themselves.

However unjust this opinion may be, it is natural enough for planters and farmers, burdened with heavy taxes, and frequently dragged from their familys upon military duty, on the continual alarms occasioned by the superiority of the British fleet. They see their property daily exposed to destruction, they see with what facility the British troops are removed from one part of the continent to another, and with what infinite charge and fatigue ours are, too late, obliged to follow ; and they see too very plainly, that a strong French fleet would have prevented all this. If our allies had a superior fleet here, I should have no doubt of a favorable issue to the war, but without it, I fear we are deceiving both them and ourselves, in expecting we shall be able to keep our people much longer firm, in so unequal an opposition to Great Britain. France surely intends the separation of these States forever from Great Britain. It is highly her interest to accomplish this; but by drawing out the thread too fine and long, it may unexpectedly break in her hands.

God bless you, my dear child! and grant that we may again meet, in your native country, as freemen, otherwise, that we never see each other more, is the prayer of

Your affectionate father,
G. MASON.[1]

It seems not unlikely that this latter interesting and patriotic letter may have had some influence with the French Court, and hastened the arrival of the French fleet. The Honorable James M. Mason, who possessed a copy of it which he transcribed for the "Virginia Historical Register," wrote to the editor that "the indorsement on [the copy] shows that the original had been by Dr. Franklin put into the hands of the Count de Vergennes—doubtless from the tenor of the letter, intended by Dr. F. to stimulate the government of France to send to the revolted colonies the promised succour. The concluding paragraph," adds Mr. Mason, "you will agree with me, I think, would have adorned the ages of Brutus and Manlius."

In Gen. John Mason's recollections of his childhood he mentions that the last tutor that his father had at "Gunston" was a Mr. Constable, who was a native of Scotland, and was engaged in that country to come over to Virginia as a teacher in Colonel Mason's family. In 1781 Mr. Constable wished to leave Virginia to make his home in the West Indies, and Colonel Mason wrote to Thomas Nelson, then governor of the State, to obtain a passport for him.

FAIRFAX COUNTY, GUNSTON HALL,
September 3d, 1781.

SIR:

A young gentleman (Mr. David Constable) a native of Scotland, from the college of Aberdeen, has lived in my family ever since the year 1774, as a tutor to my children, during which time he has supported a very good character, and his behaviour has been un-

---

[1] Niles' "Principles and Acts of the Revolution," p. 126; "Virginia Historical Register," vol. ii., p. 32; "Virginia Calendar Papers," vol. ii., p. 141.

exceptionable, in every instance, but refusing the oath of allegiance to the commonwealth, which he told me at the time he was induced to do from some expectations he had from his friends in the British West Indies, where he intended to settle, after the expiration of his engagements in my family. He has an elder brother who has lived many years in the island of St. Christopher's, where he has had the management of some estates belonging to gentlemen residing in Great Britain, and has acquired considerable property. From this brother Mr. Constable has very lately received a letter, informing him that he should return to Britain the beginning of next winter, to repair a constitution injured by long residence in a warm climate, pressing him to come to St. Christopher's immediately, and promising if he arrived while he remained there, to give him an estate he has in the island and put all his agencies into his hands. This is so much beyond anything Mr. Constable can expect in Virginia or may ever meet with hereafter, that out of friendship to a man who has lived so many years in my family, and behaved so well in it, I wish him enabled to avail himself of it, and for that purpose must entreat your Excellency to grant him a passport or permit, to go with a flag to Lord Cornwallis's army, from whence he may readily obtain a passage to the West Indies. And his speedy arrival there being of the utmost importance to him, you will oblige me exceedingly in transmitting me such a passport by the next post. This favor I flatter myself will be granted as an act of the last session of Assembly invests the governor and council with such a power ; as Mr. Constable's detention here would materially injure him as an individual, without the smallest benefit to the American cause, and as it is not in his power to give any useful intelligence to the enemy, or if it was, I know him to be a man of more honor than to abuse any indulgence you shall be pleased to grant him, and can venture to engage for his conduct.

I am, with the greatest esteem and respect

Sir, your most obedient, humble servant

G. Mason.

P. S. If Mr. Constable is permitted to go by water it will enable him to carry his books and other effects which he could not well carry by land.[1]

[1] MS. Letter.

Lafayette passed through Colchester, the little post town near "Gunston," in the spring of 1781, and the tax commissioners, one of whom was Martin Cockburn, George Mason's friend, and another Richard Chichester, whose daughter married one of Colonel Mason's sons, gave out to the Marquis a quantity of wheat for his command.[1] It is very likely that Lafayette visited "Gunston" at this time and brought messages from Washington to its proprietor. The army of Washington was on its way in September to the memorable field of Yorktown, and great preparations were made for its approach in the counties it would have to traverse from Georgetown to Dumfries. The militia were instructed by the county lieutenants, through letters from the commander-in-chief, to repair the roads and make them passable for wagons. The baggage wagons of the American and French forces, the cavalry, and the beef cattle were all to take this route. Washington wrote to request the gentlemen of the neighborhood, as a pleasing mark of attention, to assist the French officers, Rochambeau, Chastellux, and others, with their carriages, from point to point. From "Mt. Vernon" they were to be furnished with carriages to Dumfries, where new relays were requested to take them to Fredericksburg. Colonel Mason must have met these distinguished strangers at this time, and in all probability his equipage was at their command. Washington arrived at "Mt. Vernon" on the 9th of September, Rochambeau, Chastellux, and their suites the following day. A dinner-party was given at "Mt. Vernon" on the 11th, and the next morning the journey to Williamsburg was resumed, lasting two days longer. This was the first time Washington had been home since 1775.

Thomson Mason, who was living at his country-seat in Loudon County, wrote to Washington offering the services of his two sons in the proposed campaign.

[1] "Virginia Calendar Papers," vol. ii., p. 128.

RASPBERRY PLAIN, Sept. 26th, 1781.

MY DEAR GENERAL:

I must sincerely congratulate your Excellency upon your safe return to your native country, and look upon it as a happy presage of putting a glorious period to the present war.

But do not flatter yourself that your fatigues are to end with this war. No, more glorious ones are yet reserved for you, in ridding your country of its domestic enemies, more silent indeed, but not less destructive, than its foreign invaders ; and in fixing some permanent constitution that may render us happier than the present ever can ; it is my most ardent wish and expectation, that you will accomplish all this.

Nothing but my crazy constitution should have restrained me from thanking your Excellency in person for the benefits which I as a private citizen, am likely to enjoy from your labors; but as my health will not permit me to undertake so long a journey, this will be handed to you by one of my two eldest sons. The first Stevens Thomson is equipped as a volunteer horseman, the second having served out his tour of duty as an ensign in the Loudon militia, is also desirous of serving the remainder of the campaign as a volunteer, to which I have consented and sent him a horse. From the retired privacy in which they have been brought up, I have no expectation that they can render their country any effectual service. But to pay a grateful respect to General Washington is a duty due from every citizen of America, and for that reason only, do they wait upon your Excellency. In whatever capacity you may employ them for the remainder of the campaign, (and I can part with them no longer,) I will be answerable they will discharge their duty with bravery, secrecy and integrity ; and the oldest is tolerably ready at most kinds of business.

I have the honor to be, with the greatest respect and esteem, your Excellency's most devoted, obliged and affectionate, humble servant,

THOMSON MASON.

The surrender of Cornwallis took place on the 19th of October, and a few days later Colonel Mason had occasion

---

[1] Washington MSS., State Department.

to write to Robert Carter of "Nomini," when he refers to the recent victory.

GUNSTON HALL, October 27th, 1781.

DEAR SIR:

The bearer, Capt. Cleon Moore, a neighbor and particular friend of mine waits on you to rent some of your lands in Prince William County. As I thought it probable that the abuses too frequent among tenants might make you cautious of renting lands to a stranger, I take the liberty of introducing Capt. Moore to you, as a gentleman whose integrity and punctuality in whatever contract he makes with you, I think may be relied on, and one to whom I would most readily rent lands myself, if I had any which suited him.

I congratulate you on the late signal success of our arms, which there is reason to hope will lay the foundation of a safe and lasting peace.

I beg my compliments to your lady and family, and am,

Dear Sir,

Your most obedient servant,

G. MASON.

Hon. Robert Carter,

Nominy, Westmoreland.

In Congress at this time the land companies were pushing their claims to the Western territory, and they were supported in their pretensions by those States whose selfish and short-sighted policy was opposed to the acknowledgment of Virginia's charter rights—rights in which a principle was involved most important to the autonomy of all the States. Madison wrote indignantly from Philadelphia to Jefferson in January, 1782, on this subject. The memorial of the Indiana Company had been justified by Congress, in spite of the emphatic protest of the Viginia delegates, though so clearly an infringement upon Virginia's sovereignty. Madison wished to receive from Virginia "an accurate and full collection of the documents which relate to the subject."

[1] MS. Letter.

He sent the proceedings of Congress to his State while the Assembly was in session, but to his mortification they were not received in time. He had hoped that Jefferson would have undertaken the task of preparing and forwarding these papers; and as it was, he found himself left without adequate material to contradict the calumnies and misrepresentations that were rife. He had evidently written to George Mason to aid him, for he adds: "Colonel Mason's industry and kindness have supplied us with some valuable papers and remarks." There had also been sent Joseph Jones "some judicious remarks" by Edmund Pendleton.[1]

Jefferson at this time was at "Monticello" by the bedside of his sick wife, and no assistance could be expected from him. At the spring session of the Assembly in 1782, a committee had been appointed "to state the title of Virginia to western territory," and this committee consisted of Jefferson, George Mason, Edmund Randolph, Arthur Lee, and Dr. Thomas Walker. Though Colonel Mason was not in the Assembly, his name was the first one proposed, as Randolph tells us. He was known to be an authority on this subject, and in the task assigned the committee it was anticipated that he would take the lead. Edmund Randolph writes to Arthur Lee: "I expected the first movement from him [George Mason], as being the first in nomination. Mr. Jefferson's domestic happiness is threatened with too great an interruption by the illness of his wife, to suffer him to enter into the researches which our subject requires. Should I be so unfortunate as not to hear from Col. Mason on this weighty business, notwithstanding your request to him to communicate with me, I shall certainly write to him, urge him to assist his country, and through me correspond with Mr. Jefferson and Dr. Walker."[2]

In response to this call upon him, George Mason wrote the following statement of Virginia's title, in a letter to Edmund Randolph.

[1] "Madison Papers," vol. i., p. 109.
[2] Lee Papers, *Southern Literary Messenger*, 1858.

GUNSTON HALL, October 19, 1782.

DEAR SIR:

Your favor of the 30th of August was so long on the road that it did not reach me until a few days ago. I must beg pardon for not writing sooner to you and the other gentlemen of the Committee for stating the title of Virginia to her western territory. The truth is I was somewhat embarrassed by an appointment, which I was far from desiring or expecting; and which I had not an opportunity of refusing, as I should have done, had I received notice of it before the last session ended. I quitted my seat in the House of Delegates, from a conviction that I was no longer able to do any essential service. Some of the public measures have been so contrary to my notions of policy and of justice that I wished to be no further concerned with, or answerable for them; and to spend the remnant of my life in quiet and retirement. Yet with all her faults, my country will ever have my warmest wishes and affections; and I would at any time, most cheerfully sacrifice my own ease and domestic enjoyments to the public good. But though I look upon asserting the right to our western territory, and thereby putting a stop to the dangerous usurpations of Congress, before they shall have been established into precedents, to be a matter of the utmost importance, I do not know that it is in my power to give the committee any assistance. My distance from the seat of government, and the public archives, disables me from investigating the subject. What evidence had occurred to me I sent you last year by our friend Mr. May; and I have since put into the hands of Dr. Lee an official copy of all the council-entries for lands upon the western waters. These necessarily imply an equal extension of our laws and jurisdiction; and upon the exercise of jurisdiction, under the former as well as the present government, our title, in my opinion, in a great measure depends. Among the council-entries there is one for fifty thousand acres of land, near forty years ago, upon the Mississippi, beginning at the confluence of the Ohio and Mississippi, and running up both rivers to include the quantity. And the royal instructions to Sir William Gooch, respecting the Ohio Company in 1749, is to grant lands on either side the Ohio river, "within our colony of Virginia." Governor Dinwiddie, by proclamation in 1754, offered a bounty of two hundred thousand acres of land, upon the Ohio River, to the officers and soldiers of the First Virginia Regiment, commanded by Colonel Washington (now his Excellency, General Washington), which was afterwards surveyed accordingly, and patents granted, in the time of Lord Botetourt and Lord Dunmore. There were, besides, a great many patents and surveys upon record, and in the secretary's office, under the former government, some of them of pretty old standing ; and a great number of inhabitants settled in that part of Augusta County which lay beyond the Alleghany mountains (upon the different branches of the western waters), under the particular encouragement of the Virginia laws, which, having received the royal assent, were constitutional acts of the British government. Dr. Walker is better acquainted with the extent and dates of these settlements, surveys, and grants than most men in America, and knows that the principal water-courses, &c., received their names from Virginia settlers. Col. Thomas Lewis is also very capable of giving information upon this subject. If I mistake not, two or three counties (Botetourt and Fincastle, besides the district of West-Augusta) were separated from that part of Augusta County which lay beyond the Alleghany mountains ; civil and military jurisdiction regularly exercised, and representation in the Virginia legislature enjoyed there, before the present Revolution. And that more counties were not erected there was owing to a royal instruction of a very alarming and tyrannical nature, restraining the governor from assenting to any law for erecting new counties, unless a clause was inserted to deprive such new counties of the right of representation in the legislature ; which being evidently calculated to maintain an undue influence of the crown in our General Assembly, no such clause was submitted to. The governor had recourse to the power of the prerogative, and instead of a new county, established the district of West-Augusta (to the north-westward) over the Alleghany mountains ; in which he commissioned civil magistrates and militia officers, and courts were regularly held there, suits brought, judgments granted, deeds recorded, &c. In the year 1775, the district of West-Augusta sent two representatives, John Harney and George Roots, Esqrs., to the general convention at Richmond, where they were received ; and the inhabitants of the said district continued to send

their representatives to the Virginia legislature, until the same
was formed into three distinct counties, Ohio, Monongalia, and
Youghyoughgaine ; which counties have regularly ever since
sent representatives to the House of Delegates and the Senate.
Soon after the present Revolution, the county of Kentucky was
separated from Botetourt and Fincastle, upon the Ohio, to the
south-westward ; which has since been divided into three counties, Fayette, Lincoln, and Jefferson.   Towns have been laid
off, courts established, and civil and military jurisdiction regularly
exercised in these counties, and each of them represented in the
Virginia legislature ; several thousand inhabitants are settled in
them, all deriving their titles from Virginia, subject to her laws,
and to all intents and purposes her citizens.   The British posts,
within our chartered territory, at Kaskaskie upon the Mississippi,
and St. Vincents upon the Obache, have been reduced by Virginia
militia, without any assistance from or charge to the United
States, and a garrison, as well as the civil establishment, under
the sole direction and at the sole expense of the Virginia government, has been maintained there.

The purchase at the Treaty of Lancaster in 1743 was made
with Virginia money ; and if I remember right, there is a clause
showing that it was made for the use and benefit of the colony
of Virginia, as far westward as his majesty should at any time
choose to extend the settlements.   It is evident, from the royal
instructions in 1749 to Sir William Gooch, Lieutenant-Governor
of Virginia, that the crown directed the settlements to be
extended over the Ohio river ; and several subsequent laws
were made for their encouragement.   The purchase of Lancaster
was made in the reign of *George the second*, when just regard
was paid to the constitutional rights of the American colonies.
It was made by Virginia commissioners appointed for that
purpose ; and from the proceedings upon record, it appears that
the whole transaction was fair, open, and in the presence of the
commissioners and governors of the other colonies, particularly
the province of New York, which a select committee of Congress
have lately discovered had always the right to these lands.
The purchase at Fort Stanwix (which in fact was only
purchasing the same lands over again; for ministerial purposes, which had been before purchased and paid for) was

made in the reign of *George the third*, in the year 1768, when the rights of the colonies had been repeatedly violated, and under the direction of that ministry which formed the system for enslaving America, one of the first steps to which was dismembering the old colonies, and erecting new ones more immediately dependant upon the crown and the commands of the ministry. The whole transaction wore the face of mystery and knavery ; for though Dr. Walker was there as a public commissioner for Virginia, he was refused access to the conferences, the greatest caution was used to conceal from him what they were about, and every thing until the business was finished, was conducted privately with the Indian chiefs, by Sir William Johnston and the traders. The substance of these facts was proved by the oath of Dr. Walker, on his examination in the House of Delegates, upon the hearing of the Indiana Company's title. It was also proved by the depositions on the same trial, that the tributaries of the Six Nations had been totally expelled from this side the Ohio to the other (from whence they never returned) and the country conquered in the course of the last war ; and that before the treaty at Fort Stanwix, there were several Virginia settlers upon the very lands purchased by Trent and Sir William Johnston for the Indiana Company. But if these damning circumstances were not in the case, the purchase made by the crown at the treaty of Fort Stanwix ought not to operate to the injury, but inure to the benefit of the colony to whom the country had been originally granted, as all the former purchases from the Indians had done. If such purchases could operate against the title of Virginia, they would have operated against the title to the Northern Neck, the greater part of which was possessed by the Indians when the grant was made by Charles II., and not purchased from them for many years after. So late as Queen Anne's reign (when Governor Spotswood presided here) the Blue Ridge of mountains was by a solemn treaty fixed as the boundary between the English subjects and the Indians, yet in the reign of George the second the king and council gave Lord Fairfax a judgment for the lands to the fountain head of Potomac river, fourscore miles beyond the Blue Ridge. As our settlements were extended, the wild game destroyed, and the country rendered unfit for the savage life, the Indians have been forced to remove further, for the convenience of hunting. As they retired, purchase after purchase hath been made from them, and temporary lines and boundaries, for the sake of peace, from time to time accordingly settled between them and the English inhabitants here, but none of them have ever been considered as at all affecting the title of Virginia. When the colony of Virginia was first settled, it was without any previous purchase from the Indians. The first lands purchased from the Indians were only upon and near the mouths and larger parts of the rivers, then to the falls of the said rivers, then to the Blue Ridge of mountains, and afterwards (before the unnecessary purchase at Fort Stanwix) as far westward as the claim of Great Britain extended. Most of these purchases were made subsequent to the actual settlement and occupation of part of the lands purchased. It is about sixty years ago since the people of Virginia settled the country over the Blue Ridge, and near forty years since they began to settle beyond the Appalatian or Alleghany mountains ; but the purchase at Lancaster was not made until 1743, nor the purchase at Fort Stanwix till 1768. It has been objected to the treaty at Lancaster, and urged as a proof that the Indians were imposed on, that they sold their whole country, or in the common phrase, that they sold themselves out of house and home ; but this is a false suggestion. The country back of New York adjacent to Lake Ontario, was originally and still is the country and habitation of the Iroquois or Six Nations ; and this it will be found (I believe upon due examination) was the country which they put under the protection of the New York government, and perhaps also their beaver-hunting country, between that and the great lakes. The country upon the Ohio, above the Tennessee river, was what they called their conquered lands, from which they had totally extirpated the original inhabitants, and afterwards permitted the Delawares from the river Delaware, and the Shawnese from Potomac, with some other small tribes, to live there as their tributaries : These lands being of little use to them, and their right precarious, it may be presumed they were desirous to sell. If according to the opinion of the best writers, the occupation of a few hordes of savages cannot give right to an extensive territory, as being contrary to the primary laws of nature, a conquest which utterly extirpates the inhabitants, and leaves the country desolate, being more contrary to the laws of nature, can confer no right on the conqueror. If the country is considered in the light of derelict lands, which the first possessor without any other claim, has a right to occupy and enjoy, *a fortiori* had the colony of Virginia, having a previous title, a right to possess and occupy them, as it has done.

The English and American maps have uniformly laid down Virginia across the continent, to the westward, until the Treaty of Paris in 1762, and since to the river Mississippi, that having been then established the boundary between the British and French dominions. Many solemn acts of the British government, at different periods, have recognized the right of Virginia to her western territory, nor can there be found any one act of government impeaching or invalidating it, until the conclusion of the last war, and after the adoption of that system, which by compelling America to assert her rights with the sword, has produced the present Revolution. Long before the Articles of Confederation (and I think previous to the American Declaration of Independence) the Virginia legislature, in that act which formed our constitution, had plainly described and declared the extent of our western territory. This was notorious to Congress, when the Articles of Confederation were formed, the sovereignty of each State respectively secured to it, the mutual guarranty stipulated, and the proviso inserted "that no State shall be deprived of territory for the benefit of the United States." It was upon these express conditions that Virginia acceded to the Articles of Confederation; the present attempt, therefore, to dismember Virginia, without her consent, is a flagrant breach of public faith, and if carried into execution dissolves the federal compact, and renders it no longer obligatory upon this commonwealth. Congress are properly the delegates of the different States, with certain powers defined and limited by the Articles of the Confederation; these they can not be permitted to exceed, without establishing an arbitrary and tyrannical aristocracy; for if under pretence of public utility, necessity, or under any pretence whatsoever, they can, in one instance, exceed the powers delegated to them, they may in another, or in a hundred; every usurpation will be urged as a precedent for others, and maintained by the command which they have (and must have) of our fleets and armies. They may in time proceed to fill up their own vacancies, vote themselves members for life, and what not !

The only natural and safe remedy is, for every State to have a watchful eye over this great American council, to keep them constantly within the lines of the Confederation, and to resist and reprobate their first attempts to exceed them. This was intended, about two years ago, by the General Assembly of Virginia, in their Remonstrance, but an ill-judged timidity (miscalled delicacy) in our delegates at that time (I believe) prevented its being entered on the journals of Congress. If experience shall prove that the present powers of Congress are, in some instances, insufficient, let them be increased by additional Articles to the Confederation, acceded to, after due deliberation, by all the States; but upon no pretence, however plausible, without.

It is strongly provided by the Articles of Confederation (without which they would never have been acceded to by the different States) that "each State retains its sovereignty, freedom and independence, and every jurisdiction and right, which is not by this Confederation expressly delegated to the United States in Congress assembled." Yet the claim of Congress to the unappropriated lands is founded upon the assertion that the sovereignty of Great Britain hath, on the present Revolution, descended to them, as representatives of all the States, though it is as clear as the sun at noonday, that it has not descended to them, but remains to each individual State, respectively, in its own right, by whom alone it can be safely exercised. This doctrine of sovereignty, teeming with oppression, and striking at the vitals of American liberty, has been eagerly patronized by Congress, and echoed by P[ain]e, W[harto]n, and every mercenary party-scribbler.

Posterity will reflect with indignation that this fatal lust of sovereignty, which lost Great Britain her western world, which covered our country with desolation and blood, should even during the contest against it, be revived among ourselves, and fostered by the very men who were appointed to oppose it !

There is not a single word in the Articles of Confederation giving Congress a power of limiting, dividing, or parcelling out any of the thirteen States, or of erecting new ones. The fourteenth article declares that "*Canada* acceding to this Confederation, and joining in the measures of the United States, shall be entitled to all the advantages of this Union, but *no other colony* shall be admitted into the same, unless such admission be agreed to by nine States." This evidently relates to the other British colonies of Nova Scotia and the Floridas, neither of which is to be admitted into the Union, without the concurrence of nine States. Yet under color of this article, Congress assumes the power of curtailing and dividing the different States, of depriving them of territory for the benefit of the United States (directly contrary to the Confederation), of demanding cessions, and of erecting new States. There is no power whatsoever which they may not with equal propriety arrogate to themselves, and pretend to derive it from the Articles of the Confederation. Did the different States view this subject impartially, as they ought, no little jealousy, envy, or pique to any particular State, no local or party views would induce them to connive at innovations and unwarranted assumptions of power, which if continued, must end either in the dissolution of the federal Union or the destruction of American liberty. To show, therefore, the total absence of power in Congress on this occasion, and to expose the danger of their usurping it, I should conceive a very useful part of the work confided to the committee ; and preserving good manners and decency of language, I think the subject can hardly be too freely treated.

It is worthy of observation that the arguments against the chartered title of Virginia to the country on the north-west side the Ohio, if they prove anything, will prove it part of the new British province of Quebec or Canada. Because by an act of Parliament in the latter end of 1773, or the beginning of 1774, the boundaries of the province of Quebec or Canada were extended so as to include the whole country between the Ohio and the Mississippi rivers ; and this being done before the separation of the colonies, or the Declaration of Independence, when we professed ourselves British subjects, and acknowledged the obligation of their laws, except on the subject of taxation, the authority of Parliament to make the said act can not be impeached upon any other ground than the title of some of the old colonies, under their charters, to the country so included ; and that the British government had no right to add to their new province of Quebec what had been, long before, solemnly granted to others. Aware of this, and to prevent too sudden an alarm or opposition, a proviso was inserted in the act, saving to the other colonies the lands within their respective charters. If, therefore, Congress taking upon itself the insidious and dangerous work of curtailing the boundaries of the different States, should set aside the title of Virginia, and Virginia acquiesces in it, that country will thenceforward be placed in the same predicament with the undisputed part of Canada, and the other British provinces of Nova Scotia, and the East and West Floridas ; and what claim or demand could the United States or any of them, have upon it, unless they can conquer and hold it by force of arms ? Or upon a negotiation of peace with Great Britain, what argument could we fairly urge for contracting the lately extended boundaries of Canada and reducing it to its former limits ? Or what would any neutral or mediating power probably say to us upon such an occasion ? The consequences of suffering a British colony to surround great part of the United States, and extend itself between them and the numerous tribes of western Indians, are too obvious to need explanation ; and this subject is the more important, as it may easily be foreseen that settling the bounds of Canada will be one of the most difficult objects of a treaty.

I have not by me the copies of the Virginia charters in 1606 and 1609, or I should have made some remarks on them, endeavoring to show that Payne's construction of them is capricious and absurd, as several of his other strictures are, and some of them founded in misrepresentation and falsehood ; that the description and boundaries are intelligible, and admit a natural and easy construction, the charter of 1609 confirming and enlarging, not destroying that of 1606 ; that though the Virginia Company was dissolved, and the government resumed by the crown, the charter, so far as the settlers and their posterity are interested, or affected, remains valid, and among other things, the covenant in the charter of 1606, that no new colony should be settled to the westward, which seems to have been one of the causes of the great western extension of the second charter, whereby the repetition of the former clause became unnecessary ; that the ancient method of granting lands, established by the Virginia Company in virtue of their charter, always continued under the king's government ;

that the charter granted to the colony of Virginia in 1667, by King Charles the second, has reference to the country described in the former charter of 1609, and by recognising and confirming the ancient custom of granting lands for the importation of inhabitants, the privileges of the people, and the jurisdiction of the colony, has forever barred the crown from dismembering the colony, or refusing to grant lands to persons coming hither to settle, or importing others ; that the crown has always considered the charter of 1667 in this light, and acted accordingly, until the present reign, when all reverence to law and justice was thrown aside, and a resolution formed to abolish the ancient constitution of the colonies, annihilate their charters, and establish despotism and slavery in their stead ; that the proclamation of 1763 therefore was absolutely illegal and void, as well as the scheme for erecting the new province of Vandalia, even if no lands had been previously granted, or inhabitants settled beyond the Alleghany Mountains. And as to what has been said of the acquiescence and approbation of the government of Virginia, the utmost that is asserted only shows that the *privy-council of Virginia* (holding their places at pleasure, and totally dependent upon the ministry) did not venture to oppose it.

The charters, I presume, may all be found in the House of Delegates' office : I had them all in my possession (made up in one bundle) when I was formerly appointed to settle some matters of jurisdiction in Chespeake Bay and Potomac River with the State of Maryland, but our Assembly not thinking it prudent to enter into any engagement with that State, while it refused confederating, I returned the charters into the House of Delegates at the clerk's table. If any of the observations which I have scattered up and down, without method or order, will be of use, they are very much at the committee's service. And though I hope to be excused from taking any particular part in this business, for the reasons I have already given, yet if the gentlemen of the committee conceive I can be useful to them on any occasion, I will wait on them (my health permitting) at any time and place they shall be pleased to appoint, for I can truly say there are no men in the United States in whom I can more cordially confide, or with whom I would more cheerfully act.

I must entreat them to consider this long epistle as a general letter, and excuse my not writing to each particular member. I must entreat them, too, to proceed in the business, without delaying it on account of

Dear Sir,

Your affectionate and obedient servant,

G. MASON.

Edmund Randolph, Esquire,
Attorney-General.[1]

George Mason, Jr., was still in France, and John Adams, who was in Paris in the winter of 1782–3 negotiating the treaty of peace, mentions in his journal Mr. Mason among other Americans to whom he extends his hospitality. The following letter from Colonel Mason to his son gives some public as well as personal details which are not without interest. There would seem to have been a number of his countrymen abroad, at this time, in embarrassed circumstances, to whom Mr. Mason had given assistance, and his father endorses this liberality in the same spirit of openhanded sympathy.

" GUNSTON HALL, January 8th, 1783.

. . . .

" As to the money you have spent in Europe, provided you can satisfy me that it has not been spent in extravagance, dissipation, or idle parade, I don't regard it. It is true, I have a large family to provide for ; and that I am determined, from motives of morality and duty, to do justice to them all ; it is certain also that I have not lost less than ten thousand pounds sterling by the war, in the depreciation of paper money and the loss of the profits of my estate ; but think this a cheap purchase of liberty and independence. I thank God, I have been able, by adopting principles of strict economy and frugality, to keep my principal, I mean my country estate, unimpaired, and I have suffered little by the depredations of the enemy. I have at this time, two years' rents (you know mine are all tobacco rents) in arrear and two crops uninspected ; so that if a peace happens, it will find me plentiful handed in the article of tobacco, which

[1] Mason Papers.

will then be very valuable.   The money it has cost you to relieve the distresses of your unfortunate countrymen was worthily expended, and you will receive retribution, with large interest, in heaven—but in order to shorten the time of credit and also to entitle myself to some proportion of the merit, I shall insist upon replacing to you every shilling of it here ; I hope you will therefore keep an exact account of it.

"I beg you will freely communicate to me the situation of your affairs ; and if there should be a necessity of making you remittances, I will endeavor to do it at all events, though it must be by selling some of the produce of my estate at an undervalue. I am now pretty far advanced in life, and all my views are centred in the happiness and welfare of my children—you will therefore find from me every indulgence which you have a right to expect from an affectionate parent.

"I have been for some time in retirement and shall not probably return again to public life ; my anxiety for my country in these times of danger, makes me sometimes dabble a little in politics, and keep up a correspondence with some men upon the public stage. You know I am not apt to form opinions lightly and without due examination. And I can venture to say that the French court and nation may confide in the honor and good faith of America. We reflect with gratitude on the important aids France has given us ; but she must not, and I hope will not, attempt to lead us into a war of ambition or conquest, or trail us around the mysterious circle of European politics. We have little news worth communicating—nothing of consequence has happened here this campaign, the enemy having generally kept close within their lines, and the American army not strong enough to force them. We have a long time expected the evacuation of Charlestown, the enemy having dismantled their outworks and embarked their heavy artillery and some of their troops. However, by the last accounts (in December) they had still a garrison there. By late accounts from Kentucky, we are informed that General Clarke, with twelve hundred volunteers, had crossed the Ohio river and destroyed six of the Shawnese towns, destroying also about two thousand barrels of their corn and bringing off furs and other plunder to the value of three thousand pounds, which was sold, and the money divided among his men ; this will probably drive these savages near the lakes or the Mississippi. Upon Clarke's return the Chickasaws sent deputies to him to treat for peace. Everything was quiet in the new settlements, and upwards of five thousand souls have been added to them since last September. The people there are extremely uneasy lest the free navigation of the Mississippi to the sea should not be secured to them upon a treaty of peace. If it is not, it will occasion another war in less than seven years. The inhabitants think they have a natural right to the free, though not the exclusive, navigation of that river, and in a few years they will be strong enough to enforce that right." [1]

[1] Niles, " Principles and Acts of the Revolution," p. 127.

CHAPTER II.

THE YEAR OF THE PEACE.

1783.

In March, 1783, Colonel Mason addressed a letter to General Washington, in behalf of the latter's young kinsman, Lawrence Washington, of Chotank, who had been engaged in a duel with Mr. Philip Alexander, in which he had mortally wounded his antagonist. The father of Lawrence, whom George Mason designates as "old Mr. Lawrence Washington," was evidently the same person to whom General Washington left a bequest in his will, speaking of him and his cousin, Robert Washington, as the "acquaintances and friends of his juvenile years." They were descendants of Lawrence, the brother of Col. John Washington. Lund Washington was one of this same family.[1]

VIRGINIA, GUNSTON HALL,
March 19th, 1783.

DEAR GENERAL:

My motives for troubling your Excellency at this particular time are motives of humanity. Mr. Lawrence Washington, Junr., who will deliver this has been unfortunately engaged in a duel, or rather an affray, with Mr. Philip Alexander of Chotanck; in which his antagonist was mortally wounded and died six or seven days after. I have taken some pains to inform myself of the real truth of the case, and have seen several testimonials, signed by

---

[1] "George Washington and Mount Vernon"; Moncure D. Conway, "Memoirs of the Long Island Historical Society," vol. iv.

unprejudiced persons of credit, and though Mr. Washington may not be strictly justifiable in a legal sense, I am entirely of opinion that he has done no more than any man of sensibility and honour would have thought himself obliged to do under the same circumstances of provocation. Mr. Alexander appears to have been, in every instance, the aggressor; the provocation given Mr. Washington was of the most interesting and aggravating kind—an attempt to blast the reputation of a young lady of family and character, allied to him by the nearest ties of blood. This is one of the few cases which does not admit the usual reparation of other wrongs, in a court of justice; a young lady's character being of too delicate a nature to be submitted to such an investigation; and however false the defamation, however generally disbelieved, the injury is lasting. The custom of the world, the manners of the age we live in, the voice of nature calls upon relations and friends to redress an injured person, who from the natural weakness and incapacity of her sex is deprived of the means of doing it.

Mr. Alexander after refusing to accept a challenge, and professing to act upon the defensive, added fresh injuries to those he had already offered, and continued to insult and abuse Mr. Washington in the grossest manner; and when they afterwards met at a public place and walked out together, fired his pistol first (at not more than a yard's distance) with a manifest intention to kill the other, before he knew whether it was Mr. Washington's design to act offensively or not; the ball missed him, though so very close that the powder burned his face. Mr. Washington instantly stepped back, and drawing a pistol from his belt, under his great-coat, shot the other in the body, which brought him to the ground. This was done in the sight of many people, and I think proves that Mr. Washington, in firing his pistol, acted upon the defensive. The only circumstances against him are his former challenge and his having desired Mr. Alexander, that day, to walk aside with him. Upon the whole, though I think Mr. Washington may safely stand his trial, and trust himself in the hands of an honest and impartial jury, yet he has been judiciously advised to absent himself for the present, until men's passions and prejudices have subsided, as he must first be tried by an examining court in the county where the deceased had many relatives and friends : and the circumstances of Mr. Alexander's remaining wounded and his life despaired of, several days before he died, during which time most of the neighbors visited him, has contributed not a little to heighten the prejudices against Mr. Washington.   Such spectacles naturally excite our compassion and, of course, our resentment against the man who has been the cause ; our passions are inflamed too much to consult our reason ; and it is not until cool reflection returns that we are capable of inquiring into the merits.   For these reasons, Mr. Washington has determined to pass a month or two in the army, if you shall be pleased to permit him to act in it as a volunteer.

I am well apprized of your Excellency's strict attention to the authority of the civil power, and thoroughly sensible how greatly and justly it has endeared your character to your fellow-citizens ; I should therefore be one of the last men in the world who would presume to recommend to your countenance or protection either a criminal or a fugitive from justice ; but I think, in my conscience, that this young gentleman has been rather unfortunate than culpable ; and am assured and convinced he means to return and submit himself to a fair trial, by the laws of his country ; if the friends of the deceased, after due reflection, shall judge fit to prosecute him ; which according to the best of my judgment I think I should not do, if Mr. Alexander had been my nearest relation.

I can truly declare that I have not the smallest connection, or even acquaintance with either of the parties.   I own I can't help feeling, as a man and as a father, for old Mr. Lawrence Washington, who is a very worthy man, and is exceedingly distressed by this unhappy accident.   Your Excellency's permitting his son to remain, for a short time, in the army will alleviate his present distress, and, in a little time, I hope, he will have nothing to fear. I sincerely wish you health, and every felicity ; and with sentiments of the highest respect and esteem, I have the honour to be

Your Excellency's most affectionate and obedient servant,

G. MASON.

His Excellency General Washington,
　　　　Head Quarters.
P. favour—Mr. Lawrence Washington, Junr.[1]

[1] MS. Letter.

Thomson Mason, who was employed to defend Mr. Washington, also wrote to the Commander-in-chief on the same subject, the 17th of March, from "Chappawamsic." He enclosed a detailed statement of the difficulty between Mr. Lawrence Washington "second son of that very worthy man, Mr. Lawrence Washington of Chetauque," and "Mr. Philip Alexander, a son of John Alexander of the same place." Thomson Mason's letter concludes in these words:

"Permit me now, sir, to return you my warmest acknowledgments for your very great kindness showed to my son Stevens Thomson at the siege of York, of which both my son and self retain the most grateful sense. The success of that siege, so glorious to your Excellency, gave none of your numerous friends more unfeigned pleasure than your Excellency's most obedient and most obliged humble servant,

"THOMSON MASON." [1]

The preliminaries of the treaty of peace were signed by the European powers in January, 1783. The Tory ministry of Lord North had given place to the Whigs under the Marquis of Rockingham. Fox was at the head of the foreign department, and Lord Shelburne had charge of the colonies. Fox and Shelburne differed on the question of the status of the colonies, whether they should be treated as already independent, or as made so by the treaty. Lord Shelburne supported the latter view, and carried his point. It was finally decided, through the suggestion of John Adams, that the United States would not require from Great Britain a formal declaration of their independence, if the same form was used by the British commission treating with them as was used in treating with other powers. [2]

Thomson Mason, in a letter to be given later, compares a certain party in the Virginia Assembly to the Shelburne faction in Parliament. The following letter was written by Colonel Mason to Arthur Lee, then in Congress:

[1] Washington MSS., State Department.
[2] "Life of John Adams," p. 216: American Statesmen Series.

VIRGINIA, GUNSTON HALL,
March 25, 1783.

DEAR SIR:

I thank you for your several favors since I had the pleasure of seeing you last, the receipt of which I should have acknowledged earlier, but have been a long time disabled, by a very sore finger, from holding a pen.

Since your last of the 12th instant, informing me of the arrival of Capt. Barney, &c., I have seen a printed hand bill containing the preliminary Articles between Great Britain and the United States, and so far as I am able to judge, they are, upon the whole, as favorable as America, in her present situation, has a right to expect. The grand points are ceded to her, and as for the payment of debts contracted before the war, it is no more than justice requires, nor do I think it would have been sound policy in us to have abrogated them, had it been in our power. The far-fetched distinctions which have been attempted to be shown between this and other wars would hardly have been approved, as understood by mankind in general ; and with what degree of faith could the merchants of other nations have trusted their effects here, if their private property was in danger of being wrested from them and applied to our own use, upon any national quarrel, and upon arguments and principles in which we should be both judges and parties. There can't, therefore, be a stronger proof of the weakness or wickedness of our Assembly, than their late instructions to our delegates in Congress.

I once thought that we ought to risk a long war in order to bring the remaining British colonies into our Union, but time and reflection have altered my opinion. I have seen that lust of power, so natural to the mind of man, prevailing in Congress at a much earlier period than could well have been expected. I have seen some of the States, from partial, local, temporary views, conniving at, and fostering principles which would inevitably end in their own destruction. I have seen our legislatures trampling under foot the obligations of morality and justice, and wantonly invading the sacred rights of their fellow-citizens. It may not be amiss to have some rival power at their door, some powerful motives to restrain them within the bounds of moderation. It will at least be a comfortable reflection, that if our government should grow intolerable (which, judging of the future from the past, is neither impossible nor improbable) a man would have some place of refuge, the means of sheltering himself from anarchy, ignorance and knavery. But I hope everything from peace. I hope then to see our great national council, as well as our different assemblies, filled with men of honest characters, and of independent circumstances and principles, for until this shall be the case, our affairs can never go well. I therefore hope that the preliminary articles agreed to by our commissioners at Paris, will be ratified by Congress; that Capt. Barney may return with them as speedily as possible; and that nothing on our part may be wanting to hasten so desirable an event, for I presume his passport from the King of Great Britain is both in and out. I am anxious to hear the determination of Congress upon this important subject, and if there is no injunction of secrecy (and I don't see why there should) shall be much obliged to you for the earliest communication.

The refugee barges are lately returned, and again plundering on the shores of Potomac. One of their crews was lately pretty roughly handled by a small party of Northumberland militia. They lost two of their rascally officers and a few men, upon which they fled with the greatest precipitation. It is a mortifying reflection, and accords badly with the ideas of sovereignty and independence, that the power of two States is not sufficient to protect us from a band of robbers.

I have lately received two or three letters from Europe, *via* Philadelphia, every one of them broken open and sealed up again there, or at some of the intervening post-offices, as almost all the letters I have had these two years past from Europe have been. The post-office is a considerable tax upon the people; under proper regulations and in honest hands, it would be a great convenience and benefit to the public, but by such vile practices as these it is likely to become a nuisance to society. If Congress fails to put it under better regulations, or don't compel the postmaster-general to be more circumspect in the appointment of his deputies, the different States will soon be under the necessity of taking it out of their hands into their own.

I sincerely wish you health, and am with great esteem and respect,

Dear sir, your most obedient servant,

G. MASON.

P. S.—I beg leave to trouble you with the three inclosed letters to Mr. Johnson of Nantes, covering letters to my son George, and as they are duplicates, beg the favor of you to forward them by different vessels.[1]

Captain Joshua Barney, the celebrated naval hero of the Revolution, had sailed for France the preceding November carrying despatches to Dr. Franklin, and he had returned now with the welcome preliminaries of peace, and also with a loan of money from the French king.

The Virginia Assembly met in May, and was confronted with the important issues of the peace, as they affected Virginia and her section, as also with matters of internal government, and the powers of the Federal Congress. George Mason wrote to two of his friends in the Assembly, William Cabell and Patrick Henry, on the same day, asking them for their interest in support of a project of his son's, Thomson Mason, jr. Colonel Mason discusses public affairs in these letters, and, as was natural, writing them both at one sitting probably, he uses the same language frequently to his two correspondents. But there is a sufficient variety in their contents to warrant the publication of both letters.

FAIRFAX CO., GUNSTON HALL,
May 6th, 1783.

DEAR SIR :

I congratulate you most sincerely, upon the establishment of American liberty and independence. Happiness and prosperity are now within our reach ; but to attain and preserve them must depend upon our own wisdom and virtue. I hope the Assembly will revise several of our laws, and abolish all such of them as are contrary to the fundamental principles of justice. This and a strict adherence to the distinctions between right and wrong for the future, is absolutely necessary, to restore that confidence and reverence in the people for the legislature, which a contrary conduct has so greatly impaired, and without which their laws must ever remain little better than a dead letter. Frequent interference with private property and contracts, retrospective laws destructive of all public faith, as well as confidence between man and man, and flagrant violations of the Constitution must disgust the best

[1] MS. Letter.

and wisest part of the community, and occasion a general depravity of manners, bring the legislature into contempt, and finally produce anarchy and public convulsion.

I write to you with the freedom and sincerity of a friend, knowing that you detest such measures as much as I do. They drove me out of the Assembly, with a thorough conviction that it was not in my power to do any manner of good. The love of my country is not extinguished by it, and if I recover tolerable health, and have just cause to think I can do any essential public service, I shall return again into the legislature.

We are told here that the present Assembly intend to dissolve themselves to make way for a general convention to new model the Constitution. Will such a measure be proper, without a requisition from a majority of the people? If it can be done without such requisition, may not the caprice of future Assemblies repeat it from time to time, until the Constitution shall have lost all stability, and anarchy introduced in its stead? Or at any rate, will it not be better to defer it a year or two, until the present ferment (occasioned by the late sudden change) has subsided, and men's minds have had time to cool? We are very much alarmed, in this part of the country, least the Assembly should pass some laws infringing the Articles of Peace, and thereby involve us in a fresh quarrel with Great Britain, who might make reprisals upon our shipping or coasts, without much danger of offending the late belligerent powers in Europe, but I trust that more prudent and dispassionate councils will prevail.

One of my sons and one William Allison have lately erected a snuff manufactory in this county, and have already made a large quantity of snuff, which they intend to send soon into different parts of the country. Fearing the attempts of the British merchants [to send] such a manufacture here, they have presented a petition to the Assembly, for laying a duty upon snuff imported from foreign countries. The reasons for this are fully stated in their petition, which I beg the favor of you to examine, and if you think their request just and reasonable, I flatter myself they will be favored with your interest in the General Assembly.

I am with much respect and esteem, Dear sir,

Your most obedient servant,   G. MASON.[1]

To Col. William Cabell.

[1] " Virginia Historical Register," vol. iii., p. 84.

FAIRFAX COUNTY, GUNSTON HALL,
May 6, 1783.

DEAR SIR :

Although it is a long time since I had the honor of hearing from you, I reflect, and ever shall reflect, with pleasure on our former acquaintance and the proofs I have experienced of your esteem and friendship. I have enjoyed but indifferent health since I retired from public business : should I recover a better state of health, and have just cause to think I can render any essential public service, I shall return again to the Assembly.

I congratulate you most sincerely on the accomplishment of what I know was the warmest wish of your heart, the establishment of American independence and the liberty of our country. We are now to rank among the nations of the world, but whether our independence shall prove a blessing or a curse, must depend on our own wisdom or folly, virtue or wickedness ; judging of the future by the past, the prospect is not promising. Justice and virtue are the vital principles of republican government ; but among us a depravity of manners and morals prevails to the destruction of all confidence between man and man. It greatly behooves the Assembly to revise several of our laws ; to abolish all such as are contrary to the fundamental principles of justice, and by a strict adherence to the distinctions between right and wrong for the future to restore that confidence and reverence in the people for the legislature which has been so greatly impaired by a contrary conduct, and without which our laws can never be much more than a dead letter. It is in your power, my dear sir, to do more good and prevent more mischief than any man in this State ; and I doubt not that you will exert the great talents with which God has blessed you in promoting the public happiness and prosperity. We are told that the present Assembly intend to dissolve themselves, in order to make way for a general convention to new-model the constitution of government. Will such a measure be proper without a requisition of the people ? If it can be done without such requisition, the caprice of future Assemblies may repeat it from time to time until the stability of the constitution is totally destroyed and anarchy introduced in its stead. Or at any rate will it not be better to defer it a year or two until the present ferment (occasioned by the late sudden change) has subsided and men's minds have had time to cool ?

The people in this part of the country are made very uneasy by the reports we have from below, that the Assembly will make some laws or resolutions respecting British debts which may infringe the articles of the peace, under the mistaken idea that Great Britain will not risk a renewal of the war on account of such an infraction of the treaty. We see by the late public papers that the terms of peace with America are so strongly censured in both houses of Parliament, that it has occasioned or will occasion a total change in the ministry. A new ministry averse to the treaty, or even the ministry who concluded it, might resent or avenge any infraction of its provisions in any particular State, by reprisals upon the ships or coasts of such State, or by sending two or three frigates to intercept their trade, without danger of involving themselves in a new war; for the power of war and peace and of making treaties being in Congress and not in the separate States, any such act would be considered as an unwarrantable assumption of power in the State adopting it; and we have no reason to expect that either the late belligerent powers in Europe, or even the American States in general, would make a common cause of it. It is easy to foresee that, in such an event, our situation would be neither safe nor honorable. Had it been in the power of the American commissioners (which it certainly was not) to have abolished the British debts here, it would have been but short-sighted policy to have done so. The far-fetched arguments which have been used to show the distinction between this and other wars, would not have been approved or comprehended, by the bulk of mankind; and with what degree of confidence would foreign merchants have ventured their effects here, if upon any national quarrel they were liable to confiscation? I could have wished, indeed, that some reasonable time had been allowed for the payment of the British debts, and that the interest on them had been relinquished. As to the first, the desire of the British merchants to reinstate themselves in their trade here will probably prevent their pressing their debtors, and as to the last, their bond-debts only will carry interest. It is notorious, that the custom of giving interest upon common accounts was introduced by the partiality of the merchants of whom the jurors at the general court were chiefly composed for several years before the late Revolution. Under our present circumstances, I think the accounts of the British creditors may be safely trusted to the Virginia juries without any interposition of the legislature. In conversation upon this subject we hear sometimes a very absurd question : "If we are now to pay the debts due to British merchants, what have we been fighting for all this while ?" Surely not to avoid our just debts or to cheat our creditors ; but to rescue our country from the oppression and tyranny of the British government, and to secure the rights and liberties of ourselves and of our posterity, which we have happily accomplished. The ministry in Great Britain and the Tories here have indeed constantly accused us of engaging in the war to avoid the payment of our just debts ; but every honest man has denied so injurious a charge with indignation. Upon the whole we have certainly obtained better terms of peace than America had cause to expect ; all the great points are ceded to us, and I cannot but think it would be highly dangerous and imprudent to risk a breach of it.

The people here too are greatly alarmed at a prevailing notion, that those men who have paid the British debts into the Treasury in depreciated paper money, instead of making up the real value to their creditors, will now attempt to throw the difference upon the shoulders of the public and raise it by taxes upon the people. I should hope that such an iniquitous scheme will be rejected with the contempt it deserves. If it is adopted it will probably cause some violent convulsion ; the people being determined, in many parts of the country, to form associations against it, and to resist the payment of any taxes imposed on them for discharging the private debts of individuals.

I hope the Assembly will, as soon as they meet, postpone the collection of taxes (which by an act of last session were to be paid in this month) until August or September ; the war being ended, the delay will occasion no material inconvenience to the public, and though it will not diminish the revenue a shilling, it will lessen the taxes upon the people 100 % by enabling them to pay with one half the tobacco or other produce which it would at this time require. If the people are compelled to pay immediately, the merchants taking advantage of their necessity will keep down the price of tobacco in a manner that may affect the market through the whole season ; whereas if the collection of taxes be postponed, the people will be under no necessity of selling until the arrival of a great many ships has increased the demand, and raised the price of country produce. In short, the immediate collection of the taxes will, in a great measure, deprive the people of the benefits of peace this year.

One of my sons and one William Allison (who have in partnership erected a snuff manufactory in this county) have presented a petition to the Assembly for laying a duty upon snuff imported from foreign countries; the reasons in support of it being fully stated in their petition, I will not trouble you with a recapitulation, but beg the favor of you to examine the petition, and if you think it just and reasonable I flatter myself it will have your support and patronage. My son George (who is still in Europe) desires me to present his most respectful compliments to you, with his thanks for the testimonial you were so kind as to give him under the seal of the commonwealth; it has been of great service in recommending him to the notice of many gentlemen of rank and fortune. I have lately received a letter from him dated Paris the 20th February, in which he gives very strong hints of great duplicity in some articles of European politics, such as, he says, he does not care to venture upon paper that is to cross the Atlantic, but shall reserve the communication until he arrives in America, which he expects will be about the middle of July; and he concludes with the following expression: "I wish America would put her trust only in God and herself, and have as little to do with the politics of Europe as possible." He tells me our old friend Mazzey [Mazzei?] was then in Paris and preparing to return to America.

I have reason to apologise for this long letter, but I hope your candor will excuse it and ascribe it to its true cause, the unfeigned esteem and regard with which I am, dear sir,

Your affectionate and obedient servant,

G. Mason.

To Hon. Patrick Henry.[1]

After seven years of war the land was blessed with peace. After the long struggle to secure the autonomy they had established, the independence of the American States was acknowledged by all the world. Small wonder that men's

[1] MS. Letter.

minds were in a "ferment" through the "late sudden change." This was no time for remodelling the State constitution George Mason felt. What Virginia's duties were, and what the crisis demanded from her representatives in the Assembly, Colonel Mason states clearly and forcibly in "The Address and Instructions of their Constituents" to Alexander Henderson and Charles Broadwater, the delegates from Fairfax County at this time. Though no names are signed to this paper there can be no doubt, to those who are familiar with his style and his opinions, that George Mason was the writer of it; and as the leading citizen of his county, and on so many previous occasions its spokesman, the presumption is most natural that the like office was assigned to him at this time.

" May 30th, 1783.

"GENTLEMEN :

"We have committed to you the greatest and most sacred trust, which a free people can repose in any of their fellow-citizens; the care of our dearest and most important interests, the protection of our rights and liberty, and the power of making, on our behalf, those laws by which we are to be governed, and this commonwealth preserved in safety and prosperity. And although we confide thoroughly in your integrity and attachment to the public good, yet we judge it expedient, at this critical and important season, to communicate to you our sentiments, and to exercise our undoubted right of instructing you, as our immediate Representatives in the Legislature.

" And first, Gentlemen, we desire and expressly instruct you, that you give not your assent to, and on the contrary, that you oppose, to the utmost of your power, the smallest infraction of the late Treaty of Peace, either with respect to the payment of debts, or in any other matter whatsoever, whereby the public faith, solemnly pledged by the American Commissioners duly authorized, may be violated, and this country again involved in the calamities of war, or the danger of reprisals.

"We also direct and instruct you, that you use your utmost endeavors to enact a law for repayment of the principal and interest to each and every individual, who hath paid paper money into the public treasury, in discharge of debts due to British creditors, according to its real value in specie, to be adjusted by the legal scale of depreciation, at the time each sum was respectively placed in the Treasury ; and that such debts, as well as all other private debts and contracts, be thereafter left to the common course of the laws of the land. And in case of any division of the House, upon either of these subjects, or upon any other important matter, whereby the rights of the people, and the safety of the Commonwealth may be endangered, the maxims of justice contravened, or the fundamental principles of the Constitution violated ; we desire and instruct you to call for and cause to be published, the yeas and nays upon the state of the question, that so the people may, at least, be enabled to distinguish their country's foes from its friends, and hereafter to separate the *tares* from the *corn*.

"We desire and instruct you, that you give not your assent to, and that you firmly oppose, granting any exclusive privileges or advantages in our trade, to any particular kingdom or nation, other than what may be stipulated in the Commercial Treaties concluded by the authority of Congress, it being the true and permanent interest of America to admit the trade of all nations, upon equal terms, without preference to any, further than the goodness and cheapness of their commodities may entitle them to.

"We desire and instruct you that you give not your assent to, and that you oppose, any further occlusion of the Courts of Justice ; as withholding the due and regular administration of justice in any country, must loosen the bonds of society, corrupt the morals of the people, and tend to produce anarchy and public confusion.

"We desire and instruct you to oppose all future emissions of paper money ; all interference of the Legislature in private contracts, they being properly cognizable in the judiciary departments of the State ; all *ex post facto* laws, except such only as are warranted by the greatest emergencies, and the plain principles of justice ; and that you endeavour to procure a revisal or repeal of all laws, which may have been heretofore made, contrary to such principles.

"We desire and instruct you to oppose any further delay in the collection of this year's taxes than will be absolutely necessary to give the people the benefit of this summer's market, for their commodities now on hand ; all such delays being highly injurious to public credit.

"We desire and instruct you to promote a strict enquiry into the expenditure of public money, and the bringing to speedy account and punishment all public delinquents and defaulters.

"We desire and instruct you to endeavour to procure ample justice to the officers and soldiers of the American army ; who though constantly surrounded with uncommon distress and difficulties, have so bravely defended the rights and liberties of their country.

"We desire and instruct you that you assent not to, and that you oppose repealing the law for preventing extensive credits upon open accounts ; and also that you assent not to, but oppose the imposition of any greater duty upon imported iron or cordage than shall be imposed upon other imported goods, for the reasons respectively given in our petitions to the Assembly upon these subjects.

"We desire and instruct you strenuously to oppose all encroachments of the American Congress upon the sovereignty and jurisdiction of the separate States ; and every assumption of power, not expressly vested in them, by the Articles of Confederation. If experience shall prove that further powers are necessary and safe, they can be granted only by additional articles to the Confederation, duly acceded to by all the States ; for if Congress, upon the plea of necessity, or upon any pretence whatever, can arrogate powers not warranted by the Articles of Confederation, in one instance, they may in another, or in an hundred ; every repetition will be strengthened and confirmed by precedents.

"And in particular we desire and instruct you to oppose any attempts which may be made by Congress to obtain a perpetual revenue, or the appointment of revenue officers. Were these powers superadded to those they already possess, the Articles of Confederation, and the Constitutions of Government in the different States would prove mere parchment bulwarks to American liberty,

"We like not the language of the late address from Congress to the different States, and of the report of their committee upon the subject of revenue, published in the same pamphlet. If they are carefully and impartially examined, they will be found to exhibit strong proofs of lust of power : They contain the same kind of arguments which were formerly used in the business of ship money, and to justify the arbitrary measures of the race of Stuarts in England. ·And the present king and council of Great Britain might not improperly adopt great part of them, to prove the expediency of levying money without consent of Parliament. After having reluctantly given up part of what they found they could not maintain, they still insist that the several States shall invest *the United States in Congress assembled with a power to levy*, for the use of the United States, the following duties, &c., and that the revenue officers shall be amenable to Congress. The very style is alarming. The proposed duties may be proper, but the separate States only can safely have *the power of levying taxes*. Congress should not have even the appearance of such a power. Forms generally imply substance, and such a precedent may be applied to dangerous purposes hereafter. When the same man, or set of men, holds both the sword and the purse, there is an end of liberty. As little are we satisfied with the resolution of Congress of the 10th of October, 1780, lately renewed, engaging that *the unappropriated lands* 'that may be ceded or relinquished to the United States by any particular States, shall be disposed of for the common benefit of the United States.' Who is to judge of the quality and legality of pretended appropriations? And will this vague resolution be a sufficient bar to Congress against confirming the claims under Indian purchases, or pretended grants from the Crown of Great Britain, in which many of their own members are interested as partners, and by which great part of the ceded lands may be converted to private, instead of public purposes? The intrigues of the great land companies, and the methods by which they have strengthened their interest are no secret to the public. We are also at a loss to know whence Congress derives the powers of demanding cessions of lands and of erecting new States before such powers have been granted them by their constituents.

"And finally we recommend it to you (for in this we will not presume to give positive instructions) to endeavour to obtain an instruction from the General Assembly to the Virginia delegates in Congress, against sending ambassadors to the courts of Europe; it being an expence which (in our present circumstances) these United States are unable to support. Such appointments can hardly fail of producing dangerous combinations, factions, and cabals, in the great council of America. And from the great

distance and the difficulty of knowing and examining their conduct, there is danger, too, that some of the persons so sent, may
be corrupted and pensioned by the courts where they reside. We
are of opinion, that consuls to superintend our trade (at less than a
tenth part of the charge of ambassadors) will be sufficient to
answer every good purpose. And nature having separated us, by
an immense ocean, from the European nations, the less we have to
do with their quarrels or politics, the better. Having thus, Gentlemen, given you our opinions and instructions, upon such subjects
as we deem at this time most important, we remain, with sentiments of great respect and esteem, your friends and fellow-
citizens." [1]

Thomson Mason was in the Assembly during this session,
and his views upon public affairs were given to his constituents in the following letter:

To the Freeholders of Stafford County:

RICHMOND, June 10th, 1783.

GENTLEMEN :

I return you my sincere thanks for the confidence you have
placed in me, in electing me a delegate to represent you in the
General Assembly ; and I shall now, in return, lay before you the
views and motives which induced me to offer myself a candidate at
your late election. It is needless to assert, that no private interest
of my own actuated me, because from your acquaintance with me
from my youth, you know it did not. The fears of some of you,
that I would endeavour to prevent the Treaty of Peace from
being ratified, or the payment of British debts, were groundless ;
no man was more desirous of a peace, or entertained a more fixed
regard for the strict rules of justice than myself, and my disposition
is not vindictive ; but I think the safety of my country depends
upon excluding from the rights of citizenship those who joined the
enemy and not only deserted us in the hour of distress, but by
their arms and false councils assisted our enemies in prolonging
the war against us. And those who remained among us, and
avowed principles incompatible with American liberty, I think also

[1] *The Virginia Gazette*, June 7, 1783.

ought never to be trusted with any office, civil or military, nor even to be allowed to vote for any man who is to guide our public councils. I wished also to suspend all executions on judgments obtained for debts contracted before the war, so as to issue for one fourth or fifth part of the debt annually, till the whole was discharged, in order to place the debtor as near as we could in the same flourishing situation that he was when that debt was contracted ; for I really dreaded, that if Tory and refugee creditors were suffered to return and harass their debtors with that rapacious and vindictive spirit which we have reason to suppose they will, that those citizens who had been most active in defence of the liberties of their country would be the devoted victims of their fury, and in the present scarcity of money, great part of the property of this country would centre in the hands of the avowed enemies to liberty ; and as power is the constant, the necessary attendant on property, that after all the struggles of the virtuous, the wicked would at last prevail, and introduce a more slavish dependence upon Britain than that from which we have just emerged.

I wished also to prevent the money paid into the Treasury, either for British debts or loans, from being accounted for on any other terms, than at the real depreciation at the time it was paid in. I wished to introduce some regular system into our revenue laws, so as to pass several distinct laws establishing separate substantial funds ; first for the support of our civil government, secondly, for the annual payment of the interest of our foreign debt, thirdly, for the payment of the annual interest of the debt due to the army, and fourthly, for that due to our own citizens ; that these funds should be most sacredly applied to the separate purpose for which each was designed, and the overplus go towards sinking the principal of each ; and I was not without hopes that the increase of our inhabitants, commerce, and wealth would be so rapidly great, that the excess of each fund would pay off that principal in less than twelve years.

I wished to encourage the culture of hemp, by giving a bounty to the makers of it, and laying such a duty on imported cordage as would pay that bounty, that we might not be altogether dependent upon foreigners for the means of fitting out vessels, either for necessary defence or the extension of our commerce.

And I wished to place our bay and river trade, and above all our fisheries, on such a foundation, as to render them useful nurseries of free seamen ; on the increase of which our naval strength and the extension of our commerce so materially depend.

Whether I shall succeed in all or any of these views, I shall be better able to inform you when I return ; in the meantime think me not guilty of inconsistency, if you find by the journals that I should often vote against measures which by them seem to be proposed by myself ; for where there are a large number to deliberate upon any measure, in which a majority are to agree, the measure is often so altered as to make it exceedingly different from what it was first intended to be.

I am, gentlemen, with the highest sentiments of gratitude and esteem, your sincerely affectionate,

THOMSON MASON.[1]

The great question before the Assembly, in the estimation of Madison, Jefferson, and Joseph Jones was the report on the federal impost. The duty law passed at a previous session had been repealed, it was said through the agency of the Lees, Richard Henry, and Arthur, but it was now hoped that it would be re-enacted. Jefferson wrote to Madison, on the 3d of May, giving a somewhat cynical sketch of the House, and the attitude of its prominent members in regard to the articles proposed by Madison covering this subject. The Lees were against them : " Henry, as usual, is involved in mystery" ; Thomson Mason " is a meteor whose path cannot be calculated. All the powers of his mind seem at present to be concentrated in one single object—the producing a convention to new-model the State constitution. This is a subject much agitated, and seems the only one they will have to amuse themselves with till they shall receive your propositions." [2]   Joseph Jones hurried from his seat in Congress to attend the Assembly, and he wrote regularly to Madison while in Richmond to report the progress of affairs. Patrick Henry and Richard Henry Lee he describes as the

[1] *Virginia Gazette*, June 14, 1783.
[2] Bancroft's " History of the Constitution," vol. i., Appendix, p. 310.

" two great commanders " in the House, but he intimates that there is too much said and too little done. On the 21st of June he wrote :

" We are now as usual putting to sleep many of the bills that have employed our time and attention for great part of this session. Among them two, one for the benefit of debtors, the other for regulating the proceedings in the county courts. These were thought to have some connection and ought to rest together. Mr. Mason introduced and patronized the debtors' bill. I was not in the House when it was read, but understand it allowed all creditors to obtain judgment, but suspended execution, rather permitted it for a fifth of the debt annually, for five years, comprehending as well foreign as domestic credits. I came into the House during the debate and from the observations of R. H. L [ee] and those who opposed the bill its principle was severely reprobated. Mr. Mason and C. M. T. [Charles Minn Thruston] warmly supported it and pronounced it indispensably necessary to preserve the people from ruin and the country independent. The disposition of the members, however, was so prevalent for lopping off all business not really necessary that the latter gentlemen were obliged to submit to its being referred to the next session. This bill, at least so far as respected British creditors, would have had more advocates but for the late period at which it was introduced, and because there already existed and will continue in force until the 1st of December a law that prohibits suits for or on account of British subjects." [1]

A letter from Thomson Mason to John Francis Mercer, half-brother to George and James Mercer, and at this time in the Continental Congress, gives a graphic account of Virginia politics, and brings before us in lively colors the aspect of the Assembly which was just about to close its session.

MY DEAR SIR :   RICHMOND, 22d June, 1783.

I must entreat your forgiveness in having so long neglected to answer your very obliging favor of April, but have really been so much engaged in the duties of my profession, and the business of

---

[1] " Letters of Joseph Jones," p. 120.

the public, that I have scarce had a moment's leisure. Add to this the very infirm state of my health, and at times the total disability of my better hand, and you will be convinced that my silence proceeded not from any disrespect, for believe me, sir, I esteem you as I ought.

I thank you most sincerely for the very interesting intelligence you gave me, of which I endeavoured to avail myself to promote the public good, though I am sorry to say to little purpose, as the Shelborne faction, as I have christened them, are yet very powerful though they lose ground.

·I never saw the provisional Treaty of Peace till I reached Garrard's, in my way to this place, and did not determine upon the part I afterwards took on that occasion, till I knew whether I could prevail on my son who was here to declare himself for Loudon, and till I had consulted your brother whether it might not interfere with your election. The result of these conferences ended in both my son and myself writing up to our respective counties, that we would serve if they chose us. In my letter to my son John which I desired him to make public, I expressed my wishes that all my friends would also be yours, and was not without hopes that we should both have been elected, and we certainly should have been so, but a particular party, having made several unsuccessful attempts to raise you up an opponent, had after I left the county, prevailed on young Col. Garrard to set up in professed opposition to you, in partnership with Col. Carter. He rode from house to house in the county, and supported by Col. Carter prevailed upon many to promise him, even before my intentions were known. Notwithstanding this, if our election had been managed properly you would have run Col. Carter hard ; but instead of our staunch friends (which actually formed a majority of those present) pushing us both from the beginning, which they ought to have done, as both the other candidates were our professed enemies, they only pushed in such who were only for one of us, and they giving one vote, some to Garrard and some to Carter, added to those who were their staunch friends, run those gentlemen so far ahead that our friends began to be apprehensive we should both be dropped, and Garrard having declared that he would resign his pretensions if you were withdrawn, outwitted your friends so far as to withdraw you, expecting by so doing that I should then be certainly elected, as Garrard would then withdraw. But here they found themselves deceived ; Garrard and Carter still continued to push their elections, and my friends threw their votes upon Carter till they got me about a dozen votes ahead of Garrard, who finding he had not another vote resigned, and upwards of thirty of my friends then thought it unnecessary to vote at all, not duly considering that this might possibly have overturned my election in case of a controversy. Your old friend Col. Mountjoy quarrelled with his brother-in-law on account of his conduct in setting up in opposition to you. Thus I have given you a particular account of the election as stated to me, for I was not there ; if I had [been] I think you would have run my colleague hard ; if not have turned him out, though many untruths, and the inconvenience of serving in Congress and Assembly, were I am told urged much to your prejudice.

The Assembly have passed an act to render members of Congress ineligible in future for the Assembly. I fancy some maneuvering was intended to your prejudice in the ballot for members of Congress. It was the general sense of gentlemen without doors, that there would be no election till the November session ; but upon my going up to defend Mr. Lawrence Washington of King George (who was discharged from further trial for the death of Mr. Alexander) the House in that week proceeded to ballot for members of Congress, and you were not even put in nomination for some time, which my son Stephens perceiving, got so far the better of his false modesty, as to propose you, and afterwards supported your interest warmly without doors. Mr. Jefferson, Mr. Hardy, yourself, Dr. Lee and Col. Monroe were elected. It was lucky for Dr. Lee that the election came on so soon, as I am told the part he took two days afterwards against a French ship, which having been seized through the ignorance of the captain, he petitioned for the interposition of the Assembly and obtained it, against the violent opposition of several who always have been staunch Whigs. Dr. Lee joined in this opposition, and by so doing gave great umbrage to many who had before voted for him, as a delegate to Congress, but declared they would never do so again. So much for private intelligence.

I am really alarmed at the critical situation we stand in with Great Britain, and the more so from their refusal to deliver up to several of the citizens of this State their slaves, when demanded under the authority of the Executive, by their respective masters, in direct violation of the Treaty. I cannot entirely agree with you in your sentiments on the subject of British debts. The occlusion of the courts of justice by any law, would certainly be a legal impediment, but still I think that even this might be justly done without infringing the treaty, if we made no distinction between the British and domestic creditor, for every country has an inherent right of regulating her internal police, and surely where there is no discrimination, a British sovereign has no right by the law of nations, to expect, much less to demand greater privileges from us for his subjects than we grant to our own citizens. And the present situation of our country is such, that the justice we owe our citizens, renders it necessary to place them before they are called upon to pay their debts, in the same situation they were in when those debts were contracted. Under this idea I drew and introduced a bill for the relief of debtors, and another for the security of creditors. Under the last I placed our courts in such a situation as to enable the creditor in all cases where no defence could be made, to obtain a judgment in six months at the farthest, and in all other cases in fifteen months. By the first bill I enabled all debtors upon giving an additional security, who were also to be liable to execution upon the judgment against the principal, in case of non-payment, to pay off the judgments when obtained in five annual payments ; the judgments to carry interest, and remain in force for six years without being revived by *Sci: fa.*, and an execution to issue annually for one fifth of the judgment, and interest against principal and security, till the whole was discharged. All interest during the war was to cease, and no debts to be affected by this act contracted after the passing of it ; with a proviso that it should not extend to any debts contracted with foreigners during the war by individuals.

These laws being for the mutual advantage of debtor and creditor, and a mere regulation of our internal police, in which the British subject was placed on the same footing with our own citizens (indeed the word British was not even mentioned in the bill) nor any kind of distinction set up, I well hoped would have gone down ; but the Shelborne faction were apprehensive it might possibly give umbrage to Britain, and induce them to infringe the treaty. They put off the consideration of the first bill to the next session of the Assembly, and I myself moved for putting off that for speedy trials to the same time, and after a pretty warm opposition succeeded.

We have also been warmly engaged upon a bill to declare who should in future become citizens of this State. The bill as I had modelled it (for it was first brought in with great severity and too little discrimination) excluded all persons who being residents of the United States after the Declaration of Independence had aided and assisted the enemy, from ever becoming citizens or residing amongst us for any longer or other time than was or should be stipulated in the provisional articles or definitive treaty of peace ; that all others who either left us or, remaining amongst us, had avowed principles inimical to the independence of America, should be incapable of holding any post, civil or military, of sitting in either House of Assembly, of voting at any election, or of participating in our councils for the preservation of that independence which they had endeavoured to prevent. Here again the Shelborne faction took the alarm, and the threat of being here a week longer when harvest was approaching, induced a majority to postpone the consideration of this also till the next session of Assembly, for which, as I had the yeas and nays taken, I fancy their constituents will not thank them much on their return.

The plan proposed by Congress for placing in their hands a permanent fund for the discharge of the federal debt was rejected by a great majority as a precedent dangerous to liberty upon this principle, that as we had already entrusted them with the sword, if we were to give them the purse also, the control we should afterwards have over them would be but a feeble barrier against future encroachments ; for such was the lust of power, that whoever was in possession of it would still endeavour to extend it, and though we should even change our members of Congress annually it would be immaterial to us whether we chose A. B. C. or X. Y. Z., since every letter of the alphabet, whilst they were members of any body, would endeavour to support and extend the power of that body, and I candidly confess, my friend, that I joined with the majority in this opinion. Yet sensible of the necessity of establishing funds, we have laid an impost of five per cent. ad valorem and the duties recommended by Congress exactly agreeable to their idea of this matter, as to the quantum, but it is to be collected by our own officers, and paid by them to the Congressional receiver, who is to give a receipt for it, to be carried to our account and credited to this State upon a future settlement, and this is to continue till the whole debt is discharged. But this act is not to be applied to this purpose until the other States have passed laws similar to it. This fund it is calculated will amount to forty-thousand pounds, and we have added to it our whole land tax, which amounts at this time to ninety-five thousand pounds annually, and will be an increasing fund as our back lands are rapidly settling. This tax is to be paid by the sheriffs to our treasurer and by him paid to the Continental receiver, who is to give a receipt for the same, and carry it to our credit on a future settlement ; and if these funds should fall short, the deficiency is to be made good out of the slave tax, which amounts to one hundred and twenty thousand pounds annually, but as we do not expect that this last fund will ever be called on, in aid of the others, we have ventured to appropriate part of the slave tax to other purposes. That I may be perfectly understood upon this subject, the duties upon imposts and the land tax are appropriated to Congress till the whole of the Continental debt is discharged, without having any other regard to this State's particular quota of that debt than to have credit at a future settlement of what we may pay more than our quota amounts to.

Without regard to our internal police of revenue we have passed a law to establish a fund for paying the annual interest of the certificates granted our officers and soldiers, and the principal at eight annual payments, the first payment to be made the first day of January, 1786. To do this we have laid an additional tax of *1d. per bushel upon salt*, ⚹ 2 / per ct. on imported hemp, 1 / per ct. on imported cordage, 1 / per lb. on imported snuff, 4d. per gallon on imported spirits, 6 per gallon upon wine, a duty upon tea, sugar and some other articles which I do not recollect, and *5 / per hogshead on tobacco.*⚹ [Mr. Mason makes this marginal note : " N. B. I think the articles marked thus ⚹ ought not to have been taxed, because the first being a necessary of life will fall heavy upon the poor especially in the back parts where it will raise the price of salt even in Loudon to 7 or 8 / and in counties further back to double that sum, and tobacco is an export."] This it is thought will amount to thirty thousand pounds. The deficiency is to be made good by the slave tax. It is presumed that a fund of seventy thousand pounds will answer the ends proposed by this law.

For my own part I think this law an unwise one, because no new tax ought ever to be appropriated to any purpose but to the contingent charges of government, till experience has evinced that the commodity taxed will bear it with convenience, and some certain estimate can be made of what it will produce, as when it is once appropriated to a permanent fund it cannot afterwards be discontinued, however inconvenient, without a breach of public faith. I should therefore have been better pleased that the whole seventy thousand pounds had been drawn from the State tax, and these duties appropriated to the contingent charges of government, and then they might have been altered hereafter as experience might have convinced us was necessary. Besides there not being a particular portion of the slave tax fund set apart for this use, and the civil list, the deficiencies to Congress and the deficiency to the officers and soldiers, all being quartered upon that fund, without pointing out what proportion of it shall be applied to each, will introduce confusion ; some creditors will get all, some none, and our credit be thereby impaired, for I am convinced our funds are amply sufficient, but from want of system and method in that department alone, all our distresses arrive. To illustrate this I will state the true situation of our debts and funds as nearly as I can from memory, which though not strictly right will be nearly so.

Annual land tax	£ 95,000 increasing rapidly.
Impost	40,000
	£135,000
Part of slave tax	15,000
	£150,000 to be paid to Congress.
Annual balance of slave tax	£105,000
Additional imposts	30,000
Poll tax upon whites, rapidly increasing	50,000
Upon horses, cattle and wheel carriages	40,000
Upon ordinary and marriage licences	5,000
	£230,000

Officers' and soldiers' certificates	£70,000
Civil list expenditures, including the executive, judiciary and legislative and members to Congress	30,000
Loan Office certificates, 250,000, is	15,000
British debts paid into the treasury when settled a depreciation 50,000	3,000
Foreign and domestic debt 150,000	15,000
Contingent charges of government	20,000
	£153,000
Balance to be applied towards paying the principal . . .	£77,000

We yesterday received the report from a committee to whom was referred Mr. Simon Nathan's claim to a large quantity of tobacco, under an award given by some gentlemen in Philadelphia to whom it was submitted by our delegates in Congress at the request of the governor. The committee had voted it reasonable, upon a supposition that the State was bound by the acceptance of the bills by the governor, and the award in Philadelphia ; but it appearing manifestly that the bills were drawn for paper currency at a depreciated value, only equal to £1500, though the bills were for £13,000, and that the governor had actually paid 200,000 tobacco at 25 per ct., a large majority refused to pay more, upon this principle, that the governor being deceived or even mistaken at the time of his acceptance, that acceptance was not binding for more than was actually due ; and it appearing upon the face of the award, that the arbitrators were mistaken in the matter of fact, viz. that they were drawn for specie value the State was not bound by it, since that would be a sufficient foundation for setting aside an award in any court of judicature. The matter is again to be referred to arbitrators in Maryland.[1]

Thus I have now given you a particular account of all our public affairs worth mentioning. And now let me ask my young friend if none of the young ladies of Philadelphia have had influence enough with you to resign the name given you by some ladies in Prince William ? I presume you have heard that your acquaintance my son Stephens was married the first of May. He and his

[1] Compare the letter of Edmund Randolph on this subject, Conway's " Life of Randolph," p. 51. Thomson Mason gives good reasons for the so-called " repudiation."

lady (formerly Miss Polly Armistead) who are both in town, present their compliments to you.

Adieu my dear sir, and believe me to be

Your sincerely affectionate

THOMSON MASON.[1]

George Mason wrote from "Gunston Hall," the 27th of August to Messrs. Hunter, Allison, and Company, merchants in Alexandria, a letter of business relating to his tobacco sales, and in a postscript he gives the news he had lately received from Europe. "I have a letter," he writes, "from my son George, dated in Nantes, June 20th, where he has been waiting six or seven weeks for a passage in the *Hannibal,* Capt. Cunningham. He says the definitive treaty is proceeding slowly, on account of the difficulties of adjusting matters with the States-General. The court of London, have in the meantime made provision by proclamation, for a commercial intercourse with the United States of America. The Algerines have fitted out a small fleet on purpose to cruise against American vessels, notwithstanding the Emperor of Morocco's orders to his Admiral. I very much suspect this a British intrigue to discourage our trade in the Mediterranean." [1]

General Greene, returning from the South in the fall of 1783, records in his diary the incidents of his journey. Near Dumfries his carriage was overturned, and he was much bruised. But he spent an agreeable evening there at Colonel Grayson's, and dined on the 13th of September at "Mount Vernon." At Alexandria he was taken ill with fever, which prevented him from accepting the public dinner the citizens wished to give him. He writes from Alexandria:

"R. H. Lee and many others came to see me, but I was too unwell to enjoy company, and most part of the time to see any. . . . Colonel [name illegible] and his son William, an amiable youth, was to see me, and carried off Major Hyrné on a visit to

[1] MS. Letter.

Mr. Mason's, where one of the young ladies made a great impression on his heart." [1]

This was probably Colonel Mason and his son William Mason.

At the meeting of the Assembly in October, General Nelson presented a bill to invest the United States with a power to lay certain duties for the use of the United States. This power of taxation was the one the States least liked to entrust to Congress, but an urgent public necessity eventually forced the measure from them. On the 26th of November, the speaker laid before the House a letter from Edmund Randolph, respecting the proceedings of the persons appointed to vindicate the title of Virginia to western territory, stating the progress made in that business. Rives, in his "Life of Madison," says of the work appointed the committee that it does not appear the task was ever executed. A defence, however, was prepared, as would appear from this letter of Edmund Randolph to the Speaker of the House. In it he speaks of the difficulty of getting the committee together, and adds:

"Mr. George Mason has already, however, perused and approved about a third of the composition. If the General Assembly will therefore permit the work to go into print under the correction of Mr. Mason and myself, we may probably be able soon to concert the measures necessary for its publication, as I shall see him on my way to Alexandria about the 24th of next month, whither I am going on business of Mr. Nathan." [2]

On the 8th of December the House resolved:

"That the delegates of this State to the Congress of the United States be instructed and fully authorized to convey, by proper instrument, in writing on the part of this State to the Congress of the United States, all right, title and claim, which the said Commonwealth hath to the lands northward of the Ohio, upon

---

[1] "Life of Genl. Nathaniel Greene," vol. ii., George Washington Greene, p. 508.

[2] MS. Letter, State Library, Richmond.

the terms contained in the act of Congress of the thirteenth September last : *Provided* that lands be reserved out of these hereby proposed to be ceded sufficient to make good the several military bounties agreed to be given to sundry officers by resolutions of both Houses of Assembly : the lands hitherto reserved being insufficient for that purpose."

And on the 15th Joseph Jones presented a bill in accordance with this resolution.[1] This cession was accepted by Congress and, as Hinsdale says in his able work on this subject, it ended the long struggle between Virginia and the States in Congress opposed to her rights, leaving Virginia substantially victorious. She retained, as she had desired, the lands now forming the States of Kentucky and West Virginia, "the territory south-east of the Ohio, the sole question at issue."[2] In the interests of peace and union, Virginia had made a generous gift to the Confederacy. She parted with two hundred and seventy thousand, five hundred and fifty square miles of territory, which by its sale since to private individuals has enriched the Federal treasury to the extent of more than a hundred million of dollars.[3] George Mason, as has been seen, first sketched the terms of this cession, and by his influence, in and out of the Assembly, aided in securing its adoption by his State.

What Colonel Mason thought of the measures of the Assembly at this session we learn through a letter from Madison to Jefferson, written after his return from Congress then sitting at Annapolis :

" ORANGE, December 10th, 1783.

.   .   .   .

"I took Col. Mason in my way, and had an evening's conversation with him. I found him much less opposed to the general impost than I expected. Indeed he disclaimed all opposition

[1] Journal of the Assembly.

[2] " The Old Northwest," p. 245. A part of this territory was torn from Virginia, in direct violation of the Constitution, and erected into a new State, within our own time.

[3] Bill introduced into the Virginia Assembly, February, 1888.

to the measure itself, but had taken up a vague apprehension, that, if adopted at this crisis, it might embarrass the defence of our trade against British machinations. He seemed, upon the whole, to acquiesce in the territorial cession, but dwelt much on the expediency of the guaranty. On the article of a convention for revising our form of State government, he was sound and ripe, and, I think would not decline a participation in the work. His heterodoxy lay chiefly in being too little impressed with either the necessity or the proper means of preserving the Confederacy." [1]

Jefferson wrote to Madison from Annapolis on the following day, making anxious inquiries as to the sentiments of the recluse at "Gunston" on the subject of the State Constitution:

"You have seen G. M. I hope, and had much conversation with him. What are his sentiments as to the amendment of our constitution? What amendments would he oppose? Is he determined to sleep on, or will he rouse and be active? I wish to hear from you on this subject." [2]

His compatriots were all desirous to know George Mason's views, and to see him back again in public life. Joseph Jones wrote to Jefferson on the 29th of December in regard to the British debt question and other important subjects that would come before the Assembly at its next session. And he feared the abilities of this body would not be equal to the trust: "Madison's aid I think we may depend on"; he adds, "perhaps old Mr. G. Mason's, as the business of the land offices requires revision, and his apprehensions on that subject, if nothing else, may draw him from his retirement." [3]

Washington resigned his commission in December, and left Annapolis in time to reach "Mount Vernon" Christmas-eve. From a young lady's letter, Miss Lewis of Fredericks-

[1] "Madison Papers," vol. i., p. 579.
[2] Bancroft's "History of the Constitution," vol. i., p. 335, Appendix.
[3] "Letters of Joseph Jones," p. 137.

burg, probably the daughter of Colonel Fielding Lewis, General Washington's brother-in-law, we obtain a lively picture of the home-coming of the chief and the attendant festivities. And the foremost figure among the guests was Colonel Mason, whose appearance is pleasantly portrayed by the pen of his fair young admirer:

"I must tell you what a charming day I spent at Mount Vernon with Mama and Sally. The general and madame came home on Christmas Eve, and such a racket the servants made, for they were glad of their coming! Three handsome young officers came with them. All Christmas afternoon people came to pay their respects and duty. Among them were stately dames and gay young women. The general seemed very happy, and Mistress Washington was busy from daybreak making everything as agreeable as possible for everybody. Among the most notable of the callers was Mr. George Mason, of Gunston Hall, who was on his way home from Alexandria, and who brought a charming granddaughter with him, about fourteen years old. He is said to be one of the greatest statesmen and wisest men in Virginia. We had heard much of him and were delighted to look in his face, hear him speak, and take his hand, which he offered in a courtly manner. He is straight in figure but not tall, and has a grand head and clear gray eyes. He has few white hairs, though they say he is about sixty years old." [1]

[1] "Mary and Martha Washington," B. J. Lossing, p. 229.

CHAPTER III.

VIRGINIA'S COMPACT WITH MARYLAND.

1784–1787.

The following letter, found among Monroe's papers,[1] is believed to have been written by him to George Mason, to whom the younger statesman had applied for advice on the several important public questions before the country. Monroe was at this time in Congress at Annapolis:

" ANNAPOLIS, February, 1784.

" DEAR SIR :

"Your favor of the 5th ultimo did not reach me till a few days since from the difficulty the severity of the season hath created in passage of the rivers. I am particularly happy to receive it as it promises to me, in the office which I hold, the aid of your age, judgment and experience. I have paid great attention to your reasoning, and think that in two instances, viz., the peace establishment and the seat for the residence of Congress, it is conclusive. If no European power had possessions on the continent I should suppose the idea of a standing army would never have been brought upon the carpet. The Indian incursions or trade, as you observe, would more regularly come within the cognizance of the State exposed or to derive advantage from it. But the possessions of these powers, and particularly of Great Britain, is a matter of more serious import. The impolicy of New York hath already thrown a considerable body of people into Nova Scotia ; and Canada, in tracts at present uninhabited, is certainly capable

[1] Evidently the rough, first draft of the letter sent to his correspondent. There was some doubt at first as to its authorship, but Mr. Bancroft, to whom the MS. was shown, pronounced it unmistakably Monroe's handwriting.

68

of maintaining extensive settlements. Many European countries, in a higher northern latitude, are thickly settled, and the lands of Canada are perhaps richer than those of the Swiss Cantons, Denmark, Sweden or Russia. These provinces are also well timbered, and at the same time that the inhabitants promise to be an hardy and robust race of men give them all the advantages from their situation of a nursery for seamen, dock-yards for building ships and a share in our carrying business.

" The court of London hath turned its attention to the Indies, proposing to attempt such arrangements as may compensate to the nation the loss of America. But what can Great Britain promise [herself] from the Indies which she doth not now possess. If colonies are established upon the footing we lately stood, and emigration is encouraged, how long will they be connected with the parent country? And will not such establishments which take the Indies out of the Company induce the necessity of standing armies and respectable fleets to prevent insurrection, and turn the tide of commerce into the bosom of the parent country, and will not this expense be thrown upon the state? And as the climate suits a despotic government, and the general in command may be popular with his troops, is it not rational to suspect he will seek the sovereignty himself? If these questions could be answered in the negative, I think it will be granted that the possession of India will only prove a commercial advantage. The inhabitants of these provinces will have but little attatchment to the parent country, and will personally be never brought to add to its number or increase its strength in any European operation, While this trade and government are in the possession of a company, the nation is free from the expense of these troops or fleets. Considering therefore all the relative circumstances, I think it a doubtful question whether this change would be of public advantage, while most certainly it would prove very materially injurious to the Crown. The Crown now has the advantage of the sale occasionally of the renewal of the charter to the Company, and of this it would of course be deprived. I think therefore the conclusion just that the monopoly of the trade and expense of the government will remain with the Company, and that any arrangement the court of London may make with respect to that country will only tend to create dependants on the Crown and increase its influence in the Parliament without effecting any material change in the constitution of India. View the prospects of Britain as we will in the East and I cannot see how in any event any arrangements can turn to any great national advantage. Will the population of India increase the number of British citizens? Will any Eastern arrangement increase the fleet or add to the army but to guard itself? I am therefore of opinion that if the court of London are wise they will be cautious how they interpose in the affairs of the East.

"I am therefore of opinion that the Court of London will still turn her attention to this continent in every consideration she may have in view to add to or increase her national strength. Passion or folly may sometimes govern her councils, but in time she will observe her error and attempt to correct the fault. I think as national advantages are to be derived from it, she will turn her attention to these provinces, and there is a kind of energy in the natives of that country which is not to be found in the peasantry of any of the monarchies of Europe. When any of the countries are overstocked in France or Spain the overplus turn beggars in the street or starve; but the people of England seek a dwelling in foreign climes and distant countries. I suppose, therefore, these provinces will prove a drain to the surplus of citizens in Great Britain. What will be their policy with respect to these provinces, whether they will extend to them the freedom of the British Constitution, or keep in them a standing army, be this as it may, will it not be a desirable circumstance to us to prevail on them to keep few or no troops in Canada? Will not this be a proper subject for a convention between us? But if they will not acceed to it, I still think with you that the defence of the country should be thrown on the militia." [1]

Colonel Mason's friends in Fairfax County were anxious to see him again in the Assembly, and some of them, it seems, in the spring of 1784 were about to take a step that would force him to re-enter the Legislature, as they hoped. Against this proceeding he made a vigorous protest in a letter to his friend Mr. Cockburn, declaring that it was an infringement of his personal liberty:

[1] Gouverneur Collection. The MS. draft is endorsed by Monroe, "Supposed to have been written to Col. George Mason."

GUNSTON HALL, April 18, 1784.

DEAR SIR:

I have been lately informed that some people intend to open a poll for me at the election to-morrow in this county. I hope this will not be offered for I have repeatedly declared that I cannot serve the county at this time as one of its representatives. I should look upon such an attempt in no other light than an oppressive and unjust invasion of my personal liberty, and was I to be elected under such circumstances I should certainly refuse to act, be the consequences what they may. I mention this to you in your official capacity as high sheriff of the county, and if a poll is demanded for me I must request the favor of you to inform the people publicly of my resolution, and that such a demand is made against my consent or approbation. If ever I should see a time when I have just cause to think I can render the public essential service and can so arrange my domestic concerns so as to enable me to leave my family for any length of time, I will most cheerfully let the county know it, but this is not the case in either instance at present.

Your affectionate and obedient servant,

G. MASON.[1]

Others besides his constituents, as we have seen, wished to recall George Mason to the councils of the State. Madison and Jefferson were still urging changes in the Virginia Constitution. Madison wrote to his friend on this subject March 16th: "Much will depend on the politics of Mr. Henry which are wholly unknown to me. Should they be adverse, and G. Mason not in the Assembly, hazardous as delay is, the experiment must be put off to a more auspicious conjunction."[2] After the opening of the session he writes from Richmond, deploring Jefferson's departure to Europe at this time, and adds in regard to the contemplated revision of the Constitution: "As Col. Mason remains in private life, the expediency of starting the idea will depend much on the part to be expected from R. H. Lee and Mr. Henry."[3]

[1] Mason Papers. [2] "Writings of Madison," vol. i., p. 73.
[3] *Ibid.*, vol. i., p. 80.

In the meantime though George Mason was no longer in the Assembly, his State had some work for him to do which he could not refuse to undertake. On the 28th of June the following resolution was introduced in the House of Delegates:

"Whereas great inconveniences are found to result from the want of some concerted regulations between this State and the State of Maryland, touching the jurisdiction and navigation of the river Potomac ; *Resolved*, That George Mason, Edmund Randolph, James Madison, jun., and Alexander Henderson, Esqrs. be appointed commissioners ; and that they, or any three of them, do meet such commissioners as may be appointed on the part of Maryland, and in concert with them frame such liberal and equitable regulations concerning the said river, as may be mutually advantageous to the two States ; and that they make report thereof to the General Assembly."[1]

Questions of trade and revenue were much discussed at this session, and the subject of the British debts still agitated the Assembly and the people. Should the treaty of peace be carried out in all its provisions, while the British still held the western posts, was asked. At the fall session of 1784–5 the subject was renewed in the Assembly, and through Madison's influence, provision was finally made for payments of British debts in seven annual instalments. But the House adjourned before the bill was acted upon, and the matter remained practically unsettled until after the adoption of the Federal Constitution. Other subjects of interest to Colonel Mason brought before this Assembly were the assessment plan, and resolutions adding to the duties assigned the commission of which he had been appointed a member at the previous session. On the 11th of November the House resolved: "That the people of this commonwealth, according to their respective abilities, ought to pay a moderate tax or contribution annually, for the support of the Christian religion, or of some Christian church, denomination or com-

[1] Journal of the Assembly.

munion of Christians, or of some form of Christian worship."[1] Patrick Henry, who favored the resolution, was made chairman of the committee appointed to bring in a bill on the subject. Those who opposed the assessment, with Madison at their head, finally induced the Assembly to postpone consideration of the bill until the following November. It was to be published with a record of the votes upon it, in handbills, and twelve copies given to each member to be distributed in their respective counties, and the people were requested to signify their opinion respecting the adoption of such a bill to the next session of the Assembly. On the 28th of December the House came to the following resolutions :

"That the commissioners or any two of them appointed on the twenty-eighth of June last, to concert with commissioners on the part of Maryland, regulations touching the navigation and jurisdiction of the Potomac, be further authorized to unite with the said commissioners in representing to the State of Pennsylvania, that it is in contemplation of the said two States to promote the clearing and extending the navigation of the Potomac, from tide water upwards as far as the same may be found practicable ; to open a convenient road from the head of such navigation to the waters running into the Ohio ; and to render the waters navigable as far as may be necessary and proper : That the said works will require great expense, which may not be repaid unless a free use be secured to the said States and their citizens, of the waters of the Ohio and its branches so far as the same lie within the limits of Pennsylvania. That as essential advantages will accrue from such works, to a considerable portion of said State, it is thought reasonable that the legislature thereof, should by some previous act, engage that for the encouragement of the said works, all articles of produce and merchandise which may be conveyed to or from either of the said two States through either of the said rivers, within the limits of Pennsylvania to or from any place without the said limits, shall pass throughout free from all duties or tolls whatsoever other than such tolls as may be established and be necessary for reimbursing expenses incurred by the State or its

[1] *Ibid.*

citizens, in clearing, or for defraying the expense of preserving the navigation of the said rivers : And that no articles imported into the State of Pennsylvania through the channel or channels, or any part thereof to be opened as aforesaid and vended or used within the said State, shall be subject to any duties or imposts other than such articles would be subject to if imported into the said State through any other channel whatsoever : That in case a joint representation in behalf of this State and of Maryland shall be rendered by circumstances unattainable, the said commissioners or any two of them, may of themselves make such representations on the subject to the State of Pennsylvania, as will in such event become proper." [1]

We obtain a glimpse of Colonel Mason in domestic life, and of the family circle, through a letter to his daughter, Mrs. McCarty, on the death of an infant. The original letter has been carefully preserved by this lady's granddaughter :

GUNSTON HALL, February 10th, 1785.

My DEAR CHILD :

I most sincerely condole with you for the loss of your dear little girl, but it is our duty to submit with all the resignation human nature is capable of to the dispensation of Divine Providence which bestows upon us our blessings, and consequently has a right to take them away. A few years' experience will convince us that those things which at the time they happened we regarded as our greatest misfortunes have proved our greatest blessings. Of this awful truth no person has lived to my age without seeing abundant proof. Your dear baby has died innocent and blameless, and has been called away by an all wise and merciful Creator, most probably from a life of misery and misfortune, and most certainly to one of happiness and bliss.

Your sisters are both at Col. Blackburn's and not expected home before Sunday or you should immediately have their company. Your brother George and his wife are in Chotanck. I wish you could come to Gunston Hall. In the meantime I would by all means advise you to lose a little blood without delay, and

[1] *Ibid.*

to take two or three times a day twenty or thirty drops of spirits of lavender of which I send you some by the bearer. I am, my dear child,

Your affectionate father

GEORGE MASON.

P. S.—Mrs. Mason says your sisters told her they should go to Col. Cook's, and would not be at home before the middle of next week. She begs that you will come to Gunston Hall.

"Colonel Cooke" was Travers Cooke, of Stafford County, son of Sir John Cooke and grandson of Raleigh Travers. Colonel Cooke's son, John Cooke, married Mary Mason, one of George Mason's daughters.

In this same month of February, 1785, Colonel Mason lost his brother, Thomson Mason, who died on the 26th, and was buried at his place, " Raspberry Plain," in Loudoun County. He drew up his will shortly before his death. Bailey Washington, Jr., was named one of his executors. He describes himself as " Thomson Mason of Stafford County in the Commonwealth of Virginia Esq. : " He begins with the usual solemn formula, giving his soul into the hands of his Creator " to dispose of as His justice and mercy shall think fit, and I humbly beg," adds the testator, " that through the merit and mediation of my blessed Redeemer Jesus Christ the manifold sins I have committed in this life will be forgiven, and I declare that I have lived and hope to die in the belief of the Christian faith." To his widow, who was his second wife, Thomson Mason left all the estate that came to him through his marriage with her. She had been a Miss Westwood, of Elizabeth City County, and the country-seat, " Errol," in that county, which is mentioned in the will, was probably her patrimony. She was the widow of Dr. Wallace at the time of her marriage with Thomson Mason. Mrs. Mason was to receive a life estate in lands of Thomson Mason on Chappawamic Run, in Stafford County, lying below "lands of the late Mr. Moncure"; also in another plantation on the same run in Prince William County, lying below the property of Col. Burr Harrison and Robert Carter,

Esq. There were about twelve hundred and twenty acres in the two tracts, and the testator reserved out of them for his son, John Thomson Mason, his choice of fifty acres, " to be laid off in a square for a seat, on which side the run he pleases, so that it does not include the garden, orchard, or any of the housing in the county of Stafford, or any of the low grounds in the same county." John Thomson Mason was to fall heir to this Stafford and Prince William property, eventually, with other lands in the same counties, amounting in all to three thousand acres. This the third son of Thomson Mason made his home later in Maryland, where he owned a beautiful country-seat in Montgomery County, called " Montpelier." He became an eminent lawyer of Maryland. Stevens Thomson, the eldest son of Thomson Mason, was confirmed by his father's will in his possession of " Raspberry Plain," already given him by deed, with the plate and furniture belonging to it. He was also to have a square of four acres of land on which to build a public-house, with certain unimproved lots in the towns of Richmond and Manchester, " which were drawn in the late Colonel Byrd's lottery, by tickets marked with the initials of his mother's or his brother George's name." Stevens Thomson Mason was also to have the ground in Richmond " on which the public storehouse lately stood," together with the money due from the public for its valuation, etc., it having been destroyed during Arnold's raid. Other bequests of houses, lots, etc., were left to the eldest son. And to the second son, Abram Barnes Thomson, his father also left lands in Loudoun County, besides town lots drawn in Colonel Byrd's lottery.

To his only daughter, Ann Thomson Mason, her father bequeathed certain slaves and a sum of money. She married Richard McCarty Chichester, son of Richard Chichester, of " Newington," and a brother of Sarah Chichester, wife of Thomson Mason, of " Hollin Hall." Mrs. Mason, by her husband's will, was to have the household furniture at " Errol " and at " Chappawamsic," with all the stock at the former place. She was to have also a chariot and harness and four chariot horses well matched ; also the use of certain slaves, "Silvia," "Catina," and others. A square of one hundred and fifty acres of land in Loudoun County was to be laid off in half-acre lots for a town, and sold to the highest bidder for a term of twenty-one years, with a ground rent of two silver dollars on each lot. The two youngest sons of Thomson Mason, the only children of his second marriage, were very young at the time of their father's death, and in the latter's will, after naming their mother and two of their half-brothers as their guardians, he gives the following instructions as to their education. He desires " that they may be put to learning English at one of their guardian's houses till eight years of age, and that then they be kept at writing, arithmetic, and reading elegant English authors and modern languages till they are twelve years of age, and then to be kept at learning the Latin language, book-keeping, mathematics, and other useful branches of literature, till the age of eighteen, and then to be put out to such business or profession as their geniuses are best calculated for." Thomson Mason then adds a caution against the temptations of the gayer portion of the State. " I positively direct," he says, "that neither of my younger sons, Westwood Thomson Mason or William Temple Thomson Mason, shall reside on the south side of James River or below Williamsburg before they respectively attain the age of twenty-one years, lest they should imbibe more exalted notions of their own importance than I could wish any child of mine to possess." Thomson Mason provides watches for each of his children by name, except Stevens, who it is presumed was already in possession of one. His wife is to have "a new gold watch with an embossed case and equipage, suitable for a lady, of the price of thirty guineas," purchased for her. His own gold watch is to go to the youngest son. Ann Thomson is to have the "equipage that was her mother's," and a gold watch purchased for twenty guineas to go with it. The three other sons are to have each a silver horizontal watch. John is to have his father's brass barrelled pistols.

A faithful servant was rewarded after the following manner :

" I direct that my negro man Jack be allowed to settle upon any of my lands in Loudon, Stafford or Prince William and that my executors lay off for him thirty acres of good arable land and ten acres of pasturage to tend a crop for himself, build him a barn of logs twenty feet square and furnish him one cow, two sows, one ewe and a mare of ten pounds value, one bar share plow, one Dutch plow, one broad hoe, one narrow hoe, one axe, one mattock, five bushels oats, five baskets rye, five bushels of wheat and ten barrels of corn to stock his plantation and set him forward, and let him have one month's work of an able negro man and the loan of my ox cart for the same time to put his little farm in order ; with liberty to get rails and firewood off my adjacent lands."

In addition to the farm and stock, his master gave Jack the annual sum of six pounds specie. The use of the land was given him for life, the stock forever. He was to be protected in all his just rights and " subject to the control of no person whatsoever, and this provision I have made for him," concludes the testator, " as a grateful acknowledgment of the remarkable fidelity and integrity with which he has conducted himself to me for twenty years and upwards." Jack was to receive also three hundred-weight of pork. To his wife's maid, Catina, if ever she should be parted from her mistress, her master left her two hundred-weight of pork, and certain articles of clothing annually. Certain profits of the estate were to be used " in the purchase of white servants, stocks and improvements." Two " indented farming, white servants," who have four or five years to serve, were to be purchased for one of the testator's sons, " provided they do not exceed the price of thirty pounds each." Thomson Mason, like most of the Virginia planters of his day, owned thorough-bred horses and took an interest in the turf. In his will he leaves to his son, John Thomson, his " riding horse Rupert, the young St. George's mare, the two-year-old sorrel filly, her year-old Sweeper horse colt, and Camilla and her colts." To another son is left, among less distinguished steeds, "a bay Tamerlane colt," and to a third son his "Eclipse bay horse colt." [1]

In giving directions for his burial, Thomson Mason makes the one allusion to his brother that is found in his will. He desires to be buried at "Raspberry Plain," where his son George lies, and he wishes the remains of his first wife to be brought from "the family burying-ground at my brother's," to be laid beside his own.

George Mason must have felt this loss keenly. But unfortunately no letters have been preserved which allude to it. And now, while the work of the younger brother was over, the elder one was to come forward into the federal arena in a way that could have been little dreamed of by either of them in 1785. But for two years longer George Mason remained out of the Assembly. In the meantime he was not unemployed. Two months after his brother's death we find him attending a meeting of the county court of Fairfax, at Alexandria, on the 22d of March, and as the presiding justice, drawing up a protest against what he conceived to be a violation of the rights of the court by the executive:

"1785, March 22. At a court held for the county of Fairfax.
"Present:

"George Mason,	John Gibson,
Charles Broadwater,	David Stuart,
Alexander Henderson,	William Payne,
George Gilpin,	(Gentlemen Justices).

"A new commission for this county, signed by the Hon. Benj. Harrison Esq: late Governor of this Commonwealth being this day presented and read, whereby the Justices of the county are constituted and appointed *de novo*, and consequently are required to take the oath of qualifications over again, notwithstanding they

[1] Will of Thomson Mason (on record at Stafford Court House). Old copy in possession of Arthur Mason Chichester, Loudoun County, Va.

Volume ii. of Grigsby's "Convention of 1788" ("Virginia Historical Collections," vol. x.) contains sketches of Thomson and Stevens Thomson Mason.

had before taken them under the commonwealth, and several of the justices have been many years acting magistrates, by virtue of former commissions, for this county. The court, unanimously refuse to receive, and do protest against the same, for the following reasons &c.

"P. WAGENER, Clk. Ct.

"A copy of the protest to be transmitted to the executive."

The protest goes on to state that they object to such commissions because "of unnecessary multiplication and repetition of oaths, rendering them common and familiar, etc. Because such a commission would afford a dangerous precedent and tend to renew, in this commonwealth, one of the many abuses and arbitrary practices of the late monarchical government here, yielding to the secretary an unnecessary fee and to the governor and council an unjust and oppressive power of insulting or turning any man out of his office of a civil magistrate, as prejudice, malice, or caprice might dictate, without a hearing, or without a cause of complaint against him; for the constituting and appointing the former acting justices *de novo*, necessarily implies the power of vacating the former commissions; that the justices derive their office entirely from the last, and consequently, that by issuing a new commission, and misplacing any man in it, he might lose his rank, and might be degraded from the first to the last justice in the county; or by leaving out any justice's name he would thenceforward be deprived of his office, both of which, it is notorious, were frequently practised under the former government. Because it is conceived that the exercise of such a power is altogether illegal, giving to the executive power of the State an undue and dangerous influence over the courts of justice, directly contrary to the Declaration of Rights and to the fundamental principles of our free government. And although this court hath no cause to believe that the present commission was issued for any such evil purposes, yet we should think we were deficient in the duty we owe to our country and to posterity, if we suffered ourselves to become accessory to establishing a precedent evidently tending to introduce them, and by renewing the oppressive maxims and practices of the government from which we have so lately been rescued by force of arms, to sap the foundations of that liberty which has been purchased at the expense of so much blood and treasure." [1]

In this same month of March the commissioners met at Alexandria to settle the jurisdiction of the Chesapeake Bay and the Potomac and Pokomoke rivers. Maryland had suggested the time and place of meeting, and her commissioners arrived in good season. By some inadvertence, however, the Virginia commissioners were not informed when and where they were to hold the conference, and on this account only George Mason and Alexander Henderson were able to be present. By invitation of General Washington the commissioners adjourned from Alexandria to "Mount Vernon." Ten days before, Washington records in his journal a visit to Colonel Mason and some of his neighbors. Finding Lawrence Lewis, who lived at "Woodlawn," away from home, he proceeded to Colonel Mason's, where he "dined and lodged," leaving "Gunston Hall" for Mr. Cockburn's, at "Springfield," about twelve the next day. On the 20th, the diary relates:

"Major Jenifer came here to dinner, and my carriage went to Gunston Hall to take Col. Mason to a meeting of commissioners at Alexandria for settling the jurisdiction of Chesapeake Bay and the rivers Potomac and Pokomoke between the States of Virginia and Maryland. The commissioners on the part of Virginia being Col. Mason, the Attorney General, Mr. Madison and Mr. Henderson. On that of Maryland, Major Jenifer, Thomas Johnson, Thomas Stone and Samuel Chase, Esqrs." [2]

Two of the Maryland gentlemen had written to George Mason that they would stop at his house on their way to Alexandria, and they were very probably there at this time.

[1] "Virginia Calendar Papers," vol. iv., p. 16.
[2] MS. Journals, State Department.

On the 24th, General Washington writes: "Sent my carriage to Alexandria for Col. Mason according to appointment, who came in about dusk." The next day, the journal continues, about one o'clock Major Jenifer, Mr. Stone, Mr. Chase, and Mr. Henderson arrived at "Mount Vernon." This was Friday. Saturday and Monday the commissioners were in session, and Tuesday they all left for their homes. Colonel Mason drove back to "Gunston" in the "Mount Vernon" carriage, "by the return of which," adds Washington, "he sent me some young shoots of the Persian jessamine and Guelder rose." It is a very meagre chronicle, and one cannot but wish that some of the table-talk at "Mount Vernon" during these four days had been preserved for us. The commission, it will be seen, finished their work on the 28th, having been four days apparently at Alexandria and four at "Mount Vernon."

On the fifth of April Colonel Mason wrote from "Gunston Hall" to General Washington, sending him a present of some cider. He had broached, he says, four or five hogsheads, and filled the bottles with the best, though there was not much difference, "all being made of Maryland red streak and managed in the same manner." The cider this year is not so clear and fine, he tells his friend, and he does not know the reason except that he had ground his apples last fall later than usual. And Colonel Mason adds: "As the cider in bottles will not ripen for use until late in May, I have also filled a barrell out of the same, which I beg your acceptance of." He recommends that a little ginger should be put in it, as it improves sweet cider; and he sends Washington some watermelon seed which he had promised him.[1] Colonel Mason, in this letter, speaks of suffering again with the gout. He had gone back from the convention at "Mount Vernon" to the pleasant home interests and occupations, to the enjoyment of the rural tastes, which he shared with the retired commander-in-chief. But in the meanwhile he was preparing also to give an account to the Assembly of the

[1] Washington MSS., State Department.

work undertaken by the commission. The responsibility of its seeming irregularity had fallen upon him, a responsibility he would not evade, and which he felt the circumstances fully justified his assuming. Joseph Jones, however, only expressed a surprise which was natural when he wrote to Madison, June 12th, of the rumor that had reached him on the subject. He says: " I know not whether any copy of the resolution you allude to has been officially communicated to Mr. Mason. Such as Beckley copied for the executive have been, so whether *that* should have been of the number I cannot tell, as we are not yet favored with the journals by the printer, and I cannot inform myself at the clerk's office, Mr. Beckley being out of town." The Assembly now only met once a year, in October, and the resolution referred to was probably the one passed at the last session of the House, when new powers were delegated to the commission appointed the previous June. Joseph Jones adds: " I heard, but have only heard, that Mason and Henderson proceeded to execute the other branch of the business committed to the commissioners without the attendance, or call for attendance, of the other commissioners. What they have done has not come to my knowledge." [1]

Madison had already written on the 2d of June to George Mason, probably making inquiries on the subject, and the latter sent the following letter of explanation in reply :

"GUNSTON HALL, August 9th, 1785.

" DEAR SIR :

" I should have answered your favor of the second of June, long ago, had not ill health, and the absence of my sons from home, disabled me from making out the copies of the proceedings of the Virginia and Maryland Commissioners which I now enclose, and upon which I wish to be favored with your sentiments.

" We thought ourselves unfortunate in being deprived of yours and my friend the Attorney's assistance, in this important business ; and nothing but absolute necessity should have induced me to enter upon it without you. But the Maryland gentlemen

[1] " Letters of Joseph Jones," p. 144.

would have been much disgusted with a disappointment, after attending at such a distance in very bad weather. We waited some days expecting your arrival in Alexandria, when I received a letter from the Attorney, upon other business, without mentioning a word of the meeting, or of the Assembly's appointment. This convinced us that there must have been some blunder or neglect, in some of the public offices, in not giving the proper notification to the Virginia Commissioners. The Maryland gentlemen declared that nothing had been omitted on their part, that they had written an official letter to the Virginia Commissioners (addressed by their governor to the commissioners) proposing the time and place, if agreeable to them ; and if not, desiring they would name some other ; that having received no answer, they took it for granted that the time and place was accepted, and attended accordingly.

"So great has been the neglect in some of our public departments that neither Mr. Henderson or myself had been furnished with copies of the Assembly's resolutions. And I should not have known that I was one of the persons appointed, had I not by mere accident, two or three days before the meeting, been informed of it by two of the Maryland commissioners writing to me that they should endeavor to take my house in their way, and go with me to Alexandria. His Excellency General Washington happened to have a copy of the Assembly's resolutions respecting the application to be made to the government of Pennsylvania, which he very obligingly gave me, by which *any two* or more of the commissioners were empowered to proceed. And it was natural for us to conclude that these last resolutions had pursued the style of the former respecting the jurisdiction of the two States ; as well as that the subject had been taken up upon the same principles as in the year 1778, when commissioners were directed to settle the jurisdiction of the Chesapeake Bay and the rivers Potomac and Pokomoke [1] ; in which sentiments Mr. Henderson, from what he was able to recollect of the resolutions, concurred.

"Thus disagreeably circumstanced, only two of the Virginia commissioners present, and without any copy of the resolves upon the principal subject, we thought it better to proceed than to dis-

[1] George Mason, Thomas Ludwell Lee, and James Henry were the Virginia commissioners appointed, 1778.

appoint the Maryland commissioners ; who appeared to have
brought with them the most amicable dispositions, and expressed
the greatest desire of forming such a fair and liberal compact, as
might prove a lasting cement of friendship between the two
States ; which we were convinced it is their mutual interest
to cultivate. We therefore upon the particular invitation of the
General adjourned to ' Mount Vernon ' and finished the business
there. Some time after, Mr. Henderson wrote to Mr. Beckley
(clerk of the House of Delegates) for a copy of the resolves ;
upon receiving which we were surprised to find no mention made
of *Chesapeake or Pokomoke River*, that our powers were confined
to *Potomac River*, and to not less than *three* of the commissioners.
I am still inclined to think that the omission of Chesapeake Bay
and Pokomoke River was owing to a mistake or inadvertence, in
not attending to the resolves of 1778 ; and, if so, it was perhaps
lucky that we had not been furnished with a copy of the resolves ;
for the Maryland commissioners had an express instruction from
their Assembly to consider the relinquishment, on the part of Virginia, of any claim of laying tolls, &c., on vessels passing through
the capes of Chesapeake as a *sine qua non ;* and if it was refused
immediately to break off all further conference with the Virginia
commissioners.

"This blundering business, however, will give me the trouble
and expence of a journey to Richmond, next session, to apologize
for and explain our conduct ; where, if the substance of the compact is approved by the Assembly, I hope forms will be dispensed
with, especially as the breach of them has been the fault of some
of their own officers, not ours, and as I am conscious of our having been influenced by no other motives than the desire of
promoting the public good." [1]

With this letter George Mason sent to Madison drafts of
the communication of the Virginia commissioners to the Assembly, stating briefly the points that had been settled ; and
also the letter to the president of the Executive Council of
Pennsylvania from the commission on the subject of cooperation with Virginia and Maryland.[2] The following
memorandum was added as a postscript to the letter to

[1] Madison MSS., State Department. [2] Appendix 1.

Madison. The suggested correction or alteration in the compact was not made, however, as may be seen by reference to the law in the Virginia and Maryland codes.

"*Memorandum*. The concluding clause of the seventh article of the compact is not so clearly expressed as it ought to be, and is capable of a construction which was not intended ; and though it would be a strained and unnatural one, it had better be removed. The words are 'provided, &c., and that the citizens of neither State shall have a right to fish with nets or seins upon the shores of the other.' This may be construed to restrain the citizens of either State, having lands upon the river in the other, from fishing with nets or seins upon their own shores ; which would be unreasonable and unjust ; although in its present form, it seems to be the grammatical construction. The addition of two or three words will set it right—thus : 'And that the citizens of neither State shall have a right to fish with nets or seins upon the shores *of the citizens* of the other.' I never observed this circumstance till very lately, or I am sure I could easily have had it altered by the Maryland commissioners, at any time before the meeting of their Assembly. The fisheries upon Potomac River are becoming a very important object, and therefore I could wish the above clause in the compact properly amended. If the amendment goes no farther than I have mentioned, it will occasion no objection from Maryland, and I wish the article to be no otherwise altered, for this was the most difficult business we had to settle with the Maryland commissioners. The idea of the right of fishing on both shores of Potomac River is one the Marylanders are not fond of parting with ; and I trust it will be found we have obtained everything for Virginia, with respect to Potomac River, which she can desire. The exceptionable part of the article before mentioned was really a mistake. Not having time now to write to my friend the Attorney upon this subject, Mr. Madison will be pleased to mention it to him.

"And I shall be particularly obliged to Mr. Madison to inform me what is done with respect to the Northern Neck, on the subject of the records in the late proprietor's office, entering, or resurveying lands, quit-rents, &c.

"G. M."

Another subject which interested George Mason at this time was the Assessment Bill. Its fate was to be decided at the next session of the Assembly, and so energetically did its enemies work against it, its rejection was readily secured. To George Mason, in great part, this success was due. Madison, in a letter to one of Colonel Mason's grandsons, written in 1826, gives the following account of the matter:

" During the session of the General Assembly, 1784–5, a bill was introduced into the House of Delegates, providing for the legal support of Teachers of the Christian Religion, and being patronized by the most popular talents in the House, seemed likely to obtain a majority of votes. In order to arrest its progress, it was insisted with success, that the bill should be postponed till the ensuing session ; and in the meantime be printed for public consideration. That the sense of the people might be better called forth, your highly distinguished ancestor, Col. George Mason, Col. George Nicholas, also possessing much public weight, and some others thought it advisable that a remonstrance against the bill should be prepared for general circulation and signature, and imposed on me the task of drawing up such a paper. The draught having received their sanction, a large number of printed copies were distributed, and so extensively signed by the people of every religious denomination, that at the ensuing session the projected measure was entirely frustrated, and under the influence of the public sentiment thus manifested the celebrated bill ' Establishing Religious Freedom ' created into a permanent barrier against future attempts on the rights of conscience, as declared in the great charter prefixed to the Constitution of the State." [1]

The fact of Madison's authorship of the " Remonstrance " was not generally known until after his death, and there were some persons in Virginia who attributed it to George Mason.[2] Colonel Mason probably wrote to a number of his friends enclosing them this paper for signature, and two of

[1] MS. Letter. Compare Rives' " Madison," vol. i., p. 631.
[2] Oration of Mr. Williams on the death of Madison.

these letters, written, the first part of them, in identical terms, one to General Washington and one to Robert Carter of " Nomini," are preserved.   The letter to Washington is as follows:

GUNSTON HALL, October 2d, 1785.

DEAR SIR :

I take the liberty of enclosing you a Memorial and Remonstrance to the General Assembly, confided to me by a particular friend whose name I am not at liberty to mention ; and as the principles it avows entirely accord with my sentiments on the subject (which is a very important one), I have been at the charge of printing several copies to disperse in the different parts of the country.   You will easily perceive that all manner of declamation and address to passions have been avoided, as unfair in themselves, and improper for such a subject ; and although the Remonstrance is long, that brevity has been aimed at, but the field is extensive.

If upon consideration, you approve the arguments and the principles upon which they are founded, your signature will both give the Remonstrance weight, and do it honor.   I would have waited on you personally upon this occasion, but have been so shattered by a late violent fit of the convulsive cholic, complicated with the gout in my stomach, that I am hardly able to walk across the floor.   The bearer will deliver you a packet inclosing another copy for my friend Doctor Stuart.   I am in hopes he and his colleague will endeavor to forward the subscriptions in this county.   Mrs. Mason, and the family here, present their compliments to you, your lady and Miss Bassett, with,

Dear Sir,

Your affectionate and obedient servant,

G. MASON.[1]

In the letter to Robert Carter, George Mason says:

" If upon consideration you approve the reasoning and the principles upon which it is founded, I make no doubt you will endeavor to promote the subscriptions in your part of the country ; if they can be completed, and the Remonstrance

[1] Washington MSS., State Department.

sent down to the Assembly, by the first or second week in November, I presume it will be in good time." [1]

Washington wrote in reply to Colonel Mason:

MOUNT VERNON, October 3d, 1785.

DEAR SIR:

I have this moment received yours of yesterday's date, enclosing a memorial and remonstrance against the Assessment Bill, which I will read with attention. At present I am unable to do it, on account of company. The bill itself I do not recollect ever to have read; with attention I am certain I never did, but will compare them together.

Although no man's sentiments are more opposed to any kind of restraint upon religious principles than mine are, yet I must confess, that I am not amongst the number of those, who are so much alarmed at the thoughts of making people pay towards the support of that which they profess, if of the denomination of Christians, or declare themselves Jews, Mahometans, or otherwise, and thereby obtain proper relief. As the matter now stands, I wish an assessment had never been agitated, and as it has gone so far, that the bill could die an easy death; because I think it will be productive of more quiet to the State, than by enacting it into a law, which in my opinion would be impolitic admitting there is a decided majority for it, to the disquiet of a respectable minority. In the former case, the matter will soon subside; in the latter, it will rankle and perhaps convulse the State. The dinner bell rings, and I must conclude with an expression of my concern for your indisposition.

Sincerely and affectionately, I am, &c. [2]

Councillor Carter's answer to George Mason was a more emphatic condemnation of the proposed law. He wrote from " Nomony Hall," October 15, 1785:

" SIR :

" Your favor inclosing a copy of a Remonstrance and Memorial against a bill for establishing a provision for teachers of the Christian religion was put into my hands this day. The violence

---

[1] MS. Letter.
[2] "Writings of Washington," Sparks, vol. xii., Appendix, p. 404.

offered therein to the Declaration of Rights and the presumptu-
ous aid intended to Christ's visible church below, were very
alarming—and in the month of last June I joined some persons
in the lower counties in this neck in offering to the people, there,
a petition addressed to the General Assembly noting therein some
reasons against the bill and praying that it might be rejected. I
fully intend to present to the people to-morrow the Remonstrance
and Memorial." [1]

Many of the Virginia statesmen, however, still clung to the
principle of some compulsory law for the support of religion.
Edmund Randolph, Patrick Henry, Richard Henry Lee, and
John Page of " Rosewell," afterwards Governor of Virginia,
all of them members of the Church of England, favored an
assessment by the State for this purpose. John Page wrote
to Jefferson in August, 1785 : " We have endeavored eight
years in vain to support the rational sects by voluntary contributions." And the clergy of the former establishment
were many of them without the means of remaining in their
parishes. Yet churchmen such as George Mason, Madison,
and George Nicholas looked beyond the exigencies of the
hour, and were ready to sacrifice present convenience for the
sake of the principle involved. And theirs, which was the
religion of a majority of the landed gentry, was, of course,
the " rational sect " which suffered most from the new order
of things.

Colonel Mason wrote to Washington early in November,
making reference to the proceedings of the Assembly then
in session :

GUNSTON HALL, 9th November, 1785.

DEAR SIR :

The bearer waits on you with a side of venison (the first we
have killed this season), which I beg your acceptance of.

I have heard nothing from the Assembly except vague reports
of their being resolved to issue a paper currency ; upon what
principles or funds I know not ; perhaps upon the old threadbare
security of pledging solemnly the public credit. I believe such

[1] Carter Letter-Books.

an experiment would prove similar to the old vulgar adage of carrying a horse to the water. They may pass a law to issue it, but twenty laws will not make people receive it.

I intended to go down to Richmond about the fifteenth of the month to have reported the compact with the Maryland commissioners, but I have lately had so severe a fit of the convulsive colic, or the gout, in my stomach, that I dare not venture far from home ; it held me from Sunday evening till Tuesday morning, and has left me so weak that I am hardly able to walk across the floor.

We hope to hear that you, your lady, and family are well ; to whom Mrs. Mason and the family here present their best compliments, with those of, dear sir,

Your affectionate and obedient servant

G. Mason.[1]

Washington, in his diary, records a visit made to Colonel Mason on the 25th of this month. He writes : " Set out after breakfast, accompanied by Mr. G. Washington to make Mr. Mason at Colchester a visit, but hearing on the road that he had removed from there I turned in to Gunston Hall where we dined and returned in the evening."[2] The two friends doubtless discussed Assembly affairs, the Assessment Bill, the paper-money question, the commercial compact with Maryland, etc.

Madison had visited " Mount Vernon " early in September and also on the 12th of October, staying until the 14th, as we learn from Washington's diary. And it was probably on the latter occasion that he went also to " Gunston Hall." The constant attacks of illness, of which Colonel Mason makes mention in his letters at this time, had prevented him from going to Richmond with the report of the commission, which he wished to lay before the Assembly, so he was obliged to send it in a letter to the Speaker of the House. He wrote, about the same time, to Madison :

[1] Washington MSS., State Department. Bancroft's " History of the Constitution," vol. i., Appendix, p. 468.

[2] MS. Journals, Toner Transcripts.

GUNSTON HALL, December 7th, 1785.

DEAR SIR :

I have had such frequent fits of the convulsive colic, compli-cated with the gout in the stomach, since you were here, that I dare not undertake a journey to Richmond ; and therefore, after putting it off as long as I well could, in hopes of recovering such health as would permit me to present the compact with the State of Maryland, in person, I have now inclosed it in a letter to the Speaker.   I incurred a small expense of £3 15 9, in waiting three or four days in Alexandria for the Maryland commissioners ; which the Assembly may repay me if they please, otherwise I am very well satisfied without it.   I also incurred an expense equal to about £5 in specie, attending the committee upon the revisal of the laws in Fredericksburg, and about double that sum in Williamsburg, at different times, after the sessions of Assembly ended, in collecting evidence, and cross examining witnesses be-tween the Commonwealth and Colonel Richard Henderson, in the cause which I was directed to manage, by a vote of both Houses ; but I never made any particular account of it.

I must intreat you, if you find it necessary, to make my apology to the Assembly for having rather exceeded our authority. I gave you the reasons in a former letter, soon after the meeting of the commissioners ; but least you should not recollect them, I will repeat them. . . .   My paper draws to an end, and leaves me only room to beg your attention to the inclosed memorandum, to express my desire of hearing from you on the subject of the com-pact, and such other public matters as you may have time to com-municate, as soon as convenience will permit ; and to assure you that I am with the most sincere esteem and regard,

Dear sir,
Your affectionate friend and obedient servant,
G. MASON.[1]

On the 13th of December the Speaker laid before the House a letter from George Mason, Esq., enclosing the pro-ceedings of the commissioners on the compact between the States of Virginia and Maryland respecting the jurisdiction and navigation of the rivers Potomac and Pokomoke ; which

----

[1] Madison MSS., State Department.

were read and referred to the Committee on Commerce, and, on the 30th, the bill to ratify the compact passed the House.[1] The compact consisted of a dozen articles on the jurisdiction of the Chesapeake Bay and the two rivers mentioned, covering the items of tolls, fisheries, lighthouses, buoys, piracies, etc. And the letter to the Speaker from the Virginia commissioners opened up other and wider views of the commission: such as the regulation of gold and silver money passing current in the two States, bills of exchange, etc., duties on imports or exports, which it was proposed should be settled by an annual commission, appointed by the legislatures of the two States, the number of the commissioners to be not less than three or more than five from each State. The conference at " Mount Vernon," as it proved, was the first step in the direction of a new federal government. Maryland, in ratifying the compact and supplementary report of the commission, proposed that Pennsylvania and Delaware should be invited to unite in the same commercial system. The Virginia legislature went still further. On the 21st of January, 1786, at the close of the session, the following resolution passed the House:

"That Edmund Randolph, James Madison, Walter Jones, St. George Tucker, and Meriwether Smith be appointed commissioners, who, or any of them, shall meet such commissioners as may be appointed by the other States of the Union at a time and place to be agreed on, to take into consideration the trade of the United States; to examine the relative situations and trade of the said States; to consider how far a uniform system in their commercial regulations may be necessary to their common interest and their permanent harmony; and to report to the several States, such an act relative to this great object as, when unanimously ratified by them, will enable the United States in Congress effectually to provide for the same."[2]

---

[1] Journal of the Assembly. This letter of George Mason to the Speaker, etc. (as in the Madison MSS.), is in the State Library, Richmond.

[2] Journal of the Assembly.

At first only three commissioners were named, Tucker and Smith were then added by the House, and when the resolution was sent to the Senate it was amended by the addition of three others—George Mason, William Ronald, and David Ross. Ronald's name was struck out at his own desire, but the rest stood. Madison thought that there were too many, and that the multitude of associates would "stifle the thing in its birth and was probably meant to do so."[1]

There had been much excitement in the Assembly over the question of regulating trade; on the one hand, lest the power of the States should be abridged, and, on the other, lest the power of Congress should be inadequate to the purposes for which the Union had been formed. Mr. Tyler introduced the proposition of a convention at the last moment, having vainly sought an earlier opportunity to effect his object. To invest Congress with the means of regulating commerce, and yet insure certain qualifying clauses, it was thought would satisfy both the friends of Congress and the upholders of the rights of the States. Colonel Mason's opinions on the subject were not clearly known. It was suspected that he was adverse to a stronger Union, and those who favored it desired to obtain an influence so important. Monroe wrote to Madison from New York, where Congress was in session, on the 3d of September: "I consider the convention of Annapolis as a most important era in our affairs. . . . Prevail, I beg of you, on Colonel Mason to attend the convention. It will give him data to act on afterward in the State."[2] The convention met on the 11th of September, 1786, but George Mason did not attend, doubtless on account of the attacks of gout, from which he still suffered. Commissioners were present from four States only—New York, New Jersey, Pennsylvania, and Virginia. Edmund Randolph, Madison, and St. George Tucker were the three delegates who at-

---

[1] "Writings of Madison," vol. i., p. 217. The names do not appear in the printed journal of the Senate.

[2] Rives' "Life of Madison," vol. ii., p. 123.

tended from Virginia. The convention adjourned on the 14th, proposing that all the States should meet in the following May at Philadelphia " to render the Constitution adequate to the exigencies of the Union."

Monroe was uneasy at this time concerning the projects of Jay and his party. He saw in them an attempt to break up the Union, and he wrote to the prominent men in Virginia to ascertain and influence their views on the subject. In a letter to Madison of the 29th of September, he says:

"I wrote some weeks since to Colonel Mason upon this subject, at the time I wrote Governor Henry, but have received no answer from him, from which circumstance, as well as that of R. H. Lee's being in the opposite sentiment, there is room to conjecture he is not with us."[1]

It was generally taken for granted, it seems, that Lee and Mason would concur in their political views. General Henry Lee, who was in Congress at this time, also wrote to General Washington, incidentally giving his testimony to the consideration in which George Mason was held, and the desire that was felt to bring him back into public life. In regard to the navigation of the Mississippi, which Spain, in the projected treaty with her Jay was negotiating, proposed to close to the United States for thirty years, he says: " Should this matter come before our Assembly, much will depend on Mr. Mason's sentiments." And Washington replies on the 31st:

"Colonel Mason is at present in a fit of the gout. What his sentiments on the subject are, I know not, nor whether he will be able to attend the Assembly during the present session. For some reasons, however, which need not be mentioned, I am inclined to believe he will advocate the navigation of that river."[2]

There was another subject on which much was expected from George Mason; this was the question of emitting

---

[1] Bancroft's " History of the Constitution," vol. ii., p. 397.
[2] " Correspondence of the American Revolution," Sparks, vol. iv., p. 140; " Writings of Washington," Sparks, vol. ix., p. 205.

paper money. And on the 12th of August Madison had written to Jefferson, referring to the action of the several States who advocated the measure : " Whether Virginia is to remain exempt from the epidemic malady, will depend on the ensuing Assembly. My hopes rest chiefly on the exertions of Colonel Mason, and the failure of the experiment elsewhere."[1] Bancroft says that aided by an unfavorable balance of trade and the burden of heavy taxation, an effort, it was known, would be made by Meriwether Smith and others to issue a paper medium in 1786 : "Aware of the danger, Washington insisted that George Mason should be a candidate for the Assembly ; and his election proved a counterpoise to the public cry."[2] Colonel Mason had not consented to serve again in the Assembly, but the honor was forced upon him ; and Washington, in his journal of April 17, 1786, speaks of going "up to Alexandria to an election of delegates to represent the county, Colo. Mason and Doctr. Stuart elected." And he adds, the "suffrages of the people fell upon the first contrary to, and after he had declared he could not serve, and on the other whilst he was absent at Richmond. Capt. West who had offered his services and was present was rejected. The votes were, for Col. Mason 109, for Dr. Stuart 105, and for Capt. West 84."[3] George Mason's health did not permit him to attend at this year's session of the Assembly, but he was present the following October. The question of paper money was brought up 1786–7, and was defeated ; its emission was denounced as "unjust, impolitic, and destructive of public confidence, and of that virtue which is the basis of republican government."[4] George Nicholas headed the long list of those who voted in favor of this resolution, and doubtless George Mason's influence was felt here, as in the assessment controversy, though he was not present. On

[1] " Writings of Madison," vol. i., p. 245.
[2] " History of the Constitution," vol. i., p. 238.
[3] Washington's MS. Journals. Toner Transcripts.
[4] Journal of the Assembly.

the 4th of December, 1786, the Assembly appointed seven
deputies to the convention in Pennsylvania, George Washington, Patrick Henry, Edmund Randolph, John Blair,
James Madison, George Mason, and George Wythe.[1] Patrick Henry declined the appointment, and James McClurg
was nominated in his place.

But one letter of George Mason's, written in 1786, has
been preserved. This was addressed to "Col. John Fitzgerald, Merchant in Alexandria." It is on the subject of
Colonel Mason's tobacco shipments to Bordeaux, where he
hears of the failure of a certain house to which his consignments had been sent: " I should think," he writes, "it will
be proper for me, without loss of time, to write to some
merchant of credit in Bordeaux, authorizing him to take
possession of the tobacco and sell it on my account, for
which purpose perhaps a power of attorney from me may
be necessary in case the authority merely of a letter should
be disputed. Mercantile transactions are so out of my line
of life that I am really at a loss how to proceed, and shall
be obliged to you for your advice."[2]

The year 1787 was to bring George Mason out of his
retirement into a wider field of action than he had ever
before entered. He had come forward at the call of his
State to serve in the Federal Convention, a council to which
all were now anxiously looking as the final effort to amend
the Union. It was to meet in Philadelphia in May. Madison, who was an ardent advocate of a stronger federal government, wrote from Congress to Jefferson on the 23d of
April:

" The prospect of a full and respectable convention grows
stronger every day. . . . Our Governor, Mr. Wythe, Mr.
Blair, and Col. Mason will pretty certainly attend. The last,
I am informed, is renouncing his errors on the subject of the
confederation, and means to take an active part in the amendment of it."

[1] Journal of the Assembly.   [2] MS. Letter.

Vol. II.—7

Colonel Mason's "errors," in the eyes of Madison, consisted undoubtedly in his wholesome fears of drawing too tight the bonds of union. With Patrick Henry and Richard Henry Lee he was jealous of unnecessary encroachments on the sovereignty of Virginia. Edmund Randolph, then governor, was at this time of the same party. The following letters were written to Edmund Randolph in reply to the latter, who had given Colonel Mason notice of the time appointed for the meeting of the convention, and informed him that the money to defray his expenses would be provided by the State.

GUNSTON HALL, April 12th, 1787.

DEAR SIR :

I have received your favour, notifying the time appointed for the meeting of the deputies of the different States in the city of Philadelphia, and informing me that the money was ready in the treasury to be advanced us, for defraying our expenses ; this last is, at present, an article of such importance to me, that without it, I could hardly have attended ; having been disappointed in the payment of several sums of tobacco sold ; so that I have lately been obliged to commence suits in Virginia and Maryland, for nearly the amount of six thousand pounds, upon contracts, in which I expected punctuality.

I have desired the bearer, my neighbor Col. Wagener, to bring me up, from the treasury, the sum of sixty pounds. Should our stay in Philadelphia prove shorter than I expect, whatever money may remain, more than my due, shall be punctually returned. You will oblige me exceedingly in giving whatever directions may be necessary from the Executive, for remitting the said sum of sixty pounds to me by Col. Wagener ; as I shall not probably meet with another safe hand, in time.

I hope I shall have the pleasure of seeing you at Gunston Hall, on your way to Philadelphia ; and have the honor to be, with greatest respect,

Dear Sir,

Your most obedient servant,

G. MASON.[1]

[1] MS. Letter. The address is missing in the original.

GUNSTON HALL., April 23d, 1787.

DEAR SIR :

I have received your favor by Col. Wagener with the sum of sixty pounds from the treasury. I was unacquainted with the sum allotted for each deputy, and was afraid of exceeding it. Considering the number of deputies from the different States, the great distance of some of them, and the probability that we may be obliged to wait many days before a full meeting can be obtained, we may, perhaps, be much longer from home than I at first expected. I will, therefore, accept your very obliging offer of getting the balance of the sum of £100 (vizt. £40), invested for me in Philadelphia Bank notes, or good notes on Mr. Robert Morris, either of which, I presume, will be equal to cash in the city of Philadelphia, and you will do me the favor to bring them up with you. Whatever remains more than our allowance of six dollars per day, shall be punctually returned to the treasury.

I think to set out time enough to spend a day or two in Annapolis, in order to have a little conversation with some of the Maryland deputies on the subject of the convention, and if the weather proves fine to cross the bay there ; otherwise to go through Baltimore. I expect to have the pleasure of seeing you at Gunston Hall on your way, and if you will do me the favor to let me know at what time to expect you, I will regulate my movements accordingly. I am, with the greatest regard and esteem, dear Sir,

Your most obedient servant,

G. MASON.[1]

[1] " Virginia Calendar Papers," vol. iv., p. 272.

CHAPTER IV.

IN THE FEDERAL CONVENTION.

May–July, 1787.

Of the Convention which framed the Constitution of the United States, Flanders says:

"Over its deliberations presided Washington; the genial wisdom of Franklin illustrated its debates; the trained mind, extensive information and reflective habits of Madison; the fertile resources, the ready and trenchant talents of Gouverneur Morris; the liberal views and sound sense of Charles Cotesworth Pinckney; *the inflexible integrity and unbending republicanism of Colonel Mason;* the penetrating mind and persuasive eloquence of Rufus King, were all displayed on this conspicuous theatre, and more or less determined the course and result of the Convention." [1]

To this brilliant assemblage we now follow the subject of our memoir. Colonel Mason arrived in Philadelphia the 17th of May, and two letters of his to George Mason, Jr., and one to Arthur Lee, bring us to the threshold of the new scene in which he was to act such a conspicuous part.

" PHILADELPHIA, May 20th, 1787.

"DEAR GEORGE:

"Upon our arrival here on Thursday evening, seventeenth May, I found only the States of Virginia and Pennsylvania fully represented; and there are at this time only five—New York, the two Carolinas, and the two before mentioned. All the States, Rhode

[1] "Chief Justices of the United States," vol. ii., p. 127.

Island excepted, have made their appointments ; but the members drop in slowly ; some of the deputies from the Eastern States are here, but none of them have yet a sufficient representation, and it will probably be several days before the Convention will be authorized to proceed to business. The expectations and hopes of all the Union centre in this Convention. God grant that we may be able to concert effectual means of preserving our country from the evils which threaten us.

"The Virginia deputies (who are all here) meet and confer together two or three hours every day, in order to form a proper correspondence of sentiments ; and for form's sake, to see what new deputies are arrived, and to grow into some acquaintance with each other, we regularly meet every day at three o'clock. These and some occasional conversations with the deputies of different States, and with some of the general officers of the late army (who are here upon a general meeting of the Cincinnati), are the only opportunities I have hitherto had of forming any opinion upon the great subject of our mission, and, consequently, a very imperfect and indecisive one. Yet, upon the great principles of it, I have reason to hope there will be greater unanimity and less opposition, except from the little States, than was at first apprehended. The most prevalent idea in the principal States seems to be a total alteration of the present federal system, and substituting a great national council or parliament, consisting of two branches of the legislature, founded upon the principles of equal proportionate representation, with full legislative powers upon all the subjects of the Union ; and an executive : and to make the several State legislatures subordinate to the national, by giving the latter the power of a negative upon all such laws as they shall judge contrary to the interest of the federal Union. It is easy to foresee that there will be much difficulty in organizing a government upon this great scale, and at the same time reserving to the State legislatures a sufficient portion of power for promoting and securing the prosperity and happiness of their respective citizens ; yet with a proper degree of coolness, liberality and candor (very rare commodities by the bye), I doubt not but it may be effected. There are among a variety some very eccentric opinions upon this great subject ; and what is a very extraordinary phenomenon, we are likely to find the republicans, on this occasion, issue from the Southern and Middle States, and the anti-republicans from the Eastern ; however extraordinary this may at first seem, it may, I think be accounted for from a very common and natural impulse of the human mind. Men disappointed in expectations too hastily and sanguinely formed, tired and disgusted with the unexpected evils they have experienced, and anxious to remove them as far as possible, are very apt to run into the opposite extreme ; and the people of the Eastern States, setting out with more republican principles, have consequently been more disappointed than we have been.

" We found travelling very expensive—from eight to nine dollars per day. In this city the living is cheap. We are at the old *Indian Queen* in Fourth Street, where we are very well accommodated, have a good room to ourselves, and are charged only twenty-five Pennsylvania currency per day, including our servants and horses, exclusive of club in liquors and extra charges ; so that I hope I shall be able to defray my expenses with my public allowance, and more than that I do not wish."

PHILADELPHIA, May 21, 1787.

DEAR SIR :

I take the opportunity by Col. Carrington of returning the papers you left in my hands, when I had the pleasure of your company at Gunston Hall.

I arrived in this city on Thursday evening last, but found so few of the deputies here from the several States that I am unable to form any certain opinion on the subject of our mission. The most prevalent idea I think at present is a total change of the federal system, and instituting a great national council or parliament upon the principles of equal, proportionate representation, consisting of two branches of the legislature invested with full legislative powers upon the objects of the Union ; and to make the State legislatures subordinate to the national by giving to the latter a negative upon all such laws as they judge contrary to the principles and interest of the Union ; to establish also a national executive, and a judiciary system with cognizance of all such matters as depend upon the law of nations, and such other objects as the local courts of justice may be inadequate to.

[1] Bancroft's " History of the Constitution," vol. ii., Appendix, p. 421.

I shall do myself the honor of corresponding with you from time to time, and shall be much obliged to you for your sentiments upon the important subjects that will be agitated in this Convention, upon which the prosperity and the safety of our country will so materially depend.

I have received your favor by Major Jackson ; nothing that I have heard has yet been mentioned upon this subject among the deputies now here ; though I understand there are several candidates, which I am surprised at, as the office will be of so short duration, and merely honorary, or *possibly* introductory to something more substantial.

I am with the greatest esteem and regard
Dear Sir
Your most obedient servant
G. MASON.

The Honorable Arthur Lee, Esq :
New York.[1]

PHILADELPHIA, May 27, 1787.

DEAR GEORGE :

I wrote you by the post a few days after my arrival in this city. I shall be glad to know whether my letter has come safe to hand, as also the letters I wrote from Baltimore to your brothers William and Thomson, to which I have not yet received any answer. I wish to be informed also whether you have had any good rains and what prospect of the crops of wheat and tobacco. It is impossible to judge how long we shall be detained here, but from present appearances I fear until July, if not later. I begin to grow heartily tired of the etiquette and nonsense so fashionable in this city. It would take me some months to make myself master of them, and that it should require months to learn what is not worth remembering as many minutes, is to me so discouraging a circumstance as determines me to give myself no manner of trouble about them. I have not yet been able to do anything respecting your brother John, and fear I shall meet with much difficulty on that subject.

[1] MS. Letter (published in " Life of A. Lee," vol. ii., p. 319). On the same sheet of the original are given seven amendments to the Constitution—in the handwriting of Arthur Lee. See Appendix ii. The biographer of Arthur Lee regrets " the loss of the residue of the valuable letters of G. Mason."

We had yesterday, for the first time, a representation of seven States—New York, New Jersey, Pennsylvania, Delaware, Virginia, and the two Carolinas, and it is expected that the deputies from Massachusetts, Connecticut, and Georgia will be here by Monday or Tuesday. The State of Rhode Island has refused to appoint deputies, and although New Hampshire has appointed it is thought we shall be deprived of their representation by no provision having been made for defraying their expenses. The State of Delaware has tied up the hands of her deputies by an express direction to retain the principle in the present Confederation of each State having the same vote; no other State, so far as we have yet seen, hath restrained its deputies on any subject.

Nothing was done yesterday but unanimously appointing General Washington President; Major Jackson (by a majority of five States to two) Secretary; reading the credentials from the different States on the floor, and appointing a committee to draw up and report the rules of proceeding. It is expected our doors will be shut, and communications upon the business of the Convention be forbidden during its sitting. This I think myself a proper precaution to prevent mistakes and misrepresentation until the business shall have been completed, when the whole may have a very different complexion from that in which the several crude and indigested parts might in their first shape appear if submitted to the public eye.

Present me kindly to Betsy, to the family at Gunston, to Mr. McCarty and Sallie, and to all our friends.

> I am, dear George,
> Your affectionate father,
> G. MASON.[1]

Richard Henry Lee had declined a seat in the Convention, wishing to leave himself free to act in Congress as his convictions should determine. He wrote to George Mason, giving his views in regard to the changes to be desired, knowing that Colonel Mason would be likely to forward them.

[1] Mason Papers.

May 15, 1787, CHANTILLY.

DEAR SIR—It has given me much pleasure to be informed that General Washington and yourself have gone to the Convention. We may hope, from such efforts, that alterations beneficial will take place in our Federal Constitution, if it shall be found, on deliberate inquiry, that the evils now felt do flow from errors in that constitution ; but, alas ! sir, I fear it is more in vicious manners, than mistakes in form, that we must seek for the causes of the present discontent. The present causes of complaint seem to be, that Congress cannot command the money necessary for the just purposes of paying debts, or for supporting the federal government ; and that they cannot make treaties of commerce, unless power unlimited, of regulating trade be given. The Confederation now gives right to name the sums necessary, and to apportion the quotas by a rule established. This rule is, unfortunately, very difficult of execution, and, therefore, the recommendations of Congress on this subject have not been made in federal mode ; so that States have thought themselves justified in non-compliance. If the rule were plain and easy, and refusal were then to follow demand, I see clearly, that no form of government whatever, short of force, will answer ; for the same want of principle that produces neglect now, will do so under any change not supported by power compulsory ; the difficulty certainly is, how to give this power in such manner as that it may only be used to good, and not abused to bad, purposes. Whoever shall solve this difficulty will receive the thanks of this and future generations. With respect to the want of power to make treaties of trade, for want of legislation, to regulate the general commerce, it appears to me, that the right of making treaties, and the legislative power contended for are essentially different things ; the former may be given and executed, without the danger attending upon the States parting with their legislative authority, in the instance contended for. If the third paragraph of the sixth article were altered, by striking out the words, in pursuance of any treaties already proposed by Congress, to the courts of France and Spain ; and the proviso stricken out of the first section in the ninth article, Congress would then have a complete and unlimited right of making treaties of all kinds, and, so far, I really think it both right and necessary ; but this is very different from, and in danger far short of, giving an exclusive power of regulating trade. A minister of Congress may go to a foreign court with full power to make a commercial treaty ; but if he were to propose to such court that the eight northern States in this Union, should have the exclusive right of carrying the products of the five southern States, or of supplying these States with foreign articles, such a proposition of monopoly would be rejected ; and, therefore, no danger here from the power of making treaty ; but a legislative right to regulate trade through the States may, in a thousand artful modes, be so abused as to produce the monopoly aforesaid, to the extreme oppression of the staple States, as they are called. I do not say that this would be done, but I contend that it might be done ; and, where interest powerfully prompts, it is greatly to be feared that it would be done. Whoever has served long in Congress, knows that the restraint of making the consent of nine States necessary, is feeble and incompetent. Some will sometimes sleep, and some will be negligent, but it is certain that improper power not given cannot be improperly used.

The human mind is too apt to rush from one extreme to another ; it appears, by the objections that came from the different States, when the Confederation was submitted for consideration, that the universal apprehension was, of the too great, not the defective powers of Congress. Whence this immense change of sentiment, in a few years ? for now the cry is power, give Congress power. Without reflecting that every free nation, that hath ever existed, has lost its liberty by the same rash impatience, and want of necessary caution. I am glad, however, to find, on this occasion, that so many gentlemen, of competent years, are sent to the Convention, for, certainly, "youth is the season of credulity, and confidence a plant of slow growth in an aged bosom." The States have been so unpardonably remiss, in furnishing their federal quotas, as to make impost necessary, for a term of time, with a provisional security, that the money arising shall be unchangeably applied to the payment of their public debts ; that accounts of the application, shall be annually sent to each State ; and the collecting officers appointed by, and be amenable to the States : or, if not so, very strong preventives and correctives of official abuse and misconduct, interpose, to shield the people from oppression. Give me leave, sir, to detain you a moment longer, with a proposition that I have not heard mentioned. It is that the right of making paper money shall be exclusively vested in Congress; such a right will be clearly within the spirit of the fourth section of the ninth article of the present confederation. This appears to me, to be a restraint of the last importance to the peace and happiness of the Union, and of every part of it. Knaves assure, and fools believe, that calling paper money, and making it tender, is the way to be rich and happy; thus the national mind is kept in constant ferment; and the public councils in continual disturbance by the intrigues of wicked men, for fraudulent purposes, for speculating designs. This would be a great step towards correcting morals, and suppressing legislative frauds, which, of all frauds, is the most hateful to society. Do you not think, sir, that it ought to be declared, by the new system, that any State act of legislation that shall contravene, or oppose, the authorized acts of Congress, or interfere with the expressed rights of that body, shall be *ipso facto* void, and of no force whatsoever?

My respects, if you please, to your brethren of the Convention, from this State, and pardon me for the liberty I have taken of troubling you with my sentiments on the interesting business that calls you to Philadelphia. I have the honour to be, with affectionate esteem and regard,

Your friend and servant,

RICHARD HENRY LEE.

George Mason, Esq.[1]

The Convention met on Friday, the 25th of May, seven States being represented. On the following Monday nine other deputies took their seats, and Connecticut and Maryland were added to the number of States present. The rules as reported were read. Mr. King of Massachusetts objected to that one authorizing any member to call for the yeas and nays and have them entered on the minutes. Colonel Mason seconded the objection, adding " that such a record of the opinions of members would be an obstacle to a change of

[1] " Life of Richard H. Lee," vol. ii., p. 71.

them on conviction ; and in case of its being hereafter promulgated must furnish handles to the adversaries of the result of the meeting." [1] The rule was then rejected. Madison tells us in his report of these debates that previous to the opening of the Convention it had been a subject of discussion among the members present, as to how the States should vote in the Convention. Several of the members from Pennsylvania had urged that the large States unite in refusing to the small States an equal vote, but Virginia, believing this to be injudicious if not unjust " discountenanced and stifled the project." On the 29th the real business of the Convention was opened by Edmund Randolph, who as Governor of Virginia was put forward as spokesman by his colleagues. He began by saying that as the Convention had originated from Virginia, and the delegation from this State supposed that some proposition was expected from them, the task had been imposed on him. After enumerating the defects of the Confederation, he detailed the remedy proposed. This latter was set forth in fifteen resolutions and was called afterwards the Virginia plan of government. Charles Pinckney from South Carolina had also a draft of a federal government, which was read and like the former referred to a committee of the whole House.

The first proposition debated was a resolution presented by Edmund Randolph but formulated by Gouverneur Morris, " That a *national* government ought to be established consisting of a *Supreme* Legislative, Executive, and Judiciary." Here South Carolina asked if Mr. Randolph meant to abolish the State governments. Doubts were expressed by members from Massachusetts and South Carolina whether the deputies could discuss a system founded on different principles from the Federal Constitution. Gouverneur Morris explained the difference, as he conceived it, between a *federal* and a *national* government. The term federal, however, was to change its signification, and to be used by the advocates of a " national government " to describe themselves.

[1] " Madison Papers," vol. ii., p. 724.

George Mason spoke after Mr. Morris, and put his finger on one of the chief weaknesses of the existing system. He observed, " not only that the present Confederation was deficient in not providing for coercion and punishment against delinquent States, but argued very cogently that punishment could not in the nature of things be executed on the States collectively, and therefore that such a government was necessary as could directly operate on individuals, and would punish those only whose guilt required it." [1] This was a cardinal principle, that coercion could not be used against States. And here George Mason was in direct opposition to a clause in the sixth resolution of the Virginia plan, as presented by Edmund Randolph, which declared that the National or Federal legislature should have the power "to call forth the force of the Union against any member of the Union failing to fulfil its duty under the Articles thereof." Of all the Virginia delegation, apparently, Washington, Madison, Randolph, McClurg, and Mason, the latter alone saw clearly the danger here, and he was the first one in the Convention to suggest the solution of the difficulty which was subsequently adopted.

On the 31st of May Georgia was represented in the Convention, making ten States present. It was agreed without debate on this day that the " National Legislature " ought to consist of two branches, but the succeeding resolution, that the members of the first branch ought to be elected by the people of the several States, provoked some discussion. It was opposed, says Yates, "strange to tell by Massachusetts and Connecticut, who supposed they ought to be chosen by the legislatures; and Virginia supported the resolve, alleging that this ought to be the democratic branch of government, and as such immediately vested in the people." [2] Colonel Mason spoke first after Sherman and Gerry, and Madison followed after Wilson, of Pennsylvania, all three of the latter contending for an election of the larger branch of

---

[1] *Ibid.*, p. 748.
[2] Yates' Minutes, Elliot's " Debates," second edition, 1861, vol. i., p. 392.

Congress by the people. "It was to be," said George Mason, "the grand depository of the democratic principle of the government. It was, so to speak, to be our House of Commons. It ought to know and sympathize with every part of the community; and ought therefore to be taken, not only from different parts of the whole republic, but also from different districts of the larger members of it; which had in several instances, particularly in Virginia, different interests and views arising from difference of produce, of habits, etc. He admitted that we had been too democratic, but was afraid we should incautiously run into the opposite extreme. We ought to attend to the rights of every class of the people. He had often wondered at the indifference of the superior classes of society to this dictate of humanity and policy; considering, that, however affluent their circumstances, or elevated their situations, might be, the course of a few years not only might, but certainly would, distribute their posterity throughout the lowest classes of society. Every selfish motive, therefore, every family attachment, ought to recommend such a system of policy as would provide no less carefully for the rights and happiness of the lowest, than of the highest, order of citizens.' [1]

On the 1st of June the Convention considered the question of the Executive. It was moved that his term of office should be for seven years, though others advocated three years, providing for re-eligibility. George Mason "was for seven years at least, and for prohibiting a re-eligibility, as the best expedient, both for preventing the effect of a false complaisance on the side of the Legislature towards unfit characters; and a temptation on the side of the Executive to intrigue with the Legislature for a re-appointment." [2] And seven years was the term then agreed upon. On the mode of appointing the Executive, whether it should be by Congress, as proposed in the Virginia plan, or by the people, as was moved at this time, there was some debate. George Mason

[1] " Madison Papers," vol. ii., p. 754.   [2] *Ibid.*, p. 766.

advocated the latter mode " but thought it impracticable. He wished, however, that Mr. Wilson, who had suggested the election by the people might have time to digest it in his own form." [1] On the following day the subject was renewed, but the plan of Presidential Electors was not agreed to. In regard to a resolution " that the Executive be made removable by the National Legislature," George Mason said : " Some mode of displacing an unfit magistrate is rendered indispensable by the fallibility of those who choose, as well as by the corruptibility of the man chosen. He opposed decidedly the making the Executive the mere creature of the Legislature, as a violation of the fundamental principles of good government." [2]

The vote on the question of a single Executive was taken on Monday, the 4th of June. Colonel Mason happened not to be in the House at the time, but he was known to be opposed to the resolve. Later in the day he spoke against vesting the executive powers in a single person. Among these powers, he went on to say, was that of appointing to offices in certain cases.

" The probable abuses of a negative had been well explained by Dr. Franklin, as proved by experience, the best of all tests. Will not the same door be opened here ? The Executive may refuse its assent to necessary measures, till new appointments shall be referred to him ; and having by degrees engrossed all these into his own hands, the American Executive, like the British, will, by bribery and influence, save himself the trouble and odium of exerting his negative afterwards. We are, Mr. Chairman, going very far in this business. We are not, indeed, constituting a British government, but a more dangerous monarchy, an elective one. We are introducing a new principle into our system, and not necessary, as in the British government, where the executive has greater rights to defend. Do gentlemen mean to pave the way to hereditary monarchy ? Do they flatter themselves that the people will ever consent to such an innovation ? If they do, I venture to tell them, they are mistaken.

[1] *Ibid.*, p. 768.   [2] *Ibid.*, p. 776.

The people never will consent. And do gentlemen consider the danger of delay, and the still greater danger of a rejection, not for a moment, but forever, of the plan which shall be proposed to them? Notwithstanding the oppression and injustice experienced among us from democracy, the genius of the people is in favor of it; and the genius of the people must be consulted. He could not but consider the Federal system as in effect dissolved by the appointment of this convention to devise a better one. And do gentlemen look forward to the dangerous interval between extinction of an old, and the establishment of a new, government; and to the scenes of confusion which may ensue? He hoped that nothing like a monarchy would ever be attempted in this country. A hatred to its oppressions had carried the people through the late Revolution. Will it not be enough to enable the Executive to suspend offensive laws, till they shall be coolly revised, and the objections to them overruled by a greater majority than was required in the first instance? He never could agree to give up all the rights of the people to a single magistrate. If more than one had been fixed on, greater powers might have been entrusted to the Executive. He hoped this attempt to give such powers would have its weight hereafter, as an argument for increasing the number of the executive." [1]

George Mason's views on the subject of the Executive are further elaborated in the following speech, which is preserved in manuscript, and which is undated, but was evidently written for delivery in the Convention at this or a subsequent period.

"It is not yet determined how the Executive is to be regulated, whether it is to act solely from its own judgment, or with the advice of others; whether there is, or is not to be a council annexed to it, and if a council how far their advice shall operate in controlling the judgment of the supreme magistracy. If there is no Council of State and the executive power be vested in a single person, what are the provisions for its proper operation,

[1] *Ibid.*, p. 787.

upon casual disability by sickness or otherwise. These are subjects which must come under our consideration, and perhaps some of the most important objections would. be obviated by placing the executive power in the hands of three, instead of one person.

"There is also to be a council of revision, invested, in a great measure, with a power of negative upon the laws ; and an idea has been suggested, either within or without doors, that this council should be formed of the principal officers of the state, I presume of the members of the Treasury Board, the Board of War, the Navy Board, and the Department for Foreign Affairs. It is unnecessary, if not improper, to examine this part of the subject now, but I will venture to hazard an opinion, when it comes to be thoroughly investigated, that we can hardly find worse materials out of which to create a council of revision, or more improper or unsafe hands in which to place the power of a negative upon our laws. It is proposed, I think, sir, in the plan upon your table, that this council of revision shall be formed out of the members of the Judiciary departments joined with the Executive; and I am inclined to think, when the subject shall be taken up, it may be demonstrated, that this will be the wisest and safest mode of constituting this important council of revision. But the federal inferior courts of justice must, I presume, be fixed in the several respective States, and consequently most of them at a great distance from the seat of the federal government. The almost continual operation of the council of revision upon the acts of the national parliament, and upon their negative of the acts of the several State legislatures, will require that this council should be easily and speedily convened, and consequently, that only the judges of the Supreme Federal Court, fixed near the seat of government, can be members of it. Their number will be small. By placing the Executive in three persons, instead of one, we shall not only increase the number of the council of revision (which I have endeavored to show will want increasing), but by giving to each of the three a vote in the council of revision, we shall increase the strength of the Executive in that particular circumstance in which it will most want strength—in the power of defending itself against the encroachments of the legislature. These, I must acknowledge, are, with me, weighty considerations for vesting the Executive rather in three than in one person.

"The chief advantages which have been urged in favor of unity in the Executive, are the secresy, the dispatch, the vigor and energy which the government will derive from it, especially in time of war. That these are great advantages, I shall most readily allow. They have been strongly insisted on by all monarchical writers; they have been acknowledged by the ablest and most candid defenders of republican government; and it cannot be denied that a monarchy possesses them in a much greater degree than a republic. Yet perhaps a little reflection may incline us to doubt whether these advantages are not greater in theory than in practice, or lead us to enquire whether there is not some pervading principle in republican government which sets at naught and tramples upon this boasted superiority, as hath been experienced to their cost, by most monarchies which have been imprudent enough to invade or attack their republican neighbors. This invincible principle is to be found in the love, the affection, the attachment of the citizens to their laws, to their freedom, and to their country. Every husbandman will be quickly converted into a soldier when he knows and feels that he is to fight not in defence of the rights of a particular family, or a prince, but for his own. This is the true construction of the *pro aris et focis* which has, in all ages, performed such wonders. It was this which in ancient times enabled the little cluster of Grecian republics to resist, and almost constantly to defeat, the Persian monarch. It was this which supported the States of Holland against a body of veteran troops through a thirty years' war with Spain, then the greatest monarchy in Europe, and finally rendered them victorious. It is this which preserves the freedom and independence of the Swiss Cantons in the midst of the most powerful nations. And who that reflects seriously upon the situation of America, in the beginning of the late war—without arms—without soldiers—without trade, money or credit, in a manner destitute of all resources, but must ascribe our success to this pervading, all-powerful principle?

"We have not yet been able to define the powers of the Executive, and however moderately some gentlemen may talk or think upon the subject, I believe there is a general tendency to a strong

Executive, and I am inclined to think a strong Executive necessary. If strong and extensive powers are vested in the Executive, and that executive consists only of one person, the government will of course degenerate (for I will call it degeneracy) into a monarchy—a government so contrary to the genius of the people that they will ·reject even the appearance of it. I consider the federal government as in some measure dissolved by the meeting of this Convention. Are there no dangers to be apprehended from procrastinating the time between the breaking up of this Assembly and the adoption of a new system of government? I dread the interval. If it should not be brought to an issue in the course of the first year the consequences may be fatal. Have not the different parts of this extensive government, the several States of which it is composed a right to expect an equal participation in the Executive, as the best means of securing an equal attention to their interests? Should an insurrection, a rebellion or invasion happen in New Hampshire when the single supreme magistrate is a citizen of Georgia, would not the people of New Hampshire naturally ascribe any delay in defending them to such a circumstance and *vice versa?* If the Executive is vested in three persons, one chosen from the Northern, one from the Middle, and one from the Southern States, will it not contribute to quiet the minds of the people and convince them that there will be proper attention paid to their respective concerns? Will not three men so chosen bring with them, into office, a more perfect and extensive knowledge of the real interests of this great Union? Will not such a mode of appointment be the most effectual means of preventing cabals and intrigues between the legislature and the candidates for this office, especially with those candidates who from their local situation, near the seat of the federal government, will have the greatest temptations and the greatest opportunities? Will it not be the most effectual means of checking and counteracting the aspiring views of dangerous and ambitious men, and consequently the best security for the stability and duration of our government upon the invaluable principles of liberty? These Sir, are some of my motives for preferring an Executive consisting of three persons rather than of one."[1]

[1] Mason Papers.

Edmund Randolph advocated in the Convention this suggestion of his colleague, that the Executive should consist of three members, taken from the three sections of the country.

On Wednesday, June 6th, the important question was debated as to the election of the first branch of the legislature. Should it be by the State legislatures or by the people? The latter method, embraced in the Virginia plan, was now advocated by both Madison and Mason. "Under the existing Confederacy," said George Mason, "Congress represent the *States* and not the *people* of the *States;* their acts operate on the *States,* not on the *individuals.* The case will be changed in the new plan of government. The people will be represented; they ought therefore to choose the Representatives. The requisites in actual representation are, that the Representatives should sympathize with their constituents; should think as they think, and feel as they feel; and that for these purposes they should be residents among them. Much, he said, had been alleged against democratic elections. He admitted that much might be said; but it was to be considered that no government was free from imperfections and evils; and that improper elections in many instances were inseparable from republican governments. But compare these with the advantage of this form, in favor of the rights of the people, in favor of human nature! He was persuaded there was a better chance for proper elections by the people, if divided into large districts, than by the State Legislatures. Paper-money had been issued by the latter, when the former were against it. Was it to be supposed that the State Legislatures, then, would not send to the National Legislature patrons of such projects, if the choice depended on them."[1] The Convention recurring again to the Executive, the resolution to give the latter power, with the assistance of some of the judiciary, to revise the laws passed by the legislature, was reconsidered, and Colonel Mason was for "giving all possi-

[1] "Madison Papers," vol. ii., p. 803.

ble weight to the revisionary institution. The executive power," he thought, "ought to be well secured against legislative usurpations on it. The purse and the sword ought never to get into the same hands, whether legislative or executive." [1]

On the following day another great point in the formation of the Constitution was debated. The motion was made by Mr. Dickinson for the appointment of the Senate by the State legislatures, and carried in the affirmative. George Mason was the last one to speak on this occasion. "Whatever power," he said, "may be necessary for the national government, a certain portion must necessarily be left with the States. It is impossible for one power to pervade the extreme parts of the United States, so as to carry equal justice to them. The State Legislatures also ought to have some means of defending themselves against encroachments of the national government. In every other department we have studiously endeavoured to provide for its self-defence. Shall we leave the States alone unprovided with the means for this purpose? And what better means can we provide, than the giving them some share in, or rather to make them a constituent part of, the national establishment? There is danger on both sides, no doubt; but we have only seen the evils arising on the side of the State governments. Those on the other side remain to be displayed. The example of Congress does not apply. Congress had no power to carry their acts into execution, as the national government will have." [2] The thirteenth resolution of the Virginia plan, providing for making amendments to the Constitution without the assent of the legislature of the Union, came up for consideration on the 11th, and Colonel Mason urged the necessity of such a provision:

" The plan now to be formed will certainly be defective, as the Confederation has been found on trial to be. Amendments, therefore, will be necessary; and it will be better to provide for them

[1] *Ibid.*, p. 811. [2] *Ibid.*, p. 820.

in an easy, regular and constitutional way, than to trust to chance and violence. It would be improper to require the consent of the national legislature, because they may abuse their power, and refuse their assent on that very account. The opportunity for such an abuse may be the fault of the Constitution calling for amendment." [1]

George Mason seconded a motion made by Madison the following day, relating to the payment of members of the federal legislature. He thought " that it would be improper to leave the wages to be regulated by the States,—first the different States would make different provision for their representatives, and an inequality would be felt among them, whereas he thought they ought to be in all respects equal ; secondly, the parsimony of the States might reduce the provision so low, that, as had already happened in choosing delegates to Congress, the question would be, not who were most fit to be chosen, but who were most willing to serve." [2] The qualification for the age of Senators was fixed at thirty. Among George Mason's memoranda of the Convention are this note and resolve, showing his agency in an important part of the Convention's work:

"G. Mason begs the favor of Maj. Jackson to correct the following Resolution, in the manner it hath been agreed to by the Convention.

" 4. *Resolved,* That the members of the second branch of the legislature of the United States ought to be chosen by the individual legislatures, to be of the age of thirty years at least, to hold their offices for the term of six years, one third to go out biennially ; to be ineligible to and incapable of holding any office under the authority of the United States, except those peculiarly belonging to the functions of the second branch, during the term for which they were chosen and for one year thereafter." [3]

The Committee of the Whole had debated from day to day the resolutions contained in the Virginia plan, and on

[1] *Ibid.,* p. 844.   [2] *Ibid.,* p. 849.   [3] Mason Papers.

the 13th of June they reported nineteen resolutions based upon those of Virginia, forming a system of government in outline. On the following day Mr. Paterson, of New Jersey, asked for time to prepare another plan founded on the Articles of Confederation. This was submitted to the Convention on the 15th. The Virginia and the New Jersey plan were contrasted briefly by one of the members :

Virginia plan proposes two branches in the legislature.
Jersey, a single legislative body.
Virginia, the legislative powers derived from the people.
Jersey, from the States.
Virginia, a single executive.
Jersey, more than one.
Virginia, a majority of the legislature can act.
Jersey, a small majority can control.
Virginia, the legislature can legislate on all national concerns.
Jersey, only on limited objects.
Virginia, legislature to negative all State laws.
Jersey, giving power to the executive to compel obedience by force.
Virginia, to remove the executive by impeachment.
Jersey, on application of a majority of the States.
Virginia, for the establishment of inferior judiciary tribunals.
Jersey, no provision.[1]

Neither of these plans commended themselves to men like Hamilton, who wanted a strong government, and were afraid of democracy or giving power to the people. He thought the Virginia plan " but pork still with a little change of the sauce." The Articles of Confederation amended, as in the New Jersey plan, set forth a government approved of by the opposite wing of the Convention, consisting of men like Lansing, who professed an ultra devotion to the rights and autonomy of the States, yet strangely enough were ready to admit the use of force against them by the general government. George Mason, more consistent both as a

[1] Yates' Minutes, Elliot, vol. i., p 414.

champion of State sovereignty and a believer in the rights of the people, sought to give each idea its practical exposition in the new government. In a debate, June 20th, on giving two branches to the legislature, Colonel Mason summed up the arguments in its favor, replying to those who opposed it. Paterson's propositions had been rejected by the committee the day before, and the nineteen resolutions based on the Virginia plan were again reported. The second resolution referred to the constitution of the legislature.

"He did not expect this point would have been reagitated. The essential differences between the two plans had been clearly stated. The principal objections against that of Mr. Randolph were, the *want of power*, and the *want of practicability*. There can be no weight in the first, as the fiat is not to be *here*, but in the people. [The power in the Convention to frame an entirely new Constitution is meant here.] He thought with his colleague (Mr. Randolph) that there were, besides, certain crises, in which all the ordinary cautions yielded to public necessity. He gave as an example, the eventual treaty with Great Britain, in forming which the Commissioners of the United States had boldly disregarded the improvident shackles of Congress ; had given to their country an honorable and happy peace, and instead of being censured for the transgression of their powers had raised to themselves a monument more durable than brass. The *impracticability* of gaining the public concurrence, he thought, was still more groundless. Mr. Lansing had cited the attempts of Congress to gain an enlargement of their powers, and had inferred, from the miscarriage of these attempts, the hopelessness of the plan which he (Mr. Lansing) opposed. He thought a very different inference ought to have been drawn, viz., that the plan which Mr. Lansing espoused, and which proposed to augment the powers of Congress, never could be expected to succeed. He meant not to throw any reflections on Congress as a body, much less on any particular members of it. He meant, however, to speak his sentiments without reserve on this subject ; it was a privilege of age, and perhaps the only compensation which nature had given for the privation of so many other enjoyments ; and he should not scruple to exercise it freely. Is it to be thought that the people of America, so watchful over their interests, so jealous of their liberties, will give up their all, will surrender both the sword and the purse, to the same body,—and that, too, not chosen immediately by themselves? They never will. They never ought. Will they trust such a body with the regulation of their trade, with the regulation of their taxes, with all the other great powers which are in contemplation? Will they give unbounded confidence to a secret journal,—to the intrigues, to the factions, which in the nature of things appertain to such an. assembly? If any man doubts the existence of these characters of Congress, let him consult their Journals for the years seventy-eight, seventy-nine, and eighty. It will be said, that if the people are averse to parting with power, why is it hoped that they will part with it to a national legislature? The proper answer is, that in this case they do not part with power; they only transfer it from one set of immediate representatives to another set. Much has been said of the unsettled state of the mind of the people. He believed the mind of the people of America, as elsewhere, was unsettled as to some points, but settled as to others. In two points he was sure it was well settled,—first, in an attachment to republican government; secondly, in an attachment to more than one branch in the legislature. Their constitutions accord so generally in both these circumstances, that they seem almost to have been preconcerted. This must either have been a miracle, or have resulted from the genius of the people. The only exceptions to the establishment of two branches in the legislature are the State of Pennsylvania and Congress; and the latter the only single one not chosen by the people themselves. What has been the consequence? The people have been constantly averse to giving that body further powers.

"It was acknowledged by Mr. Paterson that his plan could not be enforced without military coercion. Does he consider the force of this concession? The most jarring elements of nature, fire and water themselves, are not more incompatible than such a mixture of civil liberty and military execution. Will the militia march from one State into another, in order to collect the arrears of taxes from the delinquent members of the republic? Will they maintain an army for this purpose? Will not the citizens of the invaded State assist one another, till they rise as one man and shake off the Union altogether? Rebellion is the only case in which the military force of the State can be properly exerted against its citizens. In one point of view, he was struck with horror at the prospect of recurring to this expedient. To punish the non-payment of taxes with death was a severity not yet adopted by despotism itself; yet this unexampled cruelty would be mercy compared to a military collection of revenue in which the bayonet could make no discrimination between the innocent and the guilty. He took this occasion to repeat, that, notwithstanding his solicitude to establish a national government, he never would agree to abolish the State governments, or render them absolutely insignificant. They were as necessary as the general government, and he would be equally careful to preserve them. He was aware of the difficulty of drawing the line between them, but hoped it was not insurmountable. The Convention, though comprising so many distinguished characters, could not be expected to make a faultless government. And he would prefer trusting to posterity the amendment of its defects, rather than to push the experiment too far."

Judge Yates, who gives his abstract of the debates in the first person always, has reported this speech of George Mason's a little differently, and of course, as he only professed to give minutes, much more briefly:

"These measures are supported by one who, at his time of life, has little to hope or expect from any government. . . . What! would you use military force to compel the observance of a social compact? It is destructive to the rights of the people. Do you expect the militia will do it? or do you mean a standing army? The first will never on such an occasion, exert any power; and the latter may turn its arms against the government which employs them. I never will consent to destroy State governments, and will ever be as careful to preserve the one as the other. . . . That the one government will be productive of disputes and jealousies against the other, I believe; but it will produce mutual safety. I shall close with observing,

[1] "Madison Papers," vol., ii., p. 912.

that though some have expressed much warmth on this and former occasions, I can excuse it, as the result of sudden passion ; and hope that although we may differ in some particular points, if we mean the good of the whole, our good sense, upon reflection, will prevent us from spreading our discontent farther." [1]

The Convention did not go again into committee of the whole, but continued to debate the nineteen resolutions from the 19th of June until the 23d of July. Some of these were referred to grand committees, consisting of one member from each State, or they were referred to select committees consisting of five members. On the question of the election of the first branch of the legislature, it was moved that it should be as each State legislature directed, when Colonel Mason was again on his feet :

" I am for preserving inviolably the democratic branch of the government. True we have found inconveniences from pure democracies ; but if we mean to preserve peace and real freedom, they must necessarily become a component part of the national system. Change this necessary principle, and if the government proceeds to taxation, the States will oppose your powers." [2]

When the motion was considered of the election of the first branch for two years, George Mason observed, " that the States being differently situated, such a rule ought to be formed as would put them as nearly as possible on a level. If elections were annual, the middle States would have a great advantage over the extreme ones. He wished them to be biennial, and the rather as in that case they would coincide with the periodical elections of South Carolina, as well of the other States." [3] On the subject of the " fixed stipends to be paid out of the national treasury " to the representatives, Colonel Mason moved to change the phraseology of the resolve ; that is to say, " to receive an

[1] Elliot's " Debates," vol. i., p. 429.
[2] *Ibid.*, p. 433.
[3] " Madison Papers," vol. ii., p. 930.

adequate compensation for their services, and to be paid out of the treasury," which motion was agreed to.[1]

Jefferson, in characterizing George Mason's merits as a public speaker, notices the "touch of biting cynicism" which sometimes seasoned his arguments. Examples of this quality are to be found in the following passages. The question of the age required for members of Congress was brought up by Colonel Mason, and he moved to insert "twenty-five years of age as a qualification for members of the first branch." He "thought it absurd that a man to-day should not be permitted by the law to make a bargain for himself, and to-morrow should be authorized to manage the affairs of a great nation. It was the more extraordinary as every man carried with him, in his own experience, a scale for measuring the deficiency of young politicians; since he would, if interrogated, be obliged to declare that his political opinions at the age of twenty-one were too crude and erroneous to merit an influence on public measures. It had been said, that Congress had proved a good school for our young men. It might be so, for anything he knew; but if it were, he chose that they should bear the expence of their own education."[2] The exclusive clause in the third resolve being under consideration, George Mason spoke as follows:

"It seems as if it were taken for granted that all offices will be filled by the Executive, while I think many will remain in the gift of the legislature. In either case it is necessary to shut the door against corruption. If otherwise, they may make or multiply offices in order to fill them. Are gentlemen in earnest when they suppose that this exclusion will prevent the first characters from coming forward? Are we not struck at seeing the luxury and venality which has already crept in among us? If not checked, we shall have ambassadors to every petty State in Europe; the little republic of St. Marino not excepted. We must in the present system remove the temptation. I admire many parts of the British constitution and government, but I

[1] Yates' Minutes, Elliot, vol. i., p. 436.
[2] "Madison Papers," vol. ii., p. 936.

detest their corruption. Why has the power of the Crown in-creased, so remarkably increased, the last century? A stranger, by reading their laws, would suppose it considerably diminished ; and yet by the sole power of appointing the increased officers of the government, corruption pervades every town and village in the kingdom. If such a restriction should abridge the right of election, it is still necessary, as it will prevent the people from ruining themselves. And will not the same causes here produce the same effects? I consider this clause as the corner-stone on which our liberties depend ; and if we strike it out, we are erect-ing a fabric for our destruction." [1]

The subject was continued on the following day, June 23d, when Madison renewed his motion to render the mem-bers of the first branch "ineligible during their term of ser-vice, and for one year after, to such offices only, as should be established, or the emolument augmented, by the legis-lature of the United States during the time of their being members." Colonel Mason "thought the motion of his colleague but a partial remedy for the evil. He appealed to him as a witness of the shameful partiality of the legis-lature of Virginia to its own members. He enlarged on the abuses and corruption in the British Parliament con-nected with the appointment of its members. He could not suppose that a sufficient number of citizens could not be found who would be ready, without the inducement of eligi-bility to offices, to undertake the legislative service. Genius and virtue, it may be said [he here alluded to some remarks of Mr. Wilson], ought to be encouraged. Genius, for aught he knew might ; but that virtue should be encouraged by such a species of venality, was an idea that at least had the merit of being new." [2] Yates, in reporting this speech, gives the substance of the last clause in these words:

"It is asserted that it will be very difficult to find men suffi-ciently qualified as legislators without the inducement of emolu-

[1] Yates' Minutes, Elliot, vol. i., p. 437.
[2] " Madison Papers," vol. ii., p. 940.

ments. I do believe that men of genius will be deterred unless possessed of great virtues. We may well dispense with the first characters when destitute of virtue. I should wish them never to come forward. But if we do not provide against corruption, our government will soon be at an end; nor would I wish to put a man of virtue in the way of temptation. Evasions and caballing [he continued] would evade the amendment. Nor would the danger be less, if the executive has the appointment of officers. The first three or four years we might go on well enough, but what would be the case afterwards? I will add, that such a government ought to be refused by the people; and it will be refused." [1]

On the 25th of June, the vexed question of the mode of appointing the Senate was brought up, Mr. Wilson moving that the members be elected by electors chosen by the people. This was a point which divided, as a class, the large and small States, the former advocating proportional representation in both Houses, the latter opposing it, and, as Bancroft observes, the election of the Senate by the State legislatures was looked upon "as the stepping-stone to an equal representation." [2] And while Virginia's vote went with that of Pennsylvania against a doctrine so important for the preservation of the individual commonwealth, it was one of Virginia's representatives who consistently supported it as a pillar of States-rights. "It has been agreed, on all hands," said George Mason, "that an efficient government is necessary; that to render it such, it ought to have the faculty of self-defence; that to render its different branches effectual each of them ought to have the same power of self-defence. He did not wonder that such an agreement should have prevailed on these points. He only wondered that there should be any disagreement about the necessity of allowing the State governments the same self-defence. If they are to be preserved, as he conceived to be essential, they certainly ought to have this power; and the only mode

[1] Yates' Minutes, Elliot, vol. i., p. 440.
[2] "History of the Constitution," vol. ii., p. 56.

left of giving it to them was by allowing them to appoint
the second branch of the national legislature."[1] Dr. Johnson, of Connecticut, in advocating this means of self-defence
for the States, gives George Mason credit as the author
of the scheme. "This is the idea of Col. Mason, who
appears to have looked to the bottom of this matter."[2]
Much has been written, of late, on the "Connecticut Compromise," as Bancroft styles it, the equal representation of
the States in the Senate, and here is one of the three representatives from Connecticut who urged the measure upon
the Convention avowing that it was the "idea" of Colonel
Mason, that the States should appoint the members of the
Senate, the "stepping-stone" to equal representation. The
proportional representation in the first branch, which would
make the large States more powerful there, was acquiesced
in by the small States in consideration that an equality in
the Senate would give them the same voice in its councils as
their more powerful sisters. The small States, led by Connecticut, finally effected this settlement in the Convention.
But Sherman, Ellsworth, and Johnson only made practical
an idea independently evolved by the Virginia statesman,
who, wiser than his colleagues, had " looked to the bottom
of this matter." Madison, in the *Federalist*, frankly avowed
his subsequent conversion to the equality of votes in the
Senate, which he opposed throughout the sessions of the
Convention.[3]

A recent writer says:

" The adoption of different bases for the two Houses, the
House of Representatives representing the States according to
population while the Senate represented them equally, was one
of the most important pieces of work which the Convention
accomplished, as well as *the* one which it reached most unwil-

[1] Madison Papers, vol. ii., p. 958.

[2] *Ibid.*, p. 987.

[3] As John Dickinson, representing the small State of Delaware in the Convention, made the motion for the appointment of the Senate by the State legislatures, he is entitled to some of the credit for this measure.

lingly. All the States experimenting to find different bases for their two Houses, Virginia had come nearest to the appearance of the final result, in having her Senate chosen by districts and her Representatives by counties ; and as the Union already had its 'districts' formed (in the States) one might think that the Convention merely followed Virginia's experience. But the real process was far different and more circuitous."

In fact, says this writer, it was the Connecticut system, where the towns were equally represented in the lower House, while the upper one was chosen from the whole people, which was the model proposed by Connecticut delegates to the Convention.' George Mason, however, standing apart from his colleagues, did, in effect, propose the Virginia constitution, of which he was the author, as a type for the new constitution, when he advocated both ideas combined—equal and unequal representation, for the legislature of the Union, or the choice of one House by the people and of the other by the States.

In regard to the qualifications of senators, Colonel Mason thought that "one important object in constituting the Senate was to secure the rights of property. To give them weight and firmness for this purpose, a considerable duration in office was thought necessary. But a longer term than six years would be of no avail in this respect, if needy persons should be appointed. He suggested, therefore, the propriety of annexing to the office a qualification of property. He thought this would be very practicable, as the rules of taxation would supply a scale for measuring the degree of wealth possessed by every man." [2]

It was now nearly the last of June. Five weeks, as Dr. Franklin anxiously noted, had been spent in trying to reconcile the opposing views that were to be found in the Convention; to steer between the rock of centralized government and the whirlpool, as it was deemed, of a pure

[1] " The First Century of the Constitution," article in *The New Princeton Review*, Sept., 1887.
[2] Madison " Papers," vol. ii., p. 971.

confederation; to decide upon the features of the equitable *via media.* "Groping as it were in the dark to find political truth, and scarce able to distinguish it when they found it," it were well, Dr. Franklin thought to implore for themselves each day the Divine guidance. The proposal came a little late, it is true, and there might be reason to think, as was suggested, that it would alarm the people. But surely the daily consecration was needed, and the proposition should have been agreed to. On the question for allowing each State one vote in the Senate, there seemed to be at this time no hope of a settlement. It was then determined to appoint a committee, consisting of one member from each State, in order, if possible, to effect a solution of the difficulty. George Mason was the significant choice from Virginia, and the Convention adjourned from Monday the 2d, to Thursday the 5th, of July.

The following letters were written by Colonel Mason to George Mason, Jr., and to Beverley Randolph during the month of June. The solemn words to his son on the great responsibility of the work in which he was engaged, evince George Mason's profound sense of duty, and his earnest desire to carry out its obligations.

PHILADELPHIA, June 1st, 1787.

DEAR GEORGE:

. . . The idea I formerly mentioned to you, before the Convention met, of a great national council, consisting of two branches of the legislature, a judiciary and an executive, upon the principle of fair representation in the legislature, with powers adapted to the great objects of the Union, and consequently a control in these instances, on the State legislatures, is still the prevalent one. Virginia has had the honor of presenting the outlines of the plan, upon which the convention is proceeding; but so slowly that it is impossible to judge when the business will be finished, most probably not before August—*festina lente* may very well be called our motto. When I first came here, judging from casual conversations with gentlemen from the different States, I was very apprehensive that soured and disgusted with the unexpected evils we had experienced from the democratic principles of our governments, we should be apt to run into the opposite extreme, and in endeavoring to steer too far from Scylla, we might be drawn into the vortex of Charybdis, of which I still think there is some danger, though I have the pleasure to find in the convention, many men of fine republican principles. America has certainly, upon this occasion, drawn forth her first characters ; there are upon this Convention many gentlemen of the most respectable abilities, and so far as I can discover, of the purest intentions. The eyes of the United States are turned upon this assembly, and their expectations raised to a very anxious degree.

May God grant, we may be able to gratify them, by establishing a wise and just government. For my own part, I never before felt myself in such a situation ; and declare I would not, upon pecuniary motives, serve in this convention for a thousand pounds per day. The revolt from Great Britain and the formations of our new governments at that time, were nothing compared to the great business now before us : there was then a certain degree of enthusiasm, which inspired and supported the mind ; but to view, through the calm, sedate medium of reason the influence which the establishment now proposed may have upon the happiness or misery of millions yet unborn, is an object of such magnitude, as absorbs, and in a manner suspends the operations of the human understanding.

Remember me kindly to Betsy and all the family ; let me know from time to time how they do. I am, dear George,

Your affectionate father,

G. MASON.

P. S. All communications of the proceedings are forbidden during the sitting of the Convention ; this I think was a necessary precaution to prevent misrepresentations or mistakes ; there being a material difference between the appearance of a subject in its first crude and undigested shape, and after it shall have been properly matured and arranged.

I would thank you to desire Thomson to send me, if he can find it, the plan I drew, two or three years ago, for equalizing the Virginia land tax, which I have promised a copy of to the North Carolina delegates ; I believe he will find it among the loose papers on the right hand division of the second drawer in my desk and bookcase in the little parlor ; and I should be glad to have the strictures I wrote some time ago, upon the port bill ; but where it is I don't remember ; it lay among the loose papers in one of the dining-room windows, which a little before I left home I tied up in a bundle and I believe put into one of the pigeon-holes in the bookcase in the dining-room, but am not certain. Pray desire him in looking over the papers, not to dissort them, but make them up again together, in the same separate bundles, and where any of the bundles are endorsed, to make them up again with the endorsations on the outside.

G. M.[1]

George Mason to Hon. Beverley Randolph :

PHILADELPHIA, June 30th, 1787.

DEAR SIR :

The Convention having resolved that none of their proceedings should be communicated during their sitting, puts it out of my power to give you any particular information upon the subject. *Festina lente* seems hitherto to have been our maxim. Things, however, are now drawing to that point on which some of the fundamental principles must be decided, and two or three days will probably enable us to judge—which is at present very doubtful—whether any sound and effectual system can be established or not. If it cannot, I presume we shall not continue here much longer ; if it can, we shall probably be detained 'til September.

I feel myself disagreeably circumstanced in being the only member of the Assembly in the Virginia delegation, and, consequently, if any system shall be recommended by the Convention that the whole weight of explanation must fall upon me ; and if I should be prevented by sickness or accident from attending the Assembly, that it will be difficult for the Assembly to obtain such information as may be necessary upon the subject, as I presume that in the progress through the legislature many questions may be asked and inquiries made, in which satisfactory information, from time to time, can hardly be given but by a member of the House in his place.

[1] Mason Papers ; Niles' "Principles and Acts of the Revolution," p. 128 ; Bancroft's "History of the Constitution," vol. ii., p. 424.

We have just received information here that Mr. Wythe has made a resignation, and does not intend to return. Under these circumstances I would beg leave to submit it to the consideration of the Executive, whether it might not be proper to fill the vacancy in the delegation, occasioned by Mr. Wythe's resignation, with some member of the Assembly. Mr. Corbin being here, his appointment, if it shall be judged proper, would occasion little additional charge to the State, if the Convention should, unfortunately, break up without adopting any substantial system—that event will happen, I think—before the appointment can reach this place; if the Convention continues to proceed on the business, with a prospect of success, Mr. Corbin is on the spot; and I doubt it may be difficult to prevail on any member of the Assembly, now in Virginia, to come hither at this late stage of the business.

I beg you will do me the favor to lay this subject before the Council, and believe me, with the greatest esteem and regard,

Dear Sir,
Your most obedient servant,
G. MASON.[1]

The report of the grand committee, which was made on the 5th of July, consisted of two propositions made mutually conditional. The compromise consisted in giving the first branch of the legislature the power of originating money bills, a concession, as it was maintained, made by the small States in order that the large States should concede the equal vote in the Senate. There had been hot and hasty words in the Convention, and threats of secession, and of looking to foreign countries for assistance. And it was felt that a crisis had come and a determined effort must be made to meet it. In reply to animadversions on the report, George Mason explained that it "was meant not as a specific proposition to be adopted, but merely as a general ground of accommodation. There must be some accommodation on this point, or we shall make little further progress in the work. Accommodation was the object of the House in the

---

[1] "Virginia Calendar Papers," vol. iv., p. 310.

appointment of the committee, and of the committee in the report they had made. And however liable the report might be to objections, he thought it preferable to an appeal to the world by the different sides, as had been talked of by some gentlemen. It could not be more inconvenient to any gentleman to remain absent from his private affairs, than it was for him, but he would bury his bones in this city, rather than expose his country to the consequences of a dissolution of the Convention without anything being done." [1] A motion was made to put restrictions upon the representation of the Western States, when Colonel Mason said "the case of new States was not unnoticed in the committee; but it was thought, and he was himself decidedly of opinion, that if they made a part of the Union, they ought to be subject to no unfavorable discriminations. Obvious considerations required it." [2] And in this opinion Edmund Randolph concurred.

The minutes of Judge Yates cease at this time, as he and his colleague, Mr. Lansing, left the Convention on the 6th of July, thoroughly dissatisfied with the course matters were taking. The first proposition in the report was under discussion on this day. This fixed the representation in the first branch as " one member for every forty thousand inhabitants." It was moved by Gouverneur Morris to refer this to a select committee of five. With it went the clause relating to money bills, and Dr. Franklin thought they could not be voted for separately. George Mason then suggested a reference of the rest of the report to the committee just appointed. He urged that "the consideration which weighed with the committee [the grand committee that reported on the 5th] was, that the first branch would be the immediate representatives of the people; the second would not; should the latter have the power of giving away the people's money, they might soon forget the source from whence they received it. We might soon have an aristocracy. He had been much

[1] " Madison Papers," vol. ii., p. 1033.
[2] *Ibid.*, p. 1035.

concerned at the principles which had been advanced by some gentlemen, but had the satisfaction to find they did not generally prevail. He was a friend to proportional representation in both branches, but supposed that some points must be yielded for the sake of accommodation."[1] The clause allowing each State one vote in the second branch was taken up and agreed to on the 7th. And on the 9th the report of the committee of five on the clause fixing representation in the first branch of the legislature was given to the Convention. This altered the representation from " one member to every forty thousand inhabitants," and gave fifty-six members for the first Congress, and this number to be augmented from time to time. The change did not give satisfaction, and the first part of the report was then put into the hands of another grand committee, Madison this time being the member selected from Virginia. And here the representation was augmented to sixty-five members. But it was becoming more and more apparent that the question of the balance of power was not so much between the large and small States as between the Northern and Southern States, and the Southern members contended that the changes made in the representation of the House were unfavorable to the South. Mr. Madison proposed to double the number from each State; some of the Northern members were for a reduction, urging the expense. Mr. Gerry, however, proposed to increase the number. George Mason " admitted that the objection drawn from the consideration of expense had weight both in itself and as the people might be affected by it. But he thought it outweighed by the objections against the smallness of the number. Thirty-eight will, he supposes, as being a majority of sixty-five, form a quorum. Twenty will be a majority of thirty-eight. This was certainly too small a number to make laws for America. They would neither bring with them all the necessary information relative to local interests, nor possess the necessary confidence of the people. After

[1] *Ibid.*, pp. 1040–1042.

doubling the number, the laws might still be made by so few as almost to be objectionable on that account." [1] Mr. Madison's motion being lost, and the report of the committee of eleven agreed to, Edmund Randolph moved that the legislature take a periodical census to redress inequalities in the representation. Colonel Mason here gave expression to his fears, that the South would not be sufficiently secured in her rights by the new Constitution :

" The greater the difficulty we find in fixing a proper rule of representation, the more unwilling ought we to be to throw the task from ourselves on the General Legislature. He did not object to the conjectural ratio which was to prevail in the outset ; but considered a revision from time to time, according to some permanent and precise standard, as essential to the fair representation required in the first branch. According to the present population of America, the Northern part of it had a right to preponderate ; and he could not deny it. But he wished it not to preponderate hereafter, when the reason no longer continued. From the nature of man, we may be sure that those who have power in their hands will not give it up, while they can retain it. On the contrary, we know that they will always, when they can, rather increase it. If the Southern States, therefore, should have three-fourths of the people of America within their limits, the Northern will hold fast the majority of representatives. One-fourth will govern the three-fourths. The Southern States will complain, but they may complain from generation to generation without redress. Unless some principle, therefore, which will do justice to them hereafter shall be inserted in the Constitution, disagreeable as the declaration was to him, he must declare he could neither vote for the system here, nor support it in his State. Strong objections had been drawn from the danger to the Atlantic interests from new Western States. Ought we to sacrifice what we know to be right in itself, lest it should prove favorable to States which are not yet in existence ? If the Western States are to be admitted into the Union, as they arise, they must, he would repeat, be treated as equals, and subjected to no degrading discriminations. They will have the same pride,

[1] *Ibid.*, p. 1061.

and other passions, which we have ; and will either not unite with, or will speedily revolt from, the Union, if they are not in all respects placed on an equal footing with their brethren. It has been said, they will be poor, and unable to make equal contributions to the general treasury. He did not know but that, in time, they would be both more numerous and more wealthy than their Atlantic brethren. The extent and fertility of their soil made this probable ; and though Spain might for a time deprive them of the natural outlet for their productions, yet she will, because she must, finally yield to their demands. He urged that numbers of inhabitants, though not always a precise standard of wealth, was sufficiently so for every substantial purpose." [1]

The representation to be regulated on a census of the free white inhabitants and three fifths of the slaves was the next proposition discussed. Some of the Northern members of the Convention were opposed to any representation of the slaves, while the extreme Southern delegates insisted that they should be counted equally with the whites. The three-fifths basis was another one of the compromises of the Constitution. George Mason advocated it, and on a motion for an equal representation of the blacks, declared he " could not agree to the motion, notwithstanding it was favorable to Virginia, because he thought it unjust. It was certain that the slaves were valuable, as they raised the value of land, increased the exports and imports, and of course the revenue, would supply the means of feeding and supporting an army, and might in cases of emergency become themselves soldiers. As in these important respects they were useful to the community at large, they ought not to be excluded from the estimate of representation. He could not, however, regard them as equal to freemen, and could not vote for them as such. He added, as worthy of remark, that the Southern States have this peculiar species of property, over and above the other species of property common to all the States." [2] Mr. Sherman said that he had become convinced by the observations of Mr. Randolph and Colonel

[1] *Ibid.*, p. 1064. [2] *Ibid.*, p. 1068.

Mason that the *periods* and the *rule* of revising the representation ought to be fixed by the Constitution. George
Mason "objected to a motion [made by Rutledge] to
include wealth with population in the estimate, as requiring
of the legislature something too indefinite and impracticable,
and leaving them a pretext for doing nothing."[1] In reply
to Gouverneur Morris, who reiterated his objections to
admitting the Western country on an equal footing with the
Atlantic States, Colonel Mason, while agreeing with him,
"that we ought to leave the interests of the people to the
representatives of the people," said, that "the objection
was, that the legislature would cease to be the representatives of the people. It would continue so no longer than
the States now containing a majority of the people should
retain that majority. As soon as the southern and western
population should predominate, which must happen in a
few years, the power would be in the hands of the minority,
and would never be yielded to the majority, unless provided
for by the Constitution."[2]

Gouverneur Morris startled the Convention on the 12th
by a proposal that "taxation should be in proportion to
representation." This was a blow aimed at the Southern
proposition for a full representation of the slaves. George
Mason in reply "admitted the justice of the principle but
was afraid embarrassments might be occasioned to the legislature by it. It might drive the legislature to the plan
of requisitions."[3] Morris then limited his motion to direct
taxation, and this was agreed to. After a little further
skirmishing, it was finally decided that representation
should be proportioned to direct taxation, and both to the
number of the free white and three fifths of the slave population. On a motion to assess the inhabitants of the States,
until a census could be taken according to the number
of their representatives in the first branch, Colonel Mason
said he "did not know that Virginia would be a loser by the
proposed regulation, but had some scruple as to the justice

[1] *Ibid.*, p. 1071.   [2] *Ibid.*, p. 1075.   [3] *Ibid.*, p. 1089.

of it.   He doubted much whether the conjectural rule which was to precede the census would be as just as it would be rendered by an actual census." [1]   The equal vote in the Senate was the next disputed point taken up.   The small States refused to confederate on any other terms, and the large States as a class still opposed it.   On the 16th an adjournment was voted to enable the dissatisfied ones to talk over the subject, and the result was satisfactory, for the compromise was finally effected at this time.

[1] *Ibid.*, p. 1089.

CHAPTER V.

THE CHAMPION OF STATES-RIGHTS.

July–September, 1787.

The mode of electing the Executive was under discussion on the 17th of July. George Mason approved of an election by the legislature rather than by the people at large. In animadverting upon some of the opinions that had been expressed, Colonel Mason said:

" It is curious to remark the different language held at different times. At one moment we are told that the legislature is entitled to thorough confidence, and to indefinite power. At another, that it will be governed by intrigue and corruption, and cannot be trusted at all. But not to dwell on this inconsistency, he would observe that a government which is to last ought at least to be practicable. Would this be the case if the proposed election should be left to the people at large ? He conceived it would be as unnatural to refer the choice of a proper character for Chief Magistrate to the people, as it would, to refer a trial of colors to a blind man. The extent of the country renders it impossible, that the people can have the requisite capacity to judge of the respective pretensions of the candidates." [1]

On a motion to strike out seven years as the term of office for the Executive, and substitute " during good behaviour," Colonel Mason spoke decisively against it :

" This motion was made some time ago, and negatived by a very large majority. He trusted that it would be again negatived.

[1] " Madison Papers," vol. ii., p. 1122.

It would be impossible to define the misbehaviour in such a manner as to subject it to a proper trial ; and perhaps still more impossible to compel so high an offender, holding his office by such
a tenure, to submit to a trial.   He considered an executive during
good behaviour as a softer name only for an executive for life.
And that the next would be an easy step to hereditary monarchy.
If the motion should finally succeed, he might himself live to see
such a revolution.   If he did not, it was probable his children or
grandchildren would.   He trusted there were few men in that
House who wished for it.   No State, he was sure, had so far revolted from republican principles, as to have the least bias in its
favor." [1]

On the 18th the subject of the judiciary was discussed, and
it was proposed that the judges should be appointed " by the
Executive with the consent of the Senate," instead of by the
Senate as declared in the eleventh resolution of the report.
George Mason spoke as follows :

" The mode of appointing the judges may depend in some degree on the mode of trying impeachments of the executive.   If
the judges were to form a tribunal for that purpose they surely
ought not to be appointed by the executive.   There were insuperable objections besides against referring the appointment to
the executive.   He mentioned as one, that as the seat of government must be in some one State ; and as the executive would remain in office for a considerable time, for four, five or six years
at least, he would insensibly form local and personal attachments
within the particular State that would deprive equal merit elsewhere of an equal chance of promotion." [2]

Concerning the twelfth resolution, " that the national legislature be empowered to appoint inferior tribunals," Colonel
Mason " thought many circumstances might arise, not now
to be foreseen, which might render such a power absolutely
necessary." [3]   Objections being made to the sixteenth resolution guaranteeing a republican constitution to each State
by the United States, George Mason said, " if the general

[1] *Ibid.*, p. 1127.   [2] *Ibid.*, p. 1131.   [3] *Ibid.*, p. 1137.

government should have no right to suppress rebellions against particular States, it will be in a bad situation indeed. As rebellions against itself originate in and against individual States, it must remain a passive spectator of its own subversion." [1]

The appointment of the Executive through electors having been decided upon, the question of impeachment was resumed. Colonel Mason declared:

"No point is of more importance than that the right of impeachment should be continued. Shall any man be above justice? Above all, shall that man be above it who can commit the most extensive injustice? When great crimes were committed, he was for punishing the principal as well as the coadjutors. There had been much debate and difficulty as to the mode of choosing the executive. He approved of that which had been adopted at first, namely, of referring the appointment to the national legislature. One objection against electors was the danger of their being corrupted by the candidates, and this furnished a peculiar reason in favor of impeachment whilst in office. Shall the man who has practised corruption, and by that means procured his appointment in the first instance, be suffered to escape punishment by repeating his guilt?" [2]

On the motion to associate the judiciary "with the executive in the revisionary power," Colonel Mason said, "he had always been a friend to this provision. It would give a confidence to the executive, which he would not otherwise have, and without which the revisionary power would be of little avail." He urged again, "that the defence of the executive was not the sole object of the revisionary power. He expected even greater advantages from it. Notwithstanding the precautions taken in the constitution of the legislature, it would still so much resemble that of the individual States, that it must be expected frequently to pass unjust and pernicious laws. This restraining power was therefore essentially necessary. It would have the effect, not only of

[1] *Ibid.*, p. 1139. [2] *Ibid.*, p. 1154.

hindering the final passage of such laws, but would discourage demagogues from attempting to get them passed. It has been said (by Mr. Luther Martin), that if the judges were joined in this check on the laws, they would have a double negative, since in their expository capacity of judges they would have one negative. He would reply, that in this capacity they could impede, in one case only, the operation of laws. They could declare an unconstitutional law void. But with regard to every law, however unjust, oppressive or pernicious, that did not come plainly under this description, they would be under the necessity, as judges, to give it a free course. He wished the further use to be made of the judges of giving aid in preventing every improper law. Their aid will be the more valuable, as they are in the habit and practice of considering laws in their true principles, and in all their consequences." [1]

In regard to the appointment of judges, Mr. Madison made the motion that they should be nominated by the Executive, and the appointments so made, unless disagreed to by two thirds of the Senate, were to hold good. Governor Randolph favored the motion. Colonel Mason did not assent to it; he "found it his duty to differ from his colleagues in their opinions and reasonings on this subject. Notwithstanding the form of the proposition, by which the appointment seemed to be divided between the executive and Senate, the appointment was substantially vested in the former alone. The false complaisance which usually prevails in such cases will prevent a disagreement to the first nominations. He considered the appointment by the executive as a dangerous prerogative. It might even give him an influence over the judiciary department itself. He did not think the difference of interest between the Northern and Southern States could be properly brought into this argument. It would operate, and require some precautions in the case of regulating navigation, commerce, and imposts; but he could not see that it had any connect⸵ ⸱ with the

[1] *Ibid.*, pp. 1163–1168.

judiciary department."[1] Madison had contended that appointments by the Senate would give the balance of power to the Northern States. The committee had given the appointment of judges to the second branch of the legislature, but a motion had been made on the 18th to alter this decision, which was revived by Madison.

On the 23d the Convention debated on the mode of ratifying the Constitution. Should it be by the States through their legislatures, or by conventions of the people in each State? George Mason warmly espoused the latter alternative. He " considered a reference of the plan to the authority of the people as one of the most important and essential of the resolutions. The legislatures have no power to ratify it. They are the mere creatures of the State constitutions, and cannot be greater than their creators. And he knew of no power in any of the constitutions—he knew there was no power in some of them—that could be competent to this object. Whither, then, must we resort? To the people, with whom all power remains that has not been given up in the constitutions derived from them. It was of great moment, he observed, that this doctrine should be cherished, as the basis of free government. Another strong reason was that, admitting the legislatures to have a competent authority, it would be wrong to refer the plan to them, because succeeding legislatures, having equal authority, could undo the acts of their predecessors; and the national government would stand in each State on the weak and tottering foundation of an act of Assembly. There was a remaining consideration of some weight. In some of the States, the governments were not derived from the clear and undisputed authority of the people. This was the case in Virginia. Some of the best and wisest citizens considered the Constitution as established by an assumed authority. A national constitution derived from such a source would be exposed to the severest criticism."[2]

A motion was made that the members of the Senate

[1] *Ibid.*, p. 1174.   [2] *Ibid.*, p. 1177.

should vote *per capita*, and that the number from each State should be three. Colonel Mason thought " three from each State, including new States, would make the second branch too numerous. Besides other objections, the additional expense ought always to form one, where it was not absolutely necessary." [1] The puzzling question of the mode of electing the Executive was discussed on the 24th and 25th. Among other plans, the motion was made that he should be appointed by the legislature, and be not eligible " for more than six years in any twelve years." Colonel Mason approved the suggestion :

" It had the sanction of experience in the instance of Congress, and some of the executives of the States. It rendered the executive as effectually independent as an ineligibility after his first election ; and opened the way, at the same time, for the advantage of his future services. He preferred on the whole the election by the national legislature ; though candor obliged him to admit, that there was great danger of foreign influence, as had been suggested. This was the most serious objection, with him, that had been urged." [2]

On the 24th of July, the twenty-three resolutions which the Convention had elaborated from the nineteen resolutions reported on the 19th of June were referred to a Committee of Detail to be shaped into a constitution. This committee consisted of five members, Gorham, Ellsworth, Wilson, Randolph, and Rutledge, three Northern and two Southern men. The resolution on the Executive was not given to the committee until the 26th. On this day George Mason made the opening speech in the Convention, passing in review the various propositions that had been made in regard to the subject under discussion :

" In every stage of the question relative to the executive, the difficulty of the subject and the diversity of the opinions concerning it, have appeared. Nor have any of the modes of constituting that department been satisfactory. First, it has been proposed that the election should be made by the people at large ; that is,

[1] *Ibid.*, p. 1185.   [2] *Ibid.*, p. 1202.

that an act which ought to be performed by those who know most of eminent characters and qualifications, should be performed by those who know least; secondly, that the election should be made by the legislatures of the States; thirdly, by the executives of the States. Against these modes, also, strong objections have been urged. Fourthly, it has been proposed that the election should be made by electors chosen by the people for that purpose. This was at first agreed to; but on further consideration has been rejected. Fifthly, since which, the mode of Mr. Williamson, requiring each freeholder to vote for several candidates, has been proposed. This seemed, like many other propositions, to carry a plausible face, but on closer inspection is liable to fatal objections. A popular election in any form, as Mr. Gerry has observed, would throw the appointment into the hands of the Cincinnati, a society for the members of which he had a great respect, but which he never wished to have a preponderating influence in the government. Sixthly, another expedient was proposed by Mr. Dickinson, which is liable to so palpable and material an inconvenience, that he had little doubt of its being by this time rejected by himself. It would exclude every man who happened not to be popular within his own State; though the causes of his local unpopularity might be of such a nature, as to recommend him to the States at large. Seventhly, among other expedients, a lottery has been introduced. But as the tickets do not appear to be in much demand, it will probably not be carried on, and nothing therefore need be said on that subject. After reviewing all these various modes, he was led to conclude, that an election by the national legislature, as originally proposed, was the best. If it was liable to objections, it was liable to fewer than any other. He conceived, at the same time, that a second election ought to be absolutely prohibited. Having for his primary object—for the polar star of his political conduct—the preservation of the rights of the people, he held it as an essential point, as the very palladium of civil liberty, that the great officers of state, and particularly the executive, should at fixed periods return to that mass from which they were at first taken, in order that they may feel and respect those rights and interests which are again to be personally valuable to them."

Vol. II.—10   ¹ *Ibid.*, p. 1207.

He concluded with moving, that the constitution of the Executive, as reported by the Committee of the Whole, be reinstated, viz.: "that the executive be appointed for seven years [by the legislature] and be ineligible a second time." Mr. Dickinson's proposition had been that each State should select its best citizen, and out of the thirteen names the Executive should be chosen, either by the national legislature or by electors appointed by it. It was from Mr. Wilson of Pennsylvania, that the singular scheme emanated, which called forth George Mason's shrewd sarcasm. This was, to elect the Executive for six years, by not more than fifteen of the members of the legislature, these members to be drawn from it not by ballot but by lot, and they were to retire immediately and make the election without separating. Colonel Mason's resolution passing in the affirmative, he then moved "that the Committee of Detail be instructed to receive a clause requiring certain qualifications of landed property and citizenship of the United States, in members of the national legislature; and disqualifying persons having unsettled accounts with, or being indebted to, the United States, from being members of the national legislature." He observed "that persons of the latter descriptions had frequently got into the State legislatures, in order to promote laws that might shelter their delinquencies; and that this evil had crept into Congress, if report was to be regarded."[1] Gouverneur Morris opposed this discrimination, when Colonel Mason mentioned "the parliamentary qualifications adopted in the reign of Queen Anne, which he said had met with universal approbation." Mr. Morris retorted that these "had been disregarded in practice; and were but a scheme of the landed against the monied interest."[2] The first part of Colonel Mason's motion passed in the affirmative; the clause disqualifying public debtors was lost. He next observed "that it would be proper, as he thought, that some provision should be made in the Constitution against choosing for the seat of the gen-

[1] *Ibid.*, p. 1211.   [2] *Ibid.*, pp. 1212, 1213.

eral government, the city or place at which the seat of any State government might be fixed. There were two objections against having them at the same place, which, without mentioning others, required some precaution on the subject. The first was, that it tended to produce disputes concerning jurisdiction. The second and principal one was, that the intermixture of the two legislatures tended to give a provincial tincture to the national deliberations." He moved "that the committee be instructed to receive a clause to prevent the seat of the national government being in the same city or town with the seat of the government of any State, longer than until the necessary public buildings could be erected." There was some opposition to this, and Colonel Mason then said " he did not mean to press the motion at this time, nor to excite any hostile passions against the system. He was content to withdraw the motion for the present."[1] The Convention then adjourned from the 26th of July to the 6th of August, in order to give the Committee of Detail time to prepare a constitution.

The report of the committee delivered to the Convention on the 6th of August consisted of twenty-three articles.[2] It was taken up the following day for consideration. The preamble, "We, the people of the States of" etc., with the first and second articles, was agreed to. The third article was debated, and George Mason "doubted the propriety of giving each branch a negative on the other 'in all cases.' There were some cases in which it was, he supposed, not intended to be given, as in the case of balloting for appointments." Mr. Morris moved to insert " legislative acts," instead of " in all cases." Colonel Mason "thought the amendment of Mr. Gouverneur Morris extended too far. Treaties are in a subsequent part declared to be laws; they will therefore be subjected to a negative, although they are to be made, as proposed, by the Senate alone. He proposed that the mutual negative should be restrained to 'cases requiring the distinct assent' of the two Houses." Mr. Morris considered

[1] *Ibid.*, pp. 1218–1220.   [2] *Ibid.*, pp. 1218–1220.

this " but a repetition of the same thing; the mutual negative and distinct assent being equivalent expressions. Treaties, he thought, were not laws." [1] The whole clause in regard
to a negative was struck out at the instance of Madison,
and Gouverneur Morris' motion passed in the negative.
Discussion then followed on the concluding clause, appointing the time for the legislature to meet. Colonel
Mason "thought the objection against fixing the time
insuperable; but that an annual meeting ought to be
required as essential to the preservation of the Constitution. The extent of the country will supply business. And
if it should not, the legislature, besides *legislative*, is to have
inquisitorial powers, which cannot safely be long kept in a
state of suspension." [2] The clause received, at this time, certain alterations which proved to be final. The qualifications of
electors coming up for consideration, Mr. Morris wished to
restrain the right of suffrage to freeholders. The Constitution left it to the States to decide, each one in its own way.
George Mason said:

" The force of habit is certainly not attended to by those gentlemen who wish for innovations on this point. Eight or nine States
have extended the right of suffrage beyond the freeholders. What
will the people there say, if they should be disfranchised? A
power to alter the qualifications, would be a dangerous power in
the hands of the legislature. We all feel too strongly the remains
of ancient prejudices, and view things too much through a British medium. A freehold is the qualification in England, and
hence it is imagined to be the only proper one. The true idea, in
his opinion, was that every man having evidence of attachment
to, and permanent common interest with, the society, ought to
share in all its rights and privileges. Was this qualification restrained to freeholders? Does no other kind of property but
land evidence a common interest in the proprietor? Does
nothing besides property mark a permanent attachment? Ought
the merchant, the monied man, the parent of a number of children whose fortunes are to be pursued in his own country, to be

[1] " Madison Papers," vol. iii., pp. 1243-1244.   [2] *Ibid.*, p. 1246.

viewed as suspicious characters, and unworthy to be trusted with the common rights of their fellow citizens ?" [1]

The second section of the fourth article required of a representative that he should have been a citizen of the United States at least three years before his election. Colonel Mason was "for opening a wide door for emigrants; but did not choose that foreigners and adventurers make laws for us and govern us. Citizenship for three years was not enough for ensuring that local knowledge which ought to be possessed by the representative. This was the principal objection to so short a term. It might also happen, that a rich foreign nation, for example Great Britain, might send over her tools, who might bribe their way into the legislature for insidious purposes." He moved that " seven "years, instead of "three" be inserted.' The motion was agreed to. It was then proposed to alter the next clause, and require a representative to be a resident for a certain term of years, of the State which should elect him. George Mason thought seven years, which was suggested, too long, "but would never agree to part with the principle. It is a valuable principle. He thought it a defect in the plan, that the representatives would be too few to bring with them all the local knowledge necessary. If residence be not required, rich men of neighboring States may employ with success the means of corruption in some particular district, and thereby get into the public councils after having failed in their own States. This is the practice in the boroughs of England." [3] He then moved, with Mr. Ellsworth, to insert "one year" for previous inhabitancy. The fifth section, giving the power of originating money-bills to the House of Representatives, again met with opposition. Colonel Mason said, "he was unwilling to travel over this ground again. To strike out the section, was to unhinge the compromise of which it made a part. The duration of the Senate made it improper. He did not object to that

---

[1] *Ibid.*, pp. 1250–1252.   [2] *Ibid.*, p. 1256.   [3] *Ibid.*, p. 1259.

duration. On the contrary, he approved of it. But joined with the smallness of the number, it was an argument against adding this to the other great powers vested in that body. His idea of an aristocracy was, that it was the government of the few over the many. An aristocratic body, like the screw in mechanics, working its way by slow degrees, and holding fast whatever it gains, should ever be suspected of an encroaching tendency. The purse-strings should never be put into its hands." [1] The section was struck out, however, on the motion of Madison. The next day Edmund Randolph and others moved to reconsider it. Dr. Franklin believed the two clauses, the originating of money-bills in the House, and the equality of votes in the Senate, were essentially connected by the compromise which had been made by the grand committee and reported the 5th of July. George Mason thought "this was not the time for discussing this point. When the originating of money-bills shall be reconsidered, he thought it could be demonstrated, that it was of essential importance to restrain the right to the House of Representatives, the immediate choice of the people." [2] On considering the first section of article fifth, Edmund Randolph wished to postpone the last sentence, "each member shall have one vote." It was observed that this could not be necessary, "as in case the sanction as to originating money-bills should not be re-instated, and a revision of the Constitution should ensue, it would still be proper that the members should vote *per capita.* A postponement of the preceding sentence, allowing to each State two members, would have been more proper." Colonel Mason replied, "he did not mean to propose a change of this mode of voting *per capita* in any event. But as there might be other modes proposed, he saw no impropriety in postponing the sentence. Each State may have two members, and yet may have unequal votes. He said that unless the exclusive right of originating money-bills should be restored to the House of Representatives, he should—not

[1] *Ibid.,* p. 1266. [2] *Ibid.,* p. 1271.

from obstinacy, but duty and conscience—oppose through-out the equality of representation in the Senate." [1] The third section was taken up and Gouverneur Morris proposed to make fourteen year's citizenship, instead of four, a qualification for senators. Colonel Mason " highly approved of the policy of the motion. Were it not that many, not natives of this country, had acquired great credit during the Revolution, he should be for restraining the eligibility into the Senate, to natives." [2] Nine years was finally made the period of citizenship required.

In considering article sixth, section third, several of the members contended that less than a majority in each House should constitute a quorum. George Mason " opposed the change. This is a valuable and necessary part of the plan he urged. In this extended country, embracing so great a diversity of interests, it would be dangerous to the distant parts to allow a small number of members of the two Houses to make laws. The central States could always take care to be on the spot ; and by meeting earlier than the distant ones, or worrying their patience, and outstaying them, could carry such measures as they pleased. He admitted that inconveniences might spring from the secession of a small number ; but he had also known good produced by an apprehension of it. He had known a paper emission prevented by that cause in Virginia. He thought the Constitution as now moulded, was founded on sound principles, and was disposed to put into it extensive powers. At the same time he wished to guard against abuses as much as possible. If the legislature should be able to reduce the number at all, it might reduce it as low as it pleased, and the United States might be governed by a junto. A majority of the number which had been agreed on was so few that he feared it would be made an objection against the plan." [3] The right of expulsion, article sixth, section sixth, Madison observed "was too important to be exercised by a bare majority of a quorum," and he moved that " with the concur-

[1] *Ibid.*, p. 1272.   [2] *Ibid.*, p. 1274.   [3] *Ibid.*, p. 1287.

rence of two-thirds " might be inserted between " may " and
" expel," an amendment that both Randolph and Mason
approved of. The seventh section, that the yeas and nays
shall at the desire of one fifth of the members be entered on
the journal, it was proposed to alter. Some were for allowing any member to call for the yeas and nays, and others
proposed to strike them out altogether. Colonel Mason
" liked the section as it stood. It was a middle way between
two extremes." [1] Whether the clause should be retained,
that the Congress publish their proceedings from time to
time, was debated, and George Mason was in favor of it.
He " thought it would give a just alarm to the people,
to make a conclave of their legislature." The words, however, were inserted, " except such parts thereof as may in
their judgment require secrecy." [2] Recurring to article
fourth, section second, Colonel Mason's alteration requiring
citizenship of the United States for seven years as a qualification for representatives, was assailed, and four years suggested as a substitute. Mr. Sherman, in defending the
theory of the longer term, said that the United States had
not " pledged their faith " to foreigners, as was asserted,
giving them equal privileges with native citizens, but the
individual States had done this, and the former could therefore make discriminations. Mr. Madison was shocked at
this doctrine. Colonel Mason, however, was struck, as he
said, " not, like Mr. Madison, with the *peculiarity*, but with
the *propriety*, of the doctrine of Mr. Sherman. The States
have formed different qualifications themselves for enjoying
different rights of citizenship. Greater caution would be
necessary in the outset of the government than afterwards.
All the great objects would then be provided for. Everything would be then set in motion. If persons among us
attached to Great Britain should work themselves into our
councils, a turn might be given to our affairs, and particularly to our commercial regulations, which might have
pernicious consequences. The great houses of British mer-

[1] *Ibid.*, pp. 1291, 1292.　　　　　　　[2] *Ibid.*, p. 1294.

chants would spare no pains to insinuate the instruments of their views into the government." [1] The important section fifth of article fourth was reconsidered again, and Edmund Randolph moved to alter the clause in regard to originating money-bills by inserting " for the purpose of revenue," and allowing amendments by the Senate with certain restrictions. Colonel Mason spoke at length on this subject :

" This amendment removes all objections urged against the section, as it stood at first. By specifying *purposes of revenue*, it obviated the objection that the section extended to all bills under which money might incidentally arise. By authorizing amendments in the Senate it got rid of the objections that the Senate could not correct errors of any sort, and that it would introduce into the House of Representatives the practice of tacking foreign matter to money bills. These objections being removed, the arguments in favor of the proposed restraint on the Senate ought to have their full force. First, the Senate did not represent the *people*, but the *States*, in their political character. It was improper therefore that it should tax the people. The reason was the same against their doing it, as it had been against Congress doing it. Secondly, nor was it in any respect necessary, in order to cure the evils of our republican system. He admitted that, notwithstanding the superiority of the republican form over every other, it had its evils. The chief ones were, the danger of the majority oppressing the minority, and the mischievous influence of demagogues. The general government of itself will cure them. As the States will not concur at the same time in their unjust and oppressive plans, the general government will be able to check and defeat them, whether they result from the wickedness of the majority, or from the misguidance of demagogues. Again the Senate is not like the House of Representatives, chosen frequently, and obliged to return frequently among the people. They are to be chosen by the States for six years—will probably settle themselves at the seat of government—will pursue schemes for their own aggrandizement—will be able by wearying out the House of Representatives, and taking advantage of their impatience at the close of a long session, to extort measures for that

[1] *Ibid.*, p. 1304.

purpose. If they should be paid, as he expected would be yet determined and wished to be so, out of the national treasury, they will, particularly, extort an increase of their wages. A bare negative was a very different thing from that of originating bills. The practice in England was in point. The House of Lords does not represent nor tax the people, because not elected by the people. If the Senate can originate, they will, in the recess of the legislative sessions, hatch their mischievous projects, for their own purposes, and have their money bills cut and dried (to use a common phrase) for the meeting of the House of Representatives. He compared the case to Poyning's law,[1] and signified that the House of Representatives might be rendered by degrees like the parliament of Paris, the mere depository of the decrees of the Senate. As to the compromise, so much had passed on that subject that he would say nothing about it. He did not mean by what he had said, to oppose the permanency of the Senate. On the contrary he had no repugnance to an increase of it, nor to allowing it a negative, though the Senate was not, by its present Constitution, entitled to it. But in all events he would contend that the purse strings should be in the hands of the representatives of the people."[2]

When article sixth, section ninth, regarding the ineligibility of members of Congress to office, was debated, and a motion was made to alter it, George Mason proposed ironically " to strike out the whole section, as a more effectual expedient for encouraging that exotic corruption which might not otherwise thrive so well in the American soil; for completing that aristocracy which was probably in the contemplation of some among us; and for inviting into the legislative service those generous and benevolent characters, who will do justice to each other's merit, by carving out offices and rewards for it. In the present state of American morals and manners, few friends, it may be thought, will be

---

[1] Poyning's Act, made under the administration of Sir Edward Poyning, Vicegerent of Ireland in the reign of Henry VII. Under this law no measure could be opened in the Irish Parliament unless it had been examined and passed by the king in council.

[2] " Madison Papers," vol. iii., p. 1308.

lost to the plan, by the opportunity of giving premiums to a mercenary and depraved ambition." [1] The tenth section provided that members be paid by their respective States. The Convention discussed it with special reference to the Senate, when Colonel Mason remarked " that the clause as it now stands makes the House of Representatives also dependent on the State legislatures; so that both Houses will be made the instruments of the politics of the States, whatever they may be." [2] It was finally agreed to pay the members of the legislature out of the treasury of the general government. It was proposed to amend section twelfth so as to read :

" Each House shall possess the right of originating all bills, except bills for raising money for the purposes of revenue, or for appropriating the same, and for fixing the salaries of the officers of the government, which shall originate in the House of Representatives ; but the Senate may propose or concur with amendments as in other cases."

George Mason seconded the motion. " He was extremely earnest to take this power from the Senate, who, he said, could already sell the whole country by means of treaties." [3] Mr. Mercer then contended " that the Senate ought not to have the power of treaties"; a power which belonged to the executive department, adding "that treaties would not be final, so as to alter the laws of the land, till ratified by legislative authority." Colonel Mason, to whose observations Mr. Mercer had alluded, replied that he " did not say that a treaty would repeal a law ; but that the Senate by means of treaties might alienate territory, &c., without legislative sanction. The cessions of the British islands in the West Indies, by treaty alone, were an example. If Spain should possess herself of Georgia, therefore, the Senate might by treaty dismember the Union. He wished the motion to be decided now, that the friends of it might know how to conduct themselves." [4]

[1] *Ibid.*, p. 1318.
[2] *Ibid.*, p. 1327.
[3] *Ibid.*, p. 1331.
[4] *Ibid.*, p. 1332.

The Convention proceeding to article seventh, the first section, first clause, giving the legislature power " to lay and collect taxes, duties, imposts and excises," was considered, and Colonel Mason " urged the necessity of connecting with the powers of levying taxes, duties, &c., the prohibition in article seventh, section four, ' that no tax should be laid on exports.' He was unwilling to trust to its being done in a future article. He hoped the Northern States did not mean to deny the Southern this security. It would hereafter be as desirable to the former, when the latter should become the most populous." He professed his jealousy for the productions of the Southern, or Staple States, as he called them. He moved the following amendment : " Provided, that no tax, duty, or imposition shall be laid by the legislature of the United States on articles exported from any State." But the question was left to be decided later. The clause giving Congress the power to " emit bills on the credit of the United States," it was proposed to strike out. Colonel Mason " had doubts on the subject. Congress, he thought, would not have the power, unless it were expressed. Though he had a mortal hatred to paper money, yet as he could not foresee all emergencies, he was unwilling to tie the hands of the legislature. He observed that the late war could not have been carried on, had such a prohibition existed." He was still " averse to tying the hands of the legislature *altogether*," he added later. " If there was no example in Europe, as just remarked [by Pierce Butler], it might be observed, on the other side, that there was none in which the government was restrained on this head." But the motion for striking out was agreed to.[1] In regard to the clause to appoint a treasurer by ballot, Mr. Read moved that this appointment should be left to the Executive. George Mason, in opposition to Mr. Read's motion, " desired it might be considered, to whom the money would belong; if to the people, the legislature, representing the people, ought to appoint the keepers of it."[2] In the clause " to de-

[1] *Ibid.*, pp. 1339–1344.   [2] *Ibid.*, p. 1347.

clare the law and punishment of piracies and felonies," etc., Madison moved to strike out " and punishment." Colonel Mason doubted " the safety of it, considering the strict rule of construction in criminal cases. He doubted also the propriety of taking the power in all these cases wholly from the States." [1] It was moved to insert " declare " war instead of " make " war, and Colonel Mason was against giving the power of war to the Executive, as was suggested, " because not safely to be trusted with it; or to the Senate, because not so constructed as to be entitled to it. He was for clogging, rather than facilitating war; but for facilitating peace." He preferred " declare " to " make," and the motion was agreed to.

On the 18th of August Madison submitted certain powers to be added to those of the general legislature, and George Mason introduced the subject of regulating the militia. He thought " such a power necessary to be given to the general government. He hoped there would be no standing army in time of peace, unless it might be for a few garrisons. The militia ought, therefore, to be the more effectually prepared for the public defence. Thirteen States will never concur in any one system, if the disciplining of the militia be left in their hands. If they will not give up the power over the whole, they probably will over a part, as a select militia." He moved to refer to the Committee of Detail, " a power to regulate the militia," as one of the prerogatives of the federal legislature. But he was led later to change his mind on this point. Mr. Rutledge wished to refer a clause to the committee, " that funds appropriated to public creditors should not be diverted to other purposes." Colonel Mason said he " was much attached to the principle, but was afraid such a fetter might be dangerous in time of war. He suggested the necessity of preventing the danger of perpetual revenue, which must of necessity subvert the liberty of any country. If it be objected to on the principle of Mr. Rutledge's motion, that public credit may require

[1] *Ibid.*, p. 1347.

perpetual provisions, that case might be excepted, it being declared that in other cases no taxes should be laid for a longer term than . . . years. He considered the caution observed in Great Britain on this point as the palladium of public liberty."[1] And Colonel Mason interposed later a motion that the committee prepare a clause for restraining perpetual revenue, which was agreed to *nem. con.* A grand committee was appointed to consider the necessity and expediency of the United States assuming all the State debts, and George Mason was the member from Virginia placed on this committee. Returning to the subject of the militia, Colonel Mason moved to give Congress power "to make laws for the regulation and discipline of the militia of the several States, reserving to the States the appointment of the officers." He considered "uniformity as necessary in the regulation of the militia throughout the Union."[2] Mr. Ellsworth "was for going as far in submitting the militia to the general government, as might be necessary ; but thought the motion of Mr. Mason went too far." And Mr. Dickinson thought the States ought not to give up all power over the militia. Colonel Mason then alluded to his idea of a select militia. He "was led to think that would be, in fact, as much as the general government could advantageously be charged with. He was afraid of creating insuperable objections to the plan. He withdrew his original motion, and moved a power 'to make laws for regulating and disciplining the militia, not exceeding one tenth part in any one year, and reserving the appointment of officers to the States.'"[3] General Pinckney renewed Colonel Mason's original motion. In the course of the debate that followed, Mr. Sherman "took notice that the States might want their militia" for their own defence and for other purposes. Colonel Mason "thought there was great weight in the remarks of Mr. Sherman," and moved an exception to his motion, "of such part of the militia as might be required by the States for their own use," and the two motions were

[1] *Ibid.*, p. 1356.   [2] *Ibid.*, p. 1361.   [3] *Ibid.*, p. 1362.

referred to the grand committee,[1] of which Mason was a member.

George Mason about this time moved to enable Congress " to enact sumptuary laws." No government, he urged, " can be maintained unless the manners be made consonant to it. Such a discretionary power may do good, and can do no harm. A proper regulation of excises and of trade, may do a great deal; but it is best to have an express provision. It was objected to sumptuary laws, that they were contrary to nature. This was a vulgar error. The love of distinction, it is true, is natural ; but the object of sumptuary laws is not to extinguish this principle, but to give it a proper direction." [2] The motion, however, was not carried.

On the 20th the Convention discussed the second section of article seventh, concerning treason. Colonel Mason was in favor of pursuing the statute of Edward III. In the course of the discussion it was contended that there could be no treason against a particular State. Colonel Mason replied : " The United States will have a qualified sovereignty only. The individual States will retain a part of the sovereignty. An act may be treason against a particular State, which is not so against the United States. He cited the rebellion of Bacon in Virginia, as an illustration of the doctrine." [3] The section was amended so as to read " Treason against the United States shall consist only in levying war against them, or in adhering to their enemies "; when Colonel Mason moved to insert the words, " giving them aid and comfort," as restrictive of " adhering to their enemies," etc. The latter, he thought, " would be otherwise too indefinite." And this motion was agreed to. On the 21st George Mason called for the twelfth section of article sixth, which had been postponed on the 15th. He " wished to know how the proposed amendment, as to money-bills, would be decided, before he agreed to any further points "; but the subject was again postponed, and the section of the seventh article on the power of taxing exports was debated. George Mason said :

[1] *Ibid.*, p. 1364.　　　[2] *Ibid.*, p. 1369.　　　[3] *Ibid.*, p. 1373.

" If he were for reducing the States to mere corporations, as seemed to be the tendency of some arguments, he should be for subjecting their exports as well as imports to a power of general taxation. He went on a principle often advanced and in which he concurred, that a majority, when interested, will oppress the minority. This maxim had been verified by our own legislature [Virginia]. If we compare the States in this point of view, the eight Northern States have an interest different from the five Southern States; and have, in one branch of the legislature, thirty-six votes, against twenty-nine, and in the other in the proportion of eight against five. The Southern States had therefore ground for their suspicions. The case of exports was not the same with that of imports. The latter were the same throughout the States; the former very different. As to tobacco, other nations do raise it, and are capable of raising it, as well as Virginia, &c. The impolicy of taxing that article had been demonstrated by the experiment of Virginia." [1] The power to tax exports was denied to the general government, and Virginia's vote against it was due to Mason, Randolph, and Blair.

The clause allowing the importation of slaves called forth a heated debate. George Mason, in opposition to Mr. Sherman, of Connecticut, who was for leaving the clause as it stood, made a speech of some length. "This infernal traffic," he said, "originated in the avarice of British merchants. The British Government constantly checked the attempts of Virginia to put a stop to it. The present question concerns not the importing States alone, but the whole Union. The evil of having slaves was experienced during the late war. Had slaves been treated as they might have been by the enemy, they would have proved dangerous instruments in their hands. But their folly dealt by the slaves as it did by the Tories. He mentioned the dangerous insurrection of the slaves in Greece and Sicily; and the instructions given by Cromwell to the commissioners sent to Virginia, to arm the servants and slaves, in case other means of obtaining its

[1] *Ibid.*, p. 1387.

submission should fail. Maryland and Virginia, he said, had already prohibited the importation of slaves expressly— North Carolina had done the same in substance. All this would be in vain, if South Carolina and Georgia be at liberty to import. The Western people are already calling out for slaves for their new lands; and will fill that country with slaves, if they can be got through South Carolina and Georgia. Slavery discourages arts and manufactures. The poor despise labor when performed by slaves. They prevent the emigration of whites, who really enrich and strengthen a country. They produce the most pernicious effect on manners. Every master of slaves is born a petty tyrant. They bring the judgment of heaven on a country. As nations cannot be rewarded or punished in the next world, they must be in this. By an inevitable chain of causes and effects, Providence punishes national sins by national calamities. He lamented that some of our Eastern brethren had, from a lust of gain, embarked in this nefárious traffic. As to the States being in possession of the right to import, this was the case with many other rights, now to be properly given up. He held it essential in every point of view, that the general government should have power to prevent the increase of slavery."[1] George Mason's attitude here must not be misunderstood. He was no *abolitionist* in the modern sense of the term. While he regretted the existence of slavery in the South and opposed the slave trade, at the same time he insisted that the rights of his section in this species of property should be protected, and he wished for a guarantee in the Constitution to insure it. He is himself an instance that the effect of slavery on manners was not essentially deleterious. No doubt this was the case in individual instances, but, as a class, there were no nobler men nor more gracious women than the old slave-holding aristocracy of the South, from whence came the patriots and sages of 1776, and the generation that gave equally shining names to history in 1861. As the Virginia poet sings:

[1] *Ibid.*, p. 1391.

" Who shall blame the social order
　Which gave us men as great as these ?
Who condemn the soil of th' forest
　Which brings forth gigantic trees ? "

After some further debate on this clause relating to slavery, Gouverneur Morris proposed that the whole subject be committed, including the clauses regarding taxes on exports and a navigation act. " *These things may form a bargain among the Northern and Southern States,*" said Morris. This was the beginning of the compact so reprobated by Colonel Mason, which altered the Constitution, as he declared, fundamentally, and made it impossible for him to subscribe to it. The committee was appointed, a grand committee, including one member from each State, and Madison, as might be expected, was the choice from Virginia.

While the seventh article was under consideration somewhat later, it was moved to add, as an additional power to be given to the general legislature, a negative on all the laws of the several States interfering with the interests of the Union, provided two thirds of each House assent to the same. Colonel Mason " wished to know how the power was to be exercised. Are all laws whatever to be brought up? Is no road nor bridge to be established without the sanction of the general legislature ? Is this to sit constantly in order to receive and revise the State laws ? He did not mean by the remarks, to condemn the expedient ; but he was apprehensive that great objections would lie against it." [1] The grand committee, to whom the subject had been referred, had given to the United States power to assume the several State debts, making their report on the 21st, and on the 25th the Convention modified this decision, simply affirming " that the engagements of the Confederation should be equally valid against the United States under this Constitution." Colonel Mason " objected to the term ' *shall*' fulfil the engagements and discharge the debts, &c., as too strong. It may be impossible to comply with it. The creditors should

[1] *Ibid.,* p. 1410.

be kept in the same plight. They will in one respect be necessarily and properly in a better. The government will be more able to pay them. The use of the term *shall* will beget speculations, and increase the pestilential practice of stock-jobbing. There was a great distinction between original creditors and those who purchased fraudulently of the ignorant and distressed. He did not mean to include those who have bought stock in the open market. He was sensible of the difficulty of drawing the line in this case, but he did not wish to preclude the attempt. Even fair purchasers, at four, five, six, eight for one, did not stand on the same footing with the first holders, supposing them not to be blamable. The interest they received, even in paper, is equal to their purchase money. What he particularly wished was, to leave the door open for buying up the securities, which he thought would be precluded by the term ' shall ' as requiring *nominal payment*, and which was not inconsistent with his ideas of public faith. He was afraid, also, the word ' *shall* ' might extend to all the old continental paper." [1] On this same day the report of the committee of eleven delivered into the Convention the twenty-fourth, allowing the importation of " such persons as the several States now existing, shall think proper to admit " etc., was discussed. Gouverneur Morris was for making this clause read "the importation of slaves into North Carolina, South Carolina and Georgia shall not be prohibited," etc. George Mason was not " against using the term ' slaves,' but against naming North Carolina, South Carolina and Georgia, lest it should give offence to the people of those States.' [2] The year 1800 was fixed in the report as the term when the importation of slaves should cease. This was changed to 1808. Objections were made by Sherman to the tax on slaves as acknowledging them to be property, to which Colonel Mason replied, " not to tax, will be equivalent to a bounty on, the importation of slaves." [3] Gouverneur Morris remarked, that as the clause stood it implied that the legislature might tax freemen im-

[1] *Ibid.*, p. 1425.   [2] *Ibid.*, p. 1428.   [3] *Ibid.*, p. 1429.

ported ; to which Colonel Mason replied : " The provision, as it stands, was necessary for the case of convicts, in order to prevent the introduction of them." It was finally amended so as to read " importation " only, instead of " migration and importation," as in the report of the committee.[1]

Certain propositions made in regard to regulating trade were referred to a grand committee, and George Mason was the member selected for Virginia, the choice being made as usual by ballot.[2] Colonel Mason and Mr. Madison moved to add to the oath to be taken by the supreme executive " and will, to the best of my judgment and power, preserve, protect, and defend the Constitution of the United States," which amendment passed. Article eleven, section second, having reference to the salaries of the judges, was considered, and it was urged to reinstate the words " increased or," before the word " diminished." Colonel Mason contended strenuously for the motion. " There was no weight," he said, " in the argument drawn from changes in the value of the metals, because this might be provided for by an increase of salaries, so made as not to affect persons in office ; and this was the only argument on which much stress seemed to have been laid."[3] The amendment, however, was not made. A proposition followed, to prohibit the States from interfering in private contracts, and Mr. Madison conceived " that a negative on the State laws could alone secure the effect." George Mason replied : " This is carrying the restraint too far. Cases will happen that cannot be foreseen where some kind of interference will be proper and essential. He mentioned the case of limiting the period for bringing actions on open account—that of bonds after a certain lapse of time —asking whether it was proper to tie the hands of the States from making provision in such cases."[4] A motion was made restricting the power of the States, in the words, " nor pass bills of attainder, nor retrospective laws," which received the assent of the Convention, Virginia, however,

[1] *Ibid.*, p. 1430.
[2] *Ibid.*, p. 1432.
[3] *Ibid.*, p. 1437.
[4] *Ibid.*, p. 1443.

voting against it. Madison then moved to insert "nor lay embargoes." Colonel Mason thought "the amendment would be not only improper but dangerous, as the general legislature would not sit constantly, and therefore could not interpose at the necessary moments. He enforced his objection by appealing to the necessity of sudden embargoes, during the war, to prevent exports, particularly in the case of a blockade."[1] The motion was lost. Madison moved next that the prohibition, "nor lay imposts or duties on imports," be transferred from article thirteen, where the consent of the general legislature may license the act, to article twelve, which would make the prohibition absolute. To this George Mason observed, "that particular States might wish to encourage, by impost duties, certain manufactures, for which they enjoyed natural advantages, as Virginia the manufacture of hemp, &c."[2] This motion was lost; but coming to article thirteen it was moved to insert after the word "imports" the words "or exports," which passed by a majority of one only, all the Southern States except North Carolina being in the negative.

On the 29th of August the Convention took up the important section of article seven relating to navigation acts, which the committee of eleven had, in accordance with the compromise before mentioned, reported to be struck out. This provision required the assent of two thirds of the members present in each House to pass a navigation act. Mr. Pinckney moved to postpone the report in favor of the following proposition: "That no act of the legislature for the purpose of regulating the commerce of the United States with foreign powers, among the several States, shall be passed without the assent of two thirds of the members of each House." Colonel Mason spoke with much feeling on the subject:

"If the government is to be lasting it must be founded in the confidence and affections of the people; and must be so con-

[1] *Ibid.*, p. 1444.   [2] *Ibid.*, p. 1445.

structed as to obtain these. The *majority* will be governed by their interests. The Southern States are the *minority* in both Houses. Is it to be expected that they will deliver themselves bound, hand and foot, to the Eastern States, and enable them to exclaim, in the words of Cromwell, on a certain occasion—'the Lord hath delivered them into our hands'?"[1]

The question to postpone was lost, South Carolina joining with the Northern States in their unanimous vote against it. The report striking out section sixth was agreed to, and thus the die was cast and the way made easy for that sectional legislation which was to lead at length to the Nullification crisis, and was to be one of the causes of the war between the States.

In considering article seventeen relating to the admission of new States, Gouverneur Morris made a fresh motion, putting restrictions on them, and Madison and Mason both opposed him. Colonel Mason said: "If it were possible by just means to prevent emigration to the western country, it might be good policy. But go the people will, as they find it for their interest; and the best policy is to treat them with that equality which will make them friends not enemies."[2] On the question of filling the blank in article twenty-one naming the number of States sufficient for ratifying the Constitution, thirteen, ten, nine, and eight were all suggested. George Mason was for "preserving ideas familiar to the people. Nine States had been required in all great cases under the Confederation, and that number was on that account preferable."[3] Article twenty-second was taken up: "This Constitution shall be laid before the United States in Congress assembled, for their approbation, etc.," and it was moved by Mr. Gerry to postpone it. George Mason "seconded the motion, declaring that he would sooner chop off his right hand, than put it to the Constitution as it now stands. He wished to see some points, not yet decided, brought to a decision, before being compelled to give a final opinion on this article. Should these points be improperly

[1] *Ibid.*, p. 1453.   [2] *Ibid.*, p. 1457.   [3] *Ibid.*, p. 1473.

settled, his wish would then be to bring the whole subject before another general convention." [1]   Gouverneur Morris on the 3d of September, moved to amend the report concerning the respect to be paid acts, records, etc., of one State in other States so as to read, "and the legislature shall, by general laws, prescribe the manner in which such acts, records, and proceedings shall be proved, and the effect thereof," instead of "and the effect which judgments obtained in one State shall have in another."   Colonel Mason favored the motion, particularly if the "effect" was to be restrained to judgments and judicial proceedings. [2]

Certain parts of the Constitution had been referred to a grand committee on the 31st of August, Madison being the delegate from Virginia on the committee, and their report was made the 4th of September.   Much of it referred to the Executive, the manner of his election, etc.   He was to be balloted for by electors, not chosen by the legislature, was to serve for four years instead of seven, but in case more than one candidate had a majority of votes, then *the Senate* was to choose by ballot one of these candidates for President. Colonel Mason " confessed that the plan of the committee had removed some capital objections, particularly the danger of cabal and corruption.   It was liable, however, to this strong objection, that nineteen times in twenty the President would be chosen by the Senate, an improper body for the purpose." [3]   The question was debated the following day, when George Mason spoke as follows.   He " admitted that there were objections to an appointment by the legislature, as originally planned.   He had not yet made up his mind, but would state his objections to the mode proposed by the committee.   First, it puts the appointment in fact into the hands of the Senate, as it will rarely happen that a majority of the whole vote will fall on any one candidate ; and as the existing President will always be one of the five highest, his reappointment will of course depend on the Senate.   Secondly, considering the powers of the President and those of

[1] *Ibid.*, p. 1475.   [2] *Ibid.*, p. 1480.   [3] *Ibid.*, p. 1490.

the Senate, if a coalition should be established between these two branches, they will be able to subvert the Constitution. The great objection with him would be removed by depriving the Senate of the eventual election." [1] He accordingly moved to strike out the words " if such number be a majority of that of the electors." This would make the person having the highest number of votes, though not a majority, President. Gouverneur Morris thought the point of no great consequence, and that it was probable that a majority of votes would fall on the same man. Colonel Mason replied : " Those who think there is no danger of there not being a majority for the same person in the first instance, ought to give up the point to those who think otherwise." [2] George Mason's motion was lost by a large majority. Then, after several other propositions made by different members, Colonel Mason moved to strike out the word " five " and insert the word " three," as the highest candidates for the Senate to choose from, which motion was also lost. He continued his objections : " As the mode of appointment is now regulated, he could not forbear expressing his opinion that it is utterly inadmissible. He would prefer the government of Prussia to one which will put all power into the hands of seven or eight men, and fix an aristocracy worse than absolute monarchy." [3] This question coming up again the following day, it was proposed that an eventual choice should be made by the House in conjunction with the Senate, and finally that the House of Representatives be substituted for the Senate. Colonel Mason " liked the latter mode best as lessening the aristocratic influence of the Senate," and the motion was agreed to by an almost unanimous vote. [4] Other amendments were made which met with George Mason's approval, and the clause received its final form.

In considering the section, " the Vice-President shall be *ex-officio* president of the Senate," Colonel Mason spoke at

[1] *Ibid.*, p. 1499.
[2] *Ibid.*, p. 1499.
[3] *Ibid.*, p. 1503.
[4] *Ibid.*, p. 1511.

some length. He " thought the office of Vice-President an
encroachment on the rights of the Senate, and that it mixed
too much the legislative and the executive, which, as well as
the judiciary department, ought to be kept as separate as
possible. He took occasion to express his dislike of any
reference whatever, of the power to make appointments, to
either branch of the legislature. On the other hand, he was
averse to vest so dangerous a power in the President alone.
As a method for avoiding both, he suggested that a privy
council, of six members, to the President, should be established, to be chosen for six years by the Senate, two out of
the Eastern, two out of the Middle, and two out of the
Southern quarters of the Union ; and to go out in rotation, two every second year, the concurrence of the Senate
to be required only in the appointment of ambassadors, and
in making treaties, which are more of a legislative nature.
This would prevent the constant sitting of the Senate, which
he thought dangerous, as well as keep the departments
separate and distinct. It would also save the expense of
constant sessions of the Senate. He had, he said, always
considered the Senate as too unwieldy and expensive for
appointing officers, especially the smallest, such as tide-
waiters, &c. He had not reduced his idea to writing, but it
could be easily done, if it should be found acceptable." [1]
This idea of a council was supported by Mr. Wilson, but
opposed by Mr. King. Colonel Mason then said, " that in
rejecting a council to the President we were about to try an
experiment on which the most despotic governments had
never ventured. The Grand Seignior himself had his divan.
He moved to postpone the consideration of the clause
[" and may require the opinion in writing of the principal
officer in each of the Executive Departments, upon any subject relating to the duties of their respective offices,"] in
order to take up the following : ' That it be an instruction
to the Committee of the States to prepare a clause or
clauses for establishing an Executive Council, as a Coun-

[1] *Ibid.*, p. 1518.

cil of State, for the President of the United States, to consist of six members, two of which from the Eastern, two from the Middle, and two from the Southern States, with a rotation and duration of office similar to those of the Senate: such Council to be appointed by the Legislature or by the Senate.' " [1]

This motion, seconded by Dr. Franklin and approved of by Madison and others, was rejected by the Convention.

The Constitution on the 8th of September was referred to a committee of five to revise the style. Johnson, Hamilton, Morris, Madison, and King composed this committee, and the final draft of the Constitution was the work of Gouverneur Morris. The clause referring to the Senate the trial of impeachments against the President was taken up by the Convention on the 8th, and George Mason inquired:

"Why is the provision restrained to treason and bribery only? Treason, as defined in the Constitution, will not reach many great and dangerous offences. Hastings is not guilty of treason. Attempts to subvert the Constitution may not be treason, as above defined. As bills of attainder, which have saved the British constitution, are forbidden, it is the more necessary to extend the power of impeachments."

He moved to add, after "bribery," "or maladministration." Colonel Mason was seconded by Mr. Gerry, but Madison objecting to the vagueness of the term "maladministration," he withdrew it and substituted "other high crimes and misdemeanours" [against the State]. The question then passed in the affirmative.[2] The word "State" was afterwards struck out and "United States" unanimously inserted, to prevent ambiguity. But these words "United States" were finally struck out by the committee on style. On the 10th Edmund Randolph stated at some length his objections to the Constitution as now formulated. He made a motion to submit the system to the Congress, thence to the State legislatures and conventions, the pro-

[1] *Ibid.*, p. 1523. [2] *Ibid.*, p. 1528.

cess to close with another general convention, with power
to adopt or reject amendments proposed by the State conventions. Colonel Mason "urged and obtained that the
motion should lie on the table for a day or two, to see what
steps might be taken with regard to the parts of the system
objected to by Mr. Randolph." On the 12th the Committee
of Style and Arrangement reported the Constitution, and it
was moved to reconsider the clause requiring three fourths
of each House to overrule the negative of the President, and
insert two thirds. Gouverneur Morris said the difference in
the two proportions amounted "in one House to two members only; and in the other to not more than five." George
Mason said he "had always considered this as one of the
most exceptionable parts of the system. As to the numeri-
cal argument of Mr. Gouverneur Morris, little arithmetic was
necessary to understand that three fourths was more than
two thirds, whatever the numbers of the legislature might
be. The example [given by Morris and Hamilton] of New
York depended on the real merits of the laws. The gentlemen citing it had no doubt given their own opinions. But
perhaps there were others of opposite opinions who could
equally paint the abuses on the other side. His leading
view was to guard against too great an impediment to the
repeal of laws."[1] The amendment was made, Virginia's
vote counting in the negative, however, as Mason and
Randolph were opposed by Washington, Blair, and Madison. It was then observed that no provision was made for
juries in civil cases, to which Mr. Gorham replied: "It is
not possible to discriminate equity cases from those in which
juries are proper." Colonel Mason said he "perceived the
difficulty mentioned by Mr. Gorham. The jury cases cannot be specified. A general principle laid down, on this
and some other points, would be sufficient. He wished the
plan had been prefaced with a Bill of Rights, and would
second a motion if made for the purpose. It would give
great quiet to the people; and with the aid of the State

[1] *Ibid.*, p. 1563.

Declarations, a bill might be prepared in a few hours." Mr. Gerry concurred in the idea, and moved for a committee to prepare a Bill of Rights, George Mason seconding the motion. Mr. Sherman thought it was not required, as the State Declarations of Rights were not repealed by this Constitution. Colonel Mason replied: "The laws of the United States are to be paramount to State Bills of Rights." On the question for a committee to prepare a Bill of Rights, five States voted in the affirmative and the five Southern States in the negative. Massachusetts was absent.[1] Virginia's vote probably went as before, Washington, Blair, and Madison against Mason and Randolph.

The clause relating to exports was reconsidered at the instance of Colonel Mason, who urged " that the restrictions on the States would prevent the incidental duties necessary for the inspection and safe-keeping of their produce, and be ruinous to the Staple States, as he called the five Southern States. He moved as follows: " Provided nothing herein contained shall be construed to restrain any State from laying duties upon exports for the sole purpose of defraying the charges of inspecting, packing, storing, and indemnifying the losses in keeping the commodities in the care of public officers, before exportation." In answer to a remark which he anticipated—to wit, that the States could provide for these expenses by a tax in some other way, he stated the inconvenience of requiring the planters to pay a tax before the actual delivery for exportation. Mr. Madison seconded the motion, but the Convention soon after adjourned without further action in the matter. The next day George Mason, who was the first to address the Convention, said he " had moved without success for a power to make sumptuary regulations. He had not yet lost sight of his object. After descanting on the extravagance of our manners, the excessive consumption of foreign superfluities, and the necessity of restricting it, as well with economical as republican views, he moved that a committee be appointed

[1] *Ibid.*, p. 1566.

to report articles of association for encouraging, by the advice, the influence, and the example of the members of the Convention, economy, frugality, and American manufactures." The motion was seconded and without debate agreed to, and a committee of five appointed, Colonel Mason at the head of it. But no report, it seems, was ever made by this committee. George Mason renewed at this time his proposition of the day before " on the subject of inspection laws, with an additional clause giving to Congress a control over them in case of abuse—as follows : ' Provided, that no State shall be restrained from imposing the usual duties on produce exported from such State, for the sole purpose of defraying the charges of inspecting, packing, storing, and indemnifying the losses on such produce, while in the custody of public officers; but all such regulations shall, in case of abuse, be subject to the revision and control of Congress.' " There was no debate, and the question passed in the affirmative.[1]

In considering the section, " Each House shall keep a journal of its proceedings, and from time to time publish the same, excepting such parts as may in their judgment require secrecy," Colonel Mason and Mr. Gerry moved to insert after the word " parts " the words " of the proceedings of the Senate," so as to require publication of all the proceedings of the House of Representatives. But the question passed in the negative.[2] Dr. Franklin moved to add to the powers vested in Congress " to provide for cutting canals where deemed necessary." Madison wished to enlarge the motion, " to grant charters of incorporation, &c." Colonel Mason was for " limiting the power to the single case of canals. He was afraid of monopolies of every sort, which he did not think were by any means already implied by the Constitution, as supposed by Mr. Wilson."[3] The motion, however, limiting the power to the case of canals, was lost. Colonel Mason, " being sensible that an absolute prohibition of standing armies in time of peace might be unsafe, and

[1] *Ibid.*, p. 1569.   [2] *Ibid.*, p. 1573.   [3] *Ibid.*, p. 1577.

wishing at the same time to insert something pointing out and guarding against the danger of them, moved to preface the clause (Art. I., Sect. 8), 'to provide for organizing, arming, and disciplining the militia, &c.,' with the words 'and that the liberties of the people may be better secured against the danger of standing armies in time of peace.'"[1] Both Randolph and Madison were in favor of the motion, but only two States, Virginia and Georgia, voted for it. George Mason then moved to strike out from the clause (Art. I., Sect. 9) "no bill of attainder, nor any *ex post facto* law, shall be passed," the words "nor any *ex post facto* law." He "thought it not sufficiently clear that the prohibition meant by this phrase was limited to cases of a criminal nature; and no legislature ever did or can altogether avoid them in civil cases."[2] All the States opposed the motion, however. In Article I., Section 9, it was moved by Colonel Mason to insert the words "or enumeration" after, as explanatory of, "census." He also moved a clause requiring "that an account of the public expenditures should be annually published." The motion was altered by striking out "annually" and inserting "from time to time," and passed in this form.[3] The subject of inspection laws was again taken up, and, in consequence of the proviso moved by George Mason, and agreed to by the Convention on the 13th, this part of the section was laid aside in favor of the form now in the Constitution (Art. I., Sect. 10). But a motion to strike out the last words of the paragraph, "and all such laws shall be subject to the revision and control of the Congress," passed in the negative. All the States then agreed to the substitute except Virginia.[4] Messrs. McHenry and Carroll, of Maryland, moved that "no State shall be restrained from laying duties of tonnage for the purpose of clearing harbours and erecting light-houses." Colonel Mason, in support of this motion, "explained and urged the situation of the Chesapeake, which peculiarly

[1] *Ibid.*, p. 1578.
[2] *Ibid.*, p. 1579.
[3] *Ibid.*, p. 1581.
[4] *Ibid.*, p. 1584.

required expenses of this sort." But in place of this right reserved the motion passed "that no State shall lay any duty on tonnage without the consent of Congress."[1] On the subject of the power of the Executive to grant reprieves and pardons, Edmund Randolph moved to except "cases of treason," and Colonel Mason supported the motion. Madison thought the Senate should share this power with the President, if it was to be given to the latter. Colonel Mason replied "that the Senate has already too much power. There can be no danger of too much lenity in legislative pardons, as the Senate must concur; and the President moreover can require two thirds of both Houses."[2]

The motion received the support of only two States, Virginia and Georgia. George Mason thought the plan of amending the Constitution "exceptionable and dangerous. As the proposing of amendments is in both the modes to depend, in the first immediately, and in the second ultimately, on Congress, no amendments of the proper kind would ever be obtained by the people, if the government should become oppressive, as he verily believed would be the case."[3]

Returning for the last time to a subject which he considered of vital importance, Colonel Mason expressed "his discontent at the power given to Congress, by a bare majority to pass navigation acts, which he said would not only enhance the freight, a consequence he did not so much regard, but would enable a few rich merchants in Philadelphia, New York and Boston, to monopolize the staples of the Southern States, and reduce their value perhaps fifty per cent." He then moved "that no law in the nature of a navigation act be passed before the year 1808, without the consent of two thirds of each branch of the Legislature."[4] Maryland, Virginia, and Georgia were the only States that voted in the affirmative on this motion. North Carolina was absent, and South Carolina apparently regarded herself as pledged to Northern

---

[1] *Ibid.*, p. 1586.
[2] *Ibid.*, p. 1588.
[3] *Ibid.*, p. 1591.
[4] *Ibid.*, p. 1593.

interests here.   Edmund Randolph animadverted on the indefinite and dangerous power given by the Constitution to Congress, and he made a motion "that amendments to the plan might be offered by the State conventions, which should be submitted to, and finally decided on by, another general convention."   George Mason seconded the motion, and followed Randoph in strictures " on the dangerous power and structure of the government, concluding that it would end either in monarchy, or a tyrannical aristocracy ; which, he was in doubt, but one or other, he was sure.   This Constitution had been formed without the knowledge or idea of the people.   A second convention will know more of the sense of the people, and be able to provide a system more consonant to it.   It was improper to say to the people, Take this or nothing.   As the Constitution now stands, he could neither give it his support or vote in Virginia ; and he could not sign here what he could not support there.   With the expedient of another convention, as proposed, he could sign." [1]   This was Colonel Mason's last utterance in the Federal Convention.   He was followed by Elbridge Gerry, who stated briefly his objections to the proposed system. Then, on the proposition of Edmund Randolph for a second convention, all the States voted in the negative.   This was on Saturday, the 15th of September.   On Monday, the 17th, the engrossed Constitution was read and signed by all the members present except George Mason, Edmund Randolph, and Elbridge Gerry.

George Mason told Jefferson that the Constitution as agreed to only a fortnight before met with his approval.   It was, however, somewhat earlier that the changes were made which so altered its character as to render it, in Mason's opinion, no longer a safe charter of government.   Luther Martin, in answering an assertion of one of his political adversaries, in 1788, that he had cautioned certain members of the Convention to be on their guard against the wiles of Elbridge Gerry, " for that he and Mason held private meet-

[1] *Ibid.*, p. 1594.

ings, where the plans were concerted to aggrandize, at the expense of the small States, 'Old Massachusetts and the Ancient Dominion,'" gives an account of the efforts of the States-rights party to restore the Constitution to the form first "agreed to." "Some time in the month of August," he says, "a number of members who considered the system, as then under consideration, and likely to be adopted, extremely exceptionable, and of a tendency to destroy the rights and liberties of the United States, thought it advisable to meet together in the evenings, in order to have a communication of sentiments, and to concert a plan of *conventional* opposition to, and amendment of, that system, so as, if possible, to render it less dangerous. Mr. Gerry was the first who proposed this measure to me, and that before any meeting had taken place, and wished we might assemble at my lodgings ; but not having a room convenient we fixed upon another place. There Mr. Gerry and Mr. Mason did hold meetings ; but with them also met the delegates from New Jersey and Connecticut, a part of the delegation from Delaware, an honorable member from South Carolina, [Charles Pinckney?] one other from Georgia and myself. Those were the only 'private meetings' that ever I knew or heard to be held by Mr. Gerry and Mr. Mason—meetings at which I myself attended until I left the Convention—and of which the sole object was *not* to aggrandize the *great* at the expense of the *small*, but to protect and preserve, if possible, the existence and essential rights of *all* the States, and the liberty and freedom of their citizens." [1]

Hoping against hope and vigilant to the end, Colonel Mason is to be seen at his post in the last weeks of the Convention, striving to bring about alterations of more or less signficance and value. The vote of the 29th of August had been a great disappointment to him, but he still sought to reverse its decision. Among his manuscripts is to be found a paper showing the points of the Constitution to which he

[1] *Maryland Journal and Baltimore Advertiser*, March 18, 1788. Letter of Luther Martin.

took exception and the amendments designed by him at this time. Opposite most of these notes, of which there are twenty in all, George Mason has marked in the margin "agreed" or "refused," as the case might be. One of them, endorsed as "not proposed," is as follows:

"Sect. 2—Art. 4. The citizens of one State having an estate in another, have not secured to them the right of removing their property as in the Fourth Article of the Confederation. Amend by adding the following clause: And every citizen having an estate in two or more States shall have a right to remove his property from one State to another."

George Mason's reference to Article V fixes the date of the manuscript to some extent. He says:

"By this article Congress only have the power of proposing amendments at any future time to this Constitution, and should it prove ever so oppressive the whole people of America can't make, or even propose alterations to it; a doctrine utterly subversive of the fundamental principles of the rights and liberties of the people."

Here Colonel Mason's watchfulness was of great service in detecting and bringing to light a device of Gouverneur Morris to prevent the States from having the power to propose amendments. George Mason gave an account of the circumstance to Jefferson, who thus reports it:

"One morning Gouverneur Morris moved an instrument for certain alterations (not one half the members yet come in). In a hurry and without understanding, it was agreed to. The committee [on style] reported so that Congress should have the exclusive power of proposing amendments. George Mason observed it on the report and opposed it. King denied the construction. Mason demonstrated it, and asked the committee by what authority they had varied what had been agreed. Gouverneur Morris then imprudently got up and said, By authority of the Convention, and produced the blind instruction before mentioned, which was unknown by one half the house, and not till then understood by the other. They then restored it as it originally stood." [1]

Morris was not scrupulous, as his own admissions show, in his desire to secure a centralized government. He tells how, in his capacity of draftsman for the committee on style, he sought by the wording of another portion of the Constitution, the article on the judiciary, to give it a more decided bias in the desired direction.[2] Mason and Morris were types of opposing political views, and it is noticeable in the debates of the Convention how often they engaged one another in combat. They were strongly contrasted in character also, which made the antagonism more complete.

George Mason's last and cardinal amendment is given in this manuscript as originally proposed by him:

"No law in the nature of a Navigation Act shall be passed without the assent of two thirds of the members present in each House."

In another hand, the qualifying phrase is inserted which it was believed might make it more acceptable—"before the year 1808." [3] Among George Mason's manuscripts, relating to the period of the Federal Convention, is a draft of a constitution in the handwriting of Edmund Randolph. It is discussed at length by Mr. Moncure D. Conway in his biography of Randolph.[4] This paper, full of details, and with marginal notes by John Rutledge, was evidently used in one of the Convention committees. Other manuscripts, chips preserved by George Mason from the Convention workshop, are a fragment of a speech of his, and some suggestions, in an unknown hand, on the subject of the judiciary.[5]

[1] " Jefferson's Works." vol. ix., Anas, p. 119.
[2] " Life and Writings of Gouverneur Morris," Sparks, vol. iii., p. 323.
[3] Appendix ii.
[4] " Life of Edmund Randolph," p. 73.
[5] Appendix ii.

CHAPTER VI.

LAST YEAR IN THE VIRGINIA ASSEMBLY.

1787–1788.

Washington notes in his journal September 17, 1787 :

"Met in Convention, when the Constitution received the unanimous assent of eleven States, and of Col. Hamilton from New York, the only delegate from thence in Convention, and was subscribed to by every member present, except Governor Randolph and Colonel Mason from Virginia, and Mr. Gerry from Massachusetts. The business being thus closed the members adjourned to the City Tavern, dined together, and took a cordial leave of each other. After which I returned to my lodgings, did some business with and received the papers from the Secretary of the Convention, and retired to meditate on the momentous work, which had been executed, after not less than five, for a large part of the time six, and sometimes seven hours' sitting every day (except Sundays and the ten days' adjournment to give a committee an opportunity and time to arrange the business) for more than four months."[1]

We have no record of George Mason's last day in the Convention. But his meditations upon the "momentous work" there executed were, doubtless, of a very different nature from Washington's. He went home, perhaps, in company with his neighbor of "Mount Vernon," and discussed by the way the Constitution and its shortcomings. Alexandria is said to have been strongly in favor of the new

[1] "Writings of Washington," Sparks, vol. ix. (Appendix), p. 541.

government. And such was certainly the bias of a Philadelphia paper, which published in its editorial columns a
remarkable story purporting to be a veracious account of
George Mason's reception in Alexandria on his return from
the Convention. "We hear from Alexandria," says this
Baron Munchausen, " that on the arrival of Mr. Mason (one
of the delegates in Convention) at Alexandria, he was waited
on by the Mayor and Corporation of that town, who told
him, they were *not* come to return him their thanks for his
conduct in refusing to sign the Federal Constitution, but to
express their abhorrence to it, and to advise him to withdraw
from that town within an hour, for they could not answer
for his personal safety from an enraged populace should he
exceed that time." [1] George Mason was too much respected
by the mayor and corporation of Alexandria to have received
from them any such treatment as is here described, even had
the town been so foolish as to resent the action of their representative, which is by no means proved. And as neither
Washington nor George Mason refer to any such incident,
in their letters, it may well be dismissed as completely fictitious. Edmund Randolph, too, would most likely have
reported it to Madison, if his "dissenting colleague" had
met with such an experience, when he wrote from Bowling
Green, September 30th :

" In Alexandria the inhabitants are enthusiastic [*i. e.* in favor
of the Constitution], and instructions to force my dissenting colleague to assent to a convention are on the anvil. I wrote to
him yesterday suggesting to him this expedient : to urge the
calling of a convention as the first act of the Assembly : if they
should wish amendments let them be stated and forwarded to the
States. Before the meeting of the convention an answer may be
obtained. If the proposed amendments be rejected, let the constitution immediately operate : if approved by nine States, let the
assent of our convention be given under the exceptions of the
points amended. This will, I believe, blunt the opposition, which
will be formidable, if they must take altogether or reject." [2]

[1] *The Pennsylvania Journal,* October 17, 1787.
[2] " Life of Edmund Randolph," M. D. Conway, p. 95.

This letter of Edmund Randolph to George Mason has been lost, and it is not very clear, partly owing to the fact that the sentence is not punctuated at all in the manuscript, what the Governor meant, as he described his scheme to Madison. On the subject of calling a convention, George Mason did not need any prompting, either from his Alexandria constituents or from Edmund Randolph. He had prepared, in the last days of the Convention, his "Objections to the Constitution." These he enclosed to Washington, in a letter dated October 7th. He writes:

"I take the liberty to enclose to you my objections, to the new constitution of government, which a little moderation and temper at the latter end of the Convention might have removed. I am, however, most decidedly of opinion, that it ought to be submitted to the people for that special purpose, and should any attempt be made to prevent the calling of such a Convention here, such a measure shall have every opposition in my power to give it. You will readily observe that my objections are not numerous (the greater part of the enclosed paper containing reasonings upon the probable effects of the exceptionable parts), though in my mind some of them are capital ones."

Colonel Mason in his letter then leaves politics for agriculture, and tells his correspondent of the failure of some of his crops, and that Dr. Williamson and Colonel Davie, of North Carolina, whom he had met at the Convention, had shown him letters mentioning large crops of corn in their State. He proposes to supply himself there, and will write to Dr. Williamson at Edenton for this purpose. And George Mason offers to make a contract for Washington also, should the latter desire it.[1]

George Mason wrote out his objections to the Constitution before leaving the Convention, apparently, as they are found on the edition of the Constitution printed for the benefit of the members, and given to them September 13th. This was the "Report" of the "Committee on Style and Arrange-

[1] Washington MSS., State Department.

ment." George Mason's copy,[1] which is among the few that have been preserved, is full of interlineations and marginal notes, having been used, no doubt, in Committee of the Whole. The "Objections," as they appeared afterwards in pamphlet form, were somewhat expanded, and there were changes in the style here and there.[2] They were not a great many, as George Mason told Washington, but they covered the whole ground, and were dwelt upon fully in the debates of the Virginia Convention some months later. In the " Address of the Sixteen Seceding Members of the Legislature of Pennsylvania," September 29th,[3] as Washington wrote Madison, George Mason's objections are detailed, and no doubt he was in communication with the Antifederalists of Pennsylvania and gave them the benefit of his views. His objections were circulated among his friends in manuscript before they appeared in print, and Madison wrote a reply to them in a letter to Washington, October 18th.[4] It is evident they excited a great deal of interest and no little alarm among the Federalists, though Madison affected to think them of small importance. They were published in Richmond, " Addressed to the Citizens of Virginia,"[5] probably in November or December, 1787, and it is said they were also published in Boston, "mutilated of that which pointed at the regulation of commerce."[6] An answer to them appeared in the *Massachusetts Centinel* of the 18th of December, copied from the *Connecticut Courant*, which was supposed to have been written by Ellsworth, or Sherman, or some equally able champion of the Constitution.[7] The most elaborate reply to George Mason's " Objections " was that made by James Iredell, of North Carolina, published in the biography of the latter, and reprinted among the pamphlets

[1] Owned by Mrs. St. George Tucker Campbell, of Philadelphia.
[2] Appendix ii.
[3] *American Museum*, vol. ii., p. 362.
[4] " Writings of Washington," Sparks, vol. ix., App. vi.
[5] " Pamphlets on the Constitution," Paul L. Ford, p. 390.
[6] " Writings of Washington," Sparks, vol. ix., p. 288.
[7] " The Republic of Republics," p. 444, P. C. Centz, Appendix A, No. 1.

collected by Mr. Ford. James Wilson, of Pennsylvania, was one of the most prominent advocates of the Constitution, in its unamended shape, and his pamphlet in its defence is considered the ablest on that side that appeared at this period. An amusing " Recipe for an anti-Federalist essay," which was published in one of the newspapers of the day, brings Wilson and Mason together as typical men of the two parties. The phrase " well-born," alluded to as a shibboleth of the Federalists, belonged to John Adams, and will be met with later in the debates of the Virginia Convention :

" Take ' well-born ' nine times ; ' aristocracy ' nine times ; ' liberty of the press ' thirteen times ; ' liberty of conscience ' once ; ' negro slavery ' once ; ' trial by jury ' seven times ; ' great men ' six times ; ' Mr. Wilson ' forty times ; and lastly, ' George Mason's right hand in a cutting-box ' nineteen times. Put all together, boil or roast or fry, and dish at pleasure. After being once used the remains of the same dish may be served a dozen times *ad libitum.*" [1]

Edmund Randolph published a letter embodying his objections to the Constitution, and Richard Henry Lee wrote very ably in advocacy of amendments to the charter of government as it then stood. As Mason and Randolph had been the Virginia Antifederalists of the Convention, so Richard Henry Lee and William Grayson were leaders of this party in Congress. The following letter from Richard Henry Lee to George Mason, written in reply to one from the latter, giving an account of the last days of the Convention, details the action of Lee in Congress in his efforts to advance the cause which he had at heart. Unfortunately, all the letters of Mason to Lee written at this period have been lost. Tradition says that the wife of Ludwell Lee, son of R. H. Lee, converted many of these letters into covers for her preserve-jars, and so like similar treasures among the Bland Papers, which served to line baskets of eggs, they perished ignobly.

[1] Review in *The Nation,* January 17, 1889.

New York, October 1st, 1787.

Dear Sir:

I have waited until now to answer your favor of September 10th from Philadelphia, that I might inform you how the Convention plan of government was entertained by Congress. Your prediction of what would happen in Congress was exactly verified. It was with us, as with you, this or nothing; and this urged with a most extreme intemperance. The greatness of the powers given, and the multitude to be created produces a coalition of monarchy men, military men, aristocrats and drones, whose noise, impudence and zeal exceeds all belief. Whilst the commercial plunder of the South stimulates the rapacious trader. In this state of things the patriot voice is raised in vain for such changes and securities as reason and experience prove to be necessary against the encroachments of power upon the indispensable rights of human nature. Upon due consideration of the Constitution under which we now act, some of us were clearly of opinion that the Thirteenth Article of the Confederation precluded us from giving an opinion concerning a plan subversive of the present system, and eventually forming a new Confederacy of nine instead of thirteen States. The contrary doctrine was asserted with great violence in expectation of the strong majority with which they might send it forward under terms of much approbation. Having procured an opinion that Congress was qualified to consider, to amend, to approve or disapprove, the next game was to determine that though a right to amend existed, it would be highly inexpedient to exercise that right, but merely to transmit it with respectful marks of approbation. In this state of things I availed myself of the right to amend, and moved the amendments, a copy of which I send herewith, and called the ayes and nays to fix them on the journal. This greatly alarmed the majority and vexed them extremely; for the plan is to push the business on with great dispatch, and with as little opposition as possible, that it may be adopted before it has stood the test of reflection and due examination. They found it most eligible at last to transmit it merely, without approving or disapproving, provided nothing but the transmission should appear on the journal. This compromise was settled and they took the opportunity of inserting the word *unanimously*, which applied only to simple transmission, hoping to have it mistaken for an unanimous approbation of the thing. It states that Congress having received the Constitution unanimously transmit it, &c. It is certain that no approbation was given. This Constitution has a great many excellent regulations in it, and if it could be reasonably amended would be a fine system. As it is, I think 't is past doubt, that if it should be established, either a tyranny will result from it, or it will be prevented by a civil war. I am clearly of opinion with you that it should be sent back with amendments reasonable, and assent to it withheld until such amendments are admitted. You are well acquainted with Mr. Stone and others of influence in Maryland. I think it will be a great point to get Maryland and Virginia to join in the plan of amendments and return it with them. If you are in correspondence with our chancellor Pendleton it will be of much use to furnish him with the objections, and if he approves our plan, his opinion will have great weight with our Convention ; and I am told that his relation Judge Pendleton of South Carolina has decided weight in that State, and that he is sensible and independent. How important will it be then to procure his union with our plan, which might probably be the case if our chancellor was to write largely and pressingly to him on the subject, that if possible it may be amended there also. It is certainly the most rash and violent proceeding in the world to cram thus suddenly into men a business of such infinite moment to the happiness of millions. One of your letters will go by the packet and one by a merchant ship.

My compliments, if you please, to your lady and to the young ladies and gentlemen.

I am, dear sir, affectionately yours,

RICHARD HENRY LEE.

Suppose when the Assembly recommended a Convention to consider this new Constitution they were to use some words like these : It is earnestly recommended to the good people of Virginia to send their most wise and honest men to this Convention that it may undergo the most intense consideration before a plan shall be without amendments, adopted that admits of abuses being practised by which the best interests of this country may be injured and civil liberty greatly endangered. This might perhaps give a decided tone to the business.

Please to send my son Ludwell a copy of the amendments proposed by me to the new Constitution sent herewith.[1]

These amendments correspond almost entirely with the "Objections" of George Mason. The chief variation is in the manner of composing the Executive Council. Washington wrote to Madison on the 10th of October, soon after receiving George Mason's letter with his "Objections to the Constitution":

"As far as accounts have been received from the southern and western counties, the sentiment with respect to the proceedings of the Convention is favorable. Whether the knowledge of this or a conviction of the impropriety of withholding the Constitution from the State conventions, has worked most in the breast of Col. Mason, I will not decide; but the fact is, he has declared unequivocally, in a letter to me, for its going to the people. Had his sentiments, however, been opposed to the measure, his instructions (for the delegates of his county are so instructed) would compel him to vote for it. Yet I have no doubt, that his assent will be accompanied by the most tremendous apprehensions which the highest coloring can give to his objections. To alarm the people seems to be the groundwork of his plan. The want of a qualified navigation act is already declared to be a means by which the price of produce in the Southern States will be reduced to nothing, and will become a monopoly of the Eastern and Northern States. To enumerate the whole of his objections is unnecessary, because they are detailed in the address of the seceding members of the Assembly of Pennsylvania, which, no doubt, you have seen."

Comparing George Mason and Richard Henry Lee, Washington adds:

"The political tenets of Col. M. and Colonel R. H. L. are always in unison. It may be asked which of them gives the tone? Without hesitation I answer the latter because I believe the latter

[1] Mason Papers.

will receive it from no-one.   He has, I am informed, rendered himself obnoxious in Philadelphia by the pains he took to dis- seminate his objections among some of the leaders of the seceding members of the legislature of that State.   His conduct is not less reprobated in this country.   How it will be relished generally is yet to be learned by me." [1]

The late commander-in-chief clearly belongs to the " mili- tary men " of whom Richard Henry Lee speaks in his letter to Mason.   He advocated a strong government, and could see no need for bills of rights.   He was not in a temper to appreciate the motives of the opposition leaders.   But it is difficult to see why he should think it necessary to take from George Mason the credit of originality, on a subject which had been so thoroughly canvassed by him in the Federal Convention, and to suppose that Lee gave the " tone " to his " political tenets."   Two independent thinkers may be " always in unison," it has been often seen, upon principles which each one has arrived at by his own method.   So the mere fact that Mason's " Objections " antedated Lee's " Amendments " would not be an argument against Lee's originality, though his paper closely resembled that of his friend.   Five days later Washington wrote to Henry Knox:

" It is highly probable that the refusal of our Governor and Colonel Mason to subscribe to the proceedings of the Convention will have a bad effect in this State ; for as you well observe, they must not only assign reasons for the justification of their own conduct, but ˙it is highly probable that these reasons will be clothed in most terrific array for the purpose of alarming." [2]

The Virginia Assembly met on the 15th of October.   It was the last Assembly under the old freer life of the Confederation; and it was to be Colonel Mason's last session in the Virginia Legislature.   Besides the regular business of the Assembly, the all-important question of the new Federal Constitution was to come up, incidentally, in the recommendation of a

[1] Bancroft's " History of the Constitution," vol. ii., p. 443 (Appendix).
[2] " Writings of Washington," Sparks, vol. ix., p. 270.

convention. Madison wrote from Congress to Washington on the 28th, expressing his anxiety as to the attitude on this point of George Mason and Patrick Henry. He had heard from one of his correspondents in the Assembly " that Colonel Mason had not got down, and it appears that Mr. Henry is not at bottom a friend." He is therefore " not without fears that their combined influence and management may yet create difficulties." [1] The resolution of Congress transmitting the Constitution to the several State legislatures came under consideration on the 19th, when Patrick Henry declared that it must go before a convention of the people, as the Assembly had no power to decide the matter. George Mason must have arrived in the Assembly by the 23d, as on this day Edmund Randolph wrote to Madison from Richmond : " Mr. Mason has declared in Assembly that although he is for amendments, he will not quit the Union even if they should not be made." Then follows a phrase in this letter showing that there had been some display of feeling on Mason's part, apparently, against Madison, which is not to be wondered at under the circumstances. The indistinct manuscript reads : " Colonel Mason has said *nothing good* [sic] and you may rest yourself in safety in my hands, for I will certainly repel the smallest insinuation." [2] If Madison feared the influence of Mason, it might well be that Mason returned the compliment. Already the *Federalist* had begun its work, in which Madison's pen was to be so potent. And George Mason must have viewed with chagrin a publication which was to do so much towards establishing political views of which he emphatically disapproved. However, as will be seen subsequently, the two statesmen, if estranged for a short period, renewed later their former friendly relations.

On the 25th of October the House debated the question of calling a convention, and the following account is given of the proceedings in a letter from Petersburg to a Phila-

[1] " Correspondence of the American Revolution," Sparks, vol. iv., p. 185.
[2] " Life of Edmund Randolph," M. D. Conway, p. 97.

delphia newspaper, dated November 1st, the only record that has been preserved of the debate, it would seem. The writer says: "On Thursday last the House of Delegates of this State took under consideration the resolution of Congress by which the appointment of a State Convention was recommended." The debate was opened by Francis Corbin, who "spoke with approbation of the new plan of government." He closed his speech with a resolution that a convention be called according to the recommendation of Congress. Patrick Henry rose to oppose the resolution, as it then stood.

"He did not question the propriety or necessity of calling a Convention. No man was more truly Federal than himself, but he conceived that, if this resolution was adopted, the Convention would only have it in their power to say that the new plan should be *adopted*, or *rejected*, and that however defective it might appear to them, they would not be authorised to propose amendments. There were errors and defects in the Constitution, and he therefore proposed the addition of some words to Mr. Corbin's resolutions by which the power of proposing amendments might be given."

Mr. Corbin defended his resolution, and George Nicholas seconded his defence.

"He warmly reprobated Mr. Henry's amendment, because it would give the impression that the Virginia Assembly thought amendments might be made to the new government, whereas he believed there was a decided majority in its favor. At the same time he did not deny the right of the Convention to propose amendments."

The writer goes on to say:

"Mr. Mason, who had just taken his seat in the House, rose to second Mr. Henry's motion. He told the Committee that he felt somewhat embarrassed at the situation in which he then stood. He had been honored with a seat in the Federal Convention, and all knew that he had refused to subscribe to their proceedings. This might excite some surprise, but it was not necessary at that hour, he said, to make known his reasons ; at a proper season they should be communicated to his countrymen. He would, however, declare that no man was more completely federal in his principles than he was : that from the east of New Hampshire to the south of Georgia, there was not a man more fully convinced of the necessity of establishing some general government : that he regarded our perfect union as the rock of our political salvation : but, that he had considered the new federal government according to that measure of knowledge which God had given him—that he had endeavored to make himself master of the important subject ; that he had deeply and maturely weighed every article of the new Constitution ; and with every information which he could derive, either from his own reflection, or the observations of others, he could not approve it. He said : ' I thought it wrong, Mr. Chairman,—I thought it repugnant to our highest interests, and if with these sentiments I had subscribed to it, I might have been justly regarded as a traitor to my country. I would have lost this hand before it should have marked my name to the new government.' "

John Marshall spoke next :

" He thought Mr. Corbin's resolution improper for the reason given by Mr. Henry. He thought Mr. Henry's amendment improper for the reasons given by Mr. Nicholas. He wished that the future Convention should have the fullest latitude in their deliberations, etc., but he thought, with Mr. Nicholas, that the people should have no reason to suppose that their Legislature disapproved the new federal government, and therefore he proposed this resolution : That a Convention should be called, and that the new Constitution should be laid before them for their free and ample discussion."

This resolution passed without opposition. The other speakers in the debate were Prentis, Bland, Thruston, and Benjamin Harrison. And it was decided that the convention should meet in May, the election of members to take place in March.[1]

The first mention of George Mason's name in the printed

---

[1] *Pennsylvania Packet,* November 10, 1787.

journal of the Assembly occurs on the 26th of October, the day after the debate just given, when he is added to the Committees on Revenue and Trade.   Between this date and the 8th of November there is no further reference to him in the journal, but we learn from other sources how he was employed.   On Saturday, the 3d of November, he answered the expectations of his friends by giving the death-blow to paper currency.   In a letter to Washington, written a few days later, he tells of the petitions before the House for an emission of paper money, and other similar expedients, against which he argued, maintaining that they were founded upon fraud and knavery.   Though he called upon the advocates of these measures to come forward and explain their motives, not one of them was bold enough to enter the lists against such a champion, and the resolutions which he had prepared passed unanimously.

"*Resolved, &c.*, That the present scarcity of circulating money has been, in a great measure, caused by the general fear and apprehension of an emission of paper currency ; inducing monied men to lock up their gold and silver, or remit it to Europe, and prefer receiving a very low interest for it there, to the risk of lending or letting it out here ; That money, by the common consent and custom of commercial nations, is and ought to be considered as a scale or standard by which to estimate the comparative value of commodities ; and that nothing can be more improper and unjust than to substitute such a standard as would be more uncertain and variable than the commodities themselves. That an emission of paper money would be ruinous to trade and commerce, and highly injurious to the good people of this Commonwealth ; and that by weakening their confidence in the laws and government, corrupting their manners and morals, destroying public and private credit and all faith between man and man, it would increase and aggravate the very evils it is intended to remedy ; That the making paper currency, or anything but gold and silver coin, a tender in discharge of debts contracted in money is contrary to every principle of sound policy as well as justice." [1]

[1] Journal of the Assembly.   *Virginia Gazette*, November 22, 1787.

In the first resolution an amendment was made, striking out " remit to Europe, &c.," and inserting " preferring the loss of interest." George Mason enclosed a copy of these resolutions in his letter to Washington. And he tells his correspondent of a resolution which passed on the third also, prohibiting the importation of spirits and some other things, all of which he thought impolitic. Madison ascribes this resolution to Patrick Henry.[1] A plan was before the House, Mason writes, for " a three years' instalment of all debts," which he thought exceptionable, but as he had no hope that the opposition against it would be effective he meant to try and change it by making the consent of the creditor necessary and the instalments voluntary. Colonel Mason also enclosed Washington the " resolutions upon the proposed Federal government." On the 8th of November, the House in committee on the state of the commonwealth came to the following resolution :

" That the delegates of this Commonwealth in Congress ought to be instructed to urge that honorable body to allow a credit to this State against the present existing requisitions of Congress for the ascertained amount of the claim of this Commonwealth against the United States for expenses incurred on account of the territory ceded to Congress by this State."[2]

The committee of ten appointed to prepare these instructions included George Mason, Patrick Henry, and James Monroe. Four days later other important resolutions were passed by the House. The question of the free navigation of the Mississippi was still unsettled, and the Assembly now restated Virginia's position on the subject in these resolutions :

" That the free use and navigation of the western streams and rivers of this Commonwealth and of the waters leading to the sea, do of right appertain to the citizens thereof, and ought to be considered as guaranteed to them by the laws of God and nature

---

[1] " Writings of Madison," vol. i., p. 366.
[2] Journal of the Assembly.

as well as compact ; That every attempt in Congress or elsewhere
to barter away such right ought to be considered as subversive
of justice, good faith and the great foundations of moral rectitude, and particularly destructive of the principles which gave
birth to the late Revolution as well as strongly repugnant to all
confidence in the Federal Government, and destructive to its
peace, safety, happiness and duration ; That a committee ought
to be appointed to prepare instructions to the delegates representing this State in Congress to the foregoing import, and to
move that honorable body to pass an act acknowledging the
rights of this State, and that it transcends their power to cede or
suspend them ; and desiring the said delegates to lay before the
General Assembly such transactions as have taken place respecting the cession of the western navigation." [1]

Mason and Henry were appointed on the committee here
recommended. But a subject was presently to be considered
where these two leaders are found on opposite sides.   This
was the controversy respecting the immediate payment of
British debts.   Should all legal obstacles be removed in the
way of their liquidation, in accordance with a provision in
the treaty of peace, or should they remain on the statute
books until Great Britain fulfilled her part in evacuating the
posts on the western frontier? George Mason supported
the resolutions for repealing the former legislation in this
matter, while Patrick Henry opposed them. The former
was ably seconded here by George Nicholas. The contest
lasted three days, but at length George Mason triumphed.
He gives an interesting account of the debate in a letter to
Washington of the 27th of November. The journal of the
Assembly records that on the 17th, the committee of the
whole House resolved: "That all and every act or acts of
Assembly now in force in this Commonwealth repugnant to
the treaty of peace between the United States and the King
of Great Britain, or any article thereof, ought to be repealed ;
but the operation of this law shall be suspended until the
executive shall be informed by Congress that the other

[1] *Ibid.*

States in the Union have passed similar laws of repeal." A motion was made by Patrick Henry to strike out from the word " repealed " to the end of the sentence, and insert " but the operation of such repeal ought to be suspended until the treaty of peace is complied with on the part of Great Britain." This amendment passed in the negative. Another amendment was then proposed, to insert after the word " repealed " " and that an act ought to pass, to compel the payment of all debts due to British subjects, in such time and manner as shall consist with the exhausted situation of this Commonwealth." This was also negatived, and the main question then passed in the affirmative.[1] The committee of ten to whom the resolution was then referred, to prepare the necessary bill, consisted of Francis Corbin, George Mason, George Nicholas, and others, concluding with Monroe and Marshall. George Mason wrote Washington how " Mr. C———n, with the vanity so natural to a young man," undertook to draw up the bill without consulting his colleagues, and did his work so injudiciously that it would require to be " regenerated " in the committee before it could be presented. On the 24th a bill passed the House declaring tobacco receivable in payment of certain taxes for the year 1787. George Mason voted against it, and in his letter to Washington he speaks of it as " a foolish and injudicious project." Colonel Mason, on this day, was added to the committee " to amend the several acts making provision for the poor." On the 26th he was made chairman of a committee of seven who were to bring in a bill explaining and amending " the act for preventing fraudulent gifts of slaves." The following day, leave was given to bring in a bill " to remedy abuses in certain cases, and for the relief of debtors," and George Mason was one of a committee of six appointed to prepare it.[2] In his letter to Washington of this date, Colonel Mason says : " Little progress has yet been made on the subject of revenue. I shall use my best endeavors to prevent the receipt of public securities of any kind

[1] *Ibid.*   [2] *Ibid.*

in taxes. . . . By way of experiment, and to show the members the utility of such a plan, we have this day, against a strong opposition, ordered about £6,000 now in the treasury to be immediately applied to that purpose," [*i. e.*, purchasing the securities up at the market-price]. On the 28th, the House in committee of the whole on the state of the commonwealth, resolved : " That the executive ought to be authorized to dispose of the public tobacco now in the treasury, in such manner and for specie, or such public securities, whether State or Continental, as may seem to them best for the public interest." And George Mason was appointed on the committee to prepare the necessary bills.

Two days later, resolutions passed the House, making provision " for ascertaining the privileges and defraying the expenses " of the members of the Convention, which was to meet the first Monday in the following June, instead of May as at first decided on. And it was further resolved, that if this Convention " should deem it proper to send a deputy or deputies to confer with the Convention or Conventions of any other State or States in the Union, the General Assembly will make provision for defraying the expenses thereof." [1] Patrick Henry and George Mason were placed second and third on the committee appointed for this purpose. This last resolution was considered a triumph for the Antifederalists, and gave the other party no small alarm. Bushrod Washington wrote an account of the matter, three days later, December 3d, to his anxious relative at " Mount Vernon." He says :

" I am sorry to inform you, that the Constitution has lost so considerably that it is doubted whether it has any longer a majority in its favor. From a vote which took place the other day, this would appear certain, though I cannot think it so decisive as its enemies consider it. It marks, however, the inconsistency of some of its opponents. At the time the resolutions calling a Convention were entered into, Colonel Mason sided with the friends of the Constitution, and opposed any hint

[1] *Ibid.*

being given, expressive of the sentiments of the house as to amendments [?]. But, as it was unfortunately omitted at that time to make provision for the subsistence of the Convention, it became necessary to pass some resolution on the subject ; when a resolution was added, providing for any expense which may attend an attempt to make amendments. As Colonel Mason had, on the former occasion, declared that it would be improper to make any discovery of the sentiments of the House on the subject, and that we had no right to suggest anything to a body paramount to us, his advocating such a resolution was matter of astonishment. It is true, he declared, it was not declaratory of our opinion. But the contrary must be very obvious. As I have heard many declare themselves friends to the Constitution since the vote, I do not consider it altogether decisive of the opinion of the House with regard to it." [1]

There was some debate in the Assembly, evidently, on these resolutions. But it may be certain, whatever George Mason said on the 30th of November was not inconsistent with the opinions so emphatically expressed by him on the 25th of October.

On the 1st of December, Colonel Mason and several other members were appointed to prepare a bill " to supply the defect of evidence of the Royal assent to certain Acts of Assembly under the former government." And on this day the vexed question of the British debts was again before the House, and two amendments were made to the bill. The first two clauses, including the preamble, were stricken out and the following was inserted :

" Whereas it is stipulated by the fourth article of the treaty of peace between the king of Great Britain and the United States of America in Congress assembled, that creditors on either side shall meet with no lawful impediment in the recovery of the full value in sterling money, of all *bona fide* debts heretofore contracted. Be it therefore enacted, &c.—That such of the act or acts of the legislature of this Commonwealth, as have prevented, or might prevent, the recovery of debts due to British

[1] " Writings of Washington," Sparks, vol. ix., p. 273.

subjects, according to the true intent and meaning of the said treaty of peace, shall be and are hereby repealed."

This first amendment may have been due to the making over in the committee of the illy drawn instrument as it came from Mr. Corbin's hands. But the second amendment showed Patrick Henry's influence, and in fact was meant to nullify the whole bill. The proviso that the operation of the law shall be suspended until the Governor with the advice of the Council shall, by his proclamation declare the same to be in force; which proclamation he is hereby empowered and directed, with the advice aforesaid to issue on receiving official information from Congress that the other States in the Union have passed laws enabling British creditors to recover their debts agreeably to the terms of the treaty, was struck out and in its place was inserted:

" Provided that this act shall be suspended until the Governor with the advice of the Council shall, by his proclamation notify to this State that Great Britain hath delivered up to the United States the posts therein now occupied by British troops, which posts were stipulated by treaty to be given up to Congress immediately after the conclusion of peace ; and is also taking measures for the further fulfilment of the said treaty, by delivering up the negroes belonging to the citizens of this State taken away contrary to the seventh article of the treaty, or by making such compensation for them as shall be satisfactory to Congress." [1]

Patrick Henry "carried his point," as Madison wrote Jefferson.[2]

No doubt the subject was warmly debated this day also between Mason and Henry. There was much to be said on both sides, and that side advocated by Patrick Henry was the one most likely to appeal to popular favor. An attack was made on the church glebes at this time, on a petition of the Presbyterians praying a repeal of the law reserving to

[1] Journal of the Assembly.
[2] "Writings of Madison," vol. i., p. 379.

the Episcopal Church the church buildings and glebes. George Mason was not prepared to go the length of depriving the Church of her rightful property, and he voted against the resolution to sell the glebe lands in the parishes which were without a rector. And it was not until some years after Colonel Mason's death that the spoliation was effected. On the 6th of December the House in committee of the whole, considering that "the distresses of the people, arising from a variety of causes, are such, that property taken in execution to satisfy debts and contracts, does not in most cases sell for near its value, thereby in the end tending to the ruin both of debtor and creditor. Resolved &c. That some act of the legislature ought to pass for remedy thereof; That an act ought to pass for establishing district courts, and for reforming the county courts." George Mason, Patrick Henry, and George Nicholas were on the committee of sixteen, who were to prepare a bill for these purposes.[1] A resolve which Colonel Mason enclosed to Washington in his letter of November 27th was on this subject of debts, and suggested a measure for the accommodation of both debtor and creditor. A few days later George Mason was made chairman of a committee to amend two acts concerning roads, to repair some and open others. These roads passed through Colonel Mason's own neighborhood, so it was a matter in which his constituents were specially interested. The former acts, it seems, had proved oppressive, in requiring tolls from those who received no benefit by the turnpikes. The new bill, as drawn up by George Mason remedied this injustice. As much travelling in those days was done by private conveyance, the subject of tolls was an important one to the country gentlemen. The report of the treasurer's account was referred to a committee of which Colonel Mason was a member. And on the seventeenth he was appointed one of a committee of five to prepare a bill "concerning debts due to and from citizens, partners with British subjects." A committee, con-

---

[1] Journal of the Assembly.

sisting of Nicholas, Mason, Cabell, Monroe, Corbin, and Henry, was appointed to amend the acts " for sequestering British property and enabling those indebted to British subjects to pay off such debts, and directing the proceedings in suits where such subjects are parties."

George Mason was also at this time appointed chairman of a committee of six, who were " to call on the commissioners now engaged in liquidating and adjusting the expenses incurred by this commonwealth, for the northwestern territory ceded to Congress, and request of them a statement of their proceedings therein &c." [1] On the 22d of December George Mason was appointed chairman of a committee of six to prepare a bill " for regulating the rights of cities, towns and boroughs, and the jurisdiction of corporation courts." This act recites :

" Whereas the accumulating different and distinct offices of power and authority in the same persons has a tendency to introduce abuses, and to create an improper and dangerous influence in a few individuals, contrary to the spirit and genius of republican government, and naturally productive of oppression and subversive of liberty : Be it therefore enacted by the General Assembly, that from and after the first day of March next, no person being a member of any corporation court, court of hustings or common council be capable of acting as a justice of any county court."

And in conclusion it is enacted that,

" Whereas it is contrary to the true principles of representation, that a freehold estate in any particular place should enable the possessor to vote in the elections of different and distinct places, so the citizens of a town etc., sending a delegate to the Assembly are not to vote in the county elections." [2]

In its statesman-like recurrence to fundamental principles this bill is easily traceable to George Mason's pen. A week later, Colonel Mason reported a bill to the House, " pro-

[1] *Ibid.*   [2] Hening's " Statutes," vol. xii.

viding for the regular payment of the expenses accruing from the trial of criminals in the county and corporation courts." In a bill providing for the manumission of slaves, an amendment was proposed and lost, that those emancipated should leave the State within twelve months or be sold at public auction. Colonel Mason voted for the amendment. On the last day of December an act was passed by the Assembly for establishing and incorporating the *Randolph Academy*, which was to be situated in the western part of the State, in one of the following counties: Harrison, Monongalia, Randolph, and Ohio. One sixth of the fees appropriated to the support of William and Mary College was to go to the aid of this new institution. Edmund Randolph, Benjamin Harrison, Patrick Henry, George Mason, and George Nicholas were among the trustees named, and they were to hold their first meeting on the second Monday in the following May, at Morgantown in Monongalia.[1] It is not probable that Colonel Mason attended this meeting, if it was ever held. And but little is heard of the Academy in the later legislation of the Assembly. Morgantown and its neighborhood were still subject to raids from the Indians on the border, and protected by scouts and rangers from these incursions, and the inhabitants were scarcely in a situation to patronize institutions of learning. George Mason and three other members of the Assembly were appointed on the 3d of January to bring in a bill " to authorize the executive to establish fire companies." Two days later the journal of the House records a determined effort that was made, when it came to the third reading of the bill " to enable citizens, partners with British subjects to recover their proportion of debts," to postpone it until the following March. The vote was equally divided, forty-three on each side. The Speaker decided the question by a vote in the negative. George Mason, of course, voted against the postponement.

The last action of Colonel Mason in the Assembly was to

[1] *Ibid.*

give in his report from the committee appointed to confer with the commissioners engaged in liquidating and adjusting the expenses incurred by Virginia for the northwestern territory ceded to Congress. And here, it seems, it was necessary to look sharply to Virginia's interests. Congress was ungenerously anxious to evade Virginia's just claims. There had been much delay in getting the board appointed, the deed of cession dating from the spring of 1784, more than three years previously. There were three commissioners forming the board; one was appointed by the United States and one by Virginia, while the third was appointed by the two other commissioners. George Mason enclosed the resolve of the House of Delegates to the board, in a letter requesting to know at what time they could have their proceedings ready for inspection. The board from the "Office of Illinois Accounts," December 20th, responded that they were uncertain whether to comply or not, but finally decided that it was proper to notice the request, and they would submit the rough entries for perusal by Monday or Tuesday next. The commissioner appointed by Congress, however, dissented from the "propriety of our furnishing the information to the house of delegates requested by their note &c., because that as commissioners appointed to settle these accounts between the State of Virginia and the United States I think that we cannot prior to our final report, consistent with our duty to each party communicate any official information to one party without the privity or consent of the other." The committee then say that being refused information from the above commissioner they entered upon the examination of the proceedings of the board as laid before them by the other two gentlemen. The deed ceding the territory specified "that the necessary and reasonable expenses incurred by this State in subduing any British posts, or in maintaining forts and garrisons within and for the defence, or in acquiring any part of the territory so ceded or relinquished, shall be fully reimbursed by the United States." But the committee, after their examination, declare that they "find the negotiation now in such a train that Virginia, unless the General Assembly interpose, will be denied a credit for great part of the money she has actually and *bona fide* paid, in acquiring and maintaining the territory so ceded and relinquished to the United States. Questions have arisen concerning the true spirit, intent and meaning of the words 'necessary and reasonable expenses,' as used in the act of session; on the depreciation of money advanced by this State; on bills paid, *bona fide* by the State on the Illinois account, and on the expenses of establishing and maintaining forts Jefferson and Nelson &c. Your committee," as the report proceeds to state, "observing the progress of this business, so unfavorable to the interest of the State and so inconsistent with the apparent intentions of the contracting parties, requested the commissioners to reconsider the business and to do Virginia that justice to which, in the opinion of the committee, she is entitled. But the commissioner on the part of Congress and the third commissioner have informed us that they mean to proceed unless the powers given them be revoked by both the contracting parties."

Virginia had incurred expenses in subduing British posts and maintaining forts, etc., to the amount of more than two hundred and twenty thousand pounds. And yet if the accounts were settled as proposed by the commission, this would be "reduced to a pittance not worth acceptance." The General Assembly protested against these proceedings of the commissioners, and the Virginia delegates in Congress were instructed to assure that body that the General Assembly "animated by the same spirit which governed them in the cession of such a vast territory to the Union, will be satisfied with the reimbursement of such sums which she [Virginia] hath actually expended in acquiring, maintaining and defending said territory to be paid in reasonable instalments." [1] These resolutions were carried to the Senate by Colonel Mason. Instrumental as he had been in urging upon his State to make this cession, in the interest of

---

[1] Journal of the Assembly.

harmony and union, to the general government, George Mason was watchful of his "country's" rights, and he now sought, as his final work in her legislative halls, to secure to Virginia the modest and equitable terms named in her deed of gift.

The following letters from George Mason to General Washington afford an interesting view of the proceedings of the Assembly up to the latter part of November.

RICHMOND, NOVEMBER 6, 1787.

DEAR SIR :

On Saturday last, in a committee of the whole house upon the state of the commonwealth, to whom were referred sundry petitions, some praying for an emission of paper money, and others for making property at an appraised value, a tender in the discharge of debts, I moved and carried the resolutions of which I inclose a copy. During the discussion of the subject, after treating the petitions as founded upon fraud and knavery, I called upon any of the members of the House, who were advocates for such measures, if any there were, to come boldly forward, and explain their real motives. But they declined entering into the debate, and the resolutions passed unanimously. I hope they have given this iniquitous measure a mortal stab, and that we shall not again be troubled with it.

A resolution this day passed for an absolute prohibition of all imported spirits, with some others, in my opinion, almost equally impolitic, and calculated to subject the eastern part of the State to the arbitrary impositions of the western. The prohibition of the single article of rum, would cut off a net revenue of eleven thousands pounds per annum. When the bill is brought in, I think they will find such insuperable difficulties in the mode of carrying into execution, as will oblige them to abandon the project.

I take the liberty of inclosing a copy of the resolutions upon the proposed Federal Government ; by which it will appear that the Assembly have given time for full examination and discussion of the subject, and have avoided giving any opinion of their own upon the subject. I beg to be presented to your lady and family, and am, with greatest respect and regard,

GEORGE MASON.

P. S.   A plan is before the House for a three years' instalment of all debts.   Though, in my opinion, very exceptionable, it is better than the plans of that kind heretofore proposed, and I believe will be adopted, in spite of every opposition that can be made to it.   I shall, therefore, instead of pointing the little opposition I can make against the whole, endeavour to change the plan, by making the consent of the creditor necessary, and the instalments voluntary, and, in such cases, giving the force of judgments to the instalment bonds.[1]

RICHMOND, November 27, 1787.

DEAR SIR :

I this morning received your favor of the fifteenth, and shall do myself the honor of communicating such of our proceedings as are important ; though very little business, of that kind, has yet been completed.   The Instalment Plan, after being presented to the committee of the whole house upon the state of the commonwealth, and some hours' debate upon the subject, has been postponed from time to time.   From the best information I can collect, I fear there is a majority for it ; I shall therefore, whenever the committee proceed upon the consideration, endeavor to substitute the Resolve, of which I enclose a copy, and upon which I wish to be favored with your sentiments.

The performance of the treaty with respect to British debts, has taken up three days of warm debate ; Mr. Henry, General Lawson and Meriwether Smith on one side, and Col. George Nicholas (who is improved into a very useful member) and myself on the other.   The yeas and nays were demanded upon these questions on this subject ; first upon an amendment proposed by Mr. Henry for suspending the operation until the treaty should be fully performed on the part of Great Britain, which was rejected by a majority of thirty-three ; secondly upon an amendment proposed by Mr. Ronald, tantamount to an instalment of British debts.   Knowing that instalments were calculated to please a strong party, we avoided going into the subject at large, and confined ourselves to the impropriety of installing British debts, before we could know the sense of the legislature upon a general instalment of all debts ; as any discrimination would be

[1] "Correspondence of the American Revolution," Sparks, vol. iv., p. 190.

a palpable infraction of the treaty. The amendment was rejected by a majority of twenty-two ; the main question was then put upon the resolve for repealing all laws which prevented the recovery of British debts, with a clause suspending the operation of the repeal until other States shall also pass laws to enable British subjects to recover debts, and carried by a majority of forty. A bill has been brought in in consequence of the said Resolve, once read and committed to a committee of the whole house on Friday next. Some of the most respectable characters in the house were nominated a committee to prepare the bill ; but Mr. C——n with the vanity so natural to a young man, took upon himself to draw without the other gentlemen having time to consider it, and has drawn it so very injudiciously, that in its present shape, it would infallibly be thrown out on the third reading. However we will take care to regenerate it in the committee, and I make no doubt of its passing the House of Delegates ; there will be a strong but I trust a fruitless opposition in the senate. As soon as the Treaty Bill is secured we will bring forward the Sequestration business ; £275,000 paper currency of the average value of about 14*d.* in the pound having been paid into the treasury, in discharge of British debts. In the discussion of this subject, I expect we shall see some long faces.

A bill for receiving tobacco in discharge of taxes will certainly pass ; it is in my opinion a foolish and injurious project ; as such it was opposed, but to no purpose. After finding their strength, the first step was to raise the last year's price of the James river tobacco ; we had then nothing left but to endeavor to bring up the price of our tobacco in proportion, in which we, with some difficulty succeeded, and got our tobacco fixed at 28*s.*, the James river tobacco having been previously settled at 30*s.*

Little progress has yet been made on the subject of revenue. I shall use my best endeavors to prevent the receipt of public securities of any kind in taxes (as the only effectual means of digging up speculation by the roots) and appropriating a good fund for purchasing them up at the market price. By way of experiment and to show the members the utility of such a plan, we have this day, against a strong opposition, ordered about £6,000 now in the treasury, to be immediately applied to that purpose ; which I hope will have a good effect upon the minds of the members. Yet I fear the interest of the speculators is too powerful, to suffer any regular extensive system upon this subject.

The bill for prohibiting the importation of spirits stands committed to a committee of the whole house, the day after to-morrow. Dr. Stuart tells me he has sent you one of the printed bills ; you will find it fraught with such absurdities as render it perfectly ridiculous, yet I much doubt their finding them out so as to amend the bill in the committee. The opposers ought to let them go on their own way, and reserve their attack to the passage on the third reading. As the bill now stands, according to the strict grammatical construction, spirits are subject to forfeiture after they have been swallowed, and the informer will be equally subject to the penalty with the persons he informs against. But besides the nonsense of the bill, the very principle of it is impolitic as it will affect our commerce and revenue ; partial and unjust in sacrificing the interest of one part of the community to the other. I am afraid this scrawl is hardly legible, being obliged as I am to write with bad spectacles, bad light and bad ink.

I beg my compliments to your lady, and the family at Mount Vernon, and am with the most sincere respect and esteem,

Dear Sir,

Your affectionate and obedient servant,

G. MASON.

The resolution enclosed, of which the writer asked Washington's opinion, is to the following effect :

" Resolved, that it is the opinion of this committee, in order to alleviate, as far as is consistent with justice, the present distresses of the people of this commonwealth, to prevent tedious and ruinous law-suits, and by making it their mutual interest to encourage and promote voluntary and amicable settlements and compositions between debtors and creditors, that the force of judgments ought to be given to all bonds on account of debts contracted or due before the   day of   1787, which shall be entered into within one year after the . day of   by the mutual consent of debtor and creditor, for the instalment of debts by annual payments, for any number of years not exceeding six years ; and that no appeal or replevin ought to be allowed upon the judgments or executions, which shall be obtained in virtue of such instalment bonds, when they respectively become due."[1]

Madison in a letter to Jefferson of the 9th of December makes the following allusions to the Liquor Bill and the Port Bill of this session. He says:

"I find Mr. Henry has carried a Resolution for *prohibiting* the importation of rum, brandy and other spirits, and, if I am not misinformed, all manufactured leather, hats and sundry other articles are included in the *prohibition*. Enormous duties at least, are likely to take place on the last and many other articles. A project of this sort, without the concurrence of the other States, is little short of madness. . . . Col. Mason made a regular and powerful attack on the Port Bill, but was left in a very small majority. I found at the last session that that regulation was not to be shaken, though it certainly owes its success less to its principal merits than to collateral and casual considerations."[2]

The port bill was amended, however, probably in accordance with Colonel Mason's views. George Mason returned to "Gunston Hall" on the 4th of February, and Washington wrote to Madison the following day, expressing his anxiety about the approaching Convention, the election of delegates being the absorbing topic just then. He says: "Many have asked me with anxious solicitude, if you did not mean to get into the Convention, conceiving it of indispensable importance. Colonel Mason who returned but yesterday, has I am told, offered himself for Stafford county and his friends say he can be elected, not only in that, but in the counties of Prince William and Fauquier also."[3] Here we see Madison and Mason were instinctively pitted against each other in Washington's thoughts, as leaders of the two parties in the approaching struggle. George Mason, on his side was anxious to secure Richard Henry Lee as an ally in the Convention. Arthur Lee who probably visited " Gunston

[1] Washington MSS., State Department.
[2] " Writings of Madison," vol. i., p. 364.
[3] " Writings of Washington," Sparks, vol. ix., p. 313.

Hall" at this time, wrote from Alexandria to his brother on the 19th of February :

"Col. Mason laments very much that you do not stand for the Convention. He says there will be no one in whom he can confide. That you will be regarded as having deserted a cause on which you have published your persuasion of its being of the last moment to your country. That this belief will be strengthened by a report which some of your friends have propagated, that you have given up all idea of opposing the constitution because your friends think differently, and have recommended two violent constitutionalists to the freeholders of Westmoreland. He is afraid these things will injure your character so much that should another General Convention be ordered you will not be among the delegates, which he shall consider a misfortune to the country. It is his opinion that the Convention will recommend another General Convention." [1]

The letters of the public men in Virginia at this time are full of speculations as to the probable complexion of the Convention, and the result anticipated was federal or antifederal according to the bias of the writer. Madison writing to Jefferson in December, represents "the body of the people in Virginia as favorable" to the Constitution. "What change," he adds, "may be produced by the united influence of Mr. Henry, Mr. Mason, and the Governor with some pretty able auxiliaries is uncertain." [2] Cyrus Griffin gave currency to some of the extravagant rumors of the day, when he wrote from New York, February 15th :

"Col. R. H. Lee and Mr. John Page, men of influence in Virginia, are relinquishing their opposition ; but what to us is very extraordinary and unexpected, we are told that Mr. George Mason has declared himself so great an enemy to the Constitution that he will heartily join Mr. Henry and others in promoting a Southern Confederacy." [3]

[1] Lee Papers, University of Virginia. (Quoted in "Life of E. Randolph," p. 99.)

[2] "Writings of Madison," vol. i., p. 364.

[3] Bancroft's "History of the Constitution," vol. ii., p. 461.

Again, in April, he speaks of the personal characteristics of the more eminent members of the opposition in the Convention, clearly showing to which side he leaned :

" In point of virtues and real abilities the federal members are much superior. Henry is mighty and powerful, but too interested ; Mason too passionate, the governor by nature timid and undecided, and Grayson too blustering." [1]

Randolph was still looked upon as an Antifederalist by the uninitiated. Madison, about the same time, writes of the opponent whom it is probable he most feared : " Colonel Mason is growing every day more bitter and outrageous in his efforts to carry his point, and will probably in the end be thrown by the violence of his passions into the politics of Mr. Henry." [2] Washington wrote to Lafayette in April, expressing a belief that the Convention would favor the adoption of the Constitution. He adds : " There will, however, be powerful and eloquent speeches on both sides of the question. . . . Henry and Mason are its great adversaries. The Governor, if he opposes it at all, will do it feebly." [3] The position of Edmund Randolph, still undefined to the public, was evidently no secret to Washington. George Mason's ally in the Convention of 1787 was to be his foe in the Convention of 1788, and already in April had given token of his tergiversation. Washington's influence in Fairfax County had doubtless contributed to the election there in March, of Federalists to the Convention. But Stafford County elected George Mason with Andrew Buchanan. The characteristic story is told of George Mason at this time, that " he was informed that if he opposed the ratification of the Federal Constitution the people of Alexandria would mob him, [when] he mounted his horse, rode to the town, and going up the court-house steps, said to the sheriff, ' Mr. Sheriff, will you make proclamation that George Mason

[1] *Ibid.*, p. 463.
[2] " Writings of Madison," vol. i., p. 388.
[3] " Writings of Washington," Sparks, vol. ix., p. 356.

will address the people ?' A crowd assembled, and Mason
addressed them, denouncing the Constitution with bitter
invective, after which he mounted his horse and returned
home."[1] One of the opposition delegates, from Loudoun
County, was George Mason's nephew, Stevens Thomson
Mason. His vote was always given to the Antifederalists,
though his youth and modesty prevented him from speaking
in the Convention.

Two letters of George Mason, written in April and May,
are all that remain to us of his correspondence at this
period. One of them is addressed to Robert Carter, of
"Nomini," and the other to John Francis Mercer, who had
been a delegate in the Federal Convention from Maryland,
and held similar views to Mason on the subject of the Constitution. He had taken charge of some law business for
Colonel Mason on the death of Thomas Stone, which event
occurred in Alexandria the previous October :

GUNSTON HALL, April 30th, 1788.

DEAR SIR :

This will be delivered you by my son John, who is going to
settle in Bordeaux, having lately entered into partnership with
two Maryland gentlemen (Messrs. Joseph and James Fenwick)
who about a year or two ago established a house there, the firm
of which has hitherto been Joseph Fenwick and Company.
Their capital will not be large (only about 1,000 sterling each),
and their plan is to give no credit, nor even advance more than
the value of effects in their hands for any man. This at the
same time that it will enable them to send out their correspondent's goods, upon better terms than those can, who buy upon
credit, will also be the most effectual means of rendering safe
whatever property their friends shall think fit to commit to their
charge. They are determined to examine themselves, into the
prices and quality of all the goods they send to America ; and as
wines, brandy, silks, cambrics, chintz, calicoes, and several other
articles may be purchased in France, of which Bordeaux is one
of the greatest trading towns, as cheap as in any part of Europe,

[1] J. Esten Cooke in *Magazine of American History*, May, 1884.

they hope to be able to give general satisfaction ; and there being no other American house in Bordeaux they flatter themselves with considerable encouragement and preference, from their own country, so long as they continue to deserve it.   They daily expect a ship of about 300 hhds. to load in Potomac river, upon consignment, to their address.   Any tobacco, clear of trash and sound, although not of extraordinary quality, will answer the French market ; but from the number of British and Irish smugglers who frequent Bordeaux, I have reason to believe that fine, stout, dark, waxy tobacco, of the best quality, will find as good a market there as in Europe.

If you can make it convenient to encourage the house, with a consignment of some of your tobacco, I am sure you will find from them the strictest justice ; and I hope their attention to their friends' interest, by rendering the correspondence mutually advantageous, will merit a continuation of your favors,

> I am, dear sir,
> Your most obedient servant,
> G. MASON.

Robert Carter, Esq.,
> Nominy,
> > Westmoreland County.

Per Mr. John Mason.[1]

VIRGINIA, GUNSTON HALL, May 1, 1788.

DEAR SIR :

Your favor of the 18th of April did not come to hand until to-day.   I am exceedingly obliged to you for the trouble you have taken to investigate the situation of my affair with Rutland.   Had my former counsel, Mr. Stone, taken half as much, it would have saved me a great deal of vexation, and probably much loss, which, I fear, by his neglect I shall now sustain.

I thoroughly agree with you in thinking Mr. James Little's debt, under the circumstances you mention, must have preference to mine, and that my case, so far as it is affected by that debt, is without remedy.   The only thing which could be done is what you have so kindly determined to do, to see that the sale is fairly conducted, that the value, as near as circumstances will admit, may be procured for that part of the property on which the fi: fa:

---

[1] MS. Letter.

was served for Mr. Little's debt, that my security may be as little [*word illegible*] by it as possible. I should be glad to know whether Rutland's new store, or warehouse and wharf (which I conceive the most valuable part of his improvements) are upon the part advertised to be sold for Mr. Little's debt. From Rutland's account of things, I am also inclined to suspect there has been some attempt made by him and Mr. Duvall, to subject my mortgaged property to some demand of the State against them. Upon reflecting on some past circumstances, I have some hopes that, upon examination it will appear that Mrs. Rutland was of age when she relinquished her right of dower, on the twenty-second of February, 1787. Mr. Rutland went to London with a shipload of tobacco in 1783, and I remember it was reported he was engaged to this lady some time before he left the country. However, if Mrs. Rutland was not of age at the the time she relinquished her right of dower, I hope she will be prevailed on to relinquish it now ; not only from motives of justice, as I gave Mr. Rutland the indulgence I did, upon the assurance of her relinquishment of dower, but because her relinquishment will do her no injury though it may benefit me ; for the land will be sold by virtue of Mr. Carroll's mortgage made before her marriage, which I presume will bar her claim of dower against the purchaser, and her pretension of dower as to my mortgage would have no other effect than injuring me, in causing the land to sell for less than its value. I think I have been informed that Mr. Rutland had a tract of land or two, particularly one in Montgomery, Frederick or Washington, at the time of my judgment against him, which Mr. Stone did not include in my mortgage, thinking the mortgaged premises sufficient without ; and if I remember right, there is a clause in the mortgage declaring, if they should prove insufficient, that I do not lose my remedy against any other part of his property. Those lands then, if he had such at the time, are still subject to my judgment, in whatsoever hands they may now be, and it may probably be a matter of importance to me ; as I very much fear that the incumbrances upon the mortgaged premises, which I knew nothing of, confiding entirely in Mr. Stone on the occasion, will fall short of securing my debt. I beg the favor of you, my dear sir, to inquire particularly in this matter, and I must also entreat you to push my attachment against Mr. Stephen West to as speedy decision as you can ; I presume Mr. West can have no defence to make but such as tends merely to delay.

I wish to know, as soon as you can conveniently inform me, whether you have got my papers from Mr. Stone's executors, particularly the state of the case in Ross's suit against me for a tract of the Ohio Company's land, and your opinion of the said suit. I think I gave you some memorandum also respecting the Ohio Company's title to a tract of land adjoining Fort Cumberland, called the Treasury of Walnut Bottom fraudulentiy granted by Governor Eden to one French, a creature of his.

From the returns I have seen of the elections here, I think the Convention of Virginia will be so equally divided, that no man can at present form a judgment of what may be the determination. The Federalists, as they improperly style themselves, talk of a considerable majority ; but it is notorious that many of them [*torn*] honor of their cause be it spoken, stick at no falsehood or [*torn*] to accomplish their purpose. As soon as any tolerably [*torn*] judgment can be formed of the politics of our Convention I will not fail to communicate them to you.

I beg my compliments to your lady, and am, with the most sincere esteem and regard, dear sir,

> Your affectionate friend and servant,
>
> G. MASON.

Col. John Francis Mercer,
     Annapolis, Maryland.[1]

Richard Henry Lee, from his home in Westmoreland, wrote to George Mason at this time, giving his views as to the course Virginia should pursue in the coming convention.

CHANTILLY, May 7, 1788.

DEAR SIR :

Your son delivered me the letter that you were pleased to write me on the 30th instant, and I have promoted his views, as far as it is in my power at present, by directing the tobacco I had intended to sell in the country, to be put on board his vessel. I am inclined to think, for the reasons assigned by him, that the

[1] MS. Letter.

French market will be as good a one, at least, as any that we can send to.

Give me leave now, dear sir, to make a few observations on the important business that will call you to Richmond next month. It seems pretty clear at present, that four other States, viz., North Carolina, New York, Rhode Island, and New Hampshire, will depend much upon Virginia for their determination on the Convention project of a new constitution ; therefore it becomes us to be very circumspect and careful about the conduct we pursue, as, on the one hand, every possible exertion of wisdom and firmness should be employed to prevent danger to civil liberty, so, on the other hand, the most watchful precaution should take place to prevent the foes of union, order, and good government, from succeeding so far as to prevent our acceptance of the good part of the plan proposed. I submit to you, sir, whether, to form a consistent union of conduct, it would not be well for six or eight leading friends to amendments to meet privately, and, having formed the best possible judgment of the members' sentiments from knowledge of the men, to see how far it may be safe to press either for modes of amendment or the extent of amendments, and to govern accordingly. But, certainly, the firmest stand should be made against the very arbitrary mode that has been pursued in some States, that is, to propose a question of absolute rejection or implicit admission. For though it is true that the Convention plan looks something like this, yet I think every temperate man must agree that neither the Convention, nor any set of men upon earth, have or had a right to insist upon such a question of extremity. To receive the good and reject the bad is too necessary and inherent a right to be parted with. As some subtle managers will be upon the Convention, I believe you will find entrapping questions proposed at first as a ground-work of proceeding, which will hamper, confine, and narrow all attempts to proper investigation or necessary amendment, and this will be done under the plausible pretext of losing all by attempting *any* change. I judge that it will be so here, because I observe a similar conduct has been pursued in other places, as in Maryland and Pennsylvania. I trust that such uncandid and dangerous stratagems will be opposed and prevented in the Convention of Virginia, and a thorough, particular, and careful examination be first made into all its parts as a previous requisite to the formation of any question upon it. During this process a tolerable judgment may be formed of the sentiments of the generality, and a clue furnished for forming successful propositions for amendment, as the candid friends to this system admit that amendments may be made to improve the plan, but say that these amendments ought to be made, and may be obtained from the new Congress without endangering a total loss of the proposed Constitution. I say that those who talk thus, if they are sincere, will not object to this plan which, as I propose it, is something like the proceeding of the Convention Parliament of 1688 ; in the form of ratification, insert plainly and strongly such amendments as can be agreed upon, and say, that the people of Virginia do claim, demand and insist upon these as their undoubted rights and liberties which they mean not to part with, and if these are not obtained and secured by the mode pointed out in the fifth article of the Convention plan, in two years after the meeting of the new Congress, that Virginia shall, in that case, be considered as disengaged from this ratification. Under this proposition a development will be made of the sincerity of those who advocate the new plan, the beneficial parts of it retained, and a just security given to civil liberty. In the fifth article it is stated that two-thirds of Congress may propose amendments, which, being approved by three-fourths of the legislatures, become parts of the Constitution. By this mode, the new Congress may obtain our amendments without risking the convulsion of conventions, and the friends of the plan will be gratified in what they say is necessary, the putting the government in motion, when, as they again say, amendments may and ought to be obtained. By this mode, too, in all probability, the undetermined States, may be brought to harmonize, and the formidable minorities, in the assenting States, may be quieted. By this friendly and reasonable accommodation, the perpetual distrust and opposition, that will inevitably follow the total adoption of the plan, from the State legislatures, may be happily prevented, and friendly united exertions take place. Much reflection has convinced me that this mode is the best that I have had an opportunity of cultivating. I have, therefore, taken the liberty of recommending it to your serious and patriotic attention ; in the formation of these amendments *localities* ought to be avoided as much as possible.

The danger of monopolized trade may be prevented by calling for the consent of three-fourths of the United States on regulations of trade. The trial by jury, in this State, to be insisted on, as it is used under our present government, and confining the supreme federal court to the jurisdiction of *law*, excluding *fact.* The Massachusetts amendments, except the second, and extending the seventh to foreigners as well as citizens of other States, appear to me to be very good, and for their adoption the aid of that powerful State may be secured. The freedom of the press is, by no means, sufficiently attended to by Massachusetts, nor have they remedied the want of responsibility by the impolitic combination of president and senate. It does appear to me, that, in the present temper of America, if the Massachusetts amendments, with those suggested by me, being added, and inserted in our ratification as before stated, we may easily agree, and I verily believe that the most essential good consequences would be the result.

Affectionately yours,

RICHARD HENRY LEE.

George Mason, Esq. :
Gunston Hall.[1]

A curious mention is made of George Mason in a letter of Samuel Adams to Richard Henry Lee, showing that he had been, apparently, defending Mason against the strictures of the Boston Federalists. Adams writes to his Virginia correspondent on the 3d of December, 1787, discussing the new Constitution, and he adds, in a postscript: " As I have thought it a piece of justice, I have ventured to say, that I had often heard from the best patriots from Virginia, that Mr. G. Mason was an early, active, and able advocate for the liberties of America."[2] There had been no opportunity for personal acquaintance between these two representative men of their sections, it would seem. Yet we can fancy they would have had much sympathy in

[1] " Life of R. H. Lee," vol. ii., p. 88. By Richard H. Lee.
[2] *Ibid.*, p. 130.

their tastes and convictions, for in the characteristics of independence, public spirit, and absence of personal ambition there is great resemblance between them. And on the political question of the hour, Samuel Adams and George Mason held the same just views, as to the distinction, as Adams phrased it, "between the *federal* powers vested in Congress and the *sovereign* authority belonging to the several States, which is the palladium of the private and personal rights of the citizens."

CHAPTER VII.

IN THE VIRGINIA CONVENTION.

1788.

Virginia had assembled in her Convention of 1788, a remarkable body of men, the flower of her statesmen, sages, patriots. It may fairly be affirmed that no other commonwealth on the continent could have called together as great an array of abilities. And yet Virginia had not exhausted her resources; Washington, Jefferson, Richard Henry Lee, were not included in this famous Convention. William Wirt, in his rhetorical manner, has given a characterization of the most conspicuous members. There were, among the younger generation Madison, Marshall, Monroe; there were "those sages of other days, Pendleton and Wythe; there was seen displayed the Spartan vigor and compactness of George Nicholas; and there shone the radiant genius and sensibility of Grayson; the Roman energy and the Attic wit of George Mason was there; and there also the classic taste and harmony of Edmund Randolph; 'the splendid conflagration' of the high-minded Innes; and the matchless eloquence of the immortal Henry." [1]

On the one side were ranged Madison, Marshall, Pendleton, George Nicholas, Innes, and Edmund Randolph; on the other George Mason, Patrick Henry, William Grayson, James Monroe, Benjamin Harrison, and John Tyler. "Conspicuous among those who opposed the ratification of the constitution," writes Flanders, "were Patrick Henry, George

[1] Wirt's "Life of Patrick Henry," p. 263.

Mason and William Grayson; a combination of eloquence, vigor, and genius, not often surpassed and seldom equalled."[1] Says George Ticknor Curtis in his account of the opposition to the Constitution in Virginia:

" The State was to feel, it is true, the almost overshadowing influence of Washington in favor of the new system . . . But it was to feel also the strenuous opposition of Patrick Henry, that great natural orator of the Revolution, whose influence over popular assemblies was enormous, and who added acuteness, subtility, and logic to the fierce sincerity of his unstudied harangues, and the not less strenuous or effective opposition of George Mason, who had little of the eloquence and passion of his renowned compatriot, but who was one of the most profound and able of all the American statesmen opposed to the Constitution, while he was inferior in general powers and resources to not more than two or three of those who framed and advocated it."[2]

William Grayson, the least known of the great trio in opposition, was from George Mason's neighborhood, and they were doubtless intimate personal friends. Grayson's home was in Dumfries, and on his untimely death, in 1790, he was buried in the family vault at " Belle Air," the seat of his brother, the Rev. Spence Grayson, rector of Dettingen parish, Prince William County, whose country place was near the county town. The Graysons, it is believed, were first or second cousins of James Monroe, whose father's Christian name was Spence.[3]

The Convention met in Richmond on the 2d of June, at the " public buildings," or old Capitol, and Edmund Pendle-

---

[1] "Chief Justices of the United States," vol. ii., p. 328.

[2] "Constitutional History of the United States," vol. i., p. 63.

[3] Mr. William Grayson Mann, whose maternal grandfather, Robert Carter, of "Sabine Hall," married William Grayson's only daughter, writes the author: " I have at different times during the last thirty-five years attempted to collect materials for writing the life of this truly great man, but in vain. No state papers or speeches in extenso survived the destruction by fire of the old family mansion at Dumfries, a few miles south of Mount Vernon, on the Potomac. Col. Grayson had studied law at the Inner Temple, where I have found the chambers he once occupied."

ton was elected president. A committee of privileges and elections being appointed, Benjamin Harrison was named chairman, and George Mason came second on the list of members. After some preliminary business Colonel Mason moved an adjournment, the Convention to meet the next day at the " New Academy on Schockoe Hill." This building, erected in 1786 for the promotion of the arts and sciences, was used also as a theatre. It was burned down later, and near it the new theatre was built, destroyed by fire in 1811, on the site of which now stands the Monumental Church. Here at the " New Academy " the Convention held their sessions after the first day, and their meetings were open to the public, visitors coming from all parts of the State to hear the important subject under discussion. And the assemblage was a most imposing one numerically. " It was," says Grigsby, " more than four times greater than the Convention which framed the Federal Constitution when that body was full, and it exceeded it, as it ordinarily was, more than six times." It consisted, as this writer adds, " of the public men of three generations." [1] The army, the judiciary, the planters of the State, were the three interests most prominent in the representation, and the old soldiers were generally in favor of the Constitution, as the habits of the army officer naturally lead him to approve of the strong arm in government, while the lawyer looks more to the questions of principle that are involved, and is more jealous of liberty. Of all this assemblage of more or less prominent figures there were four, says our historian, who attracted the attention of strangers before all the rest. Pendleton and Wythe, leaders among the Federalists, " with George Mason and Patrick Henry, were those first sought by the spectator, as in a convention, forty years later, were Madison, Monroe, Marshall, and Fayette." [2] George Mason and Patrick Henry had rooms at the *Swan*, a famous tavern on Broad Street, still standing, and they were often seen together walking arm in

[1] " History of the Virginia Federal Convention," p. 34. Hugh Blair Grigsby.
[2] *Ibid.*, note to p. 36.

arm on their way to the Convention. "George Mason was dressed in a full suit of black, and was remarkable for the urbanity and dignity with which he received and returned the courtesies of those who passed him." [1]

A question had been decided on the 2d of June, the first day of the Convention, of which we have an account in a contemporary newspaper, with the arguments of George Mason on the subject. This was, whether Robertson (with his assistants), to whom we are indebted for our reports of the Convention, should be employed by this assembly to take down their speeches. George Mason opposed it firstly as contrary to parliamentary usage, and secondly because he believed Robertson to be a Federal partisan and, therefore, not likely to do justice to the arguments of the opposition members. A correspondent of the Fredericksburg *Virginia Herald*, one of the interested throng of spectators in attendance on the Convention in Richmond, wrote June 2d :

" It was to-day agitated whether the short-hand gentlemen should be suffered to take down the business of the house for public information. Opposed by Henry, Mason, Grayson and White with success. Mr. Mason rested his opposition upon this ground, that these gentlemen were strangers—that it was an important trust for anyone—for not only the people at large might be misinformed, but a fatal stab might be given to a gentleman of the house from a perversion of his language—that it was a breach of privilege, and had been frequently determined so by the House of Commons ; that to show the member who moved the question, that his objections proceeded from those principles, and not from a wish to be again a member of another *Conclave*, he had given his voice for an adjournment to the Theatre, where, surrounded by his countrymen, he would endeavor to speak the language of his soul. Mr. Nicholas was up several times upon this subject, and had been the first mover of it, but at last relinquished it as not tenable." [2]

George Mason refers to this matter of the short-hand writer in one of his letters to his son to be given later. The

[1] *Ibid.*, p. 4 (note).   [2] *Maryland Journal*, June 10, 1788.

prejudice against reporters lingered long in the House of Commons, and was shared, it seems, by these eighteenth-century Americans.

On the 3d of June, after the resolution of Congress on the subject of the Constitution, the report of the Federal Convention, and the resolutions of the General Assembly were read, George Mason addressed the Convention. Grigsby pictures the scene :

" In an instant the insensible hum of the body was hushed, and the eyes of all were fixed upon him. How he appeared that day as he rose in that large assemblage, his once raven hair white as snow, his stalwart figure, attired in deep mourning, still erect, his black eyes fairly flashing forth the flame that burned in his bosom, the tones of his voice deliberate and full as when, in the first House of Delegates, he sought to sweep from the statute book those obliquities which marred the beauty of the young republic, or uttered that withering sarcasm which tinges his portrait by the hand of Jefferson, we have heard from the lips, and seen reflected from the moistened eyes, of trembling age. His reputation as the author of the Declaration of Rights and of the first Constitution of a free Commonwealth ; as the responsible director of some of the leading measures of general legislation during the war and after its close ; his position as a prominent member of the General Convention that framed the Constitution, which had been adopted under his solemn protest, and his well-known resolve to oppose the ratification with all his acknowledged abilities, were calculated to arrest attention. He was sixty-two years old, and had not been more than twelve years continuously in the public councils, but from his entrance into public life he was confessedly the first man in every assembly of which he was a member, though rarely seen on the floor except on great occasions. But the interest with which he was now watched was heightened by another cause. From his lips was anxiously awaited by all parties the programme of the war which was to be waged against the new system." [1]

There was a division among the Antifederalists as to the line of policy to be pursued. Patrick Henry considered that

[1] " History of the Virginia Federal Convention," p. 70.

the General Convention had usurped powers not bestowed upon them in overthrowing the Articles of Confederation, George Mason could not take this ground as he had been a member of the Convention and approved of the change, though he was not satisfied as to the final result. And he urged now a discussion of the Constitution, clause by clause, before any general previous question be put. He wished for a full and free investigation of the subject, since they sought to secure, "as far as possible, to the latest generation, the happiness and liberty of the people." [1] This mode of discussion proved eventually of great disservice to his own party, while it helped the Federalists. But as Grigsby says:

"The main object of Mason was to prevent a premature committal of the House by a vote on any separate part of the Constitution ; for he well knew that an approval of one part would be urged argumentatively to obtain the approval of another part, and that, if the Constitution were approved in detail, it would be approved as a whole ; and so far as his motion postponed immediate voting, it was wise and well-timed." [2]

Yet, to restrict the discussion of the general tendency of the Constitution and confine the debate to single clauses gave the Federalists an advantage, as the historian of the Convention points out. However, the Antifederalists, who were fully persuaded of the injurious scope of the whole instrument, were not to be restrained from dwelling upon this fact. Tyler, in the interests of the opposition, then moved that a committee of the whole Convention should take into consideration the proposed form of government. Madison signified his assent to this arrangement, and George Mason moved his resolution, which was agreed to by the Convention.

Thus was the plan of campaign laid down at the outset by the two protagonists of the Convention, Mason and Madison. They had waged a war of principle in the Federal Convention which had been merely adjourned, as to its final issue, to the soil of their native State. Though the

[1] Appendix iii.   [2] " History of the Virginia Federal Convention," p. 72.

party of Madison had been the victor in the former assemblage, yet was there a good prospect of the amendment party triumphing here.   Henry Lee, of Westmoreland, wished the discussion to begin immediately, but the other side was not to be hurried, as many of the members had not yet arrived, and both George Mason and Benjamin Harrison advocated an adjournment until the next day.   On the 4th of June the business properly commenced, the Convention resolving itself into a committee of the whole, George Wythe in the chair.   Nicholas, Henry, Randolph, and Mason were the four speakers on this day.   Edmund Randolph showed his colors, coming out unequivocally for the unamended Constitution, he who had a few months before in .the Federal Convention declared for amendments and a "Second General Convention."   Patrick Henry did not fall into line immediately with George Mason, but rather overstepped the mark, and his first exception to the Constitution was taken in somewhat free-lance fashion.   He took issue with the Federal Convention for changing the character of the government " to the utter annihilation of the most solemn engagements of the States."   There was a confederacy of nine States to be formed to the exclusion of the other four, and this new confederacy was to form a consolidated government.   Henry then made his famous objection to the phrase in the preamble, " We, the People," etc.[1]   That it was understood by the Federal Convention in any " consolidated " sense, or as other than a convenient style of expression for the people of the several States, may be most positively denied, or George Mason's jealous ear would have been offended, and his voice have been raised against it. Since neither Mason nor any other defender of the States in the Convention saw fit to oppose the use of this phrase, it is apparent that they were quite sure of its harmless nature. However, it was to be distorted, as Patrick Henry feared, from its obvious signification, and to be used by the party of consolidation for their own purposes at a later day.

[1] " Debates of the Virginia Convention," Robertson.

The first and second sections of the first article were under consideration. Randolph had spoken after Henry. " He was followed," says Grigsby, " by Mason, whose words were now watched with an interest hardly exceeded by that which existed when he first rose to address the house ; for he too had been a member of the General Convention, and had declared in that body that, on certain conditions, none of which included the words of the preamble, he would approve the Constitution ; but though no parliamentarian, he saw the snare into which his opponents were anxious that he should fall, and adroitly avoided it by taking ground which placed him in instant communion with Henry." [1] He maintained that the clause in the second section, "giving the first hint of the general government laying direct taxes," changed the union into a "national government." He urged with great force the danger of leaving the manner of levying taxes to those who, in the nature of things, cannot be acquainted with the situation of those on whom they are to impose them, when it can be done by those who are well acquainted with it. He thought the general government should have " the power of demanding their quotas of the States, with an alternative of laying direct taxes in case of non-compliance." The same sum raised in one way, as he declared, would be very oppressive raised in another way. The second objection made by Colonel Mason was directed against that part of the same section which dealt with representation. He did not think it a full and free representation. The Constitution did not expressly provide one representative for every thirty thousand, but it states : " the number of representatives shall not *exceed* one for every 30,000." So it might be reduced without violating the letter of the law. Colonel Mason concluded with reiterating his objection to the taxing power given Congress. With this feature amended, this part of the Constitution would receive his sanction, but he regarded it as a *sine qua non.*[2] Madison closed the debate with a few remarks, reserving a fuller reply to a future occa-

[1] " History of the Virginia Federal Convention," p. 92.   [2] Appendix iii.

sion. George Mason does not seem to have spoken in the
Federal Convention against giving Congress the power of
direct taxation. He had there urged the clause against
taxing exports, and further reflection had evidently impressed him with the conviction that the power of Congress
should be limited, in this matter of revenue, to the duties
on imposts, as explained in the fourth amendment of the
Virginia Convention. Madison on the evening of the 4th of
June wrote an account of the Convention proceedings to
Washington, which the latter in turn retailed to John Jay a
few days later. It is evident the course taken by Edmund
Randolph had greatly elated the Federalists. Madison
writes disparagingly of his antagonists, Henry and Mason,
accusing them of making "a lame figure" in the recent
debate. Still he is by no means confident of the result.
" Kentucky . . . is supposed to be generally adverse, and
every kind of address is going on privately to work on the
local interests and prejudices of that and other quarters." [1]
There were fourteen representatives in the Convention from
the district of Kentucky.

Unlike the Federal Convention, which held secret sessions, the Virginia Convention, as has been said, was open
to the public, and was attended by large crowds of citizens,
who gave the most eager attention to all that was said. It
is to be regretted that there were not some fluent scribes
among these spectators, to write down their impressions of
the scenes they witnessed, and to preserve for posterity a
record of the logic and eloquence there manifested. The
reports of Robertson, as will appear, were not wholly to be
relied on. And the Federalist Madison writing under the
excitement of the contest was certainly not to be trusted
in his estimate of the Antifederalist champions opposed to
him. But with the debates before us, as they have come
down to our generation, there seems no cause for the Federalists to take any credit to themselves, up to this point of
time. George Nicholas had advocated the system of repre-

[1] " Writings of Washington," Sparks, vol. ix., p. 370 (note) and p. 373.

sentation, but the ambiguity remained unanswerable, in the wording of the provision. Edmund Randolph could only put forth in his defence of the Constitution—and of himself —the poor plea of expediency. To the three or four tangible objections made by the opposition to the first part of the Constitution there was as yet no answer given.

From the 4th of June to the 13th, though still nominally employed upon the first and second sections of the first article, the Convention in fact diverged widely from the point, and discussed the Constitution at large. The great speech of the 5th of June was made by Patrick Henry in answer to Pendleton and General Henry Lee. He brought forward new objections. " How does your trial by jury stand ? In civil cases gone—not sufficiently secured in criminal." He thought also that the militia should not be in the hands of Congress. And he dwelt upon the folly of looking for subsequent amendments when it was in their power to insist upon them beforehand. He quoted from the Virginia Bill of Rights, the third article, on the right of the people to reform or abolish their government ; the fifth article, on taxation ; the sixth article, requiring the consent of the people to suspend the laws ; and showed how each was endangered by the new Constitution. One phrase here is prophetic : " When the people of Virginia at a future day shall wish to alter their government, though they should be unanimous in this desire, yet they may be prevented therefrom by a despicable minority at the extremity of the United States." He objected to giving Congress the control of the custom-houses, and also to the inadequate representation of the people in that body. Like the other Southern patriots, Henry believed that the South would eventually be numerically stronger than the North, a pathetic illusion as was too soon made apparent. The whole scheme of the government Henry thought too extravagant, and the President, with " the powers of a king," at the head of the army might eventually overthrow American liberties. Another specific objection advanced by Henry was the control given to Con-

gress over the time, place, and manner of elections.   Again
he denounced the clause concerning the publication of the
journals " from time to time " only.   Without the obligation
to publish their proceedings, they would be without public
responsibility.   " The Senate, by making treaties, may destroy your liberty and laws for want of responsibility."
Jay's treaty, a few years later, seemed to many, just such a
case as was here anticipated.   Stevens Thomson Mason,
who was with Henry now in the Convention, mindful of this
doctrine of responsibility, which his uncle had also enforced
in the Federal Convention, was the senator, it will be
remembered, who gave Jay's treaty to the public prints in
1795.   Patrick Henry concluded his powerful speech by
beseeching the Convention not to hurry Virginia into an
acceptance of the proposed government simply because
eight States had adopted it.   They should insist upon its
being amended, and not fear this bugbear of anarchy that
was suggested.   Pennsylvania he thought had been "tricked"
into adopting the Constitution.   " If the other States who
have adopted it have not been tricked, still they were too
much hurried into its adoption.   There were very respectable minorities in several of them, and if reports be true, a
clear majority of the people are averse to it.   If we also
accede, and it should prove grievous, the peace and prosperity of our country [Virginia], which we all love, will be
destroyed." [1]   Edmund Randolph made the opening argument on the following day.   He referred to a portion of
George Mason's speech in these words : " It is objected by
the honorable gentleman over the way, that a republican
government is impracticable in an extensive territory, and
the extent of the United States is urged as a reason for the
rejection of this Constitution."   And he contended that if
the laws were wisely made and executed, the extent of the
country would be no bar to the adoption of a " good government."   For the definition of a good government, however, the factor of territory must be taken into account,

[1] " Debates of the Virginia Convention," Robertson, p. 55.

George Mason contended.   A monarchy, though repugnant
to the genius of America, might be a good government under
certain conditions.   A republic, to be a good government,
must be small, and a union of republics should be of a
marked federal character to make it secure of retaining its
freedom.   There was, of course, no exact prototype of the
government now proposed, by which the fathers could be
guided.   And the Constitution had its national as well as
federal features.   But Edmund Randolph had objected just
as strongly as George Mason to the "national" theories of
Hamilton in the Federal Convention, and it was to bring
back the Constitution from its deflections out of the orbit
originally designed for it that amendments were sought for.
Edmund Randolph in this speech animadverted severely
upon the legislation of Virginia, meaning that his reflections
should hit Mason and Henry, who had been prominent as
its law-makers.   George Mason had drafted the first land
law, and Randolph refers to complaints on this point.

Madison and George Nicholas were the other speakers at
this time.   Madison at the close of his argument showed how
little he favored consolidation, though he supported a system which came so dangerously near it.   He said of the new
Constitution : " I believe its tendency will be, that the State
governments will counteract the general interest, and ultimately prevail." [1]   His was indeed a short-sighted political
wisdom, as he lived to discern.   Francis Corbin, the young
member of the legislature of whom George Mason makes
indulgent mention in his letter from the Assembly given in
the last chapter, answered Patrick Henry.   But in spite of
Corbin's compliments to the " declamatory talents " of the
great orator, Henry appears not to have considered him a
foeman quite worthy of his steel.   And then, too, Patrick
Henry wished to make the two-sided governor declare himself at large, that the opportunity for reprisals might be more
complete.   Lord Chesterfield amused himself with a paragraph that appeared in one of the London papers relating to

[1] *Ibid.*, p. 78.

the health of Charles Townshend, who was proverbial for his fickle changes of party: " The Right Honorable Charles Townshend has been indisposed of a pain in his side, but it is not stated in which side." His Excellency, Governor Randolph had left the world equally in doubt as to "which side" must be understood as that of his intimate convictions, in the struggle going on. Patrick Henry now asked him to continue his observations as he wished to hear all that could be said in defence of a system he [Henry] found so defective. Randolph responded to the invitation, and in the course of his remarks, while on the subject of direct taxation, he argued against the "expedient, proposed by a gentleman whom I do not now see in the house [Mr. George Mason] . . . that this power shall be only given to the general government, as an alternative after requisitions shall have been refused." And again he replied to George Mason, to whom he ascribed the observation, " that there could not be a fellow-feeling between the national representatives and their constituents, and that oppression must be inseparable from their exercise of the power of imposing taxes." Madison followed Randolph, with a long speech, making quotations of which Robertson gives only the substance, a plan which he follows with a part of the speech itself. Henry closed the debate with a comprehensive reply to the arguments of the Federalists, and he took occasion to remind " His Excellency " of his former expressions of opinion. He indulged in a little excusable irony, and caught up an incautious word of Randolph's on which he dilated, much to his victim's discomfiture. Patrick Henry concluded his speech with an ultimatum, under three heads, as "indispensably necessary ": a bill of rights ; a " general positive provision securing to the States and the people, every right which was not conceded to the general government; and that every implication should be done away." [1]

The first week of the Convention had closed with Patrick Henry's speech of Saturday. On Monday the 9th of June,

[1] *Ibid.*, p. 114.

" Henry and Mason, who had, according to their usual habit, walked arm in arm from the Swan, were seen to pause a few moments at the steps of the Academy, evidently engaged in consultation, and with difficulty made their way to their seats in the house." [1] The crowd of spectators had increased and filled the floor and galleries to overflowing. Henry rose to conclude his unfinished argument. He brought forward a subject of great interest to all present, the question of the Mississippi navigation. Seven States, or the whole North, as he said, were willing to relinquish this river which it was to the interest of the six Southern States to retain, and under the new government the South would be likely to lose it. He reviewed the several dangers to which it was asserted Virginia would be liable if she did not accept the Constitution, and showed the fallacy of these assumptions. And he expatiated afresh on the objections against it already advanced. General Henry Lee was the next speaker, and after him came the irate governor. The latter poured out the vials of his wrath on Patrick Henry, and read a portion of his public letter (objecting to the Constitution), to prove that he had not been inconsistent. There was then a little scene which must have caused a good deal of excitement in the Convention. After Patrick Henry had disavowed any intention of giving offence, Edmund Randolph made answer, that but for this concession " he would have made some men's hair stand on end by the disclosure of certain facts." Henry asked him to speak if he had anything to disclose, but Randolph made no reply to this challenge, and proceeded further in his own justification, throwing down his letter on the clerk's table to lie there " for the inspection of the curious and malicious." He continued his argument, after this ebullition, and concluded it on the following day. Monroe, Marshall, Harrison, and Nicholas were the other speakers on the 10th, and the ball of debate was tossed back and forth, each side reiterating arguments and making citations to strengthen its position. Benjamin Harrison was one of the

---

[1] " History of the Virginia Federal Convention," p. 151.

amendment party, but he only spoke in the Convention on this one occasion, when he ably seconded the position of Mason and Henry.

It will be seen from Edmund Randolph's remark in his speech on Saturday, the 7th, that George Mason was not at that time in the Convention. It is not unreasonable to suppose that his absence from his seat on this day had some connection with the arrival in Richmond of Colonel Oswald, of Philadelphia, who brought pamphlets and letters from the "Federal Republican Society" in New York to the leaders of the opposition in the Virginia Convention. Madison reported the news of this portentous event in a letter on Monday to his friend and ally, Alexander Hamilton, the leader of the Federalists in New York: "Oswald of Philadelphia came here on Saturday, and has closet interviews with the leaders of the opposition."[1] On the same day Patrick Henry, William Grayson, and George Mason all wrote letters to General John Lamb, Chairman of the New York Society, to send back by Colonel Oswald. The Antifederalists had not been dilatory in their work of opposition. They had already formulated in their committee, of which Colonel Mason was chairman, a bill of rights, and some of the amendments they meant to bring forward in the Convention. Patrick Henry wrote to Lamb that four fifths of the people in Virginia were opposed to the Constitution, and south of the James River nine tenths: "And yet, strange as it may seem, the numbers in Convention appear equal on both sides, so that the majority, which way soever it goes, will be small. The friends and seekers of power have with their usual subtlety wriggled themselves into the choice of the people." In regard to General Lamb's proposition that they should form in Virginia a society like the one in New York, Henry adds:

"If they [the Federalists] shall carry their point and preclude previous amendments, which we have ready to offer, it will be-

---

[1] "Works of Hamilton," John C. Hamilton, vol. i., p. 456.

come highly necessary to form the society you mention. . . . Col. George Mason has agreed to act as chairman of our republican society. His character I need not describe. He is every way fit ; and we have concluded to send you by Col. Oswald a copy of the bill of rights, and of the particular amendments we intend to propose in our Convention." [1]

William Grayson acknowledges the letter sent him by Colonel Oswald, and says he laid it the same evening before the "Committee of Opposition," and they had "directed their chairman to answer it by Colonel Oswald. Some of our proposed amendments," he adds, "are finished in the Committee; the others will be forwarded as soon as agreed on." He speaks of their affairs as suspended by a hair, and that "seven or eight dubious characters, whose opinions are not known," will by their decisions decide the important question.[2] The following is George Mason's letter to General Lamb:

RICHMOND, June 9th, 1788.

SIR :

I have had the honor to receive your letter dated the 18th of May, in behalf of the Federal Republican Committee of New York, upon the subject of the government proposed by the late Convention to the respective States for their adoption, and have communicated it to several respectable gentlemen of the Convention now met in this city, who are opposed to the adoption without previous amendments. They receive with pleasure the proposition of your Committee for a free correspondence on the subject of amendments, and have requested me to transmit to your Committee such as we have agreed on as necessary for previous adoption.

Although there is a general concurrence in the Convention of this State that amendments are necessary, yet the members are so equally divided with respect to the time and manner of obtaining them, that it cannot now be ascertained whether the majority will be on our side or not ; if it should be so I have no doubt but that an official communication will immediately take place between the Conventions of this State and yours.

[1] "Life and Times of General Lamb." Isaac Q. Leake, p. 306.   [2] *Ibid.*

As the amendments proposed by the Convention of Massachusetts are the first which have been offered to the public, and contain in them many things that are necessary, it is deemed proper to make them the basis of such as may finally be agreed on ; and it may also be proper to observe that an Executive Council will be necessary, because power and responsibility are two things essential to a good executive, the first of which cannot be safely given, nor the latter insured where the legislative senate form a part of the Executive. The judiciary, the exclusive legislative power over the ten miles square, and the militia are subjects to which our attention will next be turned, and we shall communicate the result of our deliberations with all possible despatch.

The nature of the opposition here is such that it has not yet taken any particular form, being composed only of members of the Convention who meet to prepare such amendments as they deem necessary to be offered to the Convention. If it should hereafter become necessary to assume one, it is hoped that system and order will everywhere appear suitable to the importance and dignity of the cause. In the meantime it is recommended to communicate with you, under cover to Capt. Jacob Reed, Junr., of Queen street, New York, in order to prevent any interruption that curiosity might give. We approve of the precaution, and also advise that Mr. George Fleming, merchant of this city, be made the instrument of safe conveyance on your part.

I have the honor to be, Sir,
  Your most obedient and humble servant,
           G. MASON.
Honorable John Lamb, Esq :
  Chairman of the Federal Republican Committee
   in New York.[1]

From the 4th to the 11th of June, George Mason's voice was not heard in the Convention, but he had been busy in the Committee of Opposition, preparing the bill of rights and amendments. He had left it to Patrick Henry to speak for the cause while he was occupied in writing for it. On the 11th, which was Wednesday, he rose after Madison and

---

[1] Lamb Papers, New York Historical Society.

made a long and careful reply to the arguments of the Federalists. Grigsby says here in allusion to the circumstance that Mason succeeded Madison :

"It has been remarked by one of the most celebrated orators of the present age, that it is an advantage to a speaker of the first order of ability, and to such only, to succeed the delivery of a first-rate speech, that the attention of the audience is fixed firmly on the subject in debate, and that there is a craving for a reply. In this respect, Mason could not have been more fortunate, and in another not less so ; for the speech which had just been delivered was addressed to the reason and not to the passions of the House, and the eminent perfection of Mason rested on his logical power, in his knowledge of the British polity, and in his experience as a statesman." [1]

He remarked first on the propriety at the present juncture of discussing the Constitution at large instead of confining the debate to a single clause. He maintained that the case of Great Britain's representation, as cited by George Nicholas, was not applicable to the United States. Yet, he asked, in what respect was the American system superior as Nicholas declared, when Great Britain with a territory ten times smaller had 550 members in Parliament, while the United States had but 65 in Congress? He spoke of the ineffectiveness of the clause restraining members of Congress from holding office. There is a hiatus in the report of Mason's speech here, as Robertson says he spoke too low to be heard. He is found, however, soon after, to be dwelling upon the "unconditional power of taxation" given to the government, and fortifying his argument against it by examples of its power for evil. He then read a letter of Robert Morris to show the sort of taxes that were already in agitation. The next point made was the need for a bill of rights, as a check to the general government and a safeguard to the people of the State, threatened in their reserved powers by the second clause of the sixth article. George

[1] "History of the Virginia Federal Convention," p. 188.

Mason in speaking of the small representation of Virginia in Congress, while advocating the democratic, as opposed to the aristocratic theory of representative government, made an allusion to the famous phrase of John Adams. He said the ten members from Virginia would be chosen, " if not wholly, yet mostly from the higher order of the people, from the great, the wealthy, the *well-born*—the *well-born*, Mr. Chairman, that aristocratic idol, that flattering idea, that *exotic* plant which has been lately imported from the ports of Great Britain, and planted in the luxuriant soil of this country." John Adams while in England had written and published the first volume of his " Defence of the American Constitutions," against the strictures of Turgot. The book came out during the session of the Federal Convention, and was much read by the members, and was believed to have influenced them in favor of a strong central government. In the preface and in the conclusion, he seemed to advocate a more aristocratic government than suited the romantic republicanism of the American patriots of the day.

George Mason then referred to a statement made by Nicholas in regard to the increase of representation :

" The worthy gentleman says that the number must be increased, because representation and taxation are in proportion, and that one cannot be increased without increasing the other, nor decreased without decreasing the other. Let us examine the weight of this argument. If the proportion of each State equally and ratably diminishes, the words of the Constitution [one for every 30,000] will be as much satisfied as if it had been increased in the same manner, without any reduction of the taxes. Let us illustrate it familiarly. Virginia has ten representatives ; Maryland has six. Virginia will have to pay a sum in proportion greater than Maryland, as ten to six. Suppose Virginia reduced to five and Maryland to three. The relative proportion of money, paid by each, will be the same as before ; and yet the honorable gentleman said, that if this did not convince us, he would give up. I am one of those unhappy men who cannot be amused with assertions. A man from the dead might frighten me ; but I am sure that he could not convince me without using better arguments than I have yet heard. The same gentleman showed us that though the Northern States had a most decided majority against us, yet the increase of population among us would, in the course of years, change it in our favor. *A very sound argument indeed, that we should cheerfully burn ourselves to death in hopes of a joyful and happy resurrection!*

In the course of his remarks, after picturing Holland with its free institutions in contrast to Spain in her poverty, he added : " They tell us, that if we be powerful and respectable abroad, we shall have liberty and happiness at home. Let us secure that liberty, that happiness first, and we shall then be respectable." Then followed another caustic observation, one of those touches of ironic humor for which the speaker was famous :

" I have some acquaintance with a great many characters who favor this government, their connections, their conduct, their political principles, and a number of other circumstances. There are a great many wise and good men among them. But when I look round the number of my acquaintance in Virginia, the country wherein I was born, and have lived so many years, and observe who are the warmest and the most zealous friends to this new government, it makes me think of the story of the cat transformed into a fine lady—forgetting her transformation—and happening to see a rat, she could not restrain herself, but sprang upon it out of the chair."

Of the desirableness of a general government there was no doubt, George Mason continued. But, he added :

" I hope that it is not to the name, but to the blessings of union that we are attached. . . . The security of our liberty and happiness is the object we ought to have in view in wishing to establish the union. If instead of securing these, we endanger them, the name of union will be but a trivial consolation."

Difficulties with Maryland about the Potomac, the western lands of Virginia, the magnitude of her debts, were pleas put forward by Edmund Randolph as reasons for joining the new government. Of the first, George Mason said he could speak with authority, having been one of the commissioners to form a compact with Maryland, and he knew of no cause of alarm there. As to the second, he believed, if the Constitution were to be adopted without amendments, the Indiana Company would drive out the settlers between the Alleghany and Blue Ridge, though their rights and title had been confirmed by the Virginia Assembly. George Mason proved to be a prophet here, as to the action of the Indiana Company, as they brought suit against Virginia in the federal court, after the adoption of the Constitution. Of the third plea, Mason said: " And shall we, because involved in debts, take less care of our rights and liberties? Shall we abandon them, because we owe money which we cannot immediately pay? Will this system enable us to pay our debts and lessen our difficulties? Perhaps the new government possesses some secret, some powerful means of turning everything to gold. It has been called by one gentleman the philosopher's stone. The comparison was a pointed one, at least in this, that, on the subject of producing gold they will be both equally delusive and fallacious." Colonel Mason then proceeded to give Randolph a home thrust on the subject of his change of front:

" My honorable colleague in the late Convention seems to raise phantoms, and to show a singular skill in exorcisms, to terrify and compel us to take the new government, with all its sins and dangers. I know that he once saw as great danger in it as I do. What has happened since to alter his opinion? If anything, I know it not. But the Virginia legislature has occasioned it, by postponing the matter. The Convention had met in June, instead of March or April. The liberty or misery of millions yet unborn are deeply concerned in our decision. When this is the case, I cannot imagine that the short period between the last of September and first of June ought to make any difference." [1]

[1] Appendix iii.

Grigsby explains the story of the cat and the fine lady as having reference to a class of men in Virginia favorable to the new Constitution, who had been disaffected throughout the Revolution, who had "hung on the rear of the friends of freedom, and sought to obstruct their progress when they could effect their object safely and without suspicion." From their high positions and wide family connections it was difficult to assail·them, yet Mason had the courage to denounce their course.

Henry Lee of Westmoreland, a gallant and skilful soldier, but no match for George Mason in statesmanship, censured "the honorable gentleman last up" for his endeavor "to draw our attention from the merits of the question, by jocose observations and satirical allusions." Grigsby thinks it evident from Lee's remarks, that the story of the cat was "not the only piece of fun with which Mason relieved one of his ablest arguments," but, he adds, "there is not a shadow of humor in any other part of the reported speech" [?]. But to continue General Lee's remarks: "He [Mason] ought to know that ridicule is not the test of truth. Does he imagine that he that can raise the loudest laugh is the soundest reasoner? Sir, the judgments and not the risibility of gentlemen are to be consulted." He also found fault with Mason for showing the letter of Robert Morris, whose proposed scheme of taxation he professed to consider as merely the opinion of a private gentleman, though Morris was the financial agent of Congress. But the same principle," he added, "has also governed the gentleman when he mentions the expressions of another private gentleman— *the well-born*—that our federal representatives are to be chosen from the higher orders of the people—from the *well-born*. Is there a single expression like this in the Constitution? . . . This insinuation is totally unwarrantable. Is it proper that the Constitution should be thus attacked with the opinions of every private gentleman? I hope we shall have no more of such groundless assertions. Raising a laugh, sir, will not prove the merits, nor expose the defects of this system " [1] Evidently the Convention had shown its appreciation of Mason's shafts of satire. And they must in turn have been amused by this solemn rebuke of his levity administered to such a master of sound reasoning as George Mason.

William Grayson made his first speech in the Convention at this time, concluding his argument on the following day, and his voice was a great accession to the strength of the opposition. He too ridiculed the imaginary dangers suggested by Edmund Randolph as the alternative of rejection. And he saw evils in a Constitution where the executive was "fettered in some parts, and as unlimited in others as a Roman dictator," and where there was "an inequality of representation and want of responsibility" in the legislature. Grayson thought, with Mason and Henry, that the power of direct taxation should remain with the States: "Give up this and you give up everything, as it is the highest act of sovereignty; surrender up this inestimable jewel, and you throw a pearl away richer than all your tribe." And he made the prophecy that "this government will operate as a faction of seven States to oppress the rest of the Union." In the further consideration of this subject Grayson said:

"An observation came from an honorable gentleman (Mr. Mason) when speaking of the propriety of the general government exercising this power, that according to the rules and doctrine of representation, the thing was entirely impracticable. I agreed with him in sentiments. I waited to hear the answer from the admirers of the new Constitution. What was the answer? Gentlemen were obliged to give up the point with respect to general uniform taxes. They have the candor to acknowledge that taxes on slaves would not affect the Eastern States, and that taxes on fish or pot-ash would not affect the Southern States. They are then reduced to this dilemma. In order to support this part of the system, they are obliged to controvert the first maxims of representation. The best writers on this subject, lay it down as a fundamental principle, that he who lays a tax, should bear his proportion of paying it."

[1] " Debates of the Virginia Convention, ' Robertson, p. 197.

The other speakers on the 12th were Pendleton and Madison for the Constitution and Henry in reply. The latter said of taxation : " This government subjects everything to the Northern majority. Is there not then a settled purpose to check the Southern interest ? We thus put unbounded power over our property in hands not having a common interest with us." The navigation of the Mississippi was made the theme of discussion for the following day. And General Lee, Monroe, Grayson, Henry, Nicholas, Randolph, and Corbin all spoke. Mr. Corbin had scarcely commenced his speech, however, when a violent storm arose which compelled him to close abruptly, and the Convention then adjourned for the day.' The subject of debate on the 13th was one of great interest, as it affected Virginia and the whole South, and as a result of the eloquence and reasoning of the Antifederalists, on the danger of losing the Mississippi, ten out of the fourteen delegates to the Convention from Kentucky voted with the opposition.' Theodoric Bland, one of the Antifederalists, wrote on this day to Arthur Lee, giving an account of the position of parties and of the progress of the discussion. Bland was a personal friend of George Mason's and there was some correspondence between them, doubtless, of which there remains now no record. In one of George Mason's letters written in 1791, he alludes to the death of his " worthy friend, Col. Bland." The following extracts from Theodoric Bland's letter to Lee express the sentiments of the Antifederalists at this juncture :

" RICHMOND, June 13th, 1788.

" DEAR ARTHUR,—I was yesterday favored with yours, and assure you I am in doubt whether the pleasure or the pain on the subject of your congratulation, affects me at this time most heavily. On the one hand I see my country on the point of embarking and launching into a troubled ocean, without chart or compass to direct her ; one half of her crew hoisting sail for the land of *energy*, and the other looking with a longing aspect on the

---

[1] *Ibid.*, p. 260.   [2] " History of the Virginia Federal Convention," p. 247.

shore of *liberty*. I have but one ray of hope, and that arises from an observation that they are yet in perfectly good humour with each other. I have as yet sat as a speechless spectator, nor shall I be induced to alter that character but as a mediator, and with a view of concentrating the two parties now (after twelve days' session) almost equally divided ; each side boasting by turns of a majority of from 3 to 8, on the general question, of adopting or rejecting, although I really at this time think there is a decided majority for anterior amendments, that is who do not think it prudent to mount a high-blooded, fiery steed, without a bridle. The amendments which will be proposed will contain simple propositions guarding the rights of the States, &c. . . . The strongest efforts are made here to inculcate the absolute necessity of posterior amendments, or unconditional submission, for fear of losing, as it is called, the government, and strong dispositions are shown to precipitate the Convention into that measure, but hitherto the fear of miscarrying altogether, has restrained the gentlemen on the side of the new Constitution.

" We object not against any powers which shall not be hurtful. That the government shall want no aids for its own support or execution, provided that such restraints shall be imposed upon it as shall support and ensure the State privileges, and the liberty of the individual against oppression. We have yet proceeded no farther in the discussion than the article of direct taxation, on which point they have collected all their force, and I think they have left hitherto the advantage considerably on our side."

Colonel Bland then tells of a duel that had just taken place in Richmond, but the principals were not members of the Convention. He adds :

" I mention this to show you that the heats have not yet entered that body, although the thunders roll, and the lightnings flash every day, both in the natural and political atmosphere. [There had been danger of a duel, however, between Henry and Randolph.] Our chief-magistrate has at length taken his party, and appears to be reprobated by the honest of both sides, but this is too precious a morsel to be left out. Although lukewarm, he has openly declared for posterior amendments, or in other words, unconditional submission." [1]

On the evening of the 13th Madison wrote his version of affairs to Washington, from the standpoint of federalism.

" Appearances at present are less favorable than at the date of my last. Our progress is slow, and every advantage is taken of the delay to work on the local prejudices of particular sets of members. British debts, the Indiana claim, and the Mississippi are the principal topics of private discussion and intrigue, as well as of public declamation. . . . The business is in the most ticklish state that can be imagined. . . . Oswald of Philadelphia has been here with letters for the anti-federal leaders from New York, and probably Philadelphia. He staid a very short time here during which he was occasionally closeted with H–y, M–s–n, &c." [2]

On the 14th of June the president was ill and unable to attend the Convention, and John Tyler, an Antifederalist, was unanimously elected vice-president to preside during the inability of the executive officer. The subject of the Mississippi was postponed, the Convention deciding to discuss the Constitution clause by clause. But William Grayson had something to say on the question of the great river before the matter was dropped. He thought its possession deeply concerned the Southern States. Without it there could be no expansion westward. And he reiterated his argument as to the " national contest "—that is, whether one part of the continent should govern the other. " The Northern States have the majority and will endeavor to retain it. This is therefore a contest for dominion, for empire. I apprehend that God and nature have intended, from the extent of territory and fertility of soil, that the weight of population should be on this side of the continent. At present, for various reasons, it is on the other side." [3] The

[1] " Life of Arthur Lee," Richard H. Lee, vol. ii., p. 337.
[2] " Writings of Madison," vol. i., p. 399.
[3] " Debates of the Virginia Convention," Roberston.

third, fourth, fifth, sixth, and seventh sections of the first article were read and commented on, Tyler, Monroe, Henry, and Grayson urging objections; Randolph, Nicholas, and Madison making reply. After the reading of the eighth section George Mason made a speech on the power of Congress over the militia. He wished " such an amendment as this—that the militia of any State should not be marched beyond the limits of the adjoining State; and if it be necessary to draw them from one end of the continent to the other, I wish such a check as the consent of the State legislature to be provided." He was averse to a standing army, and thought the militia the safeguard of the state. Congress was to have the power to arm and organize the militia, but they might neglect to do this, and Colonel Mason wished that there should be an express declaration that the State governments might arm and discipline them, in case the general government neglected this duty. He also thought the militia should never be subject to martial law but in time of war.[1] The discussion of this subject was continued by Madison, Henry, C. Clay, Nicholas, and Randolph. George Mason, after reading to the Convention the sixteenth clause of this eighth section, maintained " that it included the power of annexing punishments, and establishing necessary discipline," and therefore most ignominious punishments might be inflicted by Congress, on the worthiest citizens. The speaker then reverted to the subject of representation as inadequate, which was " a conclusive reason for granting no powers to the government, but such as were absolutely indispensable, and these to be most cautiously guarded." On the power of impeachment, of which he entertained great suspicions, he said, " after a treaty manifestly repugnant to the interests of the country was made," how was the Senate to be punished ? " The House of Representatives were to impeach them. The senators were to try themselves. If a majority of them were guilty of the crime [of bribery and corruption] would they pronounce themselves guilty ? Yet this is called

[1] Appendix iii.

responsibility." Referring to the ultimate power given Congress over elections, he was called to order by George Nicholas for leaving the section under discussion, but was allowed to proceed: "He was of opinion that the control over elections tended to destroy responsibility." He could see no good reason for it and thought it was dangerous: "I have no power which any other person can take from me. I have no right of representation, if they can take it from me. I say, therefore, that Congress may, by this claim, take away the right of representation, or render it nugatory, despicable, or oppressive." After some further argument on this point, Colonel Mason took notice of a clause in the fifth section, on publishing the proceedings of Congress, and he urged that the words "from time to time" should be replaced by others less ambiguous. The Confederation had provided that their journal should be published monthly, with certain exceptions. Here was an additional want of responsibility in the new government. In conclusion, Colonel Mason urged that the provision regarding adjournment was objectionable. "Neither house can adjourn without the consent of the other for more than three days. The Senate might have it in their power to worry the House into a compliance with their wishes, by refusing to adjourn, and they could have no objection to long sessions, as they were elected for six years, and would probably make their homes in the Federal city." [1]

The eighth section was still under consideration on Monday, the 16th, and George Mason spoke seven times on this day. After a speech by Patrick Henry, Madison answered him, and concluded by having the acts of the Assembly read, which provided for calling out the militia. Colonel Mason asked for what purpose they were read. He thought "they militated against the cession of this power to Congress, because the State governments could call forth the militia when necessary, so as to compel a submission to the laws; and as they were competent to it, Congress ought not

[1] *Ibid.*

to have the power." He was not satisfied with the explanation that General Lee had given of the word *organization*. The latter maintained that it did not include the infliction of punishments. Whereas George Mason insisted that organizing and disciplining the militia embraced the power of inflicting punishments, which might be made severe and ignominious. It was said the militia would only be subject to martial law when in actual service. But what was there to hinder Congress from inflicting it always? Madison replied, and the subject was discussed by Henry, Corbin, Grayson, and Marshall. George Mason said it had been asked who were the militia, if they were not the *people* of the country. He thought they did at this time consist of the whole people, but they might at some future period be confined to the lower and middle classes, under the new government. Then ignominious punishments and heavy fines might be expected. Discriminating laws might be made by Congress exempting its members and others from militia duty. George Nicholas professed to find an inconsistency in the propositions severally advanced by William Grayson and George Mason, and asserted that they both opposed the power given Congress on " contradictory principles." Mason replied "that he was totally misunderstood. The contrast between his friend's objection and his was improper. His friend had mentioned the propriety of having select militia, like those of Great Britain, who should be more thoroughly exercised than the militia at large could possibly be. But *he*, himself, had not spoken of a selection of militia, but of the exemption of the highest classes of the people from militia service ; which would justify apprehensions of some ignominious punishments." The opponents of the Constitution all feared the power given Congress over the federal district, and George Mason spoke on the subject at this time :

" This ten miles square may set at defiance the laws of the surrounding States, and may, like the custom of the superstitious days of our ancestors, become the sanctuary of the blackest crimes. . . . If any of their [the Federal government's] officers, or creatures should attempt to oppress the people, or should actually perpetrate the blackest deed, he has nothing to do but get into the ten miles square. . . . It is an incontrovertible axiom, that, when the dangers that may arise from the *abuse* are greater than the benefits that may result from the use, the power ought to be withheld."

Such he conceived to be the case here. And, alluding to a remark of Edmund Randolph, he added :

"We are told by the honorable gentleman that Holland has its Hague. I confess I am at a loss to know what inference he could draw from that observation. This is the place where the deputies of the United Provinces meet to transact the public business. But I do not recollect that they have any exclusive jurisdiction whatever in that place, but are subject to the laws of the province in which the Hague is. To what purpose the gentleman mentioned that Holland has its Hague I cannot see."

George Mason thought that Congress should only have exclusive power as regarded the police and good government of the place.

Of the last, or "sweeping clause," as it was termed, of the eighth section, the Antifederalists had no opinion whatever. George Mason replied to Madison and Pendleton on this head : "Gentlemen say there is no new power given by this clause. Is there anything in this Constitution which secures to the States the powers which are said to be retained ? Will powers remain to the States which are not expressly guarded and reserved "? He then stated an imaginary case, not an impossible one, of oppression arising under powers exercised by the federal government, and protests being made by public writers against such misgovernment. Could not Congress call this encouraging sedition, and lay restrictions on the liberty of the press ? Here Colonel Mason anticipated exactly what took place in the sedition law of the second administration. As with the liberty of the press, he continued, so with the trial by jury and other personal rights.

He then referred to the second of the Articles of Confederation "reserving to the States respectively every power, jurisdiction, and right, not expressly delegated to the United
States. This clause has never been complained of, but
approved by all. Why not, then, have a similar clause in
this Constitution, in which it is the more indispensably
necessary than in the Confederation, because of the great
augmentation of power vested in the former?" At the conclusion of his remarks, Patrick Henry suggested that the
Bill of Rights be read to the Convention from the eighth to
the thirteenth article. George Nicholas then spoke in defence of the Constitution as it stood, and was followed in
reply by Colonel Mason. He still thought the amendment
he had proposed was necessary. The people of Virginia
had reserved certain rights when they had formed their
government, and he asked :

"Why should it not be so in this Constitution ? Was it because
we were more substantially represented in it than in the State
government ? If in the State government, where the people were
substantially and fully represented, it was necessary that the great
rights of human nature should be secure from the encroachments
of the legislature, he asked if it was not more necessary in this government, where they were but inadequately represented ? . . . He
could see no clear distinction between rights relinquished by a
positive grant, and lost by implication." [1]

Speeches were then made by Henry, Grayson, and Nicholas.
George Mason rose to correct Nicholas who had asserted
that the Virginia Bill of Rights did not prohibit torture,
whereas, in fact, it was provided against by two clauses.[2]

The ninth and tenth sections of the first article, with the
first section of the second, were debated on Tuesday the
17th. George Mason was the first to speak after the reading of the first clause; also after the reading of the second,
third, and fourth, and again after the fifth and sixth. He
called this a fatal section, " which has created more dangers

---

[1] *Ibid.*   [2] " Debates of the Virginia Convention," Robertson.

than any other." He reprobated the clause allowing the importation of slaves for twenty years. Yet at the same time that the slave-trade was continued, there was no protection for the slaves already in the country. A tax might be laid which would amount to manumission. "So that 'they have done what they ought not to have done, and have left undone what they ought to have done.'" This clause was discussed by Madison, Tyler, Henry, and Nicholas, when the next three clauses were read and George Mason said of the fourth, on the subject of a capitation or other direct tax, that it was no restriction. "It only meant that the quantum to be raised of each State, should be in proportion to their numbers. . . . But the general government was not precluded from laying the proportion of any particular State on any one species of property they might think proper." And by laying heavy taxes on slaves they might destroy this property. Madison replied to Mason, and after the reading of the fifth and sixth clauses, the latter spoke again. He objected to the publication of the Treasury accounts "from time to time" only. The expression was a loose one and might mean any time, monthly or once in seven years. It was urged that there might be matters which would require secrecy. "But he did not conceive that the receipts and expenditures of the public money ought ever to be concealed." And now occurred a second little encounter between George Mason and "Light-Horse Harry." The latter "thought such trivial arguments, as that just used by the honorable gentleman, would have no weight with the committee. He conceived the expression to be sufficiently explicit and satisfactory," etc., etc. Colonel Mason "begged to be permitted to use that mode of arguing to which he had been accustomed. However desirous he was of pleasing that worthy gentleman, his duty would not give way to that pleasure." After a justification of the clause by Nicholas, Corbin, and Madison, George Mason answered, "that in the Confederation, the public proceedings were to to be published monthly, which was infinitely better than depending on men's virtue to publish them or not, as they might please." After the reading of the seventh clause Patrick Henry made the first speech, passing in review the whole section, which he characterized as the bill of rights of the Constitution, or its substitute. And he pointed out how far its restrictions fell short of the requirements needed. Edmund Randolph replied at considerable length, and Henry rejoined that he lamented " that he could not see with that perspicuity which other gentlemen were blessed with."

After the reading of the first clause of the tenth section Patrick Henry spoke again. Madison made a rejoinder, and then George Mason took the floor. Henry had deprecated the restrictions on the States—that they could not emit bills of credit, make anything but gold and silver coin a tender in payment of debts, pass *ex post facto* laws, etc.; and he feared one effect would be that Virginia would have to pay for her share of Continental money, shilling for shilling, and he asked if there had not been State speculations in this matter. George Mason said that both States and individuals had speculated enormously. Madison had referred to the first clause in the sixth article as protecting the States. Mason considered this satisfactory as far as it went; "that is, that the Continental money ought to stand on the same ground as it did previously, or that the claim should not be impaired. . . . Neither the State legislatures nor Congress can make an *ex post facto* law. The nominal value must therefore be paid. . . . The clause under consideration does away with the pretended security in the clause which was adduced by the honorable gentleman." After speeches by Madison, Henry, Nicholas, and Randolph, George Mason again addressed the chair, maintaining that though the debt was transferred to Congress, they had no means of paying it, because they could not pass *ex post facto* laws. "And it would be *ex post facto* to all intents and purposes to pay off creditors with less than the nominal sum, which they were originally promised." He disputed the technical definition of such a law, which Edmund Randolph declared related only to criminal cases, whereas it was, according to the ordinary use of words, simply a retrospective law. The federal court would have to decide, and it would be their duty to pronounce such laws unconstitutional. He proceeded to mention a remarkable effect this Constitution would have.

" How stood our taxes before this Constitution was introduced ? Requisitions were made on the State legislatures, and if they were unjust they could be refused. . . . But now this could not be done ; for direct taxation is brought home to us. The federal officer collects immediately of the planters. When it withholds the only possible means of discharging these debts, and by direct taxation prevents any opposition to the most enormous and unjust demand, where are you ? Is there a ray of hope ? "

What was here feared from direct taxation has come to pass through another form of the power given Congress in the eighth section. Experience has proved that indirect taxation was the more dangerous prerogative. George Mason continued. It was said " the United States can be plaintiffs, but never defendants. If so it stands on very unjust grounds. The United States cannot be come at for anything they may owe, but may get what is due to them. There is therefore no reciprocity." After Madison had spoken in reply to Mason, asserting that the clause was merely declaratory, and things existed just as they were before, Mason declared himself " still convinced of the rectitude of his former opinion. He thought it might be put on a safer footing by three words. By continuing the restriction of *ex post facto* laws to crimes, it would then stand under the new government as it did under the old." Colonel Mason was the first to speak after the reading of the next clause. He objected to its restrictions upon the States, as preventing Virginia from making " any inspection law but what is subject to the control and revision of Congress. Hence gentle-

men, who know nothing of the business, will make rules
concerning it which may be detrimental to our interests.
. . . Under this clause that incidental *revenue* which is
calculated to pay for the inspection, and to defray contingent charges, is to be put into the federal treasury. But if
any tobacco house is burnt, we cannot make up the loss. I
conceive this to be unjust and unreasonable. When any
profit arises from it, it goes into the federal treasury. But
when there is any loss or deficiency from damage, it cannot
be made up. Congress are to make regulations for our
tobacco. Are men in the States where no tobacco is made
proper judges of this business? . . . This is one of
the most wanton powers of the general government."
George Nicholas defended the clause, and said a tax could
be laid to make up for the loss of warehouses destroyed by
fire. Colonel Mason replied "that the State legislatures
could make no law but what would come within the general
control given to Congress; and that the regulation of the
inspection, and the imposition of duties, must be inseparably
blended together." George Mason rose after the reading
of the first section of the second article and expressed his
unqualified disapprobation of some of its provisions. "The
great fundamental principle of responsibility in republicanism is here sapped." This referred to the election of the
President without rotation.

"It may be said that a new election may remove him, and
place another in his stead. If we judge from the experience of
all other countries, and even our own, we may conclude that, as
the President of the United States may be re-elected, so he will.
. . . This President will be elected time after time; he will
be continued in office for life."

Turning to Edmund Randolph, Colonel Mason continued:

"The honorable gentleman, my colleague in the late Federal
Convention, mentions with applause those parts of which he had
expressed his disapprobation. He says not a word. If I am

mistaken let me be put right.' I shall not make use of his name ; but in the course of this investigation I shall use the arguments of that gentleman against it."

The " honorable gentleman " must have writhed under these words, and the promise they held out of turning his own weapons against him was not reassuring to the time-serving governor. The danger of European influence was then dwelt upon. George Mason thought " some stated time ought to be fixed when the President ought to be reduced to a private station," and he advocated eight years of office out of twelve or sixteen years. As it was, he might remain in office for life. The danger here dreaded may now seem chimerical. And public opinion has decided against a third term, so that eight years is practically the limit. But none the less there remains no constitutional restriction against the possible perils inherent in the article under considera-tion. Edmund Randolph now proceeded to confute his former opinions, but George Mason made no further reply to him. The latter spoke next on the subject of the Vice-President, whom he considered an unnecessary officer. He had addressed the Convention twelve times during this day's session.²

After speeches, on Wednesday, from Monroe and Grayson, George Mason discussed the mode of electing the Executive, as open to objection :

"A majority of the whole number of electors is necessary to elect the President. It is not the greatest number of votes that is required, but a majority of the whole number of electors. If there be more than one having such majority, and an equal number, one of them is to be chosen by ballot of the House of Representatives. But if no one have a majority of the actual number of electors appointed, how is he to be chosen? From the five highest on the list, by ballot of the lower house, and the votes to be taken by

¹ The punctuation of this sentence in Robertson is evidently incorrect, and has been altered here.
² Appendix iii. " Debates of the Virginia Convention," Robertson.

States. I conceive he ought to be chosen from the two highest on the list. This would be simple and easy. Then indeed the people would have some agency in the election. But when it is extended to the five highest, a person having a very small number of votes may be elected."

And in regard to the second section of the article on the Executive, George Mason said:

" It has been wittily observed that the Constitution has *married* the President and the Senate—has made them man and wife. I believe the consequence that generally results from marriage will happen here. They will be continually supporting and aiding each other ; they will always consider their interest as united. . . . The executive and legislative powers thus connected will destroy all balances ; this would have been prevented by a constitutional council, to aid the President in the discharge of his office, vesting the Senate, at the same time, with the power of impeaching them."

Madison in his reply took issue with Mason on the construction of the phrase, " majority of the whole number of electors appointed." However, the present mode of electing the Executive, by special conventions, the electoral college simply registering the result of the vote on the nominees of the conventions, is a wide departure in practice from the theory contemplated by the Constitution.

George Mason was the first to speak after the reading of the first clause of the second section of article second. He was alarmed at the great powers given the President. That of commanding the army in person he thought very dangerous. He believed a general superintendence was sufficient, and he took occasion to remark on the virtues and magnanimity of Washington, who, had he been ambitious, might have done much harm to the country: " So disinterested and amiable a character as General Washington might never command again." He thought the President should not have the pardoning power. General Lee said the President would not necessarily command in person and might only do so in case he was a military man and the public safety required it. To this Mason retorted, that the President might command if he pleased, and might make a dangerous use of his power. George Nicholas compared the State and federal governments, in the power of the former over the militia and the latter over the army and navy, and George Mason replied that "the Governor did not possess such extensive powers as the President, and had no influence over the navy. The liberty of the people had been destroyed by those who were military commanders only. The danger here was greater by the junction of great civil powers to the command of the army and fleet." Madison animadverted upon Mason's objection to giving the Executive the pardoning power, and said that it would not be proper to vest it in the House of Representatives, because large popular bodies were more apt to be swayed by passion. He instanced the case of Massachusetts and Shay's Rebellion, where the same legislature at different sessions were actuated by exactly opposite sentiments. To this Colonel Mason answered that "they [the Assemblies] were both right; for in the first instance, when such ideas of severity prevailed, a rebellion was in existence, in such circumstance it was right to be rigid. But after it was over, it would be wrong to exercise unnecessary severity." The second clause was read, and George Mason was again on his feet, objecting to this most dangerous provision, "as thereby five States might make a treaty, ten Senators, the representatives of five States—being two-thirds of a quorum. These ten might come from the five smallest States." George Nicholas answered Colonel Mason, but the latter was not prepared to agree with him in his argument as to the superiority of the Constitution over the Confederation on this point. The subject was discussed for some time longer, both Henry and Grayson, among others, making speeches on this question of the treaty power. On Thursday, the 19th, after Grayson and Nicholas had spoken, George Mason continued his remarks on the same topic. He considered this as "one of the greatest acts of sovereignty," and thought it should be most carefully guarded.   As it was, the President had more power than the King of England.   "Could the King give Portsmouth to France?   He could not do this without an express act of Parliament—without the consent of the legislature in all its branches.   There are other things which the King cannot do, which may be done by the President and Senate in this case."   The common law of England, he said, was not the common law of this country.   And there was nothing in the Constitution to prevent the relinquishment of territory by treaty.   "No treaty to dismember the empire, ought to be made without the consent of three-fourths of the legislature in all its branches."   And only unavoidable necessity could excuse such a treaty when it would doubtless have the "general and uniform vote of the Continental Parliament."[1]   Corbin, Henry, and Madison all spoke on this occasion; the former exhibiting, as Grigsby says, "great perspicacity in anticipating the real action of the Federal Government," in regard to treaties.[2]

[1] Appendix iii.
[2] "History of the Virginia Federal Convention," p. 274.
vol. ii—17

CHAPTER VIII.

AN ANTIFEDERALIST LEADER.

1788.

The Convention had now reached, Thursday the 19th of June, a most important part of the Constitution—the first and second sections of the third article, on the federal judiciary. It was a theme, says the historian of the Convention, "which, in itself considered, possessed an importance in the eyes of our fathers that language would vainly attempt to measure, which was discussed with a fulness of learning, with a keenness of logic, and with a glow of eloquence that it might well elicit, and which, though technical, and seen through a vista of seventy [now a hundred] years, cannot fail to strike a responsive chord in the hearts of every true son and daughter of our noble Commonwealth." And it possessed an additional interest as it was to be "the last battle-ground of the parties into which the Convention was in nearly equal portions divided."[1] Grigsby reminds us that the experience of a century "will place a child apparently on the same level with a giant, and the merest tyro in politics with a Somers or a Mason," and he adds "that the fears and gloomy predictions uttered by the opponents of the Constitution have, by the vigilance and caution which they inspired, operated in a material degree in preventing their own fulfilment." Edmund Pendleton having first spoken, in favor of the proposed system, Colonel Mason said he had hoped the friends of the Constitution

---

[1] Grigsby's "History of the Virginia Federal Convention," p. 276.

would have had the candor to point out the objections that must be apparent to all. " It is with great reluctance," he added, " I speak of this department, as it lies out of my line. I should not tell my sentiments upon it, did I not conceive it to be so constructed as to destroy the dearest rights of the community." He asked what power remained to the State courts. He could see no limitation to the power of the federal courts, and Congress might establish any number of them ; while the discrimination between their jurisdiction and that of the State courts existed only in name.

" To what disgraceful and dangerous length does the principle of this go ! For if your State judiciaries are not to be trusted with the administration of common justice, and decision of disputes respecting property between man and man, much less ought the State governments to be trusted with power of legislation. The principle itself goes to the destruction of the legislation of the States, whether or not it was intended. As to my own opinion, I most religiously and conscientiously believe that it was intended, though I am not absolutely certain. But I think it will destroy the State governments, whatever may have been the intention. There are many gentlemen in the United States who think it right, that we should have one great, national, consolidated government, and that it was better to bring it about slowly and imperceptibly rather than all at once. This is no reflection on any man, for I mean none. To those who think that one national, consolidated government is best for America, this extensive, judicial authority will be agreeable ; but I hope there are many in this Convention of a different opinion, and who see their political happiness resting on their State governments."

Though George Mason had said he meant no reflection on any man, there was one member of the Convention who could not but consider his remarks as personal. Madison alone of those present who had been delegates to the Federal Convention felt a responsibility for its work. Randolph had changed sides, and George Wythe, though voting with the Federalists on that occasion, had taken no conspicuous part in the matter. Then, too, Madison was now hand in glove with Alexander Hamilton, whose views were well known to be inimical to State sovereignty. These two were at this time writing the letters of *The Federalist* for the enlightenment of the general public, while carrying on an anxious private correspondence, in which their sympathy is seen to be complete on the subject of adopting the un-amended Constitution. Madison, therefore, interrupted Colonel Mason, and asked for "an unequivocal explanation." To this challenge Mason made reply:

"I shall never refuse to explain myself. It is notorious that this is a prevailing principle. It was at least the opinion of many gentlemen in Convention, and many in the United States. I do not know what explanation the honorable gentleman asks. I can say, with great truth, that the honorable gentleman, in private conversation with me, expressed himself against it; neither did I ever hear any of the delegates from this State advocate it."

With this explanation Madison professed himself satisfied, and George Mason continued his argument. He passed in review the powers given the judiciary, approving of some unconditionally, of others under restrictions, but excepting to some altogether as "utterly inconsistent with reason and good policy." He dwelt upon the hardships and expense to a poor man in case of oppression by federal officials.

"Even suppose the poor man should be able to obtain judgment in the inferior court, for the greatest injury, what justice can he get on appeal? Can he go four hundred or five hundred miles? Can he stand the expense attending it? On this occasion they are to judge of fact as well as law. He must bring his witnesses where he is not known, where a new evidence may be brought against him, of which he never heard before, and which he cannot contradict."

While admitting that in maritime and chancery cases jurisdiction as to fact was necessary, he thought in common-

law controversies it was inexpedient and dangerous. And
he proposed an amendment, which is to be found as corresponding to the first part of the fourteenth amendment
adopted by the Convention. In regard to controversies
between citizens of different States, Colonel Mason said:

"Can we not trust our State courts with the decision of these?
If I have a controversy with a man in Maryland—if a man in
Maryland has my bond for £100, are not the State courts competent to try it? Is it suspected that they would enforce the
payment if unjust, or refuse to enforce it if just? The very idea
is ridiculous."

He dilated further upon this case, and then proceeded to
consider that of the British creditor and the citizens of Virginia, and he thought there were many instances where the
federal courts could oblige the latter to pay a debt twice
over. Again, in regard to disputed lands he saw peril to
many in the community. "I am personally endangered,"
he went on to say, "as an inhabitant of the Northern Neck.
The people of that part will be obliged, by the operation of
this power, to pay the quitrent of their lands. . . . Lord
Fairfax's title was clear and undisputed. After the Revolution, we taxed his lands as private property. After his death,
an act of Assembly was made, in 1782, to sequester the quitrents due, at his death, in the hands of his debtors. Next
year an act was made restoring them to the executor of the
proprietor. Subsequent to this, the treaty of peace was
made, by which it was agreed that there should be no
further confiscations. But after this an act of Assembly
passed confiscating this whole property. As Lord Fairfax's
title was indisputably good, and as treaties are to be the
supreme law of the land, will not his representatives be able
to recover all in the federal court?" Next he named the
great land companies, who would now come forward:

"All that tract of country between the Blue Ridge and the
Alleghany Mountains, will be claimed, and probably recovered in

the federal court, from the present possessors, by those companies who have a title to them. . . . Again, the great Indiana purchase, which was made to the westward, will, by this judicial power, be rendered a cause of dispute. . . . Three or four counties are settled on the land to which that company claims a title, and have long enjoyed it peaceably. All these claims before those courts, if they succeed, will introduce a scene of distress and confusion never heard of before. Our peasants will be, like those mentioned by Virgil, reduced to ruin and misery, driven from their farms, and obliged to leave their country—

Nos patriam fugimus, et dulcia linquimus arva."

George Mason then proposed an amendment, "that the judicial power shall extend to no case where the cause of action shall have originated before the ratification of this Constitution, except in suits for debts due to the United States, disputes between States about their territory, and disputes between persons claiming lands under the grants of different States."[1] This forms the concluding clause of the fourteenth amendment recommended by the Convention.

Grigsby observes that "Madison manifested great sensitiveness during the speech of Mason, and it is not to be disguised that he did touch doctrines in the [Federal] Convention which would have led the way to the plan denounced by Mason; for he is reported by Yates to have said that the States were never sovereign, and were petty corporations."[2] Though it was past the hour for adjournment, Madison rose to reply to Mason " to break the effect " of his speech. And on the following day Madison continued his argument. "There was an evident interest shown," says Grigsby, " to hear the speech of Madison, who, like Mason, was not a lawyer, on a topic which was beyond the usual sphere of a politician, and which had been argued with such eminent ability by Mason the day before."[3] Patrick Henry spoke in reply to Madison, and he was followed by Pendleton, who

[1] Appendix iii.
[2] " History of the Virginia Federal Convention," note to p. 285.
[3] *Ibid.*, p. 290.

sought to refute the arguments of Mason and Henry. He accused George Mason of making a mistake in his speech " on the propriety of a jury from the vicinage." Grigsby comments here :

" Pendleton sought to make mirth with those gentlemen of the law in the Convention who thought that none but lawyers can understand legal questions. The fact is that Mason was clearly right, and Pendleton clearly wrong. Mason did not contend that a jury from the vicinage was the sole benefit accruing from jury trial, but that it was an important one, as it assuredly is, which a criminal, carried a thousand miles from his home would lose. As Pendleton wholly excludes from his view this great benefit, it is he that errs, and not Mason." [1]

Pendleton also referred to the case supposed by Mason, that a Virginian holding his bond might, through malice, assign it to a citizen of a neighboring State, and asserted that this was not a well-founded objection. Colonel Mason replied :

" The honorable gentleman has said that there can be no danger in the first instance because it is not within the original jurisdiction of the Supreme Court ; but that the suit must be brought in the inferior federal court of Virginia. He supposes there can never be an appeal, in this case, by the plaintiff, because he gets a judgment on his bond ; and that the defendant alone can appeal, who therefore, instead of being injured, obtains a privilege. Permit me to examine the force of this."

And the speaker proceeded to show that his objection was a legitimate one, and he added : " The honorable gentleman recommends to me to alter my proposed amendment. I would as soon take the advice of that gentleman as any other, but though the regard which I have for him be great, I cannot assent on this great occasion." Marshall occupied the attention of the house for the remainder of the day's session. He passed in review some of George Mason's

[1] *Ibid.*, note to p. 294.

objections to the great powers given the judiciary, and pronounced them chimerical. Mason had said of the clause, "to controversies between a State and the citizens of another State," in reference to the land companies, that these claims would be tried before a federal court:

"Is not this disgraceful? Is this State to be brought to the bar of justice like a delinquent individual? Is the sovereignty of the State to be arraigned like a culprit, or private offender? . . . What is to be done if a judgment be obtained against a State? Will you issue a *fieri facias?* It would be ludicrous to say you could put the State's body in jail. How is the judgment, then, to be enforced? A power which cannot be exercised ought not to be granted."

And Marshall replied: "*I hope no gentleman will think that a State will be called at the bar of the federal court.*" Later events justified George Mason's fears, and necessitated the eleventh amendment. Edmund Randolph had a few remarks to make on Friday, to the effect "that the faults which he once saw in this system he still perceived!" He unfolded his views on the following day, after an able speech by Grayson. "It seems to have been a rule," said the latter, "with the gentlemen on the other side, to argue from the excellency of human nature, in order to induce us to grant away (if I may be allowed the expression) the rights and liberties of our country. I make no doubt the same arguments were used on a variety of occasions. I suppose, sir, this argument was used when Cromwell was invested with power. The same argument was used to gain our assent to the stamp act." [1]

Madison wrote to Alexander Hamilton on Friday the 20th, and also on Sunday the 22d. He spoke of the debates having "advanced as far as the judiciary department, against which a great effort is making." He referred to the project of the Antifederalists to bring forward a bill of rights and amendments as conditions of ratification.

[1] "Debates of the Virginia Convention," Robertson, p. 402. Appendix iii.

"The plan meditated by the friends of the Constitution is to preface the ratification with some plain and general truths that cannot affect the validity of the act, and to subjoin a recommendation, which may hold up amendments as objects to be pursued in the constitutional mode. These expedients are rendered prudent by the nice balance of numbers, and the scruples entertained by some who are in general well affected."

He was by no means sure of a majority, however, and he adds :

"It unluckily happens, that our legislature, which meets at this place to-morrow, consists of a considerable majority of Antifederal members. This is another circumstance that ought to check our confidence. As individuals they may have some influence ; and as coming immediately from the people at large they can give any color they please to the popular sentiments at this moment, and may in that mode throw a bias on the representatives of the people in Convention." [1]

The last week of the Convention opened inauspiciously for the needs of the future historian, as on this day, Monday the 23d, the short-hand writer was absent, and only very incomplete notes of the speeches were preserved. George Mason spoke four times on the 23d, and made his last heroic efforts to procure amendments. Only once again was his voice heard in the Convention, when on the 24th he rose to correct an erroneous statement made by Edmund Randolph. On the 23d the first and second sections of the third article were still under consideration. George Nicholas urged that the Convention proceed to the next section, but Henry did not consider the objections of the opposition had been answered in a manner to give satisfaction. He called in question a statement of Marshall's, relating to the trial by jury, which the latter rose to explain, declaring that it was as well secured in the Constitution as in the Virginia Bill of Rights. Henry replied to this at considerable length. George Nicholas made the succeeding speech (after Stephen), and

[1] " Works of Hamilton," John C. Hamilton, vol. i., p. 462.

in the course of his remarks gave offence to Patrick Henry. The atmospheric conditions were not favorable to coolness of temper, either in- or out-of-doors, and the crisis of political excitement had been reached, probably, on this day, with the members of the Assembly, as they arrived in Richmond, swelling the eager audience, too much interested in the work of the Convention to organize their own Houses. The president, after some heated discussion between Nicholas and Henry, observed, "that he hoped gentlemen would not be personal, that they would proceed to investigate the subject calmly and in a peaceable manner." After speeches by Monroe, Madison, Grayson, and Henry, of which we have only the outlines, George Mason spoke in conclusion, on the judiciary. "With respect to concurrent jurisdiction," said Mason in reply to Madison, who had observed "that county courts had exercised this right without complaint," the argument adduced seemed to him very unsatisfactory:

"Have Hanover and Henrico the same objects? Can an officer in either of those counties serve a process in the other? The federal judiciary has concurrent jurisdiction throughout the States, and therefore must interfere with the State judiciaries. . . . If we were forming a general government, and not States, I think we should perfectly comply with the genius of the paper before you; but if we mean to form one great national government for thirteen States, the arguments which I have heard hitherto in support of this part of the plan do not apply at all. We are willing to give up all powers which are necessary to preserve the peace of the Union, so far as respects foreign nations, or our own preservation, but we will not agree to a federal judiciary, which is not necessary for this purpose, because the powers there granted will tend to oppress the middling and lower class of people."

After further discussion of this point, Colonel Mason sat down, to rise again on the reading of the first section of the fourth article. He professed not to understand the latter part of this clause : " *Full faith and credit shall be given to all acts ;* and how far it may be proper that Congress shall declare the effects, I cannot clearly see into." After the reading of the second section, George Mason spoke again. He reverted to observations made at an earlier stage in their proceedings, " on the security of *property* coming within this section." He thought then and he was still convinced that there was no security.[1] " More than sixty years after this remark was made by Mason," says Grigsby, " one of his grandsons in the Senate of the United States drew up an act to carry this clause of the Constitution into effect." And he adds : " If it had been objected to the first clause of this section, that a Southern gentleman could not travel with his servants through another State without having them forcibly taken from him, or *in transitu* to some other State, the friends of the Constitution would have answered that from their own experience no such result would ever follow." [2]

William Grayson was the first to speak after the reading of the third section, which in its first clause related to the admission of new States, and in its second clause to the jurisdiction of Congress over federal territory. Grayson foretold the difficulty there would be in admitting new Southern States into the Union, with a Northern majority against them. George Mason here made his last speech in the Convention. But unfortunately no report of it can be said to be extant. The meagre record published by Robertson gives us only a faint reflex of its scope and purpose. He " took a retrospective view of several parts [of the Constitution] which had been before objected to. He endeavored to demonstrate the dangers that must inevitably arise from *the insecurity* of our rights and privileges, as they depended on vague, indefinite, and ambiguous implications. The adoption of a system so replete with defects, he apprehended could not but be productive of the most *alarming*

[1] Appendix iii.
[2] " History of the Virginia Federal Convention," note to p. 304.

consequences. He dreaded popular resistance to its operation. He expressed, in emphatic terms, the *dreadful effects*
which must ensue, should the people resist ; and concluded
by observing, that he trusted gentlemen would pause before
they would decide a question which involved such awful
consequences." Such is the brief synopsis of this final appeal. The eloquence and earnestness of the speaker are
barely suggested to us, not in anywise reproduced. But
their effect on his hearers was evidently not slight. Some
intimation of this may be gathered from the speech of General Henry Lee, which followed Mason's, in which the
federal advocate sought to do away with the impression his
opponent had made.' We learn, too, what Madison thought
of George Mason's speech, through a letter written by him
to Washington, on the evening of the 23d. Unfortunately
no report from the lips of friends remains to supplement the
unsympathetic relation of political adversaries. But Madison's
letter is important as filling out, to some extent, the abbre-
viated journal of the day's proceedings. And we learn in it
that Mason was answered by others beside Lee, and that
George Mason concluded his arraignment of the Constitution, and his forecast of its perils, by "declaring his determination, for himself, to acquiesce in the event, whatever it
might be." Madison wrote to his friend :

"We got through the Constitution by paragraphs to-day. . . .
The opposition will urge previous amendments. Their conversation to-day seemed to betray despair. Colonel Mason, in particular, talked in a style which no other sentiment could have
produced. He held out the idea of civil convulsions as the
effect of obtruding the government on the people. He was answered by several, and concluded with declaring his determination, for himself, to acquiesce in the event, whatever it might be.
Mr. Henry endeavored to gloss what had fallen from his friend ;
declared his aversion to the Constitution to be such that he could
not take the oath ; but he would remain in peaceable submission
to the result." [2]

[1] "Debates of the Virginia Convention," Robertson. Appendix iii.
[2] "Writings of Madison," vol. i., p. 401.

On the 24th, George Wythe proposed a resolution of ratification, and that amendments should be recommended to Congress on its first session under the Constitution. Henry declared the motion premature, and after a speech of some length he informed the committee that he had a resolution prepared, to refer a declaration of rights, with certain amendments to the most exceptionable parts of the Constitution, to the other States in the Confederacy, for their consideration, previous to ratification. These were nearly the same, Robertson says, as the amendments ultimately passed by the Convention. And there is every reason to believe that, though presented by Patrick Henry, they were written by George Mason, the chairman of the Committee of Opposition, and a transcript of them is preserved among George Mason's papers.[1] Edmund Randolph spoke after Henry, and commented on Wythe's form of ratification, declaring it sufficient, as a declaration of rights. He also passed in review the various amendments proposed by Henry. In regard to the seventh and eighth, he said:

" I have never hesitated to acknowledge that I wished the regulation of commerce had been put in the hands of a greater body than it is in the sense of the Constitution. But I appeal to my colleagues in the Federal Convention, whether this was not a *sine qua non* of the Union."

To this George Mason replied:

" It never was, nor in my opinion ever will be, a *sine qua non* of the Union. I will give you, to the best of my recollection, the history of that affair. This business was discussed at Philadelphia for four months, during which time the subject of commerce and navigation was often under consideration; and I assert, that eight States out of twelve, for more than three months, voted for requiring two-thirds of the members present in each House to pass commercial and navigation laws. . . . If I am right, there was a great majority for requiring two-thirds of the States in this business, till a compromise took place between

[1] Appendix iv.

the Northern and Southern States ; the Northern States agreeing to the temporary importation of slaves, and the Southern States conceding, in return, that navigation and commercial laws should be on the footing on which they now stand. . . . These are my reasons for saying that this was not a *sine qua non* of their concurrence." [1]

George Mason was followed by John Dawson, a young member of the opposition, who addressed the Convention now for the first time. To him succeeded Grayson, Madison, and Henry. The latter made that memorable appeal to his hearers which Wirt has so graphically described, where, as it was said, he seemed to look beyond the horizon, to the "beings of a higher order," who were witnesses of the important work then about to be consummated in behalf of posterity, and as he thrilled his auditors with his eloquence, a thunder-storm mingled its turbulence with the human emotions the orator had aroused, bringing the scene to a dramatic conclusion.

The next day, Wednesday, was the last day of the Convention. Innes, the eminent lawyer, spoke then for the first time, bringing all his powers of intellect to bear in favor of the new government ; while the clear-headed, conservative Tyler answered him in a zealous plea for the liberties of the States. Other speeches were made by less prominent members, Patrick Henry and Edmund Randolph closing the debate. The latter made a solemn justification of himself for the benefit of "some future annalist." The vote was then taken on a resolution for previous amendments, and it passed in the negative, eighty to eighty-eight. The resolution of ratification with subsequent amendments passed in the affirmative, eighty-nine for it and seventy-nine against it. Two more days were taken up with the work of preparing and voting on the form of ratification and amendments. Though the committee named to prepare the form of ratification was a purely Federalist one, consisting of Randolph,

---

[1] " Debates of the Virginia Convention," Robertson. Appendix iii.

Nicholas, Madison, Marshall, and Corbin, yet they stated in unmistakable terms the doctrine of State sovereignty in the assertion that the "powers granted under the Constitution, being derived from the people of the United States, may be resumed by them whensoever the same shall be perverted to their injury or oppression." The "people" here meant precisely what it meant in the preamble to the Constitution as expounded by Madison, "not the people as composing one great body, but the people as composing thirteen sovereignties." Virginia here declares the right of secession, as a correlative of accession, for all of the thirteen sovereignties. The committee to prepare amendments consisted of the prominent members of both parties, including on the one side Mason, Henry, and Grayson, and on the other Madison, Marshall, and Edmund Randolph. George Wythe, as chairman of this committee, reported a bill of rights and amendments on the 27th. There were twenty articles in the former paper, and twenty amendments proposed, and they correspond in substance, with one or two exceptions, to those agreed on by the Committee of Opposition, as may be seen by comparing them with the drafts among George Mason's papers. The Convention adjourned on the 27th of June. The hard-fought battle was over, but the victory was not altogether with the Federalists. They had been forced to concede most of the amendments they had so strenuously opposed, though they were not made a condition precedent to ratification. The Convention had pledged its delegates to the first Congress under the new government to recommend to its consideration the objections of the Antifederalists and their amendments; the latter to be acted upon as the Constitution required. The expediency plea put forward by Edmund Randolph, that it was a question of "union or no union," as eight States had already ratified the compact, no doubt had its effect on the weak and the wavering in the Convention, and brought over the small majority to the Federalists.

Madison wrote to Jefferson on the 24th of July from New

York, where he had gone to attend Congress, telling his correspondent of the last days of the Convention in Virginia. He anticipates no "irregular opposition to the system." He adds:

"What local eruptions may be occasioned by ill-timed or rigorous executions of the treaty of peace against British debts, I will not pretend to say. But although the leaders, particularly Henry and Mason, will give no countenance to popular violence, it is not to be inferred that they are reconciled to the event, or will give it a positive support. On the contrary, both of them declared they could not go that length, and an attempt was made under their auspices to induce the minority to sign an address to the people, which if it had not been defeated by the general moderation of the party, would probably have done mischief. Among a variety of expedients employed by the opponents to gain proselytes, Mr. Henry first, and after him Col. Mason, introduced the opinions expressed in a letter from you to a correspondent (Mr. Donald or Skipwith I believe) and endeavored to turn the influence of your name even against parts of which I knew you approved." [1]

Jefferson had written that he wished for a bill of rights and amendments. And he had made the suggestion that the object could be obtained in this way; the nine first Conventions by adopting the Constitution would secure the good that it contained, and the four latest Conventions, whichever they might be, by refusing to accede to it until amendments were secured, would force the others to assent to them. Patrick Henry, and it seemed George Mason also, though of this Robertson gives us no intimation, very naturally counting Jefferson among the Antifederalists, had sought to secure in the Convention any strength that might be obtained by bringing forward his views. But, as Henry pointed out, Jefferson's advice could not be followed, unless they were certain as to the course of the New Hampshire Convention then in session: "They tell us," said Henry, in

[1] "Writings of Madison," vol. i., p. 405.

a speech made the 12th of June, "that from the most authentic accounts, New Hampshire will adopt it [the Constitution]. Where then will four States be found to reject it, if we adopt it? Do not gentlemen see, that if we adopt, under the idea of following Mr. Jefferson's opinion, we amuse ourselves with the shadow, while the substance is given away? If Virginia be for adoption, what States will be left, of sufficient respectability and importance, to secure amendments by their rejection?" As New Hampshire adopted the Constitution on the 21st of June, she made the ninth State, and the four States that remained, containing more than a third of the population of the thirteen, would have been able, as Jefferson said, to secure amendments by refusing to ratify the compact without them. Virginia's importance in the Confederacy we are made to realize by Grigsby's statement of statistics: "Her population was over three-fourths of all that of New England. It was not far from double that of Pennsylvania. It was not far from three times that of New York. It was over three-fourths of all the population of the Southern States; . . . and it was more than a fifth of the population of the whole Union."[1] Unfortunately the slow methods of transportation at that day did not admit of the news of New Hampshire's action reaching Richmond before the adjournment of the Convention. The intelligence was received in New York on the 24th, and not until the last day of June or 1st of July was it known in Richmond by an express sent from Hamilton to Madison.

In the letter of Madison's given above, reference is made to an address prepared by Mason and Henry to be distributed among the people for their signatures. No trace of such a paper is to be found, nor is there any mention elsewhere of such a design on the part of the two great leaders of the opposition. On the contrary, an anecdote has been preserved, which represents Patrick Henry as quelling the manifestation of feeling among the Antifederalists which would lead them to obstruct the new government:

[1] " History of the Virginia Federal Convention," p. 8.

vol. ii—18

" In the evening of the day of the final vote, General Meade and Mr. Cabell assembled the *discontents* in the old Senate Chamber, and after a partial organization of the party, a deputation was sent to Patrick Henry inviting him to take the chair. The venerable patriot accepted. Understanding that it was their purpose to concert a plan of resistance to the operations of the Federal government, he addressed the meeting with his accustomed animation upon important occasions ; observing he had done his duty strenuously, in opposing the Constitution, in the *proper place*,—and with all the powers he possessed. The question had been fully discussed and settled, and that as true and faithful republicans, they had all better go home, etc." [1]

The General Assembly, which met in extra session, called together to consider a remonstrance sent them by the Court of Appeals, remained in Richmond from the 23d to the 30th of June. The governor and many delegates were members of the Convention. But while the latter was in session their attendance, of course, on its important deliberations prevented them from taking their seats in the Assembly. And in this connection, a treacherous action is charged upon Edmund Randolph, which went far to secure the federal triumph in the Convention. George Mason, as a member of the Assembly, was doubtless present there after the 27th, and some resolutions of his, evidently written to be laid before the House, are found among his papers, though there is no trace of them on the journal of the Assembly. They reflect severely on the action of Edmund Randolph, the executive, who is accused of suppressing important papers in order to further the cause of the Federalists in Virginia. Madison and others had accused the opposition of artifices to bring about their object, though what these were does not clearly appear. The counter-charge made by the other party it is difficult to disprove. Randolph, it was said, had delayed his official letter to Governor Clinton, of New York, transmitting the proceedings of the Virginia Assembly concerning the proposed

[1] *Southern Literary Messenger*, vol. i., p. 332. MSS. of late David Meade Randolph.

Convention, from December until the following March. And a letter Clinton had written to the Governor of Virginia in reply, "on the subject of a free and cordial intercourse and communication of sentiments" between the Conventions of the two States, was not only withheld by Randolph from the Convention, but was not laid before the Assembly until *after the Convention had ratified the Constitution.* The following is a copy of the resolutions of censure. In the original draft there are some erasures and interlineations not materially affecting the substance of the paper.

"Resolved, that the official letter from his Excellency, George Clinton, Esquire, Governor of the State of New York, dated March the   1788, to his Excellency Edmund Randolph, Esquire, Governor of this Commonwealth, on the subject of a free and cordial intercourse and communication of sentiments between the Conventions of the States of New York and Virginia upon the new constitution of government recommended by the late Federal Convention, which letter was laid before the General Assembly on the   day of this instant June, ought to have been laid before the Convention of this Commonwealth at their first meeting, for their consideration. Resolved, that by the said letter's being withheld from the Convention of this Commonwealth the Convention hath been precluded from exercising their judgment upon the expediency of so important a measure as that mentioned in the said letter from his Excellency Governor Clinton.

"Resolved that a committee of   be chosen by ballot, to wait on his Excellency Edmund Randolph, Esquire, to know his reasons for not laying the said letter before the delegates of the people of this Commonwealth in the late Convention, as well as for delaying to lay the same before the General Assembly until the day after the ratification of the new constitution of government ; and also to enquire from what causes the official letter from Governor Randolph to Governor Clinton, transmitting the proceedings of the General Assembly in the last session concerning the Convention of Virginia, was delayed from the   day of December to the   day of March in its conveyance to New York, and that the said committee make report of their proceedings therein to the General Assembly." [1]

[1] Mason Papers.

The letter of Governor Randolph dated December 27, 1787, is preserved among the Clinton papers, and is endorsed in George Clinton's handwriting: " Letter from Gov. Randolph, of the 27th Dec., 1787, with act respecting Convention. Ansd. 8th May, 1788." There is no statement as to when the letter was received. But in a letter from Clinton to John Dawson, a member of the opposition, written the following December, Governor Clinton, in reference to the legislature then in session, says:

" The letter of the Legislature of Virginia is not yet received and I am not without apprehensions that measures may be taken, to retard the delivery of it so as to defeat its utility. You will not, I am persuaded, ascribe my suspicion on this occasion to an undue degree of jealousy when you recollect the circumstance respecting my letter which was laid before your Convention." [1]

This letter, as we have seen, was not laid before the Convention, but was written for that purpose. And instead of being written in March, as George Mason's resolutions state, it was written in May, unless, indeed, there was a March letter of which there is now no trace. But Clinton's endorsement on Randolph's letter would seem to be conclusive, as to the May letter being the one referred to in the resolutions, and its context bears out this conclusion. It was as follows:

" NEW YORK, 8th May, 1788.
" SIR,
" Your Excellency's letter of the 27th of December, although it appears to have been committed to the post office at Richmond, did not come to my hands until the 7th of March. The Act enclosed was immediately communicated to the legislature, but it was after they had passed their resolutions for calling a Convention, and so near the close of their sessions, that no order was taken in consequence of it.
" The system of government proposed by the Federal Convention, is an object of such vast importance to the happiness of America

[1] Clinton Papers, New York Historical Society.

that it appears to me essential that the people of the different States cultivate and cherish the most friendly sentiments towards each other, especially during their deliberations on that interesting subject. The Convention of this State are to meet at Poughkeepsie on the 17th of June, to take the proposed system into consideration, and I am persuaded they will with great cordiality hold a communication with any sister State on the important subject, and especially with one so respectable in point of importance, ability and patriotism as Virginia. I think I may venture to assure your Excellency, that the people of this State are disposed to keep up that friendly intercourse, and preserve that unanimity respecting any great change of government, which appears to be the object of the Act of your legislature, and which it is the duty of every good man to promote and cherish, and I have no doubt but that our Convention will possess the same sentiments.

"As the session of your Convention will take place before that of this State, they will, I presume, commence the measures for holding such communications as shall be deemed necessary. I cannot refrain from expressing regret that a similar conduct has not been observed by the States who have already had the proposed system under consideration. Friendly communications on the subject, and temperate discussions would, it is to be presumed, have had a most happy tendency in accommodating it much more to the sentiment and wishes of the people of America than is likely to be the case in the form it is offered by the General Convention, and acceded to by some of the States. Should it be adopted by small majorities in the larger States we cannot reasonably hope it will operate so as to answer the salutary purposes designed. As I have no direction from the legislature on the subject of your communication, your Excellency will be pleased to consider this letter as expressive of my own sentiments, but I have at the same time a well-founded confidence that a majority of the people of the State over which I have the honor to preside will concur in them." [1]

Randolph's letter "appeared to have been committed to the post-office at Richmond," but *when* it was put in the post-office, or where the detention occurred, must remain a mystery. Edmund Randolph wrote to Clinton in August, asking him

[1] "Life of Edmund Randolph," M. D. Conway, p. 110.

to look at his letter enclosing the law " concerning our late Convention." He speaks of the report in Richmond, that it had been withheld " for a considerable time ": " The back of my letter," he adds, " will show the day on which it was put in the post-office ; and I am desirous of knowing the date which is impressed by the postmaster. If your Excellency can inform me of any reasons such as your absence from town, etc., which could have prevented the letter from reaching your hands, as soon as it ought, I will thank you to add them." [1]

This long delay of two months and eleven days prevented the message from Virginia reaching New York until after the Legislature of that State had concluded their business and named a date for the meeting of their Convention. The Legislature of Virginia had adjourned also, so that Clinton could make no communication to them. There is every reason to believe that had this resolution from Virginia reached New York in the proper time, the two Conventions would have co-operated and the Antifederalists would have gained previous amendments in both States. The first resolutions on the subject of the Convention, it will be remembered, passed the House of Delegates on the 25th of October. These, Governor Randolph writes Clinton, were transmitted to him on the 14th of November ; the second resolutions, which Randolph calls the " law," were passed on the 30th of November and sent on to New York the 27th of December. Here was a delay of twenty-seven days, of which there is no explanation, in sending on the Virginia resolves to New York. But the Federalists in the Legislature of Virginia opposed one of these resolutions, the one which their opponents deemed of the first importance. This was in reference to sending " a deputy or deputies to confer with the Convention or Conventions of any other State or States in the Union." Richard Henry Lee in a letter to General Lamb of June 27th, replying to one from the latter of the 18th of May, " but this day received," laments that it

[1] *Ibid.*, p. 114.

did not reach him sooner. He thought the plan of correspondence proposed by the society of which Lamb was chairman, " would have produced salutary consequences ; *as it seems to have been the idea of our Assembly when they sent the proposed plan to a Convention.*" [1] The mails seem to have been tampered with in more than one instance, in the interests of the Federalists. Governor Clinton timed his reply to the communication from Virginia so that it should reach Governor Randolph before the opening of the Convention. A letter dated the 8th of May ought to have been received in Richmond about the 15th. It was very natural that George Mason should have supposed that it had been received at that date. Randolph, in communicating it to the Legislature, as he asserts, on the 23d, the day the Assembly met, says that " immediately upon receiving " it he laid it before the council-board and requested " their opinion whether it was of a public or private nature. They conceived it to be of the former description, and therefore it is now forwarded." [2] The inference is that there had been but a short interval between its consideration by the council and its transmission to the Assembly. Who was responsible for its delay from the 15th of May, when it should have reached Richmond, and its reception by the Governor about the 22d of June ? Even then there was time, had Randolph desired to act an upright part, to have brought it before the Convention, for which it was intended. There was no quorum in the House until the 24th, and none in the Senate until the following day. The Governor's message and its important enclosure, the journal says, was only partly read on the 24th and laid over till the next day. Good care was taken evidently that the character of Clinton's letter should not be known until after the Convention had ratified the Constitution on the 25th. The Legislature was in sympathy with the opposition, and Governor Randolph and his confederates feared its influence upon the Convention. Accord-

[1] " Life and Times of General Lamb," Isaac Q. Leake, p. 306.
[2] " Life of Edmund Randolph," M. D. Conway, p. 112.

ing to George Mason, the letter of Clinton was not read in the Assembly until the 26th. Clinton's communication is not mentioned in the journal, which states only that a letter from the Governor enclosing " sundry letters and papers " was laid before the House on the 24th and " partly read " that day, and the reading resumed on the 25th. On this day a letter from the Governor, stating " *several other matters*," was received, partly read, and the reading concluded on the 26th.[1]

The Society in New York of the Federal Republicans carried on a secret correspondence with the opposition leaders in the Virginia Convention, as we have seen. And on the 21st of June, Governor Clinton wrote from the New York Convention to General Lamb, telling him that papers and letters from Virginia, of which Colonel Oswald had been the bearer, had been communicated to the Committee of Opposition in that body, and he now enclosed to Lamb for him to forward, a letter from them " to Colonel Mason, Chairman of the Virginia Committee." And he adds : " The letter to Colonel Mason, you will observe, is put under cover to Mr. George Fleming, merchant of Richmond, as advised in Mr. Mason's letter." [2] No copy of this letter has been preserved, and it is not probable that it reached its destination before the Virginia Convention adjourned, if Colonel Mason received it at all. So the Virginia Convention was precluded from all opportunity of concerting measures with the Convention in New York. And the ratification in Virginia, without previous amendments, was followed by the same course in New York a month later. North Carolina, all honor be given her, refused to ratify the Constitution without amendments, and closed her Convention, August 1st, with the passage of resolutions to this effect. Governor Clinton had sent a circular letter from the New York Convention to the several States, asking for another General Convention, to be procured in the constitutional manner.

[1] Journal of the Virginia Assembly.
[2] " Life and Times of General Lamb," Isaac Q. Leake, p. 315.

In Pennsylvania, the able letters of "Centinel," the Junius of this contest, were addressed to the country about this time through the columns of Colonel Oswald's paper, the *Independent Gazetteer*, in reply to the *Federalist*, and to James Wilson. Of the latter, this clever Antifederalist writer said, he could "bewilder truth in all the mazes of sophistry, and render the plainest propositions problematical." The "Centinel" letters called attention to the bribery of the post-riders in Pennsylvania by the Federalists, who in this way held back New York papers of importance which might have influenced the Convention in the former State. The short-hand writer in the Pennsylvania Convention was also bought up by the Federalists and only the speeches of Wilson and the one other leader of his party in this body were published, a flagrant act of political corruption. It has been noticed that the ten amendments afterwards added to the Constitution bore a marked resemblance to the fifteen amendments offered by the minority in the Pennsylvania Convention. And it is suggested "that when Madison, in 1789, drew up the amendments for the House of Representatives, he made use of those offered by the minority of the Convention of Pennsylvania."[1] These were based, however, on the objections of George Mason as given in the address of the Antifederalists in the Pennsylvania Legislature. Massachusetts, the first State to propose subsequent amendments through her Convention, no doubt took the Pennsylvania amendments as a basis for her own, as in Virginia, George Mason says the opposition had before them the Massachusetts amendments, as doubtless had been the case in Maryland and South Carolina. New Hampshire in her twelve amendments, acted, apparently, without concert with Virginia, but the thirty-one amendments of New York and the twenty-six of North Carolina were framed with the Virginia amendments as a basis, in addition to those that had gone before. The Antifederalists were substantially in accord

[1] "Pennsylvania and the Federal Convention, 1787–1788," edited by J. B. McMaster and F. D. Stone, p. 19.

throughout the country, except in case of the amendment desired by the Southern States, requiring a two-thirds vote to pass commercial laws. This point might have been settled, as George Mason believed, in a second General Convention, had Virginia united with North Carolina in making it a condition of ratification. Though it was not one of the amendments proposed by South Carolina, as it would have unhinged the "bargain" to which she was a party in the Federal Convention, it was well known that her people generally would have welcomed it.

If it is as a member of the Federal Convention only that George Mason excites a national interest, and his autograph is sought for by collectors, it is in his twofold character of the framer of her first form of government, and the consistent advocate of her State sovereignty and reserved rights, that he has a claim upon Virginia's regard and gratitude. Not Virginia alone, however, but all the States should recognize here, in George Mason's States-rights record, his patriotic wisdom and foresight. Certainly the South has had cause to know him as the advocate of its best interests. Undoubtedly had he and his party secured all that they strove for in 1788, there would have been no war in 1861.

Judge Chamberlain in a recent paper read before the American Historical Association makes the admission that the acceptance of the Constitution of 1787 was the "triumph of the legitimate successors of the Anti-Revolutionary party of 1775," and he adds that "the Revolutionary questions from 1789 to 1860 caused dissatisfaction in the States of the South as great nearly as that between the colonies and Great Britain from 1763 to 1775." He enumerates four points which were grievances under the colonial system, and which remained under altered conditions, engrafted on the government of the American Union. The colonists had complained of the King's prerogatives; under the Federal Constitution the Executive was clothed with still greater powers. The commercial laws enacted by Parliament had been felt to be burdensome and unjust; yet by the provision of the Con-

stitution relating to navigation laws, Congress was enabled
to pass in its first session an act " similar in principle and design to acts of Charles II.," which with some modifications
is still in force. So with the question of taxation without
adequate representation, as complained of in some of the
territories. And lastly, the powers of the judiciary under
the royal government were not sufficiently controlled by the
people ; the Constitution increased this grievance " to an
extent unknown to the colonies." This condition of things
to which the Federal Convention reduced the States " was
brought about only with great difficulty," says Judge Chamberlain, " for there was a large minority led by such men as
George Mason, Elbridge Gerry, and Samuel Adams, who
strenuously contended that in adopting the Constitution of
1787 the people surrendered everything, except independence, for which they had fought seven years." [1]

George Mason, as chairman of the Committee of Opposition in the Virginia Convention, left among his papers
two drafts of amendments and a draft of a bill of rights,
with several forms of a resolve that was to introduce them.[2]
This declaration of rights, which was based, as were the
other State bills of rights, on the early paper written by
George Mason in 1776, is substantially the same as that
adopted by the Convention, with the exception of one
important clause in the third section. This was, " that
whenever any government shall be found inadequate or
contrary to these purposes, [the benefit, etc., of the people]
a majority of the community hath an indubitable, unalienable, and indefeasible right to reform, alter, or abolish it,
and to establish another in such manner as shall be judged
most conducive to the public weal." [3] The Constitution
received ten amendments in the two years succeeding its
adoption. Of these, the first eight correspond to the eighth,
eleventh, thirteenth, fourteenth, fifteenth, sixteenth, seventeenth, eighteenth, and twentieth sections of the bill of

[1] " Papers of the American Historical Association," vol. iii., No. 1.
[2] Appendix iv. [3] *Ibid.*

rights recommended by the Virginia Convention. The ninth amendment corresponds to some extent with Virginia's seventeenth amendment, while the tenth amendment expresses, though not in identical terms, the principle of Virginia's first amendment. These two amendments, as has been sarcastically observed, " meant something to the mind of that generation ; to subsequent generations the meaning depended upon degrees of latitude." [1] The first Virginia amendment, as it was formulated by George Mason, was taken from the Articles of Confederation, and was as follows : " That each State in the Union shall retain its sovereignty, freedom, and independence, and every power, jurisdiction, and right which is not by this Constitution expressly delegated to the Congress of the United States." [2] A few years later, though George Mason did not live to see it, his arguments, to some extent, bore fruit in the eleventh amendment, which prohibits suits against States in the federal courts. The most important of the Antifederalist amendments which were not incorporated in the Constitution, related to the powers of Congress in regard to taxation, navigation laws, treaties, and the regulation of elections ; to the great powers given the federal judiciary, and to certain features in the composition of the executive office, and its duration. The iniquity of a federal election law, to be passed by a sectional party, which has recently menaced the Southern States, recalls the wise provision of Virginia in her sixteenth amendment (taken from the third amendment of the opposition), in which the true intent of the framers of the Constitution is clearly stated : " That Congress shall not alter, modify, or interfere in the times, places, or manner of holding elections for senators and representatives, or either of them, except when the legislature of any State shall neglect, refuse, or be disabled by invasion or rebellion to prescribe the same." [3] This was one of the questions argued in *The*

[1] *Magazine of American History,* vol. xv., p. 589. " The Virginia Convention, 1788," A. W. Clason.

[2] Appendix iv.

[3] " Debates of the Virginia Convention," Robertson.

Federalist, and explained there in accordance with the Virginia amendment. The first step in violation of this part of the Constitution was taken in 1871, by the act appointing federal supervisors of elections through the circuit judges.

Jefferson Davis, in the Senate of the United States in 1860, referring to the debates in the Federal Convention, on giving power to Congress to coerce the States, pays the following tribute to George Mason, as "one whose wisdom, as we take a retrospective view, seems to me marvellous." Mr. Davis says of him : "Not conspicuous in debate, at least not among the names which first occur when we think of that bright galaxy of patriots and statesmen, he was the man who, above all others, it seems to me, laid his finger upon every danger, and indicated the course that danger was to take."[1] One of the great dangers which George Mason had foretold soon made itself apparent, the beginning of a course of sectional legislation inflicting great injury on the South. In 1800, Jefferson writes : "While the navigating and provision States, who are the majority, can keep open all the markets, or at least sufficient ones for their objects, the cries of the tobacco makers, who are the minority, and not at all in favor, will hardly be listened to." And comparing the situation to the fable of the monkey using the cat's paws, he says: "It shows that G. Mason's proposition in the Convention was wise, that on laws regulating commerce two-thirds of the votes should be requisite to pass them."[2] Twenty-eight years later this was the result, according to Benton:

"Under federal legislation the exports of the South have been the basis of the federal revenue. Virginia, the two Carolinas and Georgia defray three-fourths of the annual expense of supporting the federal government ; and of this great sum nothing or next to nothing returns to them in shape of government expenditures—it flows northward. This is the reason why wealth disappears from the South and rises up in the North. Federal legislation does all this."[3]

[1] Speech in United States Senate, May 7, 1860.
[2] "Jefferson's Works." H. A. Washington, vol. vi., p. 323.
[3] Speech in United States Senate, 1825.

Direct or internal taxation the Antifederalists wished to reserve to the State government while giving up external or indirect taxation to the federal government. This proved to be a mistake, and it was through the tariff that the South was impoverished, yet the eighth Virginia amendment would have secured her interests, and given her "an absolute guaranty of power."[1]

How much Virginia gave up when she entered into the Union of 1787, and how great her prosperity had been previously, Grigsby points out in his invaluable history of the Convention that sealed her fate: " In the five years of peace," after the Revolution, he says, " our tobacco, grain, and other productions of the soil and the forest maintained the grandest commerce that had ever spread its wings from an Anglo-Saxon settlement in the New World towards the shores of the Old, and such as was never seen in the colony, and such as, with the exception of a short period, has never been seen in Virginia since." He calls attention to the instructive fact " that the period from the death of Charles the First in 1641 to the restoration of Charles the Second— a period of nineteen years—and the period between the peace of 1783 and the adoption of the Federal Constitution of 1788—a space of five years—have been the most prosperous in our history ; and that of the two centuries and a half of Virginia [this was written in 1858] it was during those two periods only she enjoyed the benefits of a trade regulated by her own authority, unrestricted and untaxed."[2] The mistake of the Virginia Federalists was in the false estimate they had formed of the general condition and commerce of Virginia :

"It led, in the vain hope of sudden improvement, to the hasty adoption of the present Federal Constitution without previous amendments, and to the surrender of the right of regulating its commerce by the greatest State of the confederation to an authority beyond its control. . . . It destroyed our direct

[1] " Letters and Times of the Tylers," Lyon G. Tyler, vol. i., p. 144.
[2] " History of the Virginia Federal Convention," p. 14.

trade with foreign powers. It banished the flag of Virginia from the seas. Instead of building and manning the ships which carried the product of our labor to foreign ports, and which brought back the product of the labor of others to our own ports, as some were persuaded to believe would be the result of the change, it compelled us thenceforth to commit our produce to the ships of other States, and to receive our foreign supplies through other ports than our own. It brought about the strange result that, instead of a large part of the cost of defraying the expenses of the government of Virginia being derived from the duties levied upon foreign commerce, these duties, though levied upon a scale unknown in that age, will not suffice [in 1858] to pay the expenses of collection by other hands than our own." [1]

In the last quarter of a century, or since the war, the United States government has grown rich with the high tariffs which it has imposed upon the people in violation of all sound economic law; and statesmen and social reformers see in a return to the principle of the early Republic, a tariff for revenue only, the sole cure for the labor troubles of the time. "Our present tariff laws," wrote the Secretary of the Treasury during Cleveland's administration, "are a needless oppression instead of an easy burden. All our customs revenue might be collected by strictly revenue duties upon a few score articles, instead of by extravagant or prohibitory duties upon more than four thousand articles." [2] In that year, 1886, there were a million idle working-men in the land, while the treasury was groaning under its huge surplus. The political situation since then has grown steadily worse, with a faction in power opposed to every measure of reform, and seeking to dissipate the surplus in extravagant schemes of partisan legislation. During the century that has passed since the formation of the Union, it has been seen that the powers of Congress under the "necessary and proper" clause of the Constitution have been augmented to an alarming extent. The Antifederalists in reprobating the

[1] *Ibid.*, p. 18.
[2] Letter of Secretary Manning to President Cleveland, 1886.

"sweeping clause," as they termed it, were wise indeed, in their generation, and their fears of centralization have been amply justified. The Duc de Noailles, a French observer of American government, points out that the constitutional limitations of the legislative power have been almost entirely neutralized by this dangerous clause.[1] Our great Southern statesman, Jefferson Davis, noting the tendency to centralization which is the outcome of the unbridled power of Congress, refers to Madison's fear "when the Constitution was being formulated, that young men under its provisions would not care to enter Congress, preferring the finer field opened to them by the legislatures of the sovereign States. What would he think now," adds President Davis, "could he return to earth and see what centralization has done and is doing? What would be his feelings when he saw one house of Congress passing the Blair Educational Bill, while the other was considering and finally passing a bill in regard to bogus butter?"[2] The Senate, it was believed, would by its dignity and wisdom balance any extravagant or inexpedient legislation in the larger and popular branch of Congress. But the degeneracy of the Senate is a theme for the diatribes of the American political philosopher. To a river and harbor bill the Senate attaches "indefensible jobs." Of a canal scheme, which would construct a canal entirely within the limits of a single State, "a measure that inaugurates a system that would lead to the most prodigal extravagance—the inauguration of a class of legislation that is in the face of the Constitution, if the Constitution means anything,"[3] the Senate is the patron. And the Senate is responsible for beginning the extravagant pension legislation which has become one of the crying corruptions of the federal government.

One of George Mason's amendments to the Constitution, which was not included among those adopted by the Federalists of the Virginia Convention, is as follows :

---

[1] "Cent Ans de République aux États-Unis," t. i., p. 229, Paris, 1886.
[2] *Southern Bivouac*, August, 1886, "Jefferson Davis at Home."
[3] *The Nation*, July 15, 1886.

" That there shall be a constitutional, responsible Council, to assist in the administration of government, with the power of choosing out of their own body a president, who in case of the death, resignation or disability of the President of the United States, shall act, *pro tempore*, as Vice President, instead of a vice president elected in the manner prescribed by the Constitution ; and that the power of making treaties, appointing ambassadors, other public ministers and consuls, judges of the Supreme Courts, and all other officers of the United States, whose appointments are not otherwise provided for by the Constitution, and which shall be established by law, be vested in the President of the United States with the assistance of the Council so to be appointed. But all treaties so made or entered into shall be subject to the revision of the Senate and House of Representatives for their ratification." [1]

The fear expressed by George Mason, that in case no council was provided for the President one would grow out of the great departments, " the worst and most dangerous of all ingredients in a free country," proved to be prophetic, as Washington did create such a council, and suffered its members to guide his actions.[2] The supervision over treaties which the Antifederalists desired for the House of Representatives is to-day as much a living issue as it was under the first administration. The House asserted its right in the case of Jay's treaty, and the decision left the matter an open question. It came up again with the Louisiana Purchase treaty ; and lastly in 1867, when the purchase of Alaska was made, the House reaffirmed its privilege. In the bill appropriating the amount to be paid for the new territory, the preamble attached to it in the House stated that the stipulations of the treaty were such as " by the Constitution are submitted to the power of Congress and over which Congress has jurisdiction ; and it being for such reasons necessary that the consent of Congress should be given to said stipulations before the same can have full force and effect," etc. The Senate refused to concur in this pre-

[1] Appendix iv.
[2] " Life of Edmund Randolph," M. D. Conway, p. 139.
vol. ii—19

amble and substituted another which was violently opposed, and only passed at length by a very small majority, many members not voting.

The amendment in regard to the Executive, " That no person shall be capable of being President of the United States for more than eight years in any term of sixteen years," has become, it would seem, an unwritten law, to be read between the lines of the constitutional compact. In connection with the judiciary system of the United States, a direct confirmation of George Mason's foresight may be noted in the operation of the federal courts. In his argument on the subject in the Virginia Convention, he supposes a case and says that even if a " poor man should be able to obtain judgment in the inferior court, for the greatest injury, what justice can he get on appeal ? Can he go four hundred or five hundred miles ? On this occasion they are to judge of fact as well as law. He must bring his witnesses where he is not known, where a new evidence may be brought against him, of which he never heard before and which he cannot contradict." Again in another connection he says: " How will a poor man who is injured or dispossessed unjustly, get a remedy ? Is he to go to the federal court, seven or eight hundred miles ? He might as well give his claim up. He may grumble, but finding no relief he will be contented." Owing to the fee system by which the federal official is remunerated instead of receiving a salary, the difficulty as suggested by George Mason is made even worse. The compensation of the commissioner before whom the complaint is sworn depends on the number of warrants issued, the number of days over which the hearings extend, and the number of witnesses recognized. A recent writer, who calls attention to this matter, says :

" He [the commissioner] and the marshal can readily play into each other's hands, the marshal by finding cases and the commissioner by giving the marshal processes to serve. Then usually one commissioner does all the criminal business for a district and offenders may be taken before this one from the most remote parts of the district, at great expense to the United States and hardship to themselves, as they are called on to find bail and counsel where they are strangers. The case is prejudged. The prisoner must find bail, and if he admits guilt he must stay in jail. . . . He may be in jail weeks, waiting bail for an offense punishable only by fine or a small term of imprisonment. If tried and acquitted, the attorney gets twice as much as if he pleads guilty, and if convicted he is entitled to an additional fee." [1]

George Mason in the Virginia Convention expressed his belief that the great powers given the federal judiciary tended to destroy the State governments. In 1819 we find Jefferson writing of the judiciary as "on every occasion driving us into consolidation." He described them at one time as "the corps of sappers and miners, steadily working to undermine the independent rights of the States, and to consolidate all power in the hands of that government in which they have so important a freehold estate." [2] John Randolph of Roanoke, agreed with Jefferson that "the judiciary gravitates towards consolidation," and he considered the District of Columbia "to be the πουστω and the Supreme Court to be the lever of the political Archimedes." [3] If the federal judiciary gravitated towards consolidation in the first half century of the Union, its course since has been fearfully accelerated. The modern Republican in his interpretation of the Constitution takes the place of the early Federalist and has developed his theories. The "puissant doctrine" of the implied powers, Mr. Woodrow Wilson contends, has made Congress omnipotent, and its power over the States is to be extended still further; while the privileges of the federal courts permit them to "annul State action, but State courts cannot arrest the growth of congressional power." [4] Elsewhere, in writing

[1] " Federal Criminal Procedure and the Fee System," *The Nation*, July 22, 1886.

[2] "Jefferson's Works," H. A. Washington, vol. vii., p. 134.

[3] Garland's " Life of John Randolph," vol. ii., p. 145.

[4] "Congressional Government," Boston, 1885, p. 24.

of the relations of the federal judiciary to the States of the Union he takes occasion to notice the illegality of the three last amendments to the Constitution:

" The integrity of the powers of the States has depended solely upon the conservatism, the conservative legal conscience, of the federal courts. State functions have certainly not decayed; but the prerogatives of the States have been preserved, not by their own forces of self-defense, but by the national government's grace of self-restraint."

It is admitted that this royal grace of self-restraint was not always maintained by the federal courts:

" The actual encroachments which the latter have permitted themselves . . . were not needed to prove the potential supremacy of the federal government. They showed how that potential supremacy would on occasion become actual supremacy; but they added nothing but illustration to the principle that there is no guarantee but that of conscience that justice will be vouchsafed a suitor when his adversary is both court and opposing litigant."

As an instance of the " strong instinct to keep within the sanction of the law," that inspires the federal conscience, there is adduced the case of the amendments. When these "were being forced upon the Southern States by means which were revolutionary, the outward forms of the Constitution were observed. But it was none the less manifest with what sovereign impunity the national government might act in stripping those forms of their genuineness." [1] Another political writer, in discussing the changes in the federal government since 1789, finds this alteration most marked in the department of the judiciary. He says of the courts that they " have increased steadily in power and independence, so far as their relations to the two co-ordinate branches of government are concerned. The change, silent, steady, has certainly transformed the governments

[1] *The Atlantic Monthly*, April, 1886, article by Woodrow Wilson.

within themselves, and to the Federal Union it has furnished the main bulwark of its power."[1]

The biographer of John Randolph wrote in 1850, of George Mason, calling him "the champion of the States and the author of the doctrine of State Rights." "Many of the prophecies of this profound statesman," he adds, "are recorded in the fulfilments of history—many of the ill-forebodings of the inspired orator [Patrick Henry] are daily shaping themselves into sad realities."[2] Eleven years later and Southern discontent had culminated in the sad reality of war. "The predictions of George Mason and others," writes Professor Bledsoe, "in which they foretold the wrongs and aggressions of the Northern States, if armed with the formidable powers of the new government, Mr. Madison just set aside as unfounded and uncharitable suspicions. Now in regard to this point we need not ask who was the wiser of the two, George Mason or James Madison, nor need we try the question by any imperfect notions of our own. For time has pronounced its irreversible verdict in favor of the wisdom of George Mason."[3] It was perceived very clearly by Madison as well as Mason that the Constitution was to be a compact between two sections with wholly different interests and different social institutions. And it was with the understanding that the Southern States were to be secured in all their rights that the Union of 1789 was formed. How these rights were violated, notably in questions affecting the institution of slavery, is matter of history. A systematic endeavor to repress the expansion of the South into new States was one feature of this injustice. And before the generation that formed the new government had passed away, the cloud was seen in the horizon, no larger than a man's hand, out of which in after years was to burst the storm of civil war. There were two Federalists,

[1] "American Constitutions," by Horace Davis, Johns Hopkins University Studies, Third Series.
[2] Garland's "Life of John Randolph," vol. i., p. 367.
[3] "Is Davis a Traitor?" p. 169.

members of the Convention of 1788, who lived to see and deplore the tendency of the government which they had urged upon Virginia. Madison, in his later public acts, in a measure retrieved the errors of his earlier manhood. And Francis Corbin acknowledged with grief to John Randolph in 1818 his conviction that the " centripetal force of this confederacy is greater than the centrifugal." He saw " that men of a certain description are resolved at all hazards and by all means, to break down the State sovereignties, our only barrier against Federal tyranny, and to erect on their ruins a uniform system of consolidated despotism." [1] Jefferson wrote in 1820 : " The coincidence of a marked principle, moral and political, with a geographical line, once conceived, would never be obliterated from the mind ; that it would be recurring on every occasion and renewing irritations, until it would kindle such mutual and mortal hatred, as to render separation preferable to eternal discord." [2] Again he says of the policy of the Abolitionists : " All know that permitting the slaves of the South to spread into the West will not add one being to that unfortunate condition, that it will increase the happiness of those existing, and by spreading them over a larger surface, will dilute the evil everywhere, and facilitate the means of getting rid of it." [3] There is something most pathetic in the words of this patriot of '76, as with mournful prevision he looks forward to the inevitable issue :

" What does the Holy Alliance in and out of Congress mean to do with us on the Missouri question ? . . . Are we then to see again Athenian and Lacedemonian Confederacies ?—to urge another Peloponnesian war to settle the ascendancy between them ? Or is this the tocsin of merely a servile war ? That remains to be seen ; but not I hope by you or me. Surely they will parley awhile and give us time to get out of the way." [4]

[1] In memoriam of Benjamin Ogle Tayloe, Washington, 1872.
[2] " Jefferson's Works," H. A. Washington, vol. vii., p. 158.
[3] *Ibid.*, p. 194.
[4] *Ibid.*, p. 200.

On the question of the ultimate course to be pursued, Jefferson's voice gives no uncertain sound. And we cannot doubt that George Mason would have been equally explicit. After anticipating the "longer and greater sufferings" which would justify secession, he adds: "We must have patience . . . and separate from our companions only when the sole alternatives left are the dissolution of our union with them, or submission to a government without limitation of powers. Between these two evils, when we must make a choice, there can be no hesitation." [1] So John Randolph in 1814, when New England had serious thoughts of putting in practice the principle of secession, wrote of the possible "Southern Confederacy" that would remain, and while deprecating such an issue in his letter to the inhabitants of the Eastern States, he maintained that if there was hostility between the States of the Union they should separate: "For with every other man of common sense," he adds, "I have always regarded union as the means of liberty and safety; in other words, of happiness, and not an end to which these are to be sacrificed." [2] In this connection, the words of Hamilton in *The Federalist* may be noted. Replying to the supposed case of a combination of States refusing to appoint Senators, he says, "it is not from a general and permanent combination of the States that we can have anything to fear." But granting the existence of such a combination of States, it "would suppose a fixed and rooted disaffection in the great body of the people, which will either never exist at all, or will in all probability proceed from an inaptitude of the general government to the advancement of their happiness, in which event no good citizen could desire its continuance." [3] The principle of community independence and sovereignty, proclaimed first by George Mason in the Virginia Bill of Rights, reiterated by Thomas Jefferson in the Declaration of Independence, asserted in the Articles of Confederation, and

[1] *Ibid.*, p. 427.
[2] Garland's "Life of John Randolph," vol. ii., p. 51.
[3] *The Federalist*, No. 59.

acknowledged by Great Britain in the treaty of peace, it remains for the modern exponents of the American political system to disavow. One of them gravely writes:

"There is no power granted or ' reserved ' to the local States or its people which may not be taken away without their consent. They possess no power which is not held at the will of a power higher and outside of themselves. This view may not conform to the intent of the framers of the Constitution or to later opinion as to the effect of their work, but what is of more importance, it conforms to actual facts as they exist. We have now reached a point where we can afford to see these facts as they are, and we shall escape much confusion of thought if we cease to talk of Sovereign States and a divided sovereignty."[1]

If this be so, then have we realized the worst fears of the Antifederalists. But if such was not " the intent of the framers of the Constitution," it is expedient that the people who profess to live still under the institutions of 1787–89, should see that the "actual facts" conform to the theory of the fathers. A Democratic Executive has sought in the exercise of the veto power to restrain the centralizing legislation of Congress; and recent decisions of a Republican Supreme Court tend in the same conservative direction, declaring against the dangerous principle that the Federal Legislature can supersede that of the States.[2] The doctrine of State sovereignty is indeed the anchor to which we should cling as the only hope of political liberty. To quote again from that wise Southern statesman who has just gone from us, the President of the Confederate States:

"By all that is revered in the memory of our Revolutionary sires, and sacred in the principles they established, let not the children of the United States be taught that our Federal Government is sovereign ; that our sires, after having by a long and bloody war won community independence, used the power, not

---

[1] Letter on " American Sovereignty," E. Burritt Smith, *The Nation*, Feb. 4, 1886.

[2] Decision of Supreme Court on Civil Rights Act, 1883, etc., etc.

for the end sought, but to transfer their allegiance, and by oath or otherwise bind their posterity to be the subjects of another Government, from which they could only free themselves by force of arms." [1]

The early Federalists loved to compare the Union to a house with its thirteen compartments and its one roof sheltering all. The Antifederalists might have suggested that a fit motto over the door of this house would be the words which Dante saw inscribed over the entrance to the Inferno:

" *Lasciate ogni speranza, voi ch' entrate.*"

[1] Letter to *Jackson* (Miss.) *Clarion*, June 20, 1885.

CHAPTER IX.

THE PHILOSOPHER AND SEER.

1788–1790.

Upon the adjournment of the Convention George Mason returned to " Gunston Hall," and the following letters to his son in France, written at this time, contain characteristic allusions to public events :

VIRGINIA, FAIRFAX COUNTY,
GUNSTON HALL, July 21, 1788.

DEAR JOHN :

I have been so ill for these two days past that I have been unable to sit up, and now write in great pain. You must therefore excuse the shortness of this letter.

I enclose you the two or three last days' proceedings of the Virginia Convention, by which you will see the small majority which has ratified the new project. The minority are as respectable for their weight and influence as their number, and it will require their most prudent exertion to keep the people quiet in some parts of the country. . . . The debates are not yet published, nor is there any cause to expect that they will be authentic. The short-hand man who took them down being a Federal partizan, they will probably be garbled in some such partial manner as the debates in the Pennsylvania Convention have been by Lloyd.

I have desired Captain Fenwick to send you some patterns of sundry coarse articles which being in great annual demand in all the States that have many slaves, if they could be made in France and furnished upon equal or better terms than in Great Britain, it would contribute greatly to increase the commercial intercourse between the two countries ; and would be an inducement to the country gentlemen as well as merchants here to ship tobacco to France. I enclose you a letter to Mr. Jefferson upon the subject, left open for your perusal, which you will please to seal and forward. You will perceive by it, that I have some expectation the French ministry will patronize the manufacturers in imitating these articles for the American trade. If they do, and the hint originates from your house, it may prove very advantageous to its credit, especially if the attempt succeeds. You will therefore, if you find occasion, confer with Mr. Jefferson upon the subject. I have desired Capt. Fenwick to send with the patterns, the British sterling first cost of each article. You can easily compute and accommodate the difference between the English and French measure &c. The fault of all the coarse French woolens I have seen is their being stiffened and battered up with paste or glue. The nearer the coarse woolens which our negroes have been accustomed to are imitated the better ; and particular attention should be paid to the width, which should be full three fourths of an English yard.

The hoes and irons should be made of good iron, the blades of the hoes hardened, and the axes well steeled and tempered. The workmen should be informed that tar is not put over the hoes and axes to conceal cracks or flaws, but to preserve them from rusting. I am not able to sit up longer at present, than to wish you health, and success in your business, and to desire you will let me hear from you, as often, and as particularly as you can.

I am, dear John,

Your affectionate father,

G. MASON.

VIRGINIA, GUNSTON HALL,
September 2, 1788.

DEAR JOHN :

This will be delivered you by Capt. Gregory, commander and owner of the ship *Commerce*, who brings a load of tobacco for the Farmers General to Bordeaux ; and was so obliging to call upon me, a day or two ago, to know if I had any commands to the port to which he was going, and to assure me they should be delivered with his own hands.

Notwithstanding Col. Fitzgerald's brig was delayed so long, by his negligence, I was prevented writing by her, when she sailed, by her going down the river, without my knowing it. I had wrote you by her, about a month before, at the time she was expected to have sailed, which letter, I hope has come safe to hand, but am afraid the bag of hominy I sent you by her had been so long on board, that it will be moulded or damaged. At the time I wrote you by the said brig I was extremely ill with the convulsive cholic complicated, I believe, with the gout in my stomach ; which continued with little or no intermission three days and nights, and left me in so debilitated a state, that I was not able to go out of the house for four or five weeks ; and it is not until within these few days that I have begun to recruit.

I enclose you a letter for Mr. Jefferson, respecting the French endeavoring to supply us (from patterns sent) with some particular articles of coarse manufacture, which hitherto have been imported only from Great Britain. It is a subject of much greater importance than you may at first conceive, and I think I should not exaggerate, in saying that the annual demand for them in the five Southern States, is not less than 10,000,000 of Livres. Judge then what effect the French being able to supply us with these articles upon equal or better terms than Great Britain, would have upon the commercial intercourse between the two countries, and the shipment of American produce to France. I desired Capt. Fenwick to send you the patterns by the brig, but forgot to ask him about them when he was here last. He is now down the country, endeavoring to collect tobacco for a small brig of Messrs. Forrest and Stoddert, which he has chartered, and is now loading at Georgetown, so that he will not probably have an opportunity of writing by Capt. Gregory.

A violent storm of wind and rain, which we had about the 20th of August, with the almost continual rains for many days afterwards, has done great damage to the tobacco, and I think will shorten the crops much, as well as injure the quality of the whole, which I believe will in general be unusually bad this year. I think your brothers and myself have lost between thirty and forty hogsheads of tobacco in our own crops ; our wheat has also suffered some damage, and our hay a great deal. The Indian corn appeared at first to be greatly injured, but has recovered more

than could have been expected, so that the crops of corn will be
pretty good. The shortness of the crop of tobacco will considerably affect the interest of your house; if the crop of tobacco
had been as good as it promised about the first of August, your
consignments next summer would have been very considerable.
I have written to my friends in the Eastern and Southern States
in favor of your house, which I hope will have a good effect.

I did not apply (as you desired) to Mr. Alexander; my
acquaintance with him was hardly sufficient to warrant such a
request; and his character in France (as I have heard) being
doubtful, I did not think letters from him would operate to your
advantage. My late illness has hitherto prevented my writing to
Doctor Franklin; but I will do it soon, though I doubt whether
letters from him will be of much service to your house, as his intimacies were more among the literati than the mercantile part of
the nation. I sent you in my last letter lists of the firms of most
of the mercantile houses in the lower parts of Virginia. I would
recommend it to you, to endeavor to cultivate a correspondence
with the American minister, Mr. Jefferson, which I think will be
serviceable to you, and give credit to the house. I hope you determine to persevere in the line you set out, of giving no credits
whatever in America; and I wish you to be very careful and particular in purchasing the goods you send to your correspondents
upon the best terms, it being a matter upon which your consignments will in great measure depend.

.   .   .   .

Pray write to me often, and particularly, respecting your situation, your success and prospects in business; what health you
enjoy, how you like the country you are in and what progress
you make in the language, or anything else interesting to you,
and consequently to me.

I send you by the Brig the proceedings of the Virginia Convention. I have not yet seen a publication of the debates. Notwithstanding there was in the New York Convention a majority of two to
one against the new Constitution without previous amendments, yet
after the adoption by Virginia they thought themselves under the
necessity of adopting also, for fear of being left out of the Union,
and of civil commotions. They have drawn up amendments
nearly similar to those of Virginia and recommended them unani-

mously in the strongest manner, and they have written a circular to all the other States soliciting their cooperation in obtaining the amendments by application to the new Congress at their first meeting which it is expected will be in March in New York, so there is still hope of safe and proper amendments. The North Carolina Convention has rejected the new Constitution unless previous amendments are made, by a great majority. I have not yet seen their amendments but am informed they are much the same as those recommended by Virginia. Your brothers have sent you a number of late newspapers, which will give you pretty full information of the present state of American politics.

All your brothers and sisters who are at home, have written to you by this opportunity. The family are all well, and desire to be kindly remembered to you. I am extremely anxious to hear of your safe arrival and am, dear John,

Your most affectionate father,

G. MASON.

P. S. Your friend Mr. Anthony called to see me, and spent an evening with me last week on his return from North Carolina; where he tells me he has been near three months, and is to return thither again in October. If I am not mistaken he is about committing matrimony with a Miss Hill, daughter of Mr. Whitmel Hill, the most wealthy man in the State of North Carolina.

VIRGINIA, GUNSTON HALL,
December 18, 1788.

DEAR JOHN:

Capt. Fenwick's letter from George Town last week, per the post, having miscarried (as most of my letters via Alexandria do), I knew nothing of the ship *Washington* being so near sailing, until I was informed, this evening by express from Capt. F. that the ship would be down to-night, or early to-morrow morning, so that I have very little time left to write to you by her. I have not received any letter from you since your arrival at Bordeaux, but one of the fifteenth of August per the *Coulteana*, Capt. Limebourg, via Norfolk; and that so soon after your arrival that you were then able to give me little account of your affairs or situation, or how you liked the place. I hope to be particularly informed in your next letters.

I wrote you by Fitzgerald's brig, and also by Capt. Gregory who was so obliging as to call on me on purpose, and promised to deliver the packet with his own hand. By one of these opportunities (I now forget which), I sent you the proceedings of the Virginia Convention, and informed you of the then state of American politics. North Carolina has rejected the new government unless previous amendments, almost the same with the subsequent amendments proposed by Virginia, can be obtained. Rhode Island has yet done nothing decisive on the subject. New York discouraged by the adoption in Virginia, with a majority in their Convention of two to one against the new form of government, received it upon the minority's agreeing to recommend unanimously amendments similar to those in Virginia, and voting a circular letter from their president Governor Clinton to invite the concurrence of the other States in an immediate application to the new Congress for calling another Federal Convention to consider them. The other States have all adopted ; Connecticut, Jersey, Pennsylvania, Delaware and Maryland without recommending any amendments ; New Hampshire, Massachusetts, South Carolina and I think Georgia, with recommendation of amendments. The Virginia Legislature now sitting have taken up the subject upon the ground of the New York circular letter and by a large majority have voted an application to Congress for immediately calling a Federal Convention to consider the amendments proposed by this and other States. Their address to Congress for this purpose is a very firm, and in my opinion, proper one. They have also wrote a circular to the other States desiring their concurrence. . . . Colonel R. H. Lee and Colonel Grayson are appointed members of the Senate for this State. Virginia is divided into ten districts as nearly equal as circumstances will permit, the rule of computation being the number of militia in each county, each district to choose one representative [who has been a resident of the district for twelve months last past] to the new government, and it is thought the elections will go very generally in favor of men who are for calling a Federal Convention to make amendments. Our district consists of the counties of Loudon, Fairfax, Prince William, Fauquier, Stafford, and King George. Several candidates are talked of by the other party, to wit Ludwell Lee, Dr. Stuart, Mr.

Fitzhugh of "Chatham," Leven Powell and Martin Pickett ; but they will hardly, I suppose, be foolish enough to start more than one. The gentlemen for the amendments have not yet fixed upon a candidate and I doubt we shall be at a loss for one, several who have been applied to having refused. If we can prevail upon a proper person to offer I think there will be little doubt of his succeeding. Mr. James Monroe of Fredericksburg (late member of Congress) opposes Mr. Madison in the Spottsylvania and Orange district and it is thought will carry his election. Beverley Randolph is chosen Governor of Virginia in the room of young A—ld.

Several of our late Convention acquaintance are appointed members of the Federal Senate ; John Langdon, Esq : from New Hampshire, Caleb Strong, Esq: from Massachusetts, Dr. Johnson and Oliver Ellsworth, Esq: from Connecticut, Mr. Paterson from Jersey, Robert Morris from Pennsylvania, George Read and Richard Bassett, Esqurs: from Delaware. So much for politics. For domestic occurrences I refer you to your sisters, who I make no doubt will give you a satisfactory detail.

Your partner Mr. Joseph Fenwick has written to me to desire my interest in getting him the appointment of Consul in Bordeaux. Upon talking with your brother George upon the subject, I find he had recommended the same thing to you, before you left Virginia, a circumstance I was not before apprised of. But as Mr. Fenwick has written to me to recommend him, before he knew of your previous intention (indeed before your arrival in Bordeaux) your brother George and I are both of opinion that it will be proper to make the application for him, in preference to you, for several reasons ; first because he is an older man, and consequently has more experience ; secondly because he will probably remain longer in France ; and above all, because we would avoid giving the smallest cause for any jealousy or misunderstanding between you. You may therefore assure Mr. Fenwick that what interest I may have, with our new rulers, shall be most cordially exerted in his favor, as soon as the new Congress meets ; though I have no reason to expect my interest will have much weight in the new government, having, as you know, warmly opposed it, in its present shape, both in the Federal Convention and our own. In my opinion a letter of recommendation from our Minister, Mr. Jefferson, would have a good effect. Pray excuse me particularly to Mr. Fenwick, for not writing to him by this opportunity. The ship's sailing so suddenly and unexpectedly has not left me time; and I could have said little to him but a repetition of what I have said, and shall say, to you.

The debates in the Virginia Convention are published, at least one volume of them. As soon as I can get them I will send them to you, though I believe they will be hardly worth your attention, being, I am told, very partially garbled by the short-hand writer who took them down and published them. This I always expected, as I understood the man was a federal partizan and they, you know as well as I do, stick at nothing. He had the audacity to desire the sanction of Convention authority for his work, even before he began it, and got a member to make a motion for that purpose on the first day of the Convention, but upon the impropriety and absurdity of it being properly exposed by Mr. Henry and myself, the member who made the motion (George Nicholas) was ashamed of it and withdrew it. So that they come out with no other sanction than the credit of the publishers. Some of the Federalists (as they call themselves) revised and corrected their speeches. I know that some of the principal gentlemen on the other side were privately applied to by the short-hand writer to do the same, but treated the proposal with contempt.

One thing with respect to the appointment Mr. Fenwick desires, I had almost forgot to mention; I fear some difficulties may arise from it, and being of opinion with Mr. Fenwick, that such an appointment would be advantageous to the house, I wish to have it in my power, by proper information on the subject to obviate them. Hitherto, I believe, there has been only one American consul-general in France; unless the arrangement is altered, it is probable Mr. Barclay will be continued; it may be necessary therefore to show, that a particular consul will be requisite at Bordeaux or in its neighborhood, for that part of the kingdom.

I am told there are a great many young Irishmen in Bordeaux; if we may judge of them by the samples we have here, they are neither safe nor respectable companions. I trust I am as free as most men, from illiberal national prejudices; but yet I wish you to converse with them with caution, and to avoid as far as good manners will permit, all intimacy with them. Your not being able to speak French will naturally lead you into company, and intimacies with those whom you can converse with easily ; this you must guard against, and submit to a little inconvenience to avoid greater evils ; and I hope you will soon acquire the French language.

In a letter Capt. Fenwick showed me from his brother, I observe Mr. Whitesides of London makes you an offer of a credit of £1000 sterling upon his house, &c. You are obliged to Mr. Whitesides for his friendship and ought to return him thanks for the offer, but I would, by no means, advise you to accept it ;—the custom of drawing and re-drawing being the most dangerous, in my opinion, of all mercantile expedients. Put yourselves in no man's power ; an accident, or a sudden, unexpected call for money, you could not pay, might ruin you in a moment ; a sufficient reason surely for avoiding accepting credits, further than you can clearly and safely see your way through, if you take them at all. And if the business of your house becomes considerable (as I think it will) your neighboring merchants and secret rivals will look upon you with a jealous eye, and seize any opportunity of destroying you. The older I grow, the more experience has convinced me, that there are few men to be safely confided in— *rari nantes in gurgite vasto.*

Stick to your first principles of giving no credits yourselves ; especially in America where large credits must infallibly ruin you, and small ones are not worth the charge of collecting. By giving extensive credits you may, indeed, acquire a large fortune upon paper ; but you will never have any anywhere else. Diligence, frugality and integrity will infallibly increase your business and your fortunes, if you can content yourselves with moderate things at first. You will rise, perhaps, by slow degrees, but upon a solid and safe foundation. It is a terrible thing for a man to spend the prime of his life in business, to no other purpose than to ruin himself, and others ; and yet this is the case with the greater part of those who are called men of great enterprize—men of deep speculation, &c. Your business (after the house comes to be generally known) will depend entirely upon the prices you can render for the commodities consigned you, and the prices of the articles you send in return—no man will long continue any business, unless he finds gain in it.

I have written to most of my friends in the different States, informing them of your plan, and recommending the house. From the answers I have received, I have reason to think you will meet with encouragement, both from the eastward and southward; I think it would be proper for you to write to the gentlemen of your acquaintance in the late Federal Convention, and in Boston. I have spoken also to a great many of my friends in Virginia; most of them express a desire of giving your house a preference; but vague promises of that sort are little to be relied on. I enclose you a list of some of those I would advise you to write to.

The crop of tobacco this year in Virginia is a common one, as to quantity, neither very great nor small—the quality bad, and I think the price in the country will be rather low, not more than 18/ to 20/ Virginia currency per hundred upon Potomac and Rappahannock. I applied to some of my Assembly friends lately recommending the shipping to your house a quantity of the public tobacco received for taxes; I don't yet know the result; I am sure it would be to the advantage of the public, but I fear our finances are too low, and the public too needy, to adopt such a plan.

When I saw Capt. Fenwick about a month ago, I was speaking to him, about chartering a small ship, to load with wheat, upon consignment. I think one might be speedily filled up, and could put a considerable quantity on board her myself; but I have not heard whether he has determined on doing it or not. I have not yet received any rents, or got any of my own crops prized, and therefore am unable to send you any tobacco by the *Washington*, but shall send some by the first ship which loads here for your house in the spring.

Pray let me hear from you often, and particularly, and believe me, dear John,

> Your most affectionate father,

> > > G. MASON.

P. S. Your brother Thomson, and his family, have just moved from Gunston to his own seat of Hollin Hall. Your brother Thomas is at the Academy in Fredericksburg.

John Mason, Esq.:

> Merchant in Bordeaux.[1]

> > > [1] Mason Papers.

With excellent advice to his son on the conduct of his business, and wise warnings against unseemly companions, Colonel Mason mingles in these letters shrewd suggestions of a public nature. He wished to see France, the recent ally of the Americans in the Revolution, taking the place of England in supplying the States of the South with the coarse woollen fabrics used for their negroes. And he has a proposal for the Assembly, that they should ship some of the tobacco received for taxes to Bordeaux, consigned to the house of Mason & Fenwick, a measure which would be advantageous for Virginia, as well as profitable to the firm. The political excitement of the Convention struggle had subsided; its unsettled questions lying over for adjustment, it was hoped, by the new Congress. We get echoes, however, from the late field of action; an account of the "federal partisan," the unappreciated Robertson, and his efforts to secure corrected copies of the speeches in the Convention. It is to be regretted that there was not an Antifederalist reporter there also, to whom Mason and Henry could have given their confidence. As it is, posterity is under obligations to the Federalist. George Mason's allusion to the late governor—"young A—ld"—compressed in two words all the scorn felt by his true and vehement nature for the man who, as Mason believed, had betrayed his country, Virginia, and thrown away the opportunity of securing her dearest interests.

The Virginia Assembly in the fall of this year, under the leadership of Patrick Henry, passed the resolutions, commended by Colonel Mason, for calling a second Federal Convention. This was urged upon Congress and upon the several States. And Richard Henry Lee and William Grayson, two of the most able and determined advocates of amendments, were elected to the Senate, and were pledged to bring forward the subject on the meeting of Congress. Madison, defeated for the Senate, was elected by the Federalists to a seat in the House of Representatives. The division of Virginia into Congressional districts at this session, of which George Mason speaks, has been instanced by a recent writer, upon very insufficient grounds, as the earliest example of *gerrymandering*. The charge is made that the districts were so carved out as to promote the election of the Antifederalists.[1] Just the opposite accusation was made at the time by the Antifederalists, it seems. Theodoric Bland, who calls the Federalists the "Non-Emendo-Tories," in a letter to Richard Henry Lee, tells of "their manœuvres" to prevent the latter's appointment to the Senate. "Much pains," he adds, "is taken to lay off the districts so as to include the most consequent Non-Emendo-Tories, but I expect this bill, which is almost entirely of their carving, will be hushed up and served out to the public in a more delicate form than it at present appears in."[2] As it finally passed, George Mason thought it a proper one, and he opposed, on constitutional grounds, as will be seen later, a projected alteration in the formation of his own district. The Virginia Legislature, in the fall of 1788, showed their appreciation of Colonel Mason's services to the Commonwealth by naming a county after him. An act passed for dividing the county of Bourbon in the district of Kentucky, and the new county thus formed was called Mason.

At the January court of Fairfax County in this winter of 1788–1789, George Mason, as the presiding justice, used his influence in upholding one of the great principles of free government. As the record of the court states:

"On a motion for levying tobacco for the purpose of defraying the expences of building a new court-house or repairing of the present one, it was objected that the court had no legal authority to levy any money or tobacco on the inhabitants of the county for any purpose whatever, and the question being put whether they were vested with that power or not George Mason, Charles Broadwater, Martin Cockburn, Richard Chichester [and eight others whose names are given] were of opinion that the power of

[1] Tyler's "Life of Henry," p. 313, American Statesmen Series.
[2] Lee Papers, *Southern Literary Messenger*, January, 1859.

levying taxes by the courts was destroyed by an express article in the bill of rights of this commonwealth." [1]

But ten of the justices, including Dr. David Stuart, were of the contrary opinion. And with this order is found a request of the public officers of Fairfax County asking the advice of the council and the opinion of the attorney-general concerning the power of the county courts in levying taxes. A gentleman who was living in Baltimore in 1827, wrote an account of a meeting in Alexandria, at which he had been present as a youth, when this subject was discussed. He recalled the fact of there being a score or more justices on the ground and a large crowd of gentlemen, most of them eager for the proposed measure. Just before the meeting opened it was announced that Colonel Mason was coming to oppose the project. But as public opinion was so strongly in its favor, and there were known to be so many good speakers who would advocate it, an easy triumph was antici-pated. George Mason arrived, and when the question had been argued at length by its friends, he rose and delivered such a powerful and convincing argument as to its illegality, maintaining that only the representatives of the people could properly levy taxes, and the justices present were not such representatives, that in all that hitherto confident assembly there was not one dissenting voice, and the point was won. These reminiscences, though they may possibly exaggerate the triumph of Colonel Mason, prove at least that it was owing to him that the court decided adversely to the motion, and the impression of his eloquence must have been very vivid and enduring upon his youthful hearer, since he attributed to it such signal results. It may be presumed that the council and the attorney-general supported Colonel Mason's interpretation of the law. And an act of the Assembly passed the 4th of December of this year, which empowered the justices of Fairfax County to levy a sum on the tith-able persons within the county sufficient for the new court-

[1] " Virginia Calendar Papers," vol. iv., p. 553.

house buildings and the two acres of ground on which to place them.[1]

The following letters to Capt. James Fenwick, brother of John Mason's partner, exhibit Colonel Mason in his character of a busy and careful planter and farmer, shipping his tobacco and wheat to merchants in Georgetown, to go from there to France.

GUNSTON HALL, March 8th, 1789.

DEAR SIR :

I am sorry I am disappointed in shipping all our wheat by the ship *Maryland ;* but it was impossible to help it. The bad weather which delayed Mr. McCarty's boat so long, also prevented Mr. Linton's vessel from getting out of Quantico Creek, until it was too late to send up any more wheat for this ship ; but I shall depend upon getting room for wheat we have left, in the *Becky,* and as I expect she will be quickly despatched it may probably make no great difference to me, and I beg you will get the matter so fixed, that I may not be again disappointed. The bearer, Mr. McCarty's shipper, brings up eight or nine hogsheads of tobacco for my son George. You will be pleased to let me know by a line, when he returns, at what time the ship *Becky* will certainly be ready to take in wheat, and I will begin to send ours up immediately, and if this cannot be yet known, as soon as it can you will be good [enough] to inform me by a letter per post, directed to be left at the post-office in Colchester, as I shall be anxious to get our wheat up in due time. My people went down again, as soon as the river opened, to Chickamuxon, to inspect my tobacco and despatch Messrs. F[orest] and S[toddert]'s craft, but have not yet returned. I imagine the hard frost last Wednesday night stopped up the mouth of Chickamuxon Creek, or perhaps the low tides have kept the craft aground. She will surely be up the first good day, and I hope will bring up my tobacco in time for the ship *Maryland.*

I am, dear Sir, your most obedient servant,

G. MASON.

Capt. James Fenwick,
George Town.

[1] Journal of the Assembly, 1789.

GUNSTON HALL, March 27, 1789.

DEAR SIR :

The bearer, John Hill, brings up 550 bushels of wheat by our measure which is all we have now ready ; this will fall short of the quantity I owe Messrs. Forrest and Stoddert, in return for wheat they were so kind [as] to put into the ship *Becky* upon my account. But so soon as I know the loss in this last load, by the measurement at George Town, I will desire Messrs. Fenwick, Mason, and Company to place to the credit of Messrs. F. and S. the nett proceeds of as much of my wheat in the *Becky* as I am deficient in repaying them, which I presume will be the most agreeable method to those gentlemen of settling it, as it will amount to the same thing, as repaying the whole now at Georgetown.

I will thank you to transmit me by John Hill, when he returns, a statement of all our wheat in both ships, according to their respective manifests, that I may see whether it corresponds with the statement I have given in my letters to F., M., & Co. Upon having the account of our wheat in both ships, with the measurement at George Town of the load John Hill now brings, my son William and I can easily adjust our respective quantities.

I am, dear sir, your most obedient servant,

G. MASON.

In case of Capt. Fenwick's absence, Major Stoddert will be pleased to open this.[1]

Colonel Mason wrote to his son in this same month, on the subject of the consulship which he hoped to obtain for Mr. Joseph Fenwick. This letter is of special interest, in its reference to Washington, as it bears testimony to the early and intimate character of the friendship which had subsisted between George Mason and George Washington—a friendship which the former feared was likely to be interrupted by political differences. Colonel Mason's visits to " Mount Vernon," however, had not ceased in 1788. On the 2d of November of that year, which fell on Sunday, he dined and spent the day with Washington.[2] But in the struggle over

[1] MS. Letters. Major Stoddert, Benjamin Stoddert, Secretary of the Navy under John Adams.

[2] Washington's Private Journals, Toner Transcripts.

the new Constitution, the old friends had no doubt drifted apart. George Mason, the Revolution over—in which he and Washington had been wholly of one mind,—saw now in the untried future new dangers springing up to which Washington was blind. Virginia and the South generally had cause later to know him for the wiser man of the two. But at this time he was in the party of the minority. And he seems to have felt that he must justify himself in his position of withstanding the current of public opinion. His conscience could bear witness, as he says, to the purity of his motives. A civil war bears witness now to the sound "judgment" which guided his conscience.

"GUNSTON HALL, March 13, 1789.

"DEAR JOHN :

" .   .   .   I have not yet made an application on behalf of Mr. Fenwick for the appointment of consul, as the President of the United States has the nomination to offices. I thought there was some impropriety and indelicacy in making application before General Washington has accepted the office of President, to which he has been elected by the unanimous suffrage of the electors in all the ratifying States. You may assure Mr. Fenwick that as soon as this ceremonial is adjusted I shall not fail to exert whatever interest I have in his favor. You know the friendship which has long existed (indeed from our early youth) between General Washington and myself. I believe there are few men in whom he placed greater confidence ; but it is possible my opposition to the new government, both as a member of the national and of the Virginia Convention, may have altered the case. In this important trust, I am truly conscious of having acted from the purest motives of honesty, and love to my country, according to that measure of judgment which God has bestowed on me, and I would not forfeit the approbation of my own mind for the approbation of any man, or all the men upon earth. My conduct as a public man, through the whole of the late glorious Revolution, has been such as, I trust, will administer comfort to me in those moments when I shall most want it, and smooth the bed of death. But as Shakespeare says, 'Something too much of this.' "

The letter closes with the following postscript :

" Send me by the first good ship to Potomac River insured, six half hogsheads viz. : about one hundred and eighty or ninety American gallons of good cogniac brandy in barrels or casks of about thirty gallons each, iron-bound or very well secured and tight, and covered each with a double empty cask to prevent the sailors or the craftsmen in this country from making free with it. Also a piece of silk, a pattern for your sister Betsy. I would have it a handsome but not a very expensive silk, and depend upon your taste in the choice of it. If trimmings are necessary they should be sent with it, and sewing silk to make it up." [1]

Colonel Mason wrote from " Gunston Hall " to Washington ten days later on the subject of a coachman living with him, whom the latter wanted to secure. He had been in Colonel Mason's service, and Washington wished to know his character. The man, a German, came to Maryland, " and entered into an indenture to Colonel Fitzhugh," George Mason's relative, " who thereupon paid his passage over to serve him four years." After living two years in Maryland with Colonel Fitzhugh, the latter recommended him as a coachman to Colonel Mason, and he was found to be a good driver and careful of horses, but lazy and quarrelsome. His indenture expired in October, 1787, but he had wished to remain at " Gunston," and Colonel Mason gave him then £15 a year with his clothes. He only kept him, however, he tells his correspondent, because he could get no other coachman. No servant of his own was capable of driving, and this man had never attempted to teach any one of them ; only a small negro had " ridden one of the four horses as postillion." The duties of the German were to serve as coachman, to wait at table, occasionally work in the garden, take care of the stable and horses, and keep the key of the corn house and give out the corn. But, in fact, he did little more than drive and look after the horses.[2] Probably this

[1] Mason Papers.   [2] Washington MSS., Department of State.

German coachman went from Colonel Mason's service into that of the new President, and drove for him the famous cream-colored chariot painted by Cipriani. This letter of March 23, 1789, is the last one of George Mason's letters to Washington which has been preserved.

The following letter was written by Colonel Mason to his son in France:

VIRGINIA, GUNSTON HALL,
May 14, 1789.

DEAR JOHN:

I have received your several letters, one via Norfolk and two by the brigs *Betsy* and *Nancy*, besides the former ones, the receipt whereof I had before mentioned. Your brother George has received a letter from you of a later date, via Philadelphia, wherein you mention your intention to set out for Paris the next morning. . . . I have written a long letter by this opportunity to Fenwick, Mason, & Company upon several interesting particulars, to which I refer you, to save a repetition here. I observe what you mention, with respect to overshipping goods to some particular people; perhaps in a few instances, now and then, it is difficult to avoid this, but you should avoid it as much as possible. The hazard is too great in large debts, and small debts in this country are not worth a shilling in the pound; and there are some people who would otherwise ship you tobacco, that upon getting in your debt, will immediately discontinue their correspondence. But when you were mentioning with regret your having overshipped goods to a small amount, I am surprised at your silence with respect to the more important affair of Mr. Whitesides. This has the appearance of its having been done without your participation, or of your not being intimately acquainted with the transactions and business of the house, either of which may be productive of bad consequences. You are upon the spot, ought to know, and have a right to be consulted in all important transactions. In order to entitle you with the greater propriety to this, you should spare no pains or application to make yourself well acquainted with business, so as to be able to take a proper share in the management, as well as to enable you to conduct the business of a separate house yourself whenever it becomes necessary, which probably may be soon. Notwithstanding I understand you are likely to secure yourselves, this affair gives me much uneasiness, for though I have always heard a very good character of Mr. Fenwick and that he is a diligent, attentive, discreet young man, yet this transaction shows a kind of softness and milkiness of temper liable to imposition, which both you and he ought to guard against. Pray explain this business of Mr. Whitesides, and let me know without reserve how it is like to terminate. . . . I believe your Convention acquaintance, Doctor McClurg of Richmond, has shipped you eight or ten hogsheads of tobacco per the *Washington*. I would have you write him particularly by the first convenient opportunity informing him of the prices current, and what articles can be advantageously imported from Bordeaux. It may be a means of opening you a correspondence from James River, as Dr. McClurg is a member of our Executive Council and a man of some interest in that part of the country. But you should always take care to be accurate in your quotations of the prices current at the time. This was not the case in the list of the current prices transmitted in your letters of December and January, wherein you quoted tobacco from 30 lb to 32 lb per ct. instead of 28 lb.–10.

You are under obligations to Mr. Daniel Brent, of "Richland," and his brother, Mr. Richard Brent,[1] for their utmost endeavors to promote your interest here, and I believe to very good effect. Your Stafford friends have not shipped you so generally as I expected. One reason for this is that great part of their tobacco upon low grounds was destroyed by the excessive rains last summer, and another that I believe many of them are indebted to the Scotch stores, and there is hardly a Scotch merchant in this part of the country who does not wish your house at the devil.

I hope to hear soon that you and Mr. Fenwick have got to housekeeping, for as your business is now grown considerable, and there are of course many captains of ships and others to whom it will be necessary for you to show civilities, I can't think housekeeping will be any great addition to your expences, and I am sure it will give some respectability to your house, besides that it will be much more agreeable than living in a boarding-

[1] These were sons of William Brent of "Richland," whose wife was a sister of Mrs. Robert Brent of "Woodstock."

house. I still continue of opinion that it will be very imprudent in you to come to America this year, but that it will be very proper the year after. Indeed, the more I have reflected on this subject the more I am confirmed in this opinion.

I mentioned to you in my letter by the *Becky* that it was not then in my power to ascertain the respective quantities of wheat shipped by me and your brothers Thomson and William. I now send you, on the other side, an exact statement of all the wheat we shipped you in the two ships, the *Maryland* and the *Becky*, according to which, separate accounts of sales are to be rendered us, notwithstanding the bills of lading for the whole may have been taken in my name, as I would avoid blending your brothers accounts with mine. You will observe that sixty-seven bushels of the wheat included in your brother William's quantity properly belongs to William Green, who, being very desirous to ship you something, got your brother William to include it with his, as the ship did not take in any wheat but from our family, except Forrest and Stoddert's own. For this sixty-seven bushels your brother William desires a separate account of sales may be rendered to Green, and an account rendered to himself for only his own proper wheat. It will also please Green mightily, which is some consideration, as the man seems to be much attached to you, and I believe intends to ship you his tobacco also. You will observe too that Messrs. Forrest and Stoddert are to have credit by me for the nett proceeds of fifty-four bushels of my wheat in the *Becky*, and my account debited accordingly, it being the quantity I still owe these gentlemen for what they were so kind to lend me. On the other side is also a duplicate of the list of goods I ordered in my letter per the *Becky*. I wish the brandy may arrive before the new duties take place, and I hope it will be of better quality than the brandy sent me last year by Mr. Fenwick, which, though at a very high price, is exceeding bad; the man who furnished it must have been a knave, for I make no doubt Mr. Fenwick expected it was good and paid a price accordingly. The piece of silk ordered is for your sister Betsy, and I expect you will choose it yourself.

I enclose you a list of the members of the new Congress, in both Houses, by which you will see that a considerable number of the Senate are our Convention acquaintance.

I send you by Capt. Bond a barrel containing eight hams. I wish they may arrive in good order, as I think they were exceeding good hams when they were packed up. I should be glad to know whether the barrel of hominy and smoked beef, by Capt. Rose got to hand in good order. Your brothers sent you by Capt. Rose two female and one male oppossum.

. . . . . .

We have had a mocking bird for you ever since last summer which is quite tame and domestic, and intended to send it out this spring, but it proves a female, and they seldom sing ; this hardly attempts a single note, and therefore we shall not send it abroad, to disgrace its native country. I would turn it out of the cage, but I am afraid its liberty, after such long confinement, would only make the poor thing a prey to the first hawk that came in its way. We will endeavor to raise some young ones this summer. I will also endeavor to raise a buck and doe fawn for you this summer. . . . The family at Gunston is reduced lately from a very large to a small one, consisting now only of your sister Betsy, your brother William, Mrs. Mason and myself. I most cordially wish you health and happiness, and am, dear John,

Your affectionate father,
G. MASON.

Mr. John Mason,
    Merchant in Bordeaux,
        per the *Washington*, Capt. Bond.[1]

The new Federal Government went into operation March 4, 1789, and Congress met in New York. Richard Henry Lee brought forward the Virginia amendments, and William Grayson wrote to Patrick Henry on this subject on the 29th of September :

"With respect to amendments, matters have turned out exactly as I apprehended, from the extraordinary doctrine of playing the after game ; the lower House sent up amendments which

---

[1] Mason Papers. There were 1000 bushels of wheat shipped by George Mason and his sons in the ship *Maryland*, and 1298½ bushels in the *Becky*.

held out a safeguard to personal liberty in a great many instances, but this disgusted the Senate, and though we made every exertion to save them, they are so mutilated and gutted, that in fact they are good for nothing. . . . The Virginia amendments were all brought into view and regularly rejected. . . . Their maxim seems to have been to make up by construction, what the Constitution wants in energy."

Ten amendments, however, proposed at this time were made a part of the Constitution in 1791. They were in substance equivalent to some of those on the Virginia list. The tenth amendment, which was endorsed by the Conventions of Virginia, Massachusetts, Pennsylvania, and North Carolina, as moved in the Senate by Richard Henry Lee, was in these words : " The powers not delegated by the Constitution to the United States, nor prohibited by it to the States, are reserved to the States respectively." Ellsworth, of Massachusetts, moved to add, " or to the people," a phrase which was perverted from its plain signification, " or to the people of the States," and used in later years as an argument against States-rights and the doctrine of secession.

George Mason from his retirement at "Gunston Hall" must have watched with great interest the course of events in Congress, and the action of the Virginia Legislature upon these amendments. Stevens Thomson Mason was in the Virginia Senate, and doubtless in correspondence with his uncle, by whose side he had sat in the Virginia Convention and whose principles he had made thoroughly his own. With his father no longer living, and his uncle's political career closed, Stevens Thomson Mason represented the name in public life at this time, and upon him, in some sort, the mantle of his elders had fallen. The journal of the Virginia Senate records that the House, on the 8th of December, went into committee of the whole on the resolutions of the House of Delegates ratifying the amendments (twelve in number) proposed by Congress to the Constitution of the

---

[1] " Letters and Times of the Tylers," Lyon G. Tyler, vol. i., p. 165.

United States. They came to the following resolution : That the third, eighth, eleventh, and twelfth amendments be postponed until the next session of Assembly. The others were agreed to, and then the motion was made, that all or any members who voted for the postponement of the above four articles be allowed to enter upon the journal the reasons which influenced their vote and all or any of their objections. On the 12th of December this was accordingly done, and the entry is as follows :

" The Senate of Virginia having determined to postpone until the next session of Assembly, the third, eighth, eleventh, and twelfth articles of the amendments to the Constitution of the United States, recommended by Congress, we, the underwritten members of the majority on that question, deem it incumbent on us, not only from the respect we owe to our constituents, and our responsibility to them, but in order to prevent doubt and misrepresentation, to enter on the Journals of the House the considerations which have influenced our decision on this subject, and our principal objections to those articles. We are satisfied that the people of Virginia would never have ratified the Constitution of the United States, but from a confident hope and firm persuasion of speedily seeing it much more materially altered and amended than it would be by ratifying the propositions lately submitted by Congress to the State Legislatures. That although we consider some of the amendments offered as similar, and others nearly equivalent, to a part of the amendments proposed by Virginia and other States, yet that some of them which seem analogous to other amendments so proposed, are not substantially the same and fall short of affording the same security to personal rights, or of so effectually guarding against the apprehended mischiefs of the government ; of this description we consider the 3rd, 8th, 11th and 12th articles. We conceive that the 3rd article, which seems given in lieu of the 15th, 16th, 19th and 20th articles of the bill of rights proposed by the Virginia Convention, will not bear a comparison with these articles. The 15th expressly declares the right of the people to assemble together to consult for the common good, to instruct their representatives, and to petition for redress of grievances. The 16th asserts the right of the people to freedom of speech, and of writing and publishing their sentiments, and secures the liberty of the press. The 19th and 20th hold sacred the rights of conscience, secure to every religious sect or society the most perfect equality, and effectually guard against any religious establishments.

"The 3rd amendment, recommended by Congress, does not prohibit the rights of conscience from being violated or infringed ; and although it goes to restrain Congress from passing laws establishing any national religion, they might, notwithstanding, levy taxes to any amount, for the support of religion or its preachers ; and any particular denomination of Christians might be so favored and supported by the General Government as to give it a decided advantage over others, and in process of time render it as powerful and dangerous as if it was established as the national religion of the country.

"This amendment does not declare and assert the right of the people to speak and publish their sentiments, nor does it secure the liberty of the press. Should these valuable rights be infringed or violated by the arbitrary decisions of Judges, or by any other means than a legislative act directly to that effect, the people would have no avowed principle in the Constitution to which they might resort for the security of these rights.

"The right of the people to instruct their representatives, and their right to consult with each other for the common good, seem too evident to be questioned in a republican government ; yet, these rights are denied by Congress, and they have refused to allow any amendment declaratory of them, as we discover by their Journals ; and even the humble privilege of petitioning against oppression is not fully asserted or secured ; as this privilege may be abridged or rendered nugatory without any law upon the subject ; not to mention other means, it might be defeated by a rule of either House, without violating the 3rd article of the amendments.

"This amendment then, when considered as it relates to any of the rights it is pretended to secure, will be found totally inadequate, and betrays an unreasonable, unjustifiable, but a studied departure from the amendment proposed by Virginia and other States, for the protection of their rights. We conceive that this amendment is dangerous and fallacious, as it tends to lull the apprehensions of the people on these important points, without affording them security ; and mischievous, because by setting bounds to Congress, it will be considered as the only restriction on their power over these rights ; and thus certain powers in the government, which it has been denied to possess, will be recognized without being properly guarded against abuse.

" The 8th article of the proposed amendments, so far from securing the valuable trial by jury of the vicinage in criminal prosecutions, leaves Congress the same power to abridge this right as they possess by the original Constitution. They have already by law fixed the districts co-extensive with the respective States ; and they will at all times possess the power of regulating the districts at pleasure, so that there appears to us nothing in this amendment to restrain government from carrying a man accused of a crime, out of his own neighborhood to any distance within the limits of a State, to be tried by strangers, perhaps enemies, where the advantages of this excellent mode of trial might be entirely defeated, and where a person obnoxious to Congress, might fall an innocent sacrifice to their resentment.

" We do not find that the 11th article is asked for by Virginia or any other State ; we therefore conceive that the people of Virginia should be consulted with respect to it, even if we did not doubt the propriety of adopting it ; but it appears to us highly exceptionable. If it is meant to guard against the extension of the powers of Congress by implication, it is greatly defective, and does by no means comprehend the idea expressed in the 17th article of amendments proposed by Virginia ; and as it respects personal rights might be dangerous, because should the rights of the people be invaded or called in question, they might be required to show by the Constitution what rights they have *retained ;* and such as could not from that instrument be proved to be retained, they might be denied to possess. Of this there is ground to be apprehensive, when Congress are already seen denying certain rights of the people heretofore deemed clear and unexceptionable.

" We conceive that the 12th article would come up to the 1st article of the Virginia amendments, were it not for the words ' or to the people.' It is not declared to be the people of the respective States ; but the expression applies to the people generally as citizens of the United States, and leaves it doubtful what powers are reserved to the State Legislatures. Unrestrained by the Constitution or these amendments, Congress might, as the supreme ruler of the people, assume those powers which properly belong to the respective States, and thus gradually effect an entire consolidation.

"We consider that of the many and important amendments recommended by the Conventions of Virginia and other States, these propositions contain all that Congress are disposed to grant ; that all the rest are by them deemed improper, and that these are offered in full satisfaction of the whole : and although the ratification of a part of the amendments that have been prayed for by Virginia would not absolutely preclude us from urging others, yet we conceive that by the acceptance of particular articles, we are concluded as to the points they relate to. Considering therefore that they are far short of what the people of Virginia wish, and have asked, and deeming them by no means sufficient to secure the rights of the people, or to render the government safe and desirable, we think our countrymen ought not to be put off with amendments so inadequate.

That being satisfied of the defects and dangerous tendency of these four articles of the proposed amendments, we are constrained to withhold our assent to them ; but unwilling for the present to determine on their rejection, we think it our duty to postpone them until the next session of Assembly, in order that the people of Virginia may have an opportunity to consider of them, and judge for themselves ; and that the members of the Legislature may be enabled to consult with, and know the sentiments of their constituents on the subject."

S. T. Mason was one of the eight members of the Senate who signed these resolutions, which were published shortly afterwards in the Richmond paper.[1] The House of Delegates appointed some of its members to confer with a delegation from the Senate on this subject, and Stevens Thomson Mason[2] was one of the three senators chosen for

---

[1] Journal of the Virginia Senate, 1789. *The Virginia Independent Chronicle*, January 13, 1790.

[2] Stevens Thomson Mason was the grandfather of Stevens Thomson Mason, the early "boy governor" of Michigan, one of the States carved out of Virginia's western territory.

the purpose. The Senate, on the 14th of December, ordered that Mr. Mason should acquaint the House of Delegates that they adhered to their determination not to ratify the amendments except in the conditional form declared by their resolutions. The lower House of the Virginia Legislature at this session was under the influence of such Federalists as General Henry Lee. But in the Senate, the counsels of George Mason, of Henry, Grayson, and R. H. Lee bore fruit.

Jefferson returned to America from Paris in the fall of 1789, to take his place in Washington's Cabinet. John Mason had written to him offering him a passage on one of his vessels, early in the summer; and Jefferson in replying, on the 16th of July, says: " I beg you to remember me in the most friendly terms to your father. I have put off answering his letter because I expected constantly to make my voyage to America and to see him at his own house." [1] He sailed from London to Norfolk in October, and visiting friends all along the route from Norfolk, reached " Monticello " only two days before Christmas. Setting out for New York on the 1st of March, 1790, Jefferson stopped, on his way, in Alexandria, where the mayor and citizens gave him a public reception. He did not, however, go to " Gunston Hall," owing to the badness of the roads at this season.

On the 12th of March, 1790, William Grayson, the distinguished Virginia Senator, died at Dumfries, on his way to Congress, and George Mason, it was hoped, would be induced to fill the vacancy. Governor Randolph wrote to him announcing his appointment by the Executive, as the Legislature was not in session :

RICHMOND, March 25th, 1790.

To COL. GEORGE MASON.

SIR :—I do myself the honor to enclose you a commission appointing you a senator for the State in the room of Col. Grayson deceased.

[1] Jefferson's " Works," H. A. Washington, vol. iii., p. 72.

Permit me to intreat your acceptance of this commission. The very important subjects now before Congress, so interesting to America in general, and more especially to your native State, call for the counsels of the wisest of her citizens.

Impressed with the fullest conviction of your abilities and zeal for the welfare of your country, I cannot doubt your compliance with the unanimous wishes of the Executive.

I am, &c.,

BEVERLEY RANDOLPH.[1]

The Richmond paper of the 31st of March announced: "The Hon. George Mason, Esq: is appointed a senator of the United States, in the room of the Hon. Col. William Grayson, deceased."[2]

But Colonel Mason was not to be prevailed upon to take the office, and Governor Randolph, on the same day issued the following proclamation:

Virginia to wit:

George Mason, Esq: who was duly chosen a senator for this Commonwealth in pursuance of the Constitution for the United States of America, having refused to act during the recess of the Legislature of the Commonwealth, I, Beverley Randolph, being governor or chief magistrate of the Commonwealth, have therefore thought fit and with the advice and consent of the privy council, or council of state, and by virtue of the said Constitution to appoint John Walker, Esq: to be and act as a senator for the Commonwealth until the next meeting of the Legislature thereof.

Given under my hand and the seal of the Commonwealth, this 31st day of March, 1790.

[SEAL.]   BEVERLEY RANDOLPH.[3]

At the meeting of the Assembly in the autumn of this year, James Monroe was elected to fill out Grayson's term, and for the next succeeding six years.

[1] Executive Journal, State Library, Richmond.
[2] *The Virginia Independent Chronicle*, etc., 1790.
[3] Mason Papers.

Colonel Mason alludes to his appointment to the Senate in the following letter to his son :

VIRGINIA, GUNSTON HALL,
May 20th, 1790.

DEAR JOHN :

I take the opportunity per the ship *Confidence* Capt. de Bore, to send you, via Havre de Grace (where the ship is to touch for orders) a duplicate of my letter of the 27th of April last via New York, together with a duplicate of my letter of the same date, and by the same route, to Messrs. Fenwick, Mason, & Company, covering the first bill of a letter of exchange on Messrs : Thomas Clagett & Company merchants in London for £500 sterling, payable to me, and by me endorsed to your house. I now enclose the second bill of the same etc.

Capt. Fenwick has been obliged to charter the ship *Confidence* at a very low freight rather than send her back (unchartered) in ballast, which has been the fate of many of the ships sent out to America for wheat and flour, and has reduced freights this year lower than ever they were known before. My reason for remitting the above mentioned second bill by this conveyance, via Havre de Grace, is, that it is uncertain when your ship the *Washington* will be ready to sail. I fear it will be very difficult to procure a load for her ; for the confusion and uncertain state of affairs in France makes people cautious of venturing their property there, which together with the low price of tobacco at that market last fall, discourages everybody from shipping thither, and it will not answer to purchase on your own accounts, tobacco now selling here from 18/ to 20/ per hundred Virginia currency and expected to be higher, at the same time that exchange for bills on London is at 15 to 20 per ct.

.   .   .   .

I heartily wish the French nation success in establishing their new government, upon the principles of liberty, and the sacred rights of human nature ; but I dread the consequences of their affairs remaining so long in an unsettled state. Their finances, their commerce, and some of their most important interests must suffer exceedingly by it ; besides the risk of the most respectable part of the people (which is always found in the middle walks of life) being disgusted and worn down with so long a scene of doubt and uncertainty, not to say anarchy.

. . . .

I have lately been appointed a senator for the commonwealth of Virginia, in the Senate of the United States, but have refused to serve.

. . . .

Your affectionate father,
G. MASON.

John Mason, Esquire,
    Merchant in Bordeaux.[1]

In this letter Colonel Mason speaks of having "just recovered from a three months' fit of the gout," and doubtless his state of health had something to do with his determination to remain in private life. He wrote again to his son about two weeks later:

VIRGINIA, GUNSTON HALL,
June 3, 1790.

DEAR JOHN :

This will be delivered you by your partner Mr. Joseph Fenwick, and as he proposes going by land to Boston, and embarking from thence, or from Portsmouth in New Hampshire, it will hardly come to your hands before the latter end of September, before which it is probable I shall have other different opportunities of writing to you. Mr. Fenwick's long stay in America, and the necessity you will be under of staying in Bordeaux, some time after his arrival, to adjust and fully settle your affairs, so as to take away all cause for any confusion or dispute hereafter, will, I fear, prevent your embarking for America this year ; unless you can get a passage to South Carolina, so as to arrive there in the month of November, for I would wish you to avoid a winter passage, especially after your late long ill state of health. And therefore I think you had better stay in France until next spring, than risk passage in the depth of winter ; more particularly if you come to any of the northern or middle States. Should you spend this winter in France, and find Bordeaux still disagree with your constitution, I would advise you to go to

[1] MS. Letter.

Marseilles, or some place in the south [of] France, and return to Bordeaux in the spring; as you will probably not meet with a passage from any of the ports in the Mediterranean, and even if you could, the danger of falling into the hands of the Algerines is such a shocking circumstance, as I would have you by all means avoid.

I would strongly recommend your availing yourself of every means and opportunity of making yourself acquainted with the commercial customs of France, and what of their produce or manufactures will suit the respective States here, and can be imported upon advantageous terms, so as to be able to give satisfactory information to the merchants in our different sea port towns, which you will find of infinite advantage to your house, when you make the tour you propose through the United States; which I still think it will be proper for you to do.

> Adieu, my dear John, and believe me,
> > Your most affectionate father,
> > > G. MASON.

John Mason, Esq :
   Merchant in Bordeaux.[1]

Colonel Mason had written to Jefferson recommending Mr. Fenwick as consul to Bordeaux, and Jefferson replied as follows:

NEW YORK, June 13, 1790.

DEAR SIR :—I have deferred acknowledging the receipt of your favor of March 16th, expecting daily that the business of the consulships would have been finished. But this was delayed by the President's illness, and a very long one of my own, so that it is not till within these two or three days that it has been settled. That of Bordeaux is given to Mr. Fenwick, according to your desire. The commission is making out, and will be signed to-morrow or next day.

I intended fully to have had the pleasure of seeing you at Gunston Hall on my way here, but the roads being so bad that I was obliged to leave my own carriage to get along as it could, and to take my passage in the stage, I could not deviate from the

[1] Mason Papers.

stage road. I should have been happy in a conversation with you on the subject of our new government, of which, though I approve of the mass, I would wish to see some amendments, further than those which have been proposed, and fixing it more surely on a republican basis. I have great hopes that pressing forward with constancy to these amendments, they will be obtained before the want of them will do any harm. To secure the ground we gain, and gain what more we can, is, I think, the wisest course. I think much has been gained by the late Constitution; for the former was terminating in anarchy, as necessarily consequent to inefficiency.

The House of Representatives have voted to remove to Baltimore, by a majority of 53 against 6. This was not the effect of choice, but of confusion into which they had been brought by the event of other questions, and their being hampered with the rules of the House. It is not certain what will be the vote of the Senate. Some hope an opening will be given to convert it into a vote of the temporary seat at Philadelphia, and the permanent one at Georgetown. The question of assumption will be brought on again, and its event is doubtful. Perhaps its opponents would be wiser to be less confident in their success, and to compromise by agreeing to assume the State debts still due to individuals, so as to put the States in the shoes of those of their creditors whom they have paid off. Great objections lie to this, but not so great as an assumption of the unpaid debts only. My duties preventing me from mingling in these questions, I do not pretend to be very competent to their decision. In general, I think it necessary to give as well as take in a government like ours.

I have some hope of visiting Virginia in the fall, in which case I shall still flatter myself with the pleasure of seeing you; in the meantime, I am with unchanged esteem and respect, my dear sir,

Your most obedient friend and servant.[1]

Jefferson on his return to "Monticello" in September travelled again in his own carriage, Madison with him, stopping two days at "Mount Vernon," and it is highly probable he visited "Gunston Hall" at this time. George Mason in this year, or perhaps a little earlier, resigned the

[1] "Jefferson's Works," H. A. Washington, vol. iii., p. 147.

office of justice of the peace, which he had probably held since his early manhood. His name is given, with those of Washington, McCarty, Bryan Fairfax, and others, in a list preserved of the justices of Fairfax County in 1770.[1] Twenty years later the records state that on the 21st of June, 1790, the clerk of the court of Fairfax County, after certifying that the court recommended George Augustine Washington and others for magistrates, gave a list of justices, and those marked removed, dead, etc., as a true statement of the justices of the county :

"Robert Townsend Hooe, sheriff ; George Mason, resigned ; Alexander Henderson, removed ; Charles Broadwater, dead ; George Washington, president ; Martin Cockburn, resigned ; Richard Chichester, resigned ; James Waugh, resigned."[2]

Jefferson in his letter to George Mason had referred to the question of assumption then before Congress. It was one of the " fiscal manœuvres " of Alexander Hamilton, which was believed to be a violation of the Constitution, and injurious to many of the States. The debts of the several Commonwealths were put down, on a rough estimate, as twenty millions, and the people generally assessed to pay this amount, whereas some States had a greater, some a less, indebtedness than others, and the law thus acted unfairly upon them. It was discovered also after the accounts were settled, that the estimate had been much too large. Eleven millions would have been sufficient, but by the operation of the Assumption Act, an additional debt was created, reaching in a few years to over ten millions.[3] The Virginia Assembly in December, 1790, sent a memorial to Congress protesting against this measure. They declare that "neither policy, justice, nor the Constitution warrants it " ; that a large portion of the debt is already redeemed by the collection of heavy taxes, but by this act "a heavy debt and consequently

---

[1] " Virginia Calendar Papers," vol. i., p. 263.
[2] *Ibid.*, vol. v., p. 172.
[3] Randall's " Life of Jefferson," vol. i., p. 608.

heavy taxes will be entailed on the citizens of this Commonwealth from which they can never be relieved by all the efforts of the General Assembly, whilst any part of the debts contracted by any State in the American Union, and so assumed, shall remain unpaid." The act without the smallest necessity, as they averred, extorted from the General Assembly the power of taxing their own constituents for the payment of their own debts, in such a manner as would be best suited to their own ease and convenience, etc. "Another light in which it appeared more odious and deformed" was this : During the discussions of the Federal Constitution, they, the memorialists, were taught to believe "that every power not expressly granted was retained." Under this impression they ratified the Constitution, but there was no clause in the Constitution authorizing Congress in express terms to assume the debts of the States.' Stevens Thomson Mason as a member of the Virginia Senate endorsed these views, which were those also of his illustrious uncle.

On the 10th of January, 1791, George Mason wrote two letters, one to his son John, and one giving the news he had received from France to his friend Thomas Jefferson. Unfortunately the less important of these two epistles is the only one of them that has been preserved. The one to Jefferson has been lost, and it is only through the latter's reply that anything can be known of its contents. Colonel Mason's letter to his son is as follows :

GUNSTON HALL, January 10, 1791.

DEAR JOHN :

As I presume you have left Bordeaux before this time, and that this letter may probably find you in the south of France, I enclose you a copy of my letter of this date to Fenwick, Mason, and Company to save myself the trouble of repeating its contents separately to you. This leaves me little more to add except telling you that if the *Washington* sails in time, I shall send you, as you desire, letters of introduction to some of my friends in South Carolina, particularly to Col. William Washington, a gentleman

[1] Journal of the Assembly.

for whom I have the greatest regard, and with whom you were too young to be acquainted when he went into the army. I have the pleasure to inform you that all your brothers and sisters are well, as is also the family at Gunston Hall. Mrs. Mason returns you many thanks for your acceptable present of the political fan, and gloves, and joins in our best wishes and respects to you, with, dear John,

Your affectionate father,

G. MASON.[1]

Jefferson wote to George Mason, in answer to his letter of the 10th of January :

PHILADELPHIA, February 4, 1791.

DEAR SIR :

I am to make you my acknowledgments for your favor of January 10th, and the information from France which it contained. It confirmed what I had heard more loosely before, and accounts still more recent are to the same effect. I look with great anxiety for the firm establishment of the new government in France, being perfectly convinced that if it takes place there, it will spread sooner or later all over Europe. On the contrary a check there would retard the revival of liberty in other countries. I consider the establishment and success of their government as necessary to stay up our own, and to prevent it from falling back to that kind of a half-way house, the English Constitution. It cannot be denied that we have among us a sect who believe that to contain whatever is perfect in human institutions ; that the members of this sect have many of them names and offices which stand high in the estimation of our countrymen. I still rely that the great mass of our community is untainted with these heresies, as is its head. On this I build my hope that we have not labored in vain, and that our experiment will still prove that men can be governed by reason.

You have excited my curiosity in saying there is a particular circumstance, little attended to, which is continually sapping the republicanism of the United States. What is it ?

What is said in our country of the fiscal arrangements now going on ? I really fear their effect when I consider the present

[1] Mason Papers.

temper of the Southern States. Whether these measures be right or wrong abstractedly, more attention should be paid to the general opinion. However, all will pass—the Excise will pass—the Bank will pass. The only corrective of what is corrupt in our present form of government, will be the augmentation of the numbers in the lower House, so as to get a more agricultural representation, which may put that interest above that of the stock-jobbers.

I had no occasion to sound Mr. Madison on your fears expressed in your letter. I knew before, as possessing his sentiments fully on that subject, that his value for you was undiminished. I have always heard him say that though you and he appeared to differ in your systems, yet you were in truth nearer together than most persons who were classed under the same appellation. You may quiet yourself in the assurance of possessing his complete esteem.

I have been endeavoring to obtain some little distinction for our useful customers, the French. But there is a particular interest opposed to it, which I fear will prove too strong. We shall soon see. I will send you a copy of a report I have given in as soon as it is printed. I know there is one part of it contrary to your sentiments ; yet I am not sure you will not become sensible that a change should be slowly preparing.

Certainly, whenever I pass your road, I shall do myself the pleasure of turning into it. Our last year's experiment, however, is much in favor of that by Newgate.

I am with great respect and esteem, dear Sir,

Your friend and servant. [1]

No doubt Jefferson received later an explanation of the remark which so excited his curiosity, " the particular circumstance, little attended to, which is continually sapping the republicanism of the United States." But for us there is no answer to the query, though we may surmise that it had reference to the powers given the Federal courts. The Judiciary Act of 1789, which created the inferior United States courts and so greatly extended the jurisdiction of the

[1] " Jefferson's Works," H. A. Washington, vol. iii., p. 209.

Supreme Court, doubtless filled George Mason with alarm. The fears he expresses to Jefferson lest Madison might be estranged from him, it is pleasant to know, admitted of a satisfactory reply. More and more as the years went on, and the younger statesman watched the issue of the work in which he and Mason had both been leaders, must Madison have understood that they were "nearer together" in their systems than many who were classed as of one party. Or rather Mason's system was to be acknowledged by Madison within a decade as that on which the liberties of his country-men depended. The report to which Jefferson refers was delivered on the 1st of February, 1791, and related to the cod and whale fisheries.[1]

The following letters were written in April and July to John Mason who was about to return to America :

VIRGINIA, GUNSTON HALL,
April 16th, 1791.

DEAR JOHN :

Enclosed is a letter (to which I refer) written in January and intended to have been sent *via* Baltimore or Philadelphia, but hearing of no ships from either of those places to Bordeaux, it is now sent per the *Washington*. She has been so long detained here by the winter's frost, by having considerable repairs made to her, and above all by the difficulty of procuring a load of tobacco for her, in the unsettled and uncertain state of the tobacco trade in France, that I think it probable you may have embarked for America before her arrival at Bordeaux ; neverthe-less as you may perhaps have waited her arrival, I enclose you some letters of introduction to my friends in Charles Town, South Carolina, which you will seal and deliver if you take that route, though I think it a bad season of the year to come to that warm country, and you will have a very fatiguing journey from thence to Virginia, in the latter end of the summer, which may be injurious to your health after your long indisposition. I therefore really think if you expect to arrive in America before the beginning or middle of September you had better take your

---

[1] *Ibid.*, vol. vii., p. 538.

passage to some of the Northern or Eastern States, and make a tour to the Southern States in the course of next winter, and if you purpose to establish a house in the commission line upon Potomac River, your principal American consignments here will be from the Eastern States, and therefore a tour through their principal sea port towns, on your way home, in order to settle a correspondence, may be an object of importance. However with respect to your embarking for one of the Southern or Eastern States, the season of the year, in which you expect to arrive will be your best guide. I have shipped per the *Washington* thirty-three hogsheads of tobacco. . . .

I have received your letters dated in October and November last, and rejoice to hear that your health is in a great measure restored. I rejoice also to hear that I have been mistaken in my opinion respecting the paper money, yet I think it was founded on reason as well as experience ; but really the French Revolution from the beginning has been attended with such extraordinary circumstances that the man who judges of it by comparison with anything else in the annals of mankind, will probably find himself mistaken.

No doubt you have heard that an act of Congress has passed for fixing the permanent seat of government of the Union, after ten years, upon [the] Potomac, at such place as the President should direct, between the mouth of the Eastern Branch and the mouth of Conogochieg (about sixty miles from each other) with the power of laying off ten miles square for the jurisdiction of Congress, and fixing the spot for the public buildings, confining the public buildings, however, to the eastern side of the river. The President has had the ten miles square laid off in the following manner. Beginning on the upper side of the mouth of Great Hunting Creek and running north-west ten miles (which includes the town of Alexandria), thence north-east ten miles (which crosses Potomac River a little above the Little Falls, and includes all my tract of land there of about two thousand acres), thence south-east ten miles (which includes George Town and the navigable part of the Eastern Branch), thence south-west to the beginning. He has also directed the city for the seat of government, within the said ten miles square, to be laid off in the following manner. Beginning on Potomac River on the lower side the mouth of Rock Creek (just below George Town) thence with the meanders of Potomac River to the mouth of the Eastern Branch and up the meanders of the Eastern Branch about two miles to a point called (I think) Evan's Ferry, thence a course to strike the main road from George Town to Bladensburg about half a mile from the ford, thence with the main road to the ford of Rock Creek, and with the meanders of Rock Creek to the beginning. These last boundaries contain about four thousand acres, and the proprietors, I understand, have agreed to give up the whole of the land (reserving the right of selling the wood on it) to defray the charge of the public buildings, &c, on condition of being paid the value of their houses and receiving again respectively half the lots after the town is laid off and the streets adjusted. The spot for the public buildings (which is the most important point) is not yet fixed. The Alexandrians, as usual, are very much buoyed up on the occasion and think their fortunes made forever, although it is evident to any cool, impartial, sensible man, that if the inland navigation of Potomac and Shenandoah is effectually completed and the seat of the federal government fixed near the harbor of the Eastern Branch, Alexandria must become a deserted village.

Adieu my dear son ; this, I expect will be the last opportunity I shall have of writing to you while you are in Europe. God bless you and send you safe to your native country and friends. I hope I shall soon have the pleasure of seeing you, and assuring you personally, how much I am

Your affectionate father,

G. MASON.

P. S. Your friends here are all well, except your sister Cooke's children, who are under inoculation for the small-pox, but I believe are in a good way. We shall begin to inoculate here and at " Lexington " about the end of May.

John Mason, Esquire,
 Merchant in Bordeaux.
  By the *Washington*, Capt. Chilton.[1]

---

[1] Mason Papers.

GUNSTON HALL, July 12, 1791.

DEAR JOHN:

I did not receive your letter of the 13th of May via Nantes, until Saturday the 9th instant, after that day's post had passed, so that I had no opportunity of conveying a letter to Norfolk, until this day's post. Herewith you will receive a packet (containing several letters) which I have put under cover to Mr. John Brent,[1] as you desired, and hope it will be in time; but should you have arrived, and have left Norfolk, before my packet reaches the hands of Mr. Brent, I have desired him to send it immediately after you (per post) to Petersburg or Richmond. The letters are all left open for your perusal; you will easily distinguish which are intended as complimentary introductions, merely to entitle you to civilities, and those which may be of use to you in the line of business, or in making you acquainted with the most respectable merchants, for I have myself so little acquaintance with the James River merchants, that I am not able to recommend such as it may be proper for you to confide in. Most of my letters are to gentlemen in Richmond; since the death of my worthy friend Colo. Bland, I have no intimate acquaintance nearer Petersburg than Colo. Heth and Mr. David Ross. Colo. Heth having been some years a member of the executive council in Richmond, and having married some years ago in the neighborhood of Petersburg, and lived there a good while, and from his office of collector of the upper district of James River, must be as well acquainted with the situation, and character of all the merchants there as any man in Virginia. I believe he lives near Cabbin Point, or at Bermuda Hundred. You will find him a man of information and good sense, and I am sure his friendship for me will induce him to do you every service in his power; and I think you can confide in any information he gives you. Mr. Ross is also a particular friend of mine, and I think will be ready to do you any good offices in his power. I have also received many instances of civility from Mr. Alexander, who is a very intelligent man, and well acquainted with business. He resided many years in France, and is perfectly acquainted with that country; but he is a Scotchman, and has the character of an artful, designing man. With this caution, I think he may be serviceable to you, and if it

---

[1] John Brent was a nephew of Mrs. Mason's.

does not in any way interfere with his own interest, I make no doubt will take pleasure in being so ; and I think his acquaintance is well worth your cultivating. Mr. David Ross is well acquainted with all the merchants upon James River, and is generally thought to understand commerce better than any man in the State. He is a man of uncommon penetration, and depth of understanding and judgment, by which he has acquired immense possessions, but is said to be very much in debt. He is a very plain man in his manners, and I have always found him a very friendly man, but he too is a Scotchman. I thought it necessary, however, to give you the outlines of his character. Mr. Ross spends as much of his time in Richmond as in Petersburg.

The Governor, Colo. Harvie, and Mr. Marshall are all very worthy men, and intimate friends of mine, but they have never been in any mercantile line, though they may be serviceable to you, in making you acquainted with the most respectable merchants, and in promoting connections with the country gentlemen, if you have a mind to form such. Mr. Hopkins has been many years a commissioner of the Continental Loan Office. He is well acquainted with everybody in that part of the country, has been concerned in trade, is a man of good sense, and has always supported a good character.

It is proper to inform you that Colo. Wood's, the Lieutenant Governor's lady is a distant relation, a second cousin of ours, and the daughter of the late Reverend Mr. Moncure, the most valuable friend I ever had in my life.

.   .   .   .

Should you have occasion to lodge money any time in Richmond, the iron chests in the public treasury will be the safest place. Colo. Harvie is a very intimate friend of Mr. Ambler, the treasurer, and Mr. Marshall married one of his daughters ; either of these gentlemen can procure you leave to do so. The present price of tobacco at Richmond and Petersburg I am told is from 17 /₆ to 20 / Virginia currency, upon Potomac 13 /, and I believe almost any quantity could readily be bought here at 14 / or at most 15 /. It is unfortunate you did not, immediately upon the decree with respect to tobacco, charter and send out a French ship or two. If you had at this instant three or four French ships in the Potomac, they could be readily loaded upon consignment ; but I doubt you have lost the time and that it is now too late to send orders for that purpose to France, as I have reason to believe several of the merchants here have advised their correspondents in Europe to charter French ships as speedily as they can.

Pray write to me as soon as you arrive ; a letter per post will reach me in four or five days from Norfolk, and in two or three from Richmond. I long to see you exceedingly, and so do all your brothers and sisters ; yet I think if you load the ship in James River, you had better not leave that part of the country, until you despatch her.

Your brother George is in much better health than he has been for two years past. He thinks he received much benefit, last summer, from the use of the Augusta Springs. He and your brother William spend this season there also. They set out the day before yesterday, and don't intend to return before September.

I wish to hear as soon as possible how your health is, and what effect the voyage has had upon it ; I hope a good one, and am, dear John,

Your most affectionate father,

G. MASON.[1]

Of the friends and acquaintances spoken of by Colonel Mason in this letter, several will be recognized as prominent names of contemporary statesmen. Colonel Bland, George Mason's ally in the Convention, though a silent one ; " Mr. Marshall," his able antagonist, who as Chief Justice was to do so much later towards moulding the plastic form of the new Confederation into its permanent shape, and giving it that bias towards consolidation so much to be deplored; and Colonel Harvie, a member of the Continental Congress, who was long a resident of Richmond, and afterwards removed to " Belvidere," the beautiful country-seat of the Byrds on James River. David Ross was a Scotch merchant who acquired a large landed property in various parts of Virginia's broad domain, and was the original owner of the

[1] Mason Papers.

flour mills in Richmond afterwards belonging to the Haxalls. His house, a wooden building on a cliff overlooking the James River, was still standing in 1860. Mr. Jacqueline Ambler, the Treasurer, was a son of Richard Ambler of York-town, who had been a friend and correspondent of Colonel Mason's mother. And Colonel Wood was connected with him by marriage, as he has said. Extracts from a letter of Mrs. Wood's have been given in a former chapter. Councillor Carter wrote two letters to George Mason in August, 1791, asking him "to sit as referee" in a case where his (Robert Carter's) action as trustee of his father-in-law's estate had been called in question. "The representatives" [the family of Mrs. Elizabeth Lowndes of Bladensburg, a daughter, as was Mrs. Carter, of the Hon. Benjamin Tasker], writes Colonel Carter, "are dissatisfied with my conduct in the business mentioned before, and we have mutually chosen you to hear and determine the matter of right." The 20th of September was named as the time appointed for the decision, which date apparently interfered with business of Colonel Mason's, and his correspondent therefore proposed that the former should appoint "both time and place for the hearing of the matter."[1]

[1] Carter Letter-Books.

CHAPTER X.

CONCLUSION.

1791–1792.

The new government had not been long in operation before the contingency anticipated by George Mason in respect to the Indiana Company arose—the company bringing up its claim against Virginia. There were other land schemes agitated at this time also, such as the project of Morgan and Gardoqui, which were calculated to affect seriously Virginia's interests, and which were closely watched by her representatives in Congress.[1] Colonel Morgan issued a handbill, "inviting a settlement under the authority of Spain at New Madrid, near the mouth of the Ohio, on the Spanish side," as William Grayson writes Patrick Henry in 1789. The colonists were promised the free navigation of the Mississippi, and a market at New Orleans free from duties for all the produce of their lands. Morgan was a member of the Indiana Company, and at the session of the Virginia Assembly, October, 1791, he presented a "memorial of the proprietors and share-holders of a tract of land called Indiana." It set forth "that in the year 1776 they did inform the General Assembly of the title to the said tract of land, by a memorial then presented to them; that although the legislature did afterward direct the said land to be sold for the benefit of the State, and did refuse to allow the memorialists any compensation therefor—yet they are convinced that this proceeded from a want of information

[1] "Virginia Calendar Papers," vol. iv., p. 534.

not then attainable ; and praying that their right to the said land may be investigated in the manner most satisfactory to the General Assembly, and in case it is established, that such compensation may be made to them therefor, as is consistent with equity."[1]   Roger West, one of the delegates in the Assembly from Fairfax County, consulted George Mason as to the course to be pursued, and the latter replied in the following letter, from which extracts have been given in a preceding chapter.

GUNSTON HALL, November 9th, 1791.

DEAR SIR :

Your favor of the 4th did not come to my hands until last night, and the post leaving Colchester early to-morrow morning does not leave me time to answer you upon so important a subject as the Indiana claim, either to your satisfaction or to my own. I have searched all my papers, endeavoring to find my former argument in the Assembly, when I was appointed to collect the evidence and manage the business on behalf of the Commonwealth, which (if I could have found it) would have given the fullest information, but I imagine I must have lent it to some member of the Assembly, who has never returned it, and conceiving the matter after so full an investigation and positive determination as it then had, forever at an end, I was the less careful in preserving my notes and papers.   Several depositions were then produced and some witnesses examined at the bar of the House, proving the mysterious and clandestine conduct of Sir William Johnston (the King's agent) at the treaty at Fort Stanwix, when the Indiana Company obtained their deed from the Indians.   The council books were also produced, in which were many entries, previous to the Indiana Company's purchase, for lands much further to the westward.   The Indiana Company's deed from the Indians was set aside and a declaratory act passed upon the subject, as well as my memory serves me, in the May session of 1779, principally upon the following points.   First, the purchase of the same lands from the Six Nations of Indians, at the treaty of Lancaster in the year 1744, for the use of Virginia, and paid for with our money.   The book containing the records

[1] Journal of the Assembly.

of this treaty and the deed of purchase was then produced, but I have understood has been since destroyed, as well as all the other Indian treaties, made here under the king's government, with the books and papers of the council and of the Committee of Safety, when General Arnold's troops burned the foundry at Westham in which they had been placed upon the enemy's marching towards Richmond. Second, because the Six Nations, who claimed the lands by conquest, had lost their title (even if they had not sold them at the treaty of Lancaster) by the same means by which they first gained it—conquest—their tributaries and tenants, the Shawnese and Delawares, with a mixture of the Six Nations having been expelled, and driven over the Ohio (from whence they never returned) and the lands on this side the Ohio conquered in the war which happened a little before the Indiana Company's purchase. Third, independent of the above reasons, the deed to the Indiana Company by the law of Virginia ought to have been recorded (like all other deeds) either in the county where the land lay, as in Augusta, which was the then frontier county of Virginia, or in the General Court, that for the want of this the deed (if there had been no other objection) was void as to all subsequent purchasers, and that the settlers upon the land under Virginia titles, of which there were a great many before the deed was recorded in Augusta, were in the equitable construction of the law, to be considered as purchasers. Fourth, because the consideration of the deed was a compensation to the Indian traders, for the losses they had suffered, and it was thought they had no more right to require compensation than a merchant who had his ship taken by an enemy's privateer, or any other sufferer in the common calamities of war. Fifth, because the traders to whom the Indian deed was made, being every one of them citizens of Pennsylvania, from which this trade with the Indians was carried on, if they had been entitled to compensation at all, ought to have had such compensation out of the lands under the chartered territory of Pennsylvania (for whose benefit the trade had been carried on, by her own citizens) and not out of the lands of Virginia, and this appeared in the strongest, or if I may be allowed the expression, more barefaced point of view as Pennsylvania had at that same treaty of Fort Stanwix made a large purchase from the Indians of lands within her own charter.

I presume the legislature cannot regularly give any decision in favor of the Indiana Company without repealing the before mentioned declaratory act, and the consequences of such a repeal may extend much further and produce effects which may not at first be foreseen. Among other things it would certainly open a door to the revival of Col. Henderson's and Company's claim to Kentucky, nor can any man tell when it would end.

In my humble opinion the matter's having been fully investigated, the Indiana Company heard by their counsel at the bar of the House, a dozen years ago, when there was much better evidence both written and oral, than can now possibly be had, and a solemn determination then made, is a sufficient reason against giving any decision upon it now, when some of the witnesses are dead, some removed we don't know where, and when even the record evidence has been destroyed in the events of the late war. The present applicant Mr. Morgan is entitled to as much *justice* as any other man, but surely a man who has endeavored to depopulate the United States by seducing their citizens to quit their own country and settle in the Spanish territory has little pretensions to *favor* from us.

I have thus, sir, given you the best information upon the subject the short time I had would allow. I remember the Indiana Company when their claim at their own request was before the Assembly in 1779 produced in Williamsburg some English lawyers' opinions in their favor, upon a printed state of their case. To show you (and if you think fit the Assembly) what sort of opinions the English lawyers were accustomed to give, when the poor American colonies and their rights were in question, I enclose you an opinion of Mr. Attorney-General Pratt's in the year 1760 upon a dispute between the then proprietor of Maryland and the people. Yet this is the same Mr. Pratt who has been since transformed into Lord Camden, the champion of liberty and the defender of the rights of the people. I have long kept it as a curiosity, you will therefore be pleased to take care of it and return it to me.

I thank you exceedingly for getting Mr. John Hooe's petition for a ferry postponed until the petition against it comes down. It is still out among the people of this county, but I will endeavor to get it as soon as possible and forward it to the Assembly, and have no doubt it will prove Mr. Hooe's projected new ferry not only unnecessary but productive of much injury and oppression to the people in its consequences, and calculated merely to serve a local job.

I am with great respect, dear Sir,
Your most obedient servant,
GEORGE MASON.

Roger West, Esq:
Now upon the General Assembly in Richmond.[1]

The Indiana Company brought suit in the United States Court against Virginia, and the Assembly of 1792 pronounced upon the illegality of this proceeding. The committee, after quoting from the journal of the Assembly for June 9, 1779, to show that the claim had been already decided, passed the following resolution :

" That the jurisdiction of the Supreme Court of the United States does not and cannot extend to this case, it already having been decided on before a tribunal fully competent to its decision ; that the State cannot be made a defendant in the said court, at the suit of any individual or individuals ; and that the executive be requested to pursue such measures in this case, as may seem most conducive to the interest, honor, and dignity of this Commonwealth."[2]

The claim had been prosecuted by the company for twenty-nine years at an expense of over eighteen thousand dollars, and it involved a tract of country embracing nearly three millions of acres.[3] Its final overthrow was a benefit both to Virginia and to the Union.

The opinion of Attorney-General Pratt, afterwards Lord Camden, to which George Mason refers, is doubtless the one given by him sustaining the claims made in 1757, by the upper House of the Maryland Assembly to the appointment of officers and the supervision of the acts of the lower

[1] Mason Papers.
[2] Hening's " Statutes," vol. xiii.
[3] " Virginia Calendar Papers," vol. vi.

House. The upper House was the Council and consisted of the appointees and creatures of the proprietor, Lord Baltimore. The opinion of the English lawyer concluded with these words:

" The Upper House should take care how they admit encroachments of this kind, when they are supported by arguments drawn from the exercise of the like rights in the Commons here. The constitutions of the two assemblies differ fundamentally in many respects. Our House of Commons stands upon its own laws ; whereas Assemblies in the colonies are regulated by their respective charters, usages, and the common law of England, and will never be allowed to assume those which the House of Commons are justly entitled to here, upon principles that neither can nor must be applied to the colonies." [1]

Mr. John Hooe's proposed new ferry was to have been across the Occoquan River. And it seems, from the fact that it was not established, that George Mason's views controlled the action of the Assembly. It was in this year, 1791, that Colonel Mason wrote his last political paper. It relates to the division into Congressional districts. Virginia had been divided into ten districts by the act of 1788. Of these George Mason's district embraced the six counties of Prince William, Stafford, Loudoun, Fairfax, King George, and Fauquier. It is proposed, writes George Mason, at the next Assembly to lay off the State into twenty-one Congressional districts. " The five counties of Stafford, Prince William, Fairfax, Loudoun, and Fauquier (leaving out the county of King George, to be added to some of the lower counties) will now form two complete districts, and it will be attempted to make Fairfax and Loudoun compose one of these two districts ; and Stafford, Prince William, and Fauquier compose the other district ; by which means the substance of the right of suffrage, in electing members of Congress will be taken from the people of Fairfax, and the

[1] Scharf's " History of Maryland," vol. i., p. 503.

name or shadow only left them." He gives his reasons for believing that such a result will follow, and in a footnote states what he thinks is the real motive of the " nefarious project." This was to secure the election of Richard Bland Lee, a Federalist. Colonel Mason's suggestion is that the three small counties, Stafford, Prince William, and Fairfax, should compose one district, and the two large counties, Loudoun and Fauquier, the other, as in the districts for the election of State senators, and in this way the small county of Fairfax would not lose its voice in the election, as would be the case if it was associated with a single, much larger county. In the following year, 1792, the Assembly in December, two months after George Mason's death, passed an act forming nineteen Congressional districts instead of the twenty-one anticipated. And the principle George Mason contended for seems to have been in some measure regarded. One district was formed of the large county of Loudoun with the two small ones of Fairfax and Prince William, while another district comprised the large county of Fauquier and the two small counties of Culpepper and Stafford.[1] George Mason's paper, which was probably written to be circulated among the freeholders of his county, and to be used by its representatives in the Assembly, is full of dignity, and is a clear and logical presentation of his subject, basing its argument on the fundamental principles of free government which its author had so often expounded on greater occasions. But though the matter was not one affecting a continent or a commonwealth, it involved a political right and was therefore of value to the true patriot and statesman, and makes a not unfitting close to his public labors.[2]

Colonel Mason's son John was still in Virginia, and some notes to him from his father written in December, 1791, bring to a conclusion the year's personal record for the subject of our memoir.

[1] Hening's " Statutes," vol. xiii.
[2] Appendix v.

GUNSTON HALL, December 6, 1791.

DEAR JOHN :

Having occasion to send the bearer, negro Charles, to Dr. Craik, I take the opportunity by him, of informing you that I expect my overseers, Green and Tugate, or one of them will go to Alexandria to-morrow or next day, in my little boat. I will direct them to apply to you, and you can let me know by them whether you have sold my wheat, &c. I have also to desire you will buy for me in town, upon the best terms you can for cash, and send me down by the overseers, in my boat, the articles per list on the other side. It will be best to have them ready for the overseers before they come up, that the boat may not be detained, and I will repay you the money for them when you return to Gunston. I forgot to ask you whether you had taken out for me (as I desired) from the Alexandria inspectors, the notes for my little Hunting Creek crop, of which I gave you a memorandum. If you have not pray take them out now, and bring them to me when you come to Gunston. Notes have not been issued for any of the said crop, except one hogshead, for which I gave Mitchell, the overseer an order.

Since you went away I have been reflecting upon the situation you are in with the ships you are now loading, and that if you don't get the tobacco speedily they may perhaps be stopped by the ice. Rather than you should incur this risk, I will ship you, on board of both, or either of your ships (besides the notes already delivered you), sixty-five hogsheads of tobacco, which I have by me, four of which are in Aquia, two at the Falls, and all the rest at Chickamuxon, Dumfries, Colchester, and Alexandria. Lindsay at Colchester owes me five hogsheads which he has told me were ready whenever I called for them. If they are, and I will send to him to-day to know, you may have them also, as they may enable you to leave out the tobacco at Aquia or the Falls, as may best answer your purpose. If you find it necessary to take the tobacco I offer it will be proper to advise me of it without delay. . . . The reason I did not incline to ship this tobacco when I gave you the other notes, was that it is common, ordinary, light tobacco, and I was dubious of the quality answering the French market, now that the emulation among the individual manufacturers will occasion a demand for tobaccos of superior qualities, though considering the present low price and unpromising prospects here, I think I can hardly lose by shipping in French bottoms.

I am, dear John,

Your affectionate father,

G. MASON.

GUNSTON HALL, December 15, 1791.
12 o'clock.

DEAR JOHN :

Your brother George having occasion to send to Alexandria, I take the opportunity of writing by his messenger, and wish to hear whether most of your long expected craft has arrived, and whether you have *secured* tobacco enough for both of your ships, &c. Thinking you would be glad to hear how your craft in Occoquan is going on, I sent this morning to know. Mr. Bayley writes me that the craft which took in tobacco from Colchester warehouse for you, a few days ago, got out of Occoquan yesterday, and he imagines is at Alexandria before this time ; and that another craft of yours, I presume that which went to Chickamuxon for my tobacco there, is now at the wharf at Colchester taking in 23 hhds. of my tobaccos and 5 hhds. shipped by Mr. Carter of "Nomini" and will go off this evening. The mercury is now at 40 degrees in Fahrenheit's thermometer, 8 degrees above the freezing point. If this weather holds another day it will certainly open all the creeks. Indeed I expect the creek at Dumfries will be open this afternoon, so that if the shippers of the craft do their duty, all your tobaccos from these warehouses will be up this week. About Christmas, or two or three days before, the winter's frost may probably set in, before which time I hope you may be able to get your ships loaded and down the river. After you have made your arrangements, with respect to my tobacco and got it on board the ships, give me the earliest information you can, that I may have my letters, &c., ready. You know it is my custom to enclose exact lists of the marked numbers and weights [gross, tare, and nett] of my tobacco, with the bills of lading.

Pray tell Mr. Wilson I am surprised at his not having sent a vessel for my wheat, being very anxious to have it taken away before the frost sets in ; and therefore desire the opportunity this fine weather affords may not be lost.

I am, dear John,

Your affectionate father,

G. MASON.

P. S. Please get me a good closet lock and send it by the bearer—if from Mr. Hodgson's to be charged to my account, if from any other store you will please to pay the cash for it.

John Mason, Esq :
   Alexandria.

GUNSTON HALL, December 23, 1791.

DEAR JOHN :

Enclosed you have my letters for Bordeaux and Marseilles, which I hope will be in time for the ships. Indeed I fear last night's hard frost has blocked them up, though if to-day and to-morrow turn out mild weather, the river will open again, as the ice is but thin yet. . . . And you will give the proper directions about your brother Thomas's watch, and about the four pieces of coarse grey blankets I have ordered from Bordeaux.

The overseer gave me a little bit of small cordage you sent down to see if it would answer for leading lines. Leading lines should be a very small size larger, and twisted in a different manner, viz., what is called cable-laid ; they should also be made of the soundest, strongest hemp. . . . I have ordered the bearer, Joe, to carry up a portmanteau, saddle and mail pillion, as you desired, and hope to see you at Gunston on Saturday.

I am, dear John,

Your affectionate father,

G. MASON.[1]

This last letter, written two days before Christmas, shows us that John Mason was expected home for the holidays. And no doubt there was a happy family party assembled on this occasion. George Mason from "Lexington," with his wife and children, were near enough to drive over to "Gunston" at any time. William Mason was then living with his father, though he afterwards removed permanently

---

[1] Mason Papers.

to " Mattawoman," the old Eilbeck place in Maryland. Thomson Mason's house, " Hollin Hall," on an estate in Fairfax, adjoining that of " Mount Vernon," was built for him by his father about this time. Thomas Mason lived in Alexandria in these years, though he settled later at " Woodbridge," his estate in Prince William County. John Mason, after his final return from France, made his home on Mason's Island, near Georgetown, bequeathed him in his father's will, and there called Barbadoes. Mrs. McCarty was living at " Cedar Grove," in the neighborhood of " Gunston Hall." And of the three other sisters, two of them were located in adjoining counties not far distant. Mary, Mrs. Cooke, lived at " West Farm," in Stafford County, and Elizabeth, Mrs. Thornton, at " The Cottage," in King George County. Ann, the eldest daughter and her father's house-keeper during his widowhood, had been married now some years, and her home was at " Aquasco," in Prince George County, Maryland. These brothers and sisters were an affectionate and united family, and John Mason wrote of their early home-life together as a very harmonious and happy one. And he says :

" I can add with truth as I do with infinite pleasure, and as a just tribute to the memories of my brothers and sisters, all of whom have now for some years departed this life, that the most sincere, constant affection and interchange of kindly offices subsisted afterwards among us all. And that there never was, to the best of my knowledge, a single quarrel or even a transient coolness that ever took place between any of us." [1]

The affection between George Mason and his children was very close and tender, as the letters of the former to his two sons amply testify. As the daughters were all settled so near him, but little occasion arose for correspondence no doubt, as was the case also with the three sons who did not go abroad.

[1] MS. of General John Mason.

Early in January John Mason left "Gunston" again for a trip to Philadelphia and New York. His father was suffering at the time from an attack of the gout, as we learn from this letter to his son:

GUNSTON HALL, January 23d, 1792.

DEAR JOHN :

I received your letter from Baltimore of the 7th inst. and am glad to hear you were like to meet with no disappointment in receiving my money from Messrs. Smiths, and making the payment I desired to Mr. Dulany. I was in hopes he would readily have given up the interest during the war, as I believe every British creditor who has received his debt, without a suit, has done it ; and the Supreme Courts in this State, and I believe in most, if not all the others, have constantly deducted it. There was, I understand, an opinion given in the federal court in Connecticut (though I believe not a final one) that interest upon British debts was recoverable, which I suppose is what Mr. Dulany alluded to. I wish I had thought to have desired you, just to make the experiment, whether he would not have given up the interest during the war, by telling him that upon those terms only, the money would be immediately paid. I am very anxious to hear the last news from France. I presume you got your letters by the ships, that had arrived at Baltimore from Bordeaux, the day after you wrote to me.

I am also anxious to hear that you keep your health, being apprehensive that this extreme cold weather (which is probably still more severe to the Northward) will not agree with your constitution. The snow is now as deep here as it was in the hard winter of 1740, indeed I think deeper than I ever saw it, except in the winter of 1773. It will occasion, I expect, great losses in the stocks of cattle in this part of the country, badly as it is provided with provender, from the short crops of corn and hay.

I have just recovered from the fit of the gout you left me in, and am now able to walk about the house, though still a little lame. In every other respect, thank God, I am in good health. It has proved, however, a pretty severe fit, though a regular one and remained confined to one of my feet.

Present me to my friend Col. Monroe, and tell him I should have done myself the honor of answering his letters sooner, had not the gout forbid me, for it is not without pain that I am yet able to sit at a table and write.

I have received a letter from Mr. Stoddert upon the subject of the projected bridge, in which he gives me at large the same reasons he did you to persuade me that its effects will be favorable to a town on my land on this side the river. I verily believe he is of that opinion himself, for I know him a man of great candor. I enclose you a copy of my answer to him, by which you will see I am willing to compromise with the gentlemen, upon fair and reasonable terms, though I thought it best at present to leave the matter open, to see if they are inclined to offer me such. Besides that I wish to act liberally on the occasion, I have some particular reasons for desiring to avoid any dispute with them, which I will communicate to you when I see you. The effects of the bridge as well as the practicability of the execution are very doubtful, and I am at some loss to estimate what will be a just and reasonable compensation. I would not willingly ask more nor take less. What do you think of agreeing to take, forever, a certain part (say about a fifth) of the gross tolls or money received annually for passengers &c., without my having any concern in the building, repairs or expences of the bridge? I wish you would endeavor to make yourself acquainted with, and inform me, of the tolls or rates taken at the bridge from Boston to Charles Town, and the annual amount of the money received. It is probable Mr. Gerry, or some of the Massachusetts gentlemen in Congress, can inform you. Or if you will write to Mr. Gorham he can give you the fullest information being, if I recollect right, one of the proprietors and managers. I should be glad also to know the length and breadth of the Boston bridge, the width of the spaces on each side for foot passengers, and the space in the middle for carriages. Pray let me hear from you as often as you conveniently can. Tell me how you have your health, whether you have determined to go any further eastward than New York, and when we may expect to see you again at Gunston. Your brother George and his family are well: he keeps his health this winter better than could have been expected, for I dreaded the effect of this severe weather upon him.

> I am, dear John,
>> Your affectionate father,
>>> G. Mason.

per post
  Mr. John Mason,
      Philadelphia.

If Mr. Mason should have left Philadelphia, recommended to the care of Mr. Joseph Anthony to forward to him.[1]

In May Colonel Mason wrote the following letter of business to John Francis Mercer:

GUNSTON HALL, May 12th, 1792.

DEAR SIR :

I yesterday received a letter (forwarded by Mr. Johnson) from you, dated the 23rd October, 1791, covering an old letter from Mr. Rutland to you, respecting some land he said he had upon James river. Had this letter come to my hands in Rutland's lifetime it might have enabled me to have examined into the title, situation and value of the land, and perhaps, by it, to have secured part of my debt ; at present I do not know that it will be of any use to me.

I wrote to you last fall, respecting two bonds from the late Mr. George Frazer Hawkins, to me which I had formerly put into your hands, and enclose you a memorandum of the dates and amounts of them ; but I have not been favored with any answer from you upon the subject, and Mr. Johnson tells me you do not recollect having had them. If I now had the bonds I could find means of obtaining the debt, and must entreat you to search for them. I remember, at the time I gave them to you (in my own house) seeing you put them into a pocket book you then had with you. They must certainly be somewhere among your papers, and if carefully searched for, I have no doubt may be found. In case you cannot find them, I have to request that you will advise me what manner I shall proceed to ascertain and recover the debts ; for the sum is too large for me to lose, if the loss can

---

[1] MS. Letter.

be avoided. The said bonds are regularly entered and charged in my ledger. I can prove by Col. Lyles (who transacted the business with Mr. Hawkins for me) that he took two such bonds from Mr. Hawkins, on my behalf, though perhaps he may not recollect the precise dates, or respective amounts. These bonds were both put in suit in Prince George's county court against Mr. Hawkins, and the suits abated by his death ; and it appears from the records of that court, that the two actions of debt, George Mason *vs.* George Frazer Hawkins, respectively correspond exactly with the bonds charged in my ledger ; that is, the said suits are exactly par double the sum (as the penalty) of each of the bonds charged in my ledger. Upon the abatement of the suits, on Mr. Hawkins's death, I withdrew the bonds from the clerk's office of Prince George's county, and after having kept them some time by me, gave them to you, that you might join my claim to those of some of the other creditors, who I understood had filed a bill in chancery, in order to subject Mr. Hawkins's lands to the payment of his bond-debts, during the minority of his devisees. Perhaps you may have lodged them in the chancery office for this purpose. I have cause to believe there are, or soon will be assets in the hands of his executors, or rather in the hands of his administrators, *de bonis non.* I beg you will let me hear from you upon this subject, as soon as you have had time to make the proper inquiries.

I am altogether unacquainted with the present state of my suit with Mr. David Ross. I have wrote to Mr. Luther Martin once or twice lately about it, but can get no answer from him, and have reason to believe it has been very much neglected by him. When I conversed with you about it last, you were of opinion that it would not be proper (Mr. Ross's father having obtained a patent for the land) to venture a trial at common law, upon the ejectment, until we had either obtained a patent from the land office, upon Mr. Bladen's certificate of survey, of many years' older date than Mr. Ross's patent, survey, or warrant, assigned to me by Mr. Benjamin Tasker, Mr. Bladen's attorney in fact, a patent ordered to be issued thereon to me, and the patent to me actually drawn, but before the governor had affixed the seal, and stopped by a caveat from Mr. Ross's father, and the caveat never tried. Or else that we should by a bill in chancery, endeavor either to vacate Mr. Ross's patent, or compel him to convey to me so much thereof as is included in Mr. Bladen's certificate of survey for the tract called the "Pleasant Valley." The papers and statement in yours and Mr. Martin's hands, give all the information I am able to furnish, and I hope you will now be able to attend to it, for I am extremely anxious to have the matter fairly and speedily tried, upon its real merits, so that the title may be clearly and finally settled, and enable me, if settled in my favor, to sell the land, in order to close the Ohio Company's affairs as speedily as possible.

I am, with great regard, dear Sir,

Your most obedient servant,

G. MASON.

John F. Mercer, Esq.,
Annapolis.[1]

Colonel Mason seems to have suffered some annoyances with his Maryland lawyers. First Mr. Thomas Stone, as he thinks, is a little careless of his Virginia client's interests, then Luther Martin, his Convention friend, proves forgetful and will not answer his letters, and lastly his relative, Mr. Mercer, cannot find some bonds that had been put in his hands while on a visit at "Gunston Hall." Doubtless George Mason, with his orderly habits and prompt methods, could not always make allowances for the busy advocates who were managing his affairs. Subsequent letters from George Mason of "Lexington," written after his father's death to John F. Mercer, show him winding up the Ohio Company's concerns as Colonel Mason's executor. The latter had left a statement in his own handwriting of the Ohio Company's funds. The dividend when collected would amount to £102 12s. 9d. James and John Francis Mercer, as members of the Company, were to receive their share.

The last letters of George Mason that are known to be extant were written to his son John in May and August, 1792:

---

[1] MS. Letter.

GUNSTON HALL, May 22, 1792.

DEAR JOHN :

Your man Lewis arrived here this morning with letters from you and your brother Tom.

I am glad to hear my tobacco on board the *Auguste*, Capt. Ca-bella, is insured, and thank you for the directions you have given Messrs. Cathalan's respecting it. I have never heard in what manner this vessel was lost, or whether her crew or any part of the cargo was saved ; nor have I yet heard anything of the French brig you loaded at Alexandria for Bordeaux, on board which I had fifty hogsheads of tobacco. As I understand some very good accounts of sales for good Virginia tobacco have lately been re-ceived from London, I think it probable you may be able to resell, to advantage, the tobacco you have purchased if you should find it necessary.

The prodigious fall of exchange between France and foreign countries, and the great and continuing depreciation of their assignats, are truly alarming circumstances, such as I very much fear will be productive of general dissatisfaction and confusion, and render it extremely difficult if not impracticable, to keep up an army and support an expensive war. This summer must, I presume, bring things to a crisis, and show the nation with certainty, what they are to expect from the great powers of Europe. Prussia, I have no doubt, would be ready enough to guaranty the Low Countries to the Emperor, but I think the Eng-lish government will hardly hazard so unpopular a measure.

As I shall forward this letter by the first post, I am in hopes it will find you in Norfolk, and shall therefore trouble you with the execution of a piece of business there, which though at first a trifle, is by the unexpected delay I have met with in it, now become an object of considerable importance to me. I wanted a few, a hundred feet of cypress scantling for the columns, rails, ballusters &c of the piazzas and steps to your brother Thomson's house. None of this scantling being large, it might, I dare say at any time have been procured in a fortnight, if attention had been paid to it. About this time twelvemonth or sooner, I wrote to Mr. John Brent and enclosed him an exact bill of this scant-ling and at the same time a memorandum of a large quantity of shingles I wanted, and desiring to know if they could be got at

Norfolk so as to be landed here in the course of last summer or fall. I limited the price of the shingles, but as the quantity of cypress scantling was small I limited no price to that, but desired Mr. Brent to have it got as soon as he could, and sent up by the first vessel to Potomac river, to be landed about five or six miles below Alexandria, just at the upper end of General Washington's estate, and a very little below the large Pocorson, that runs from the mouth of Great Hunting Creek two or three miles down the river. Mr. Brent wrote me that the shingles could not be procured at the price I had limited, but that I might depend upon the scantling's being immediately got and sent up by the first vessel, at all events in the course of the summer (viz. : last summer). It not coming I have wrote repeatedly to Mr. Brent, twice this spring per post, but have had no answer. The captain of the packet from Alexandria to Norfolk was desired to speak to Mr. Brent about it. Mr. Brent told him the scantling was got, but had not been brought to Norfolk but that it should be at Norfolk, ready for the packet when she came down the next trip. The next trip the same excuse was made and the same promise repeated. In short I find Mr. Brent so careless and inattentive a man that no dependence or confidence can be placed in him. When the packet was at Alexandria some time ago your brother Thomson gave the captain a bill of this scantling, and desired the captain if when he went next to Norfolk Mr. Brent had not the scantling then ready for him to depend no longer upon him, but to have the scantling got and brought to Norfolk himself and bring it up with him. The packet went from Alexandria a few days ago, and is now, I suppose, at Norfolk, where perhaps she may continue some time. I have lately got all the shingles, which with all the weather boarding are ready to put up. The house will be raised next week, and I am in danger of having the building stopped, and half a dozen workmen upon my hands, doing nothing, for want of this small quantity of cypress scantling, without which the piazzas can't be raised. What I have therefore to beg of you is to inquire immediately of Mr. Brent and the captain of the packet, and if neither of them have already had the scantling got that you will endeavor to have it got with all possible expedition, and sent up by the packet now there, or if this can't be done, by the packet the next trip, or by any other vessel which may happen to be coming to Alexandria soon. . . .

Your affectionate father,
G. MASON.

GUNSTON HALL, August 20th, 1792.

DEAR JOHN,

About four or five years ago Mr. Henderson imported from Scotland, upon annual wages, two stonemasons, James Reid and Alexander Watson, very good workmen. Since the expiration of their contract with Mr. Henderson they have been working in Dumfries and about that part of the country, and last year made some free stone chimney-pieces for Col. Cooke which I think are well done and upon reasonable terms, to the best of my recollection, a guinea each. Being desirous to get these men to make four free stone chimney-pieces for your brother Thomson's house, I sent down to Dumfries three or four days ago to get one of them to come up to take the dimensions of your brother Thomson's chimneys that they might immediately get the chimney-pieces, but was informed they are both at work at George Town, I suppose about the new bridge building over Rock Creek. I must therefore beg you will inquire them out, and see if you can get them to do your brother's chimney-pieces, as soon as the Rock Creek bridge is finished, which I am told will be by the last of this month, and that, in the meantime, the sooner the better, you will endeavor to get one of them to ride down to your brother Thomson's to take the dimensions of the four chimneys, for which he wants free stone chimney-pieces, and also of the fire place in his best room, and give directions for a marble chimney-piece to be sent for to England, unless one of those you have to dispose of will suit it, or can be made by them to do so, which you will know by getting the man to examine them after he returns from your brother's. If you can get one of these men to go down to your brother Thomson's you will be kind enough to let your man Lewis go down with him to show him the way, and you will hire a horse upon my account for the man to ride. I purpose that these men shall get the stone themselves for Thomson's chimney-pieces and hearth stones, either at Aquia or at the quarry near Dumfries, whichever they think the best stone, and I will carry them from thence to your brother Thomson's.

This letter will be delivered you by our cousin, young **George Mason** of Pohick, by whom you will let me know whether you can get these men to do the chimney-pieces; and also how common tobacco in George Town warehouse sells at present, and if likely to rise?

I see in a late Alexandria newspaper notice of an intended application to the Virginia Assembly at the next session for their projected bridge over Potomac River, opposite, or *nearly opposite* to George Town, and for a condemnation of land to join the Southern abutment to, and for a road, *if necessary*. You should take care to be fully prepared in time with a true plan and representation of the situation of the place as connected both with George Town and the federal city, the comparative width of a bridge in each of the places (that proposed by them above and that to and from the Island); the true depth of water in both places should be ascertained, in which I would not have you trust to any representation of theirs, and everything so done as to be authenticated by affidavits : the new bridge over the mouth of Rock Creek should also be laid down. And I think it would be of great importance if by writing to Mr. L'Enfant you could procure his opinion, with his reasons, in favor of a bridge at the Island, not letting the George Town people know that you make any such application.

I am something better than when you left me ; my fevers have left me, but I am still very weak and low. . . .

I am, dear John,

Your very affectionate father,

G. Mason.

John Mason, Esq :
  George Town, Maryland.
By favor of Mr. George Mason, Junr., of Pohick.[1]

What were George Mason's sentiments regarding the general government which he had seen inaugurated with so many misgivings? We have caught a glimpse of them through Jefferson's letter of February, 1791, and from the same source, in connection with a significant phrase in one of Washington's letters, George Mason's views may be very

---

[1] Mason Papers.

clearly determined. Jefferson wrote to Washington on the
23d of May, 1792, urging him to come forward for a second
presidential term, and giving him a remarkably candid
review of the objections that had been made to the administration of the government. These objections Washington
repeats in a confidential letter to Alexander Hamilton,
classifying them under twenty-one several specifications.[1]
Washington writes Hamilton on the 29th of July, from
" Mount Vernon," and says that on his way home and since
his arrival he had sought to learn " the sentiments which
are entertained of public measures." He finds that even
the moderate men, friends of the government, are alarmed
" at that system of policy and those interpretations," and he
adds : " Others less friendly, perhaps, to the government,
and more disposed to arraign the conduct of its officers
(among whom may be classed my neighbor and *quondam*
friend Col. M.), go further, and enumerate a variety of
matters, which, as well as I recollect, may be adduced under
the following heads." The " variety of matters " as given
by Washington, in Jefferson's words, are evidently to be
traced through the latter to George Mason. This is the last
time that Washington mentions his old friend, in his correspondence, and it does not seem likely there was much
intercourse just then between " Gunston Hall " and " Mount
Vernon." There is nothing, however, in George Mason's
letters to show any diminution of the friendship between
himself and Washington, though it is evident from what he
writes to his son in March, 1789, that he feared some such
alienation would arise. The objections, then, of George
Mason, Jefferson, and others, to the measures of the federal
government, related in the first place to the financial system
introduced by the Secretary of the Treasury, Alexander
Hamilton. In carrying out those schemes, affecting the
public debt, the impost, the excise, " paper speculation,"
etc., wrote Jefferson, " a corrupt squadron, deciding the

[1] " Writings of Washington," Sparks, vol. x., p. 250 ; and Appendix xii.,
p. 504.

voice of the legislature have manifested their dispositions to get rid of the limitations imposed by the constitution of the general legislature, limitations on the faith of which the States acceded to that instrument." The only hope of safety from the designs of these monarchists is in the "numerous representation which is to come forward the ensuing year" (1793). Jefferson in his letter concludes: "I can scarcely contemplate a more incalculable evil than the breaking of the Union into two or more parts," etc. Washington, giving the plural pronoun, to include George Mason and others, writes:

"They declare they can contemplate no evil more incalculable, than the breaking of the Union into two or more parts ; yet when they view the mass, which opposed the original coalescence, they consider that it lay chiefly in the Southern quarter, and that the legislature have availed themselves of no occasion of allaying it, but, on the contrary, whenever Northern and Southern prejudices have come into conflict, the latter has been sacrificed and the former soothed. . . . That the Antifederal champions are now strengthened in argument by the fulfilment of their predictions, which have been brought about by monarchical Federalists themselves. . . . They have themselves adopted the very constructions of the Constitution, of which, when advocating the acceptance before the tribunal of the people, they declared it unsusceptible ; whilst the republican Federalists, who espoused the same government for its intrinsic merits, are disarmed of their weapons, that which they denied as prophecy being now become true history. Who, therefore, can be sure, they ask that these things may not proselyte the small number, which was wanting to place the majority on the other side ? And this, they add, is the event at which they tremble." [1]

Thomas Jefferson, so soon to become the leader of a triumphant Republican (or Democratic) party, which was to carry out in the government, as far as possible, the States-rights views of George Mason, turned with the affection and

[1] *Ibid.*

reverence of a disciple to the retired sage of "Gunston Hall." It is evident that he had much correspondence with him, and was eager to know his views on all public matters. And in the spirit of Elias to the departing Elijah, the younger statesmen visited and consulted with George Mason, in the last weeks of the latter's life, gathering from his own lips the final expression of a mind still as vigorous as ever and imbued to the end with the patriot's devotion to freedom. The mantle of the prophet was to fall on the shoulders of one who, in his turn, and on a wider theatre, was to preach the creed of that political gospel on which depends the conservation of community independence and of personal liberty. Jefferson left "Monticello" on the 22d of September, on his way to Philadelphia, where Congress was to meet early in November. He stopped, on his way, both at "Mount Vernon" and "Gunston Hall." His conferences at the latter place, as recorded in the *Anas*, are prefaced with these words: "Gunston Hall, September 30th, 1792, *ex-relatione* George Mason." It was thus on the last day of September, just a week before George Mason's death, that this conversation was held. Jefferson reports the talk of his host on the subject of the Federal Convention and its work:

"The constitution as agreed to till a fortnight before the Convention rose, was such a one as he would have set his hand and heart to. 1. The president was to be elected for seven years, then ineligible for seven years more. 2. Rotation in the Senate. 3. A vote of two-thirds on particular subjects, and expressly on that of navigation. The three New England States were constantly with us in all questions,—Rhode Island not there, and New York seldom; so that it was these three States, with the five Southern States, against Pennsylvania, New Jersey, and Delaware. With respect to the importation of slaves, it was left to Congress. This disturbed the two Southernmost States, who knew that Congress would immediately suppress the importation of slaves. Those two States, therefore, struck up a bargain with the three New England States, that if they would join to admit slaves for some years, the two Southernmost States would join in changing the clause which required two-thirds of the legislature in any vote. It was done. The articles were changed accordingly, and from that moment the two Southernmost States and the three Northern ones joined Pennsylvania, Jersey and Delaware, and made the majority of eight to three against us, instead of eight to three for us, as it had been through the whole Convention. Under this coalition, the great principles of the Constitution were changed in the last days of the Convention. The Constitution as agreed to at first was, that amendments might be proposed either by Congress or the legislatures. A committee were appointed to digest and redraw. Gouverneur Morris and King were of the committee. One morning Gouverneur Morris moved an instrument for certain alterations (not one-half the members yet come in). In a hurry and without understanding, it was agreed to. The committee reported so that Congress should have the exclusive power of proposing amendments. George Mason observed it on the report and opposed it. King denied the construction. Mason demonstrated it, and asked the committee by what authority they had varied what had been agreed. G. Morris then imprudently got up and said by authority of the Convention, and produced the blind instruction before mentioned, which was unknown by one-half of the House, and not till then understood by the other. They then restored it as it originally stood."

As to the existing administration and its course :

" He [Mason] said he considered Hamilton as having done us more injury than Great Britain and all her fleets and armies. That his [Mason's] plan of settling our debt would have been something in this way. He would have laid as much tax as could be paid without oppressing the people ;—particularly he would have laid an impost of about the amount first laid by Congress, but somewhat different in several of its articles. He would have suspended all application of it one year, during which an office should have been open to register unalienated certificates. At the end of the year he would have appropriated his revenue, 1st, To pay the civil list ; 2nd, The interest of these certificates ; 3rd, Instalments of the principal ; 4th, A surplus to buy up the alienated certificates, still avoiding to make any other provision for these last. By the time the unalienated certificates should have been all paid, he supposed half the alienated ones would have been bought up at market. He would then have proceeded to redeem the residue of them." [1]

These notes of George Mason's conversation by Thomas Jefferson are the last words of his that have come down to us.

George Mason died at "Gunston Hall" in the sixty-seventh year of his age, on the afternoon of Sunday, the 7th of October, 1792, and was buried by the side of his wife in the family graveyard on the estate.[2] He had evidently been suffering for some time—from his old enemy the gout most probably—as he speaks in his letter to his son, the 20th of August, of his "fevers" having left him, but that he is still "very weak and low." On the 30th of September, however, he was able to see Jefferson, and to converse with him freely on matters of public importance. There was probably some obituary notice of Colonel Mason in the *Virginia Gazette* but no complete file of the paper for this year can be found. In the *Maryland Journal*, published in Baltimore, there is the following announcement of George Mason's death, though the date assigned is incorrect. "On the 14th ult. died, at Gunston Hall in Fairfax County, Virginia, the Hon. George Mason, Esquire. In addition to his eminent talents as a statesman, he was a gentleman of great Virtues and Patriotism." [3] *The Gentleman's Magazine* for January, 1793, contained also a notice of the death of this distinguished American patriot, and the date is there rightly given as October 7th : "At his domain of Gunston Hall, in Fairfax County, Virginia, in the 67th year of his age, Col.

[1] Jefferson MSS. In neither of the editions of "Jefferson's Works" are these extracts printed correctly. Compare vol. ix., pp. 118–120. In Randolph's "Jefferson," 1829, vol. iv., they are omitted altogether from the "Anas."

[2] Entry in the Gunston Bible.

[3] The *Maryland Journal and Baltimore Advertiser*, Friday, November 2, 1792.

George Mason." Then follows the extract from his will recommending a private station to his sons, but charging them to defend and cherish the liberties of their country.[1] There remains no account of George Mason's funeral, and unfortunately neither Washington nor Jefferson could have been present, as they had repaired to the seat of government in Philadelphia before his death occurred, Jefferson arriving there on the 5th. On the 1st of October he was with Washington at "Mount Vernon." At Washington's funeral some years later, a son of George Mason was one of the intimate circle of friends invited to attend the ceremonies. No stone, unhappily, marks the grave of George Mason. The five sons, who all survived him, doubtless proposed to pay this filial tribute to a parent so revered and beloved. But they left the purpose unaccomplished. One of the grandsons, in his generation, contemplated the erection of a suitable memorial to his great ancestor. But only the plan and inscription remain to testify to the pious design. In a letter to his cousin, Hon. James Murray Mason, George Mason of "Hollin Hall" and "Spring Bank" enclosed the projected design.

Simplicity has always appeared to me to be the true and fitting type of sepulchre, especially for those great men whose names are their highest eulogium, whose deeds are their proudest monument. I send the following as the most appropriate tomb for our immortal ancestor, and would feel much gratified to have your opinion on it :

"A granite pyramid 20 feet high on a foundation elevated 5 feet. Of course, from the top of the foundation to the apex 20 feet elevation, perpendicular. In each square of the foundation to be inlaid a marble slab (or I should say freestone, for I would

---

[1] The *Gentleman's Magazine*, January, 1793, vol. lxiii., p. 89. In the *Columbian Mirror and Alexandria Gazette*, of November 28, 1792, is this paragraph: "The following is an extract from the will of the late Colonel George Mason, deceased, of this county, which was lately admitted to record : 'I recommend it to my sons'" &c. An earlier number of this paper with the notice of George Mason's death in it cannot be found.

have it all from the rocks of his own native streams), to bear the following inscription on the front :

George Mason
Born ——
Died ——

On the opposite side, ' The Author of the Bill of Rights and the Constitution of Virginia.' On another side these words : '*Vitam impendere vero.*' [1] On that opposite to this, that sublime and sacred charge contained in his last will : 'I recommend it to my sons . . . to which themselves were born.'"

The shadow of the Civil War soon after darkened the land, and the grandsons of George Mason emerged from its gloom, to die, old men, not many years later, their fortunes ruined by the downfall of the Confederacy.

George Mason's will, dated nineteen years before his death, left his family well provided for.[2] Though his expectations from the Ohio Company's lands were not destined to be realized, he made later other purchases and investments, which proved profitable, and he was esteemed at all times a man of wealth, as wealth was estimated in those days. One of George Mason's descendants, (the same gentleman who projected the monument to him) thus sums up the condition of his ancestor's worldly affairs at the time of his death, and pays a just tribute to his practical wisdom in the care of his estates :

"While the capacity of Col. Mason, as a statesman and a writer and a speaker has been so often the subject of merited laudation, it is indeed surprising that his still more admirable talents for acquisition and economy have been entirely overlooked, not only by those who have sketched his character for the public, but even by his descendants who profited so largely through their

---

[1] This is the exalted eulogium which Lucan bestows on Cato Uticences. He says of that stern patriot, *vitam impendere vero,* " stake his life upon the truth," in every word that he uttered and every deed that he dared. If the proud Stoic deserved such praise, should it be denied to Liberty's purest and boldest votary ? [Note by the author of the inscription.]

[2] Appendix vi.

exertion. There were few men in America in his time, who evinced greater capacity for attaining honorable wealth, or exhibited a more eminent example of that only source of its maintenance, judicious economy. He undoubtedly inherited a large patrimonial estate, but that was not only greatly augmented during his life, but the foundation was laid for almost princely wealth for his descendants. He devised to his sons alone, some fifteen thousand acres, the greater part of his own acquisition, of the very best land in the Potomac region. Most of these estates were well improved, with large and comfortable mansions and all necessary outbuildings. But he left to be divided among his children what was solely acquired by himself; sixty thousand acres of among the finest lands in Kentucky, some three hundred slaves, more than fifty thousand dollars worth of other personal property, and at least thirty thousand dollars of debts, due on his books, while his own indebtedness was absolutely nothing; showing that his enterprise and economy in private fully equalled his genius and ability in public life, proving that fine talents, a highly cultivated mind, and long, laborious and eminent public services are not incompatible with that *abnormis sapiens crasque Minerva*, so indispensable to the every-day business of life. A most noble example, ever worthy the admiration, reverence and imitation of his latest posterity." [1]

Colonel Mason's library, which was divided between his five sons, as his will provided, was extensive and well selected. The present writer, however, has been unable to trace any of these books. Some of them, it is known, were literally scattered to the winds, as the leaves were torn from them and thrown into the camp-fires of Federal soldiers, when the country-seat in Loudoun County, where they were to be found, was occupied by the enemy in 1862.[2] The destruction by fire, at an early period of the house on the estate of one of George Mason's sons, and within recent years a repetition of the same casuality in the case of one of

[1] MS. Sketch by George Mason of " Hollin Hall " and " Spring Bank."
[2] This was soon after the Mason and Slidell affair, and the name of " Mason " on the fly-leaf of a book was sufficient to insure its wanton destruction.

his grandsons, will account for the loss of many of these books, as well as of valuable family papers. That in this library were many Greek and Latin classics, among which were well-used copies of Catullus and Ovid, a letter of George Mason of "Spring Bank" to John Esten Cooke attests. The editor of the "Spotswood Letters" notices the libraries, really extensive for the time, of the second William Byrd of "Westover," of Sir John Randolph of Williamsburg, and of John Mercer of "Marlboro'," and numerous others nearly as large, "among them that of George Mason of Gunston." [1] We may assume from allusions and quotations in George Mason's letters and speeches, that among his books were to be found Virgil and Tacitus, Shakespeare and Dryden and Pope; English historians, political writers and pamphleteers; the French oracle on government, Montesquieu; the Italian sage Macchiavelli; and the English Whig writer, George Mason's contemporary, whom he so much admired, the brilliant and caustic "Junius." With the aid of the astronomer's manuscripts, published works, and correspondence, and an inventory returned by his immediate descendants, scholars have been able to reconstruct the library of Galileo, arranging and classifying five hundred and twenty-one volumes. Unfortunately little material remains for the accomplishment of the same pious task in the case of any of our eighteenth-century Virginians.

In making an estimate of George Mason's character and abilities, we can but retouch the picture as portrayed by the more intelligent and sympathetic of his contemporaries. One of a famous group of historic figures, the friend and associate of Washington, Richard Henry Lee, Jefferson, Madison, Patrick Henry, they have all helped us, directly or indirectly, to see him as he lived and walked among them. Though we obtain no sketch of George Mason from the lips of Washington and Lee, we are not left in doubt as to their high regard for him. Washington's free and intimate cor-

[1] R. A. Brock, Esq. Introduction to the "Spotswood Letters," Va. Hist. Society Collections, New Series, vol. i

24

respondence, carried on through the greater part of a life-time, attests his estimation of the sterling traits of character, and the eminent talents of his friend. And this impression is scarcely impaired at the last by the few slighting words Washington suffered himself to write of Mason when his early ally and familiar companion had become his determined political opponent. Richard Henry Lee seems to have had George Mason's entire confidence all through his career, and we cannot fail to perceive how thorough was Lee's appreciation of Mason, with whom he was in complete sympathy apparently on all the great issues of the eventful years in which they labored together, first for independence of Great Britain, and secondly for the preservation of the independence of the State against federal aggression. Jefferson, from first to last, looked upon George Mason as one of the wisest of Virginians, or indeed of his contemporaries, on the theatre of the American Revolution. In his correspondence with Mason, in his " Autobiography," in his " Anas," this is fully demonstrated. Jefferson's character of Mason, as sketched in the former's " Autobiography," has been given in an earlier chapter, and need not be repeated here. These two statesmen, George Mason and Thomas Jefferson, bore the relation, more fully perhaps than Jefferson himself perceived, of master and disciple in the school of States-rights, though Jefferson, like Madison, did not at first see with the elder sage's clear vision.

Madison, in the stress and conflict of 1787–88, was not prepared to do his great opponent justice. Both Washington and Madison, as Grigsby says, " in the heat of the moment wrote about Henry and Mason—the Gamaliels at whose feet he [Washington] sat for twenty years—in a manner that betrayed more passion than judgment." And he adds: " Great as were the merits of Washington and Madison, and none rejoices in them more than I do, it is simply stating an historical fact in saying that in 1788 neither of them stood in the estimation of the Virginia of that day on the same platform with Patrick Henry and George Mason as a statesman."[1] Madison's calmer judgment gave afterwards another verdict; and he came not many years later to be considered as an expounder of the States-rights doctrines of which Mason was the early and consistent apostle. St. George Tucker, who knew personally many of George Mason's contemporaries, who had heard Richard Henry Lee speak in public and thought him the "most mellifluous orator" he had ever listened to, who had received the tradition of Thomson Mason that he was "esteemed the first lawyer at the bar," reports from Madison's own lips his estimate of Thomson Mason's great brother. Among such orators as Patrick Henry and Richard Henry Lee, in a galaxy that contained such a speaker as Innes, of whom Tucker says that he "may be compared to an eagle in the air; you looked up at him with admiration and delight," George Mason, Madison thought, was in a sense pre-eminent: "He possessed the greatest talents for debate of any man he [Madison] had ever seen or heard speak."[2] Madison, in his old age, in a letter quoted in a previous chapter, written to one of George Mason's grandsons, gives some account of the former as a public man, and adds interesting testimony to his genial, social qualities. He says to his correspondent:

"The biographical tribute you meditate is justly due to the merits of your ancestor, Colonel George Mason. It is to be regretted that, highly distinguished as he was, the memorials of him on record, or perhaps otherwise attainable, are more scanty than many of his contemporaries far inferior to him in intellectual powers and public services. It would afford me much pleasure to be a tributary to your undertaking [a biography of Mason]. But although I had the advantage of being on the list of his personal friends, and in several instances of being associated with him in public life, I can add little for the pages of your work. . . . The public situation in which I had the best opportunity of being acquainted with the genius, the opinions and the public

[1] "History of the Virginia Federal Convention," note on p. 114.
[2] Kennedy's "Life of William Wirt," vol. i., p. 352.

labors of your grandfather, was that of our co-service in the Convention of 1787, which framed the Constitution of the United States. The objections which led him to withhold his name from it have been explained by himself. But none who differed from him on some points will deny that he sustained throughout the proceedings of the body, the high character of a powerful reasoner, a profound statesman, and a devoted republican.

"My private intercourse with him was chiefly on occasional visits to 'Gunston' when journeying to and from the North, in which his conversations were always a feast to me. But though in a high degree such, my recollection, after so long an interval, cannot particularize them in a form adapted to biographical use. I hope others of his friends still living, who enjoyed more of his society, will be able to do more justice to the fund of instructive observations and interesting anecdotes for which he was celebrated." [1]

Family tradition confirms this report of George Mason's conversational powers. But alas! no Boswell has preserved for posterity the crumbs of these intellectual feasts. The "fund of instructive observations," the "interesting anecdotes," have passed into oblivion. Only one story has floated down to us on the stream of time, illustrating George Mason's quick and caustic wit. John Randolph of Roanoke, who greatly admired Mason, alludes to it, though he gives it an odd turn, when he says: "My judgment, I believe, has not deserted me, and when it does, as old George Mason said, I shall be the last person in the world to find it out." [2] John Esten Cooke narrates the anecdote in a sketch of George Mason, written in 1859, for one of the New York papers, and he repeats it in a later article. [3] In a private letter to the present writer the story is worded as follows:

"The evidence of George Mason's humor, though it would probably be more appropriate to call it wit, I thought I could

[1] Rives' "Life of Madison," vol. i., p. 162 (note). The original letter is owned by the Virginia Historical Society.

[2] Garland's "Life of John Randolph," vol. ii., p. 155.

[3] "The Virginia Declaration of Independence," *Magazine of American History*, May, 1884.

see in his *bon mot* when a candidate for the legislature. His opponent declared that the people of Stafford [Fairfax ?] knew that Colonel Mason's mind was failing, to which he replied, that when his adversary's mind failed 'nobody would ever discover it,' which I think was as biting as anything ever uttered by Talleyrand."[1]

This retort of George Mason's recalls the anecdote related of Sir John Maynard, the eminent lawyer and king's serjeant, who, when eighty-six years old, having been sixty years at the bar, was told by Jeffreys that he had got so old he forgot the law. " 'T is true, Sir George," replied Maynard, " I have forgot more law than you ever knew."

George Mason's high estimation of Patrick Henry, as he saw him first in the early years of the Revolution, he has given us through a letter to Martin Cockburn. What Patrick Henry thought of George Mason has been happily preserved for posterity in a paragraph of one of Virginia's chronicles: " When Patrick Henry was a member of the Continental Congress he said the first men in that body were Washington, Richard Henry Lee, and Roger Sherman ; and later in life [he declared] Roger Sherman and George Mason [were] the greatest statesmen he ever knew."[2] The sketch of George Mason's character, as given by Edmund Randolph in his manuscript history of Virginia, has been quoted in a former chapter. It is found in connection with the pen portraits of Patrick Henry, of Thomas Jefferson, of Peyton Randolph, of Richard Henry Lee, of Robert Carter Nicholas, Edmund Pendleton, George Washington, Richard Bland, Benjamin Harrison, George Wythe, John Blair, and Thomas Ludwell Lee. These were the Virginia leaders in 1774. A little later Madison is added to the group. This valuable work of Edmund Randolph's was never completed, and but a fragment of it, discovered in Staunton, in 1860, remains. Randolph, it seems, contemplated writing for it, and did actually prepare " parallels between the characters of certain

---

[1] MS. letter of John Esten Cooke, October 28, 1885.
[2] Howe's " Historical Collections of Virginia," p. 221.

men, such, for instance, as those between General Washington and Mr. Jefferson, President Madison and General Hamilton, *George Mason and John Dickerson*, Benjamin Franklin and John Jay, Patrick Henry and Richard Henry Lee." [1] John Dickerson, the author of the famous " Farmer's Letters" of 1767, and of able public papers in the Congress of 1774 and of 1775, was yet behindhand in patriotic sentiment in 1776, when he opposed the Declaration of Independence. An undoubted patriot, he was an extremely cautious one, and though his pen had prepared the way for revolution, his step faltered on the threshold of the new era. Learned, sensitive, pious, benevolent, pure-minded, and eminent, both as a writer and an orator, one sees in him certain points of resemblance to George Mason; though broadly outlined there is apparent a wide contrast in the man John Adams, described in 1774 as " very modest, delicate, timid," and the virile, masterful spirit of the Virginian. And as Federalist and Antifederalist in 1787–88, the opinions of the two were distinctly at variance. John Dickerson, in his letters of " Fabius," supported the Constitution, while George Mason was working in the cause of amendments to the instrument they had jointly had a share in framing. Yet Dickerson, like Madison, saw later the error of his ways.

Leaving George Mason's contemporaries for a succeeding generation, we find Henry Lee, the son of " Light-Horse Harry," Mason's martial antagonist in the Virginia Convention of 1788, repeating, doubtless, the sentiment he had heard from boyhood, when he wrote: " Among the many profound statesmen Virginia has produced, he [George Mason] was perhaps second to none in wisdom and virtue, and by many of the most renowned of his contemporaries was regarded as the wisest of them all." [2] At length his

---

[1] " Life of Edmund Randolph," M. D. Conway, p. 378.

[2] General and Governor Fitzhugh Lee, a son of Captain Sidney Smith Lee, younger brother of the great Southern chieftain, Robert Edward Lee and half-brother of Henry Lee above quoted, is descended through his mother, a daughter of General John Mason, from George Mason, of Gunston.

State determined to mark her sense of his distinguished services. And in the oration delivered by the Hon. R. M. T. Hunter, at the unveiling of the Crawford statue of Washington, in Richmond, in 1858, the following reference was made to Mason and others who were to surround

"The foremost man of Time."

"But Virginia here raises monuments to more than one of her children, and as she bends over that group of her departed sons, she may well shed the mingled tears of pride and grief. Among these she will place Lewis, her bold pioneer, who wrestled with the red man from the waters of the Holston to those of the Great Kanawa, and finally made good the title of her State to the possession of the western wilderness on the bloody field of Point Pleasant, from which he drove the Indian beyond the Ohio. There will be found Nelson, the patriotic Governor of Virginia, whose generous sacrifices and great public services called forth the thanks of Washington at the siege of York. George Mason, too, is to be placed there in the fondness of a mother's pride, he whom history will proclaim one of the apostles of civil liberty, the author of the Bill of Rights of Virginia, the orator and the sage, whose vision was so nearly prophetic, and whose wisdom and patriotism made him a great leader in his day."

Patrick Henry and Thomas Jefferson were also described in glowing terms, as among those to whom statues were decreed. But before Virginia could carry out the suggestion of her orator of 1858 and fill up her Revolutionary Pantheon with the figures of George Rogers Clark and others, the battle-fields of her second struggle for independence glorified her history, while desolating her soil, and since then her later heroes have rather thrust aside the earlier ones. But in collecting these tributes to George Mason, we come to two Virginia writers who saw, suffered in, and survived the "Confederate Revolution." John Esten Cooke wrote of George Mason in 1859:

"There was living in Virginia, at the outbreak of the Revolution, in an old mansion called 'Gunston Hall,' situated on the right bank of the Potomac, not far from 'Mount Vernon,' one of the most remarkable men, not only of his country and of his epoch, but of all countries and all time. This man, who was not yet fifty years old, had never yet held any public office, but the first statesmen of his time consulted him and looked to him for guidance. He was not a lawyer, but his opinions on government had all the force and dignity of legislative decrees. He was not an agreeable speaker [?] yet when he rose to address an assembly the greatest orators—Lee, Pendleton, Henry, and their co-mates—listened to him with avidity. Confined almost wholly to his plantation by gout, or love of retirement, he nevertheless swayed and moulded public opinion. In the most urgent crises of public affairs the great actors looked, as it were, from the rostrum to the silent figure behind the scenes. . . . His ancestors had all been honorable and public-spirited ; they had lived and died as worthy old planters, fighting bravely against the Indians, or figuring in the House of Burgesses. They cultivated their acres, and kept up the old style of living in all its profusion—mingling socially with the class which then ruled as titled persons rule at present in England. Thus, George Mason of 'Gunston Hall,' at the time of the Revolution, possessed by birth a position which entitled him to consideration. But this would never have made him what he was —not a tithe of the force which he undoubtedly stood for in his time. It was the man himself, stripped of all adventitious aids, who asserted and maintained the vast intellectual dominion which he certainly wielded over the minds of the first thinkers of that age." [1]

There are frequent allusions to this "remarkable man," as he calls him, in John Esten Cooke's later sketches and delineations of Virginia history; his last article which touches upon George Mason having been written in 1884, twenty-five years after the first strain sung in Mason's praise. General Richard Taylor writing of George Mason, in 1879, says :

"Among the wise and good who in the past century secured the independence of our country and founded its government, George Mason of Virginia holds a place second to none."

[1] *New York Century*, 1859.

And he adds :

"On the soil of Virginia rests the tomb of George Mason, within sound of the Capitol of the Union which he labored to establish, while pointing out and in vain endeavoring to strengthen the weak places in its foundation. A Virginian to the core, his sympathies extended to the uttermost limits of the colonies, and were as deeply stirred by the sufferings of Massachusetts as were those of her own great patriots, the Adamses, Warren, Hancock. Mayhap there lurks some germ of truth in the weird superstition that disembodied spirits keep watch and ward over the resting-places of their mortal remains. What changes has the spirit of Mason witnessed since his body was returned to earth ! As the mighty prophets of Israel, mournfully has he watched the fulfil-ment of his own predictions. He strove for a Union of consent and love. He has seen one of force and hate. He urged indepen-dent States to create a common servant, the Federal Government, as a useful agent. He has seen the creature they called into being rend, like Frankenstein, its creators, disperse their assemblies at the point of the bayonet, deprive their citizens of every legal right. . . . With a sadness surpassing that of Rachel, he has seen the wealth and cultivation of the South destroyed by unlettered multitudes from the interior of the continent, directed by the fanaticism of the East." [1]

Happily if George Mason's immortal spirit has seen the woes of Virginia and her sister Commonwealths of the Con-federacy, it rejoices now in 1891, in their restored prosperity; when the " New South," affectionately reverent of her recent not less than of her far off past, presses forward in a race for the prizes of the future.

In conclusion, to the award of his contemporaries and personal friends, to the discriminating eulogies of George Mason's genius found in the utterances of Virginians and Southern men of later times, may be added the impartial, well-considered judgments of a number of Northern writers,

[1] *The North American Review*, February, 1879, " A Statesman of the Colonial Era."

two or three of whom are quoted in former chapters. In the last category is found the late venerable historian Bancroft. In several paragraphs, where Virginia has been his theme, he has written in felicitous phrase of her patriot and statesman, George Mason. After noting his talents in debate and oratory, Bancroft adds :

"But his great strength lay in his sincerity, which made him wise and bold, modest and unchanging, while it overawed his hearers. He was severe, but his severity was humane, with no tinge of bitterness, though he had a scorn for everything mean, and cowardly, and low ; and he always spoke out his convictions with frank directness. He had been truly loyal ; on renouncing his King, he could stand justified to his own conscience only by the purest and most unselfish attachment to human freedom." [1]

And as General Taylor writes in the article above quoted :

" To be appreciated by the political student, who desires to understand the principles of free government and the formative history of the Federal Constitution, his work must be sought in the Declaration of Rights, Constitution and revised Code of Virginia, and in the debates of the Federal and Virginia Conventions, as must his affectionate nature in such letters to his children and friends as have been preserved ; and it may be safely asserted that no one can carefully exhaust these sources without doubting whether his own or any age has produced a man superior to George Mason in all the elements of greatness."

[1] Bancroft's " History of the United States," edition of 1876, vol. v., p. 258.

APPENDIX.

I.

LETTERS RELATING TO THE COMPACT WITH MARYLAND.

SIR :   MOUNT VERNON, March 28, 1785.

We have the honor to transmit to the General Assembly, the result of the deliberations of the Commissioners of Virginia and Maryland, appointed to settle the navigation and jurisdiction of that part of the Chesapeake Bay within the limits of Virginia, and of the rivers Potomac and Pokomoke.

We flatter ourselves that, in the execution of this important trust, the commissioners have consulted the true interest of both governments, in a compact of such just and mutual principles, that, executed with good faith, will perpetuate harmony, friendship, and good offices between the two States, so essential to the prosperity and happiness of their people. In the conference on the subject of our appointment, several matters occurred to the commissioners, which they conceived very important to the commerce of the two States ; and which, with all deference, we take the liberty to communicate.

The commissioners were of opinion, these States ought to have leave from the United States in Congress assembled, to form a compact for the purpose of affording in due time, and in just proportions between the two States, naval protection to such part of Chesapeake Bay and Potomac river which may at any time hereafter be left unprovided for by Congress. The commissioners did not consider themselves authorized to make any compact on this subject, and submit the propriety of the two governments making a joint application to Congress, for their consent to enter into compact, for the purpose aforesaid ; such compact when made to be laid before Congress for their approbation ; and to continue until mutually dissolved by these States, or Congress shall declare that such compact shall no longer exist.

It also appeared to the commissioners that foreign gold and silver coin, received in the two States, as the current money thereof, should pass at the same value, according to its fineness and weight ; and if the species of coin could be regulated at the same nominal value, it would be of great convenience to the commerce and dealings between the citizens of the two States. The damages on foreign bills of exchange protested are very different in the two States, and it is obvious that they ought to be the same, and should be considered in all cases, and to all purposes, as of equal rank with debts upon contract in writing, signed by the party, and it was suggested that fifteen pct. should be allowed, without regard to the time of negotiation, and legal interest on the principal from the time of protest. It was also conceived by the commissioners, that drafts by the merchants of either State, upon those of the other, in the nature of inland bills of exchange, should be subject by law, to official protest, by a notary public, and that the damages, for non-payment, should be the same in both States ; and it was thought, that eight pct. should be allowed upon protest, and legal interest upon the principal, from the time of protest.

It appeared to the commissioners to be essential to the commerce and revenue of the two governments, that duties on imports or exports (if laid) should be the same in both States.

If these subjects should be deemed worthy notice, it may be proper for the two legislatures, at their annual meeting in the autumn to appoint commissioners to meet and communicate the regulations of commerce and duties proposed by each State, and to confer on such subjects as may concern the commercial interests of both States. It was suggested that the number of the said commissioners should be equal, and not less than three, nor more than five, from each State ; and that they should annually meet in the third week in September, at such place as they should appoint.

We have the honor to be with the greatest respect sir,

Your most obedient servants

G. MASON.

ALEXANDER HENDERSON.

P. S. The Commissioners also beg leave to transmit to the General Assembly, the inclosed copy of their joint application to the State of Pennsylvania respecting the communication between Potomac River and the Western waters.

Honorable the Speaker of the House
    of Delegates of Virginia.

VIRGINIA, MOUNT VERNON, March 28, 1785.

SIR :

In pursuance of directions from the legislatures of Virginia and Maryland, respectively to us given, we beg leave to represent to the State of Pennsylvania that it is in contemplation of the said two States to promote the clearing, and extending the navigation of Potomac, from tide-water, upwards, as far as the same may be found practicable, to open a convenient road from the head of such navigation, to the waters running into the Ohio, and to render these waters navigable, as far as may be necessary and proper. That the said works will require great expence, which may not be repaid, unless a free use be secured to the said States, and their citizens, of the waters of the Ohio and its branches, as far as the same lie within the limits of Pennsylvania ; that as essential advantages will accrue from such works to a considerable portion of the said State, it is thought reasonable that the legislature thereof should by some previous act engage, that for the encouragement of the said works, all articles of produce or merchandise, which may be conveyed to or from either of the said two States, through either of the said rivers, within the limits of Pennsylvania, to or from any place without the said limits, shall pass throughout free from all duties or tolls whatsoever, other than such tolls as may be established and be necessary for reimbursing expences incurred by the State, or its citizens, in clearing, or for defraying the expence of preserving the navigation of the said rivers. And that no articles imported into Pennsylvania through the channel or channels, or any part thereof to be opened as aforesaid, and rendered or used within the said State, shall be subject to any duties on imports, other than such articles would be subject to, if imported into the said State through any other channel whatsoever.

We request Sir, that you will take the earliest opportunity of laying this representation, on behalf of the two States, before the legislature of Pennsylvania; and that you will communicate the result to the executives of Virginia and Maryland.

By acts of the legislatures of Virginia and Maryland for opening the navigation of the river Potomac above tide-water, the citizens of the United States have the same right of trading through the said water, which the citizens of Maryland and Virginia enjoy; and we have no doubt but the legislature of your State will, agreeably to this principle, give every encouragement to measures which have for their object, the interest and convenience of their citizens, and those of the other States in the Union.

We have the honor to be, with the greatest respect, Sir, your most obedient servants,

> G. MASON,   } Commissioners for the Common-
> ALEXANDER HENDERSON, } wealth of Virginia.
> DANIEL OF ST. THOMAS JENIFER, } Commissioners for the
> T. STONE,   } State of Maryland.
> SAMUEL CHASE,

Honorable the President of the Executive Council
of the Commonwealth of Pennsylvania.

II.

OBJECTIONS TO THE CONSTITUTION, AND OTHER PAPERS.

AMENDMENTS TO THE CONFEDERATION.

1. Impost for 25 years and the collection of it.

2. The regulation of the commerce of the United States.

3. Regulation of the Highways and Ferries throughout the United States.

4. Supreme federal Court of Error and Appeal, the judges to be appointed by Congress with supreme jurisdiction in all causes in which the United States are concerned.

5. All judges and executive officers appointed by the several States to take an oath to observe and obey the federal laws and the writs of error, decrees, judgments, orders, and warrants of the federal court in federal causes.

6. The warrant of the Chief Justice and the President of Congress to be of force throughout all the United States, and all

sheriffs, under sheriffs, constables, and other executive officers to obey and execute them.

7. A Convention shall be holden to meet the 1st Monday in May every 5 years, for the purpose of examining into the administration of the federal government for the five preceding years and proposing such amendments and additional powers as to them may seem necessary. For which purpose the said Convention shall have power to appoint a committee which shall examine the secret journals of Congress and report thereon.

(Arthur Lee on letter of George Mason's.)

NOTES ON THE CONSTITUTION IN HANDWRITING OF GEORGE MASON.

In the beginning of the 4th clause of the 3rd section of the 1st Article, strike out the words—*the vice-president of the United States*, and instead of them insert—a vice-president of the United States shall be chosen in the manner hereinafter directed who [refused]

In the 3rd clause of the 5th section of the 1st Article, after the words *such parts* add—of the journals of the senate. [refused]

At the end of the same clause add—and a regular statement and account of the receipts and expenditure of all public money shall be ~~annually~~ published from time to time, [the word "annually" is marked over as in the text and the last four words are in another hand—]. [agreed to]

In the 8th section of the 1st Article to the beginning of the clause, before the words *To provide for organizing, arming and disciplining the militia* add—That the liberties of the people may be the better secured against the danger of regular troops or standing armies in time of peace. [refused]

In the 3rd clause of the 9th section of the 1st Article strike out the words—*nor any ex post facto laws.* [refused]

In the 4th clause of the same Article after the word *census* add—or enumeration. [agreed]

In the 1st clause of the 10th section of the same Article strike out ex post facto laws—and after the words *obligation of* insert—previous. [refused]

In the latter end of the 3rd clause of the 2nd Article—enquire of the committee about the senate chusing the vice president.

In the 7th clause of the 1st section of the 2nd Article—strike out the words *during the period for which he shall have been elected* —and instead of them insert—so as in any manner to affect the person in office at the time of such increase or diminution.

At the end of the 1st clause of the 2nd section of the 2nd Article add the words—or Treason ; but he may grant reprieves in cases of treason, until the end of the next ensuing session of Congress.

At the end of the 2nd clause of the 2nd section of the 2nd Article—and which shall be established by law [added in another hand], and the Congress may by law vest the appoint-
[agreed]   ment of such inferior officers as they think proper in the president alone, in the court of law, or the heads of Departments.

Section 4th of the same Article—Inconsistency between this and the 7th clause of the 3rd section of the 1st Article—amend by inserting after the word *office* the words—and disqualified from holding or enjoying—any office of honor, trust or profit under the United States.

Article 3rd, section 1—before the word *diminished*—insert—encreased or—

In the 2nd clause of the 2nd section of the 3rd Article—strike out the word *Fact*—and insert—Equity.

In the 3rd section of 3rd Article—*corruption of blood* inaccurately expressed ; and no exception or provision for the wife, who may be innocent, and ought not to be involved in ruin from the guilt of the husband.

Section 2nd, Article 4th—The citizens of one State having an estate in another, have not secured to them the right of removing their property as in the 4th Article of the Confederation—amend
[not   by adding the following clause : and every citizen having
proposed] an estate in two or more States shall have a right to remove his property from one State to another.

Article 5th—By this Article Congress only have the power of proposing amendments at any future time to this constitution and should it prove ever so oppressive, the whole people of America can't make, or even propose alterations to it ; a doctrine utterly subversive of the fundamental principles of the rights and liberties of the people.

In the 9th section of the 1st Article after the clause—no tax or duty shall be laid on articles exported from any State

Insert

No law in the nature of a Navigation Act shall be passed [inserted in another hand "before the year 1808"] without the assent of two thirds of the members present [disagreed] in each House.

PAPER ON THE JUDICIARY—IN AN UNKNOWN HAND.

The judicial power of the United States shall be vested in one Supreme Court and in such Courts of Admiralty as Congress shall establish in any of the States. And also in Courts of Admiralty to be established in such of the States as Congress shall direct.

The jurisdiction of the supreme courts shall extend to all cases in law and equity arising under this Constitution, the laws of the United States and treaties made or which shall be made under their authority ; to all cases affecting ambassadors, other public ministers and consuls ; to all cases of admiralty and maritime jurisdiction ; to controversies to which the United States shall be a party, to controversies between two or more States ; between *citizens of the same State* claiming lands of different States, and between *a State and the citizens thereof* and foreign States, citizens or subjects.

In all cases affecting ambassadors, other public ministers and consuls, and those in which a State shall be a party, and suits between persons claiming lands under grants of different States the Supreme Court shall have original jurisdiction, and in all the other cases before mentioned the Supreme Courts shall have appellate jurisdiction as to law only, except in cases of equity and admiralty and maritime jurisdiction in which last mentioned cases the Supreme Court shall have appellate jurisdiction, both as to law and fact.

In all cases of admiralty and maritime jurisdiction, the Admiralty Courts appointed by Congress shall have original jurisdiction, and an appeal may be made to the Supreme Court of Congress for any sum and in such manner as Congress may by law direct.

In all other cases not otherwise provided for the *Superior* State Courts shall have original jurisdiction, and an appeal may be made to the Supreme federal Court in all cases where the subject in controversy or the decree or judgment of the State court shall be of the value of one thousand dollars and in cases of less value the appeal shall be to the High Court of Appeals, Court of Errors or other Supreme Court of the State where the suit shall be tried.

The trial of all crimes, except in case of impeachment shall be in the Superior Court of that State where the offence shall have been committed in such manner as the Congress shall by law direct except that the trial shall be by a jury. But when the crime shall not have been committed within any one of the United States the trial shall be at such place and in such manner as Congress shall by law direct, except that such trial shall also be by a jury.

ROUGH DRAFT OF A PAPER, APPARENTLY IN THE HAND OF G. MASON, WITH ERASURES AND INTERLINEATIONS.

At a time when our government is approaching to dissolution, when some of its principles have been found utterly inadequate to the purposes for which it was established, and it is evident that without some material alterations it can not much longer subsist, it must give real concern to every man who has his country's interest at heart to find such a difference of sentiment and opinion in an assembly of the most respectable and confidential characters in America, appointed for the special purpose of revising and amending the federal constitution, so as to obtain and preserve the important objects for which it was instituted— the protection, safety and happiness of the people. We all agree in the necessity of new regulations; but we differ widely in our opinions of what are the safest and most effectual. Perhaps this contrariety of sentiment arises from our not thoroughly considering the peculiar circumstances, situation, character and genius of the people of America, differing materially from that of any other nation. The history of other nations has been minutely investigated, examples have been drawn from and arguments founded on the practice of countries very dissimilar to ours. The treaties, leagues, and confederacies between different sovereign, independent powers have been urged as proofs in support of the propriety and justice of the single and equal representation of each individual State in the American Union; and thence conclusions have been drawn that the people of these United States would refuse to adopt a government founded more on an equal representation of the people themselves, than on the distinct representation of each separate, individual State. If the different States in our Union always had been as now substantially and in reality distinct, sovereign and independent, this kind of reasoning would have great force; but if the premises on which it is founded are mere assumptions not founded on facts, or at best upon facts to be found only upon a paper of yesterday, and even these contradictory to each other, no satisfactory conclusions can be drawn from them.

OBJECTIONS TO THIS CONSTITUTION OF GOVERNMENT.

There is no Declaration of Rights, and the laws of the general government being paramount to the laws and constitution of the several States, the Declarations of Rights in the separate States are no security. Nor are the people secured even in the enjoyment of the benefit of the common law [which stands here upon no other foundation than its having been adopted by the respective acts forming the constitutions of the several States].

In the House of Representatives there is not the substance but the shadow only of representation; which can never produce proper information in the legislature, or inspire confidence in the people; the laws will therefore be generally made by men little concerned in, and unacquainted with their effects and consequences. [This objection has been in some degree lessened by an amendment, often before refused and at last made by an erasure, after the engrossment upon parchment of the word *forty* and inserting *thirty*, in the third clause of the second section of the first article.]

The Senate have the power of altering all money bills, and of originating appropriations of money, and the salaries of the officers of their own appointment, in conjunction with the president of the United States, although they are not the representatives of the people or amenable to them.

These with their other great powers, viz. : their power in the appointment of ambassadors and all public officers, in making treaties, and in trying all impeachments, their influence upon and connection with the supreme Executive from these causes, their duration of office and their being a constantly existing body, almost continually sitting, joined with their being one complete branch of the legislature, will destroy any balance in the government, and enable them to accomplish what ursurpations they please upon the rights and liberties of the people.

The Judiciary of the United States is so constructed and extended, as to absorb and destroy the judiciaries of the several States ; thereby rendering law as tedious, intricate and expensive, and justice as unattainable, by a great part of the community, as in England, and enabling the rich to oppress and ruin the poor.

The President of the United States has no Constitutional Council, a thing unknown in any safe and regular government. He will therefore be unsupported by proper information and advice, and will generally be directed by minions and favorites ; or he will become a tool to the Senate—or a Council of State will grow out of the principal officers of the great departments ; the worst and most dangerous of all ingredients for such a Council in a free country ; [for they may be induced to join in any dangerous or oppressive measures, to shelter themselves, and prevent an inquiry into their own misconduct in office. Whereas, had a constitutional council been formed (as was proposed) of six members, viz. : two from the Eastern, two from the Middle, and two from the Southern States, to be appointed by vote of the States in the House of Representatives, with the same duration and rotation of office as the Senate, the executive would always have had safe and proper information and advice ; the president of such a council might have acted as Vice-President of the United States *pro tempore*, upon any vacancy or disability of the chief magistrate ; and long continued sessions of the Senate, would in a great measure have been prevented.] From this fatal defect has arisen the improper power of the Senate in the appointment of public officers, and the alarming dependence and connection between that branch of the legislature and the supreme Executive.

Hence also sprung that unnecessary [and dangerous] officer the Vice-President, who for want of other employment is made president of the Senate, thereby dangerously blending the executive and legislative powers, besides always giving to some one of the States an unnecessary and unjust pre-eminence over the others.

The President of the United States has the unrestrained power of granting pardons for treason, which may be sometimes exercised to screen from punishment those whom he had secretly instigated to commit the crime, and thereby prevent a discovery of his own guilt.

By declaring all treaties supreme laws of the land, the Executive and the Senate have, in many cases, an exclusive power of legislation ; which might have been avoided by proper distinctions with respect to treaties, and requiring the assent of the House of Representatives, where it could be done with safety.

By requiring only a majority to make all commercial and navigation laws, the five Southern States, whose produce and circumstances are totally different from that of the eight Northern and Eastern States, may [will] be ruined, for such rigid and premature regulations may be made as will enable the merchants of the Northern and Eastern States not only to demand an exhorbitant freight, but to monopolize the purchase of the commodities at their own price, for many years, to the great injury of the landed interest, and [the] impoverishment of the people ; and the danger is the greater as the gain on one side will be in proportion to the loss on the other. Whereas requiring two-thirds of the members present in both Houses would have produced mutual moderation, promoted the general interest, and removed an insuperable objection to the adoption of this [the] government.

Under their own construction of the general clause, at the end of the enumerated powers, the Congress may grant monopolies in trade and commerce, constitute new crimes, inflict unusual and severe punishments, and extend their powers [power] as far as they shall think proper ; so that the State legislatures have no security for the powers now presumed to remain to them, or the people for their rights.

There is no declaration of any kind, for preserving the liberty of the press, or the trial by jury in civil causes [cases] ; nor against the danger of standing armies in time of peace.

The State legislatures are restrained from laying export duties on their own produce.

Both the general legislature and the State legislature are expressly prohibited making *ex post facto* laws ; though there never was nor can be a legislature but must and will make such laws, when necessity and the public safety require them ; which will hereafter be a breach of all the constitutions in the Union, and afford precedents for other innovations.

This government will set out [commence] a moderate aristocracy : it is at present impossible to foresee whether it will, in its operation, produce a monarchy, or a corrupt, tyrannical [oppressive] aristocracy ; it will most probably vibrate some years between the two, and then terminate in the one or the other.

The general legislature is restrained from prohibiting the further importation of slaves for twenty odd years ; though such importations render the United States weaker, more vulnerable, and less capable of defence.

[This is a draft of the original "Objections" as written by George Mason on the blank sheets of the copy of the Constitution, printed for the use of the members of the Convention, and brought in September 13th. The words in brackets are those additions or alterations which appear in the "Objections" as printed later in pamphlet form. There was a change made also in the arrangement of the paragraphs, in this final form of Mason's paper, which there closes with the one beginning, "This government will commence," etc. (See "Pamphlets on the Constitution," Paul L. Ford ; and Elliot's "Debates," vol. i., p. 494).]

III.

SPEECHES IN THE CONVENTION OF 1788.

Richmond, June 2, 1788.—G. Mason put on the committee of privileges and elections. He is second on the list. B. Harrison first. Gov. Randolph third. Clerk and printer appointed. Then on motion of G. M. the Convention adjourned until the next day, to meet at the New Academy on Schockoe Hill.

Tuesday, June 3.—Serjeant-at-arms and door-keeper appointed. Rules and regulations resolved on similar to those in House of Delegates. Resolution of Congress, read of Sept. 28, report of

Federal Convention, together with resolutions of General Assembly of October 25, and act of Assembly concerning the Convention now held.

Whereupon *Mr. Mason* addressed the president [*Mr. Pendleton*] as follows : Mr. President, I hope and trust, sir, that this Convention, appointed by the people, on this great and important occasion, for securing, as far as possible, to the latest generation, the happiness and liberty of the people, will freely and fully investigate this important subject. For this purpose I humbly conceive the fullest and clearest investigation indispensably necessary, and that we ought not to be bound by any general rules whatsoever. The curse denounced by the divine vengeance will be small compared to what will justly fall upon us, if from any sinister views we obstruct the fullest inquiry. This subject, therefore, ought to obtain the freest discussion, clause by clause, before any general previous question be put ; nor ought it to be precluded by any other question.

Mr. Tyler moved that the Convention should resolve itself into a Committee of the whole Convention, to-morrow, to take into consideration the proposed plan of government, in order to have a fairer opportunity of examining its merits.

Mr. Mason, after recapitulating his former reasons for having urged a full discussion, clause by clause, concluded by agreeing with Mr. Tyler that a Committee of the whole Convention was the proper mode of proceeding.

Mr. Madison concurred with the honorable gentleman in going into a full and free investigation of the subject before them, and said he had no objection to the plan proposed. *Mr. Mason* then moved the following resolution, which was agreed to by the Convention unanimously :—

Resolved, That no question, general or particular, shall be propounded in this Convention, upon the proposed Constitution of government for the United States, or upon any clause or article thereof, until the said Constitution shall have been discussed, clause by clause, through all its parts.

Mr. Tyler said he should renew his motion &c.

Mr. Lee urged the necessity of immediately entering into the discussion.

Mr. Mason. Mr. President, no man in this Convention is more averse to take up the time of the Convention than I am ; but I am equally against hurrying them precipitately into any measure. I humbly conceive, sir, that the members ought to have time to consider the subject. Precious as time is, we ought not to run into the discussion before we have the proper means.

Wednesday, June 4.—The preamble and two first sections of Article I. were read. Mr. Nicholas made a long speech in favor of the Constitution. Patrick Henry spoke against it—animadverted on the words " *We, the people* "—thought it should have been " *We, the States.*" Gov. Randolph replied to Henry and concluded his speech thus : "In the whole of this business I have acted in the strictest obedience to the dictates of my conscience, in discharging what I conceive to be my duty to my country." He had refused his signature, but as 8 States had adopted the Constitution, he was a friend to Union.

Mr. George Mason. Mr. Chairman, whether the Constitution be good or bad, the present clause [Art. I., Sect. 2] clearly discovers that it is a national government, and no longer a Confederation. I mean that clause which gives the first hint of the general government laying direct taxes. The assumption of this power of laying direct taxes does, of itself, entirely change the confederation of the States into one consolidated government. This power being at discretion, unconfined, and without any kind of control, must carry everything before it. The very idea of converting what was formerly a confederation to a consolidated government, is totally subversive of every principle which has hitherto governed us. This power is calculated to annihilate totally the State governments. Will the people of this great community submit to be individually taxed by two different and distinct powers? Will they suffer themselves to be doubly harassed? These two concurrent powers cannot exist long together ; the one will destroy the other : the general government being paramount to, and in every respect more powerful than the State governments, the latter must give way to the former. Is it to be supposed that one national government will suit so extensive a country, embracing so many climates, and containing inhabitants so very different in manners, habits and customs? It is ascertained, by history, that there never was a government over a very extensive country without destroying the liberties of the people : history also, supported by the opinions of the best writers, shows us that monarchy may suit a large territory, and despotic governments ever so extensive a country, but that popular governments can only exist in small territories. Is there a single example, on the face of the earth, to support a contrary opinion ? Where is there one exception to this general rule ? Was there ever an instance of a general national government extending over so extensive a country, abounding in such a variety of climates, &c., where the people retained their liberty ? I solemnly declare that no man is a greater friend to a firm union of the American States than I am ; but, sir, if this great end can be obtained without hazarding the rights of the people, why should we recur to such dangerous principles ? Requisitions have been often refused, sometimes from an impossibility of complying with them ; often from that great variety of circumstances which retards the collection of moneys ; and perhaps sometimes from a wilful design of procrastinating. But why shall we give up to the national government this power, so dangerous in its nature, and for which its members will not have sufficient information ? Is it not well known that what would be a proper tax in one State would be grievous in another ? The gentleman who has favored us with a eulogium in favor of this system, must, after all the encomiums he has been pleased to bestow upon it, acknowledge that our federal representatives must be unacquainted with the situation of their constituents. Sixty-five members cannot possibly know the situation and circumstances of all the inhabitants of this immense continent. When a certain sum comes to be taxed, and the mode of levying to be fixed, they will lay the tax on that article which will be most productive and easiest in the collection, without consulting the real circumstances or convenience of a country, with which, in fact, they cannot be sufficiently acquainted.

The mode of levying taxes is of the utmost consequence ; and yet here it is to be determined by those who have neither knowledge of our situation, nor a common interest with us, nor a fellow-feeling for us. The subjects of taxation differs in three fourths, nay, I might say with truth, in four fifths of the States. If we trust the national government with an effectual way of raising the necessary sums, it is sufficient : everything we do further is trusting the happiness and rights of the people. Why, then, should we give up this dangerous power of individual taxation ? Why leave the manner of laying taxes to those who, in the nature of things, cannot be acquainted with the situation of those on whom they are to impose them, when it can be done by those who are well acquainted with it ?   If, instead of giving this oppressive power, we give them such an effectual alternative as will answer the purpose, without encountering the evil and danger that might arise from it, then I would cheerfully acquiesce ; and would it not be far more eligible? I candidly acknowledge the inefficacy of the Confederation ; but requisitions have been made which were impossible to be complied with—requisitions for more gold and silver than were in the United States.   If we give the general government the power of demanding their quotas of the States, with an alternative of laying direct taxes in case of non-compliance, then the mischief would be avoided ; and the certainty of this conditional power would, in all human probability, prevent the application, and the sums necessary for the Union would be then laid by the States, by those who know how it can best be raised, by those who have a fellow-feeling for us.   Give me leave to say, that the sum raised one way with convenience and ease, would be very oppressive another way. Why, then, not leave this power to to be exercised by those who know the mode most convenient for the inhabitants, and not by those who must necessarily apportion it in such manner as shall be oppressive ?

With respect to the representation so much applauded, I cannot think it such a full and free one as it is represented ; but I must candidly acknowledge that this defect results from the very nature of the government.   It would be impossible to have a full and adequate representation in the general government; it would be too expensive and too unwieldy.   We are, then, under the necessity of having this a very inadequate representation.   Is this general representation to be compared with the real, actual, substantial representation of the State legislatures?   It cannot bear a comparison.   To make representation real and actual, the number of representatives ought to be adequate ; they ought to mix with the people, think as they think, feel as they feel,—ought to be perfectly amenable to them, and thoroughly acquainted with their interest and condition.   Now, these great ingredients are either not at all, or in a small degree, to be found in our federal representatives ; so that we have no real, actual, substantial representation ; but I acknowledge it results from the nature of the government. The necessity of this inconvenience may appear a sufficient reason not to argue against it ; but, sir, it clearly shows that we ought to give power with a sparing hand to a government thus imperfectly constructed. To a government which, in the nature of things, cannot but be defective, no powers ought to be given but such as are absolutely necessary. There is one thing in it which I conceive to be extremely dangerous. Gentlemen may talk of public virtue and confidence ; we shall be told that the House of Representatives will consist of the most virtuous men on the continent, and that in their hands we may trust our dearest rights. This, like all other assemblies, will be composed of some bad and some good men ; and considering the natural lust of power so inherent in man, I fear the thirst of power will prevail to oppress the people. What I conceive to be so dangerous, is the provision with respect to the number of representatives ; it does not expressly provide that we shall have one for every thirty thousand, but that the number shall not exceed that proportion. The utmost that we can expect (and perhaps that is too much) is, that the present number shall be continued to us ;—" the number of representatives shall not exceed one for every thirty thousand." Now will not this be complied with, although the present number should never be increased—nay, although it should be decreased ? Suppose Congress should say that we should have one for every 200 thousand ; will not the Constitution be complied with ?—for one for every 200 thousand does not exceed one for every thirty thousand.

There is a want of proportion that ought to be strictly guarded against. The worthy gentleman tells us that we have no reason to fear ; but I always fear for the rights of the people. I do not pretend to inspiration ; but I think it is apparent as the day, that the members will attend to local, partial interests, to prevent an augmentation of their number. I know not how they will be chosen ; but, whatever be the mode of choosing, our present numbers will be ten ; and suppose our State is laid off in ten districts,—those gentlemen who shall be sent from those districts will lessen their own power and influence in their respective districts if they increase their number ; for the greater the number of men among whom any given quantum of power is divided, the less the power of each individual. Thus they will have a local interest to prevent the increase of, and perhaps they will lessen their own number. This is evident on the face of the Constitution : so loose an expression ought to be guarded against, for Congress will be clearly within the requisition of the Constitution although the number of representatives should always continue what it is now, and the population of the country should increase to an immense number. Nay, they may reduce the number from sixty-five to one from each State, without violating the Constitution ; and thus the number, which is now too small, would then be infinitely too much so. But my principal objection is, that the Confederation is converted to one general consolidated government, which, from my best judgement of it, (and which perhaps will be shown, in the course of this discussion, to be really well founded,) is one of the worst curses that can possibly befall a nation. Does any man suppose that one general national government can exist in so extensive a country as this. I hope that a government may be framed which may suit us, by drawing a line between the general and State governments, and prevent that dangerous clashing of interest and power, which must, as it now stands, terminate in the destruction of one or the other. When we come to the judiciary, we shall be more convinced that this government will terminate in the annihilation of the State governments : the question then will be, whether a consolidated government can preserve the freedom and secure the rights of the people.

If such amendments be introduced as shall exclude danger, I shall most gladly put my hand to it. When such amendments as shall, from the best information, secure the great essential rights of the people, shall be agreed to by gentlemen, I shall most heartily make the greatest concessions, and concur in any reasonable measure to obtain the desirable end of conciliation and unanimity. An indispensable amendment in this case is, that Congress shall not exercise the power of raising direct taxes till the States shall have refused to comply with the requisitions of Congress. On this condition it may be granted ; but I see no reason to grant it unconditionally, as the States can raise the taxes with more ease, and lay them on the inhabitants with more propriety, than it is possible for the general government to do. If Congress hath this power, without control, the taxes will be laid by those who have no fellow-feeling or acquaintance with the people. This is my objection to the article now under consideration. It is a very great and important one. I therefore beg gentlemen to consider it. Should this power be restrained, I shall withdraw my objections to this part of the Constitution ; but as it stands, it is an objection so strong in my mind, that its amendment is with me a *sine qua non* of its adoption. I wish for such amendments, and such only, as are necessary to secure the dearest rights of the people.

Wednesday, June 11.—*Madison* made the opening speech. Some conversation then followed on the mode of discussion— [1st and 2nd *Henry* advocating as the best plan, to discuss it at large— Sections, *Madison* approving of a regular, progressive discussion. Art. I.]

Mr. George Mason. Mr. Chairman, gentlemen will be pleased to consider that, on so important a subject as this, it is impossible in the nature of things, to avoid arguing more at large than is usual. You will allow that I have not taken up a great part of your time. But as gentlemen have indulged themselves in entering at large into the subject, I hope to be permitted to follow them, and answer their observations.

The worthy member, (Mr. Nicholas,) at a very early day, gave us an accurate detail of the representation of the people in Britain, and of the rights of the King of Britain ; and illustrated his observations by a quotation from Dr. Price. Gentlemen will please to take notice that those arguments relate to a single government, and that they are not applicable to this case. However applicable they may be to such a government as that of Great Britain, it will be entirely inapplicable to such a government as ours. The gentleman in drawing a comparison between the representation of the people in the House of Commons, in England, and the representation in the government now proposed to us, has been pleased to express his approbation in favor of the American government. Let us examine. I think that there are about 550 members in the English House of Commons. The people of Britain have a representation in Parliament of five hundred and fifty members, who intimately mingle with all classes of the people, feeling and knowing their circumstances. In the proposed American government— in a country perhaps ten times more extensive—we are to have a representation of sixty-five, who from the nature of the government, cannot possibly be mingled with the different classes of the people, nor have a fellow-feeling for them.

They must form an aristocracy, and will not regard the interest of the people. Experience tells us that men pay most regard to those whose rank and situation are similar to their own. In the course of the investigation, the gentleman mentioned the bribery and corruption of Parliament, and drew a conclusion the very reverse of what I should have formed on the subject. He said, if I recollect rightly, that the American representation is more secured against bribery and corruption, than the English Parliament. Are sixty-five better than five hundred and fifty? Bribery and corruption, in my opinion, will be practised in America more than in England, in proportion as five hundred and fifty exceed sixty-five; and there will be less integrity and probity in proportion as sixty-five is less than five hundred and fifty. From what source is the bribery practised in the British Parliament derived? I think the principal source is the distribution of places, offices, and posts. Will any gentleman deny this? Give me leave, on this occasion, to recur to that clause of the Constitution which speaks of restraint, and has the appearance of restraining from corruption, &c., but which, when examined, will be found to be no restraint at all. The clause runs thus: "No senator or representative shall, during the time for which he was elected, be appointed to any civil office, under the authority of the United States, which shall have been created, or the emoluments whereof shall have been increased, during such time; and no person holding any office under the United States shall be a member of either house during his continuance in office." This appears to me to be no restraint at all. It is to be observed that this restraint only extends to civil officers.

But I will not examine whether it be a proper distinction or not. What is the restraint as to civil officers? Only that they shall not be appointed to offices which shall have been created, or the emoluments whereof shall have been increased, during the time for which they shall have been elected. They may be appointed to existing offices, if the emoluments be not increased during the time for which they were elected.

[Here Mr. Mason spoke too low to he heard.]

Thus, after the government is set in motion, the restraint will be gone. They may appoint what number of officers they please.

They may send ambassadors to every part of Europe. Here is, sir, I think, as wide a door for corruption as in any government in Europe. There is the same inducement for corruption, there is the same room for it, in this government, which they have in the British government; and in proportion as the number is smaller, corruption will be greater.

That unconditional power of taxation which is given to that government cannot but oppress the people. If, instead of this, a conditional power of taxation be given, in case of refusal to comply with requisitions, the same end will be answered with convenience to the people. This will not lessen the power of Congress; we do not want to lessen the power of Congress unnecessarily. This will produce moderation in the demand, and will prevent the ruinous exercise of that power by those who know not our situation. We shall then have that mode of taxation which is the most easy, and least oppressive to the people, because it will be exercised by those who are acquainted with their condition and circumstances. This, sir, is the great object we wish to secure— that our people should be taxed by those who have a fellow-feeling for them. I think I can venture to assert that the general government will lay such taxes as are the easiest and the most productive in the collection. This is natural and probable.

For example, they may lay a poll tax. This is simply and easily collected, but is of all taxes the most grievous. Why the most grievous? Because it falls light on the rich, and heavy on the poor. It is most oppressive : for if the rich man is taxed, he can only retrench his superfluities; but the consequence to the poor man is, that it increases his miseries. That they will lay the most simple taxes, and such as are easiest to collect, is highly probable, nay, almost absolutely certain. I shall take the liberty, on this occasion, to read you a letter, which will show, at least as far as opinion goes, what sort of taxes will be most probably laid on us, if we adopt this Constitution. It was the opinion of a gentleman of information. It will in some degree establish the fallacy of those reports which have been circulated through the country, and which induced a great many poor, ignorant people to believe that the taxes were to be lessened by the adoption of the proposed government.

[Here Mr. Mason read a letter from Mr. Robert Morris, financier of the United States, to Congress, wherein he spoke of the propriety of laying the following taxes for the use of the United States; viz., six shillings on every hundred acres of land, six shillings per poll, and nine pence per gallon on all spirituous liquors distilled in the country. Mr. Mason declared that he did not mean to make the smallest reflection on Mr. Morris, but introduced his letter to show what taxes would probably be laid.]

He then continued: This will at least show that such taxes were in agitation, and were strongly advocated by a considerable part of Congress. I have read this letter to show that they will lay taxes most easy to be collected, without any regard to our convenience; so that, instead of amusing ourselves with a diminution of our taxes, we may rest assured that they will be increased. But my principal reason for introducing it was, to show that taxes would be laid by those who are not acquainted with our situation, and that the agents of the collection may be consulted upon the most productive and simple mode of taxation. The gentleman who wrote this letter had more information on this subject than we have; but this will show gentlemen that we are not to be eased of taxes. Any of those taxes which have been pointed out by this financier as the most eligible, will be ruinous and unequal, and will be particularly oppressive on the poorest part of the people.

As to a poll tax, I have already spoken of its iniquitous operation, and need not say much of it, because it is so generally disliked in this State, that we were obliged to abolish it last year. As to a land tax, it will operate most unequally. The man who has one hundred acres of the richest land will pay as little as a man who has one hundred acres of the poorest land. Near Philadelphia, or Boston, an acre of land is worth one hundred pounds; yet the possessor of it will pay no more than the man with us whose land is hardly worth twenty shillings an acre. Some landholders in this State will have to pay twenty times as much as will be paid for all the land on which Philadelphia stands; and as to excise, this will carry the exciseman to every farmer's house, who distils a little brandy, where he may search and ransack as he pleases.

These I mention as specimens of the kind of tax which is to be laid upon us by those who have no information of our situation, and by a government where the wealthy only are represented. It is urged that no new power is given up to the general government, and that the Confederation had those powers before. That system derived its power from the State governments. When the people of Virginia formed their government, they reserved certain great powers in the bill of rights. They would not trust their own citizens, who had a similarity of interest with themselves, and who had frequent and intimate communication with them. They would not trust their own fellow-citizens, I say, with the exercise of those great powers reserved in the bill of rights. Do we not, by this system give up a great part of the rights, reserved by the bill of rights to those who have no fellow-feeling for the people—to a government where the representatives will have no communication with the people? I say, then, there are great and important powers, which were not transferred to the State government, given up to the general government by this Constitution. Let us advert to the 6th article. It expressly declares, that "this Constitution, and the laws of the United States which shall be made in pursuance thereof, and all treaties made, or which shall be made, under the authority of the United States, shall be the supreme law of the land, and the judges in every State shall be bound thereby; anything in the Constitution or laws of any State to the contrary notwithstanding." Now, sir, if the laws and Constitution of the general government, as expressly said, be paramount to those of any State, are not those rights with which we were afraid to trust our own citizens annulled and given up to the general government? The bill of rights is a part of our own Constitution. The judges are obliged to take notice of the laws of the general government; consequently, the rights secured by our bill of rights are given up. If they are not given up, where are they secured? By implication! Let gentlemen show that they are secured in a plain, direct, unequivocal manner. It is not in their power. Then where is the security? where is the barrier drawn between the government and the rights of the citizens, as secured in our own State government? These rights are given up in that paper; but I trust that this Convention will never give them up, but will take pains to secure them to the latest posterity. If a check be necessary in our own State government, it is much more so in a government—where our representatives are to be at the distance of a thousand miles from us, without any responsibility.

I said, the other day, that they could not have sufficient information. I was asked how the legislature of Virginia got their information. The answer is easy and obvious. They get it from one hundred and sixty representatives dispersed through all parts of the country. In this government how do they get it? Instead of one hundred and sixty, there are but ten—chosen, if not wholly, yet mostly, from the higher order of the people— from the great, the wealthy—the *well-born*—the *well-born*, Mr. Chairman, that aristocratic idol—that flattering idea—that *exotic* plant—which has been lately imported from the ports of Great Britain, and planted in the luxurious soil of this country.

In the course of the investigation, much praise has been lavished upon the article which fixes the number of representatives. It only says that the proportion *shall not exceed* one for every thirty thousand.

The worthy gentleman says that the number must be increased, [Nicholas. because representation and taxation are in proportion, June 6.] and that one cannot be increased without increasing the other, nor decreased without decreasing the other. Let us examine the weight of this argument. If the proportion of each State equally and ratably diminishes, the words of the Constitution will be as much satisfied as if it had been increased in the same manner, without any reduction of the taxes. Let us illustrate it familiarly. Virginia has ten representatives; Maryland has six. Virginia will have to pay a sum in proportion, greater than Maryland, as ten to six. Suppose Virginia reduced to five, and Maryland to three. The relative proportion of money, paid by each, will be the same as before; and yet the honorable gentleman said, that if this did not convince us, he would give up. I am one of those unhappy men who cannot be amused with assertions. A man from the dead might frighten me; but I am sure that he could not convince me without using better arguments than I have yet heard. The same gentleman showed us that though the Northern States had a most decided majority against us, yet the increase of population among us would, in the course of years, change it in our favor. A very sound argument indeed, that we should cheerfully burn ourselves to death in hopes of a joyful and happy resurrection !

The very worthy gentleman who presides was pleased to tell us that there was no interference between the legislation of the general government and that of the State legislatures. Pardon me if I show the contrary. In the important instance of taxation there is a palpable interference. Suppose a poll tax ; the general government can lay a poll tax ; the State legislatures can do the same ; and yet it is said there can be no interference.

My honorable colleague in the late federal Convention, in answer to another gentleman, who had said that the annals of mankind could afford no instance of rulers giving up power, has told us that eight States had adopted the Constitution, and that this was a relinquishment of power. Ought this example to have any weight with us ? If that relinquishment was imprudent, shall we imitate it ? I will venture to assert that, out of a thousand instances where the people precipitately and unguardedly relinquished their power, there has not been one instance of a voluntary surrender of it back by rulers. He afterwards said, that freedom at home and respectability abroad would be the consequence of the adoption of this government, and that we cannot exist without its adoption. Highly as I esteem that gentleman, highly as I esteem his historical knowledge, I am obliged to deny his assertions.

If this government will endanger our liberties in its present state, its adoption will not promote our happiness at home. The people of this country are as independent, happy, and respectable as those of any country. France is the most powerful and respectable nation on earth. Would the planters of this country change their shoes for the wooden shoes of the peasants of France ? Perhaps Russia is the next greatest power in Europe. Would we change situations with the people of Russia ? We have heard a great deal of Holland. Some have called its government a democracy ; others have called it an aristocracy. It is well known to be a republic. It has arisen to uncommon power and wealth. Compared to its neighboring countries, its fortune has been surprising.

[Here Mr. Mason made a quotation, showing the comparative flourishing condition of the inhabitants of Holland, even a few years after they had shaken off the Spanish yoke ; that plenty and contentment were to be everywhere seen, the peasants well clothed, provisions plenty, their furniture and domestic utensils in abundance, and their lands well stocked ;—that, on the contrary, the people of Spain were in a poor and miserable condition, in want of every thing of which the people of Holland enjoyed the greatest abundance.]

Mr. Mason then continued : As this was within a few years after the Spanish revolution, this striking contrast could be owing to no other cause than the liberty which they enjoyed under their government. Here behold the difference between a powerful, great consolidation, and a confederacy. They tell us that if we be powerful and respectable abroad, we shall have liberty and happiness at home. Let us secure that liberty, that happiness first, and we shall then be respectable.

I have some acquaintance with a great many characters who favor this government, their connections, their conduct, their political principles, and a number of other circumstances. There are a great many wise and good men among them. But when I look round the number of my acquaintance in Virginia, the country wherein I was born and have lived so many years, and observe who are the warmest and the most zealous friends to this new government, it makes me think of the story of the cat transformed into a fine lady : forgetting her transformation, and happening to see a rat, she could not restrain herself, but sprang upon it out of the chair.

He (Governor Randolph) dwelt largely on the necessity of the union. A great many others have enlarged on this subject. Foreigners would suppose, from the declamation about union, that there was a great dislike in America to any general American government. I have never, in my whole life, heard one single man deny the necessity and propriety of the union. This necessity is deeply impressed on every American mind. There can be no danger of any object being lost when the mind of every man in the country is strongly attached to it. But I hope that it is not to the name, but to the blessings of union, that we are attached. Those gentlemen who are loudest in their praises of the name, are not more attached to the reality than I am. The security of our liberty and happiness is the object we ought to have in view in wishing to establish the union. If, instead of securing these, we endanger them, the name of union will be but a trivial consolation. If the objections be removed, if those parts which are clearly subversive of our rights be altered, no man will go farther than I will to advance the union. We are told, in strong language, of dangers to which we will be exposed unless we adopt this Constitution. Among the rest, domestic safety is said to be in danger. This government does not intend our domestic safety. It authorizes the importation of slaves for twenty odd years, and thus continues upon us that nefarious trade. Instead of securing and protecting us, the continuation of this detestable trade adds daily to our weakness. Though this evil is increasing, there is no clause in the Constitution that will prevent the Northern and Eastern States from meddling with our whole property of that kind. There is a clause to prohibit the importation of slaves after twenty years; but there is no provision made for securing to the Southern States those they now possess. It is far from being a desirable property; but it will involve us in great difficulties and infelicity to be now deprived of them. There ought to be a clause in the Constitution to secure us that property which we have acquired under our former laws, and the loss of which would bring ruin on a great many people.

Maryland and the Potomac have been mentioned. I have had some little means of being acquainted with that subject, having been one of the commissioners who made the compact with Maryland. There is no cause of fear on that ground. Maryland, says the gentleman, has a right to the navigation of the Potomac. This is a right which she never exercised. Maryland was pleased with what she had in return for a right which she never exercised. Every ship which comes within the State of Maryland, except some small boats, must come within our country. Maryland was very glad to get what she got by this compact, for she considered it as next to getting it without any compensation on her part. She considered it, at least, as next to a *quid pro quo.*

The back land, he says, is another source of danger. Another day will show that, if that Constitution is adopted without amendments, there are twenty thousand families of good citizens in the north-west district, between the Alleghany Mountains and the Blue Ridge, who will run the risk of being driven from their lands.

They will be ousted from them by the Indiana Company—by the survivors—although their right and titles have been confirmed by the Assembly of our own State. I will pursue it no farther now, but take an opportunity to consider it another time.

The alarming magnitude of our debts is urged as a reason for our adoption. And shall we, because involved in debts, take less care of our rights and liberties? Shall we abandon them because we owe money which we cannot immediately pay? Will this system enable us to pay our debts and lessen our difficulties? Perhaps the new government possesses some secret, some powerful means of turning everything to gold. It has been called by one gentleman the philosopher's stone. The comparison was a pointed one, at least in this, that, on the subject of producing gold, they will be both equally delusive and fallacious. The one will be as inapplicable as the other. The dissolution of the Union, the dangers of separate confederacies, and the quarrels of borderers, have been enlarged upon to persuade us to embrace this government.

My honorable colleague in the late Convention seems to raise phantoms; and to show a singular skill in exorcisms, to terrify and compel us to take the new government, with all its sins and dangers. I know that he once saw as great danger in it as I do. What has happened since to alter his opinion? If anything, I know it not. But the Virginia legislature has occasioned it, by postponing the matter. The Convention had met in June, instead of March or April. The liberty or misery of millions yet unborn are deeply concerned in our decision. When this is the case, I cannot imagine that the short period between the last of September and first of June ought to make any difference. The union between England and Scotland has been strongly instanced by the honorable gentleman to prove the necessity of our acceding to this new government. He must know that the act of union secured the rights of the Scotch nation. The rights and privileges of the people of Scotland are expressly secured. We wish only our rights to be secured. We must have such amendments as will secure the liberties and happiness of the people on a plain, simple construction, not on a doubtful ground. We wish to give the government sufficient energy, on real republican principles; but we wish to withhold such powers as are not absolutely necessary in themselves, but extremely dangerous. We wish to shut the door against corruption in that place where it is most dangerous—to secure against the corruption of our own representatives. We ask such amendments as will point out what powers are reserved to the State governments, and clearly discriminate between them and those which are given to the general government, so as to prevent future disputes and clashing of interests. Grant us amendments like these, and we will cheerfully, with our hands and hearts, unite with those who advocate it, and we will do everything we can to support and carry it into execution. But in its present form we never can accede to it. Our duty to God and to our posterity forbids it. We acknowledge the defects of the Confederation, and the necessity of a reform. We ardently wish for a union with our sister States, on terms of security. This I am bold to declare is the desire of most of the people. On these terms we will most cheerfully join with the warmest friends of this Constitution. On another occasion I shall point out the great dangers of this Constitution, and the amendments which are necessary. I will likewise endeavor to show that amendments after ratification are delusive and fallacious—perhaps utterly impracticable.

Saturday, June 14.—[Art. I., Section 8.]

Mr. George Mason. Mr. Chairman, unless there be some restrictions on the power of calling forth the militia, to execute the laws of the Union, suppress insurrections, and repel invasions, we may very easily see that it will produce dreadful oppressions. It is extremely unsafe, without some alterations. It would be to use the militia to a very bad purpose, if any disturbance happened in New Hampshire, to call them from Georgia. This would harass the people so much that they would agree to abolish the use of the militia, and establish a standing army. I conceive the general government ought to have power over the militia, but it ought to have some bounds. If gentlemen say that the militia of a neighboring State is not sufficient, the government ought to have power to call forth those of other States, the most convenient and contiguous. But in this case, the consent of the State legislatures ought to be had. On *real* emergencies, this consent will never be denied, each State being concerned in the safety of the rest. This power may be restricted without any danger. I wish such an amendment as this—that the militia of any State should not be marched beyond the limits of the adjoining State ; and if it be necessary to draw them from one end of the continent to the other, I wish such a check, as the consent of the State legislature, to be provided.   Gentlemen may say that this would impede the government, and that the State legislatures would counteract it by refusing their consent.   This argument may be applied to all objections whatsoever.   How is this compared to the British constitution ?   Though the King may declare war, the Parliament has the means of carrying it on.   It is not so here.   Congress can do both.   Were it not for that check in the British government, the monarch would be a despot.   When a war is necessary for the benefits of the nation, the means of carrying it on are never denied.   If any unjust requisition be made on Parliament, it will be, as it ought to be, refused.   The same principle ought to be observed in our government.   In times of real danger, the States will have the same enthusiasm in aiding the general government, and granting its demands, which is seen in England, when the King is engaged in a war apparently for the interest of the nation. This power is necessary ; but we ought to guard against danger. If ever they attempt to harass and abuse the militia, they may abolish them, and raise a standing army in their stead.   There are various ways of destroying the militia.   A standing army may be perpetually established in their stead.   I abominate and detest the idea of a government where there is a standing army.   The militia may be here destroyed by that method which has been practised in other parts of the world before ; that is, by rendering them useless—by disarming them.   Under various pretences Congress may neglect to provide for arming and disciplining the militia ; and the State governments cannot do it, for Congress has an exclusive right to arm them, &c.   Here is a line of division drawn between them—the State and general governments.   The power over the militia is divided between them.   The national government has an exclusive right to provide for arming, organizing, and disciplining the militia, and for governing such part of them as may be employed in the service of the United States. The State governments have the power of appointing the officers, and of training the militia, according to the discipline prescribed by Congress, if they should think proper to prescribe any.

Should the national government wish to render the militia useless, they may neglect them, and let them perish, in order to have a pretence of establishing a standing army.

No man has a greater regard for the military gentlemen than I have. I admire their intrepidity, perseverance, and valor. But when once a standing army is established in any country, the people lose their liberty. When, against a regular and disciplined army, yeomanry are the only defence,—yeomanry, unskilful and unarmed what chance is there for preserving freedom? Give me leave to recur to the page of history, to warn you of your present danger. Recollect the history of most nations of the world. What havoc, desolation and destruction, have been perpetrated by standing armies! An instance within the memory of some of this house will show us how our militia may be destroyed. Forty years ago, when the resolution of enslaving America was formed in Great Britain, the British Parliament was advised by an artful man [Sir William Keith] who was governor of Pennsylvania, to disarm the people; that it was the best and most effectual way to enslave them; but that they should not do it openly, but weaken them, and let them sink gradually, by totally disusing and neg- lecting the militia. [Here Mr. Mason quoted sundry passages to this effect.] This was a most iniquitious project. Why should we not provide against the danger of having our militia, our real and natural strength destroyed? The general government ought, at the same time, to have some such power. But we need not give them power to abolish our militia. If they neglect to arm them, and prescribe proper discipline, they will be of no use. I am not acquainted with the military profession. I beg to be ex- cused for any errors I may commit with respect to it. But I stand on the general principles of freedom, whereon I dare to meet any one. I wish that, in case the general government should neglect to arm and discipline the militia, there should be an express dec- laration that the State governments might arm and discipline them. With this single exception, I would agree to this part, as I am conscious the government ought to have the power.

They may effect the destruction of the militia, by rendering the service odious to the people themselves, by harassing them from one end of the continent to the other, and by keeping them under martial law.

The English Parliament never pass a mutiny **bill** but for one year. This is necessary; for otherwise the soldiers would be on the same footing with the officers, and the army would be dissolved. One mutiny bill has been here in force since the revolution. I humbly conceive there is extreme danger of establishing cruel martial regulations. If, at any time, our rulers should have unjust and iniquitous designs against our liberties, and should wish to establish a standing army, the first attempt would be to render the service and use of militia odious to the people themselves—subjecting them to unnecessary severity of discipline in time of peace, confining them under martial law, and disgusting them so much as to make them cry out, "Give us a standing army!" I would wish to have some check to exclude this danger; as, that the militia should never be subject to martial law but in time of war. I consider and fear the natural propensity of rulers to oppress the people. I wish only to prevent them from doing evil. By these amendments I would give necessary powers, but no unnecessary power. If the clause stands as it is now, it will take from the State legislatures what divine Providence has given to every individual—the means of self-defence. Unless it be moderated in some degree, it will ruin us, and introduce a standing army.

Mr. George Mason, after having read the clause which gives Congress power to provide for arming, organizing, and disciplining the militia, and governing those in actual service of the Union, declared it as his firm belief, that it included the power of annexing punishments, and establishing necessary discipline, more especially as the construction of this, and every other part of the Constitution, was left to those who were to govern. If so, he asked if Congress could not inflict the most ignominious punishments on the most worthy citizens of the community. Would freemen submit to such indignant treatment? It might be thought a strained construction, but it was no more than Congress might put upon it. He thought such severities might be exercised on the militia as would make them wish the use of the militia to be utterly abolished, and assent to the establishment of a standing army. He then adverted to the representation, and said it was not sufficiently full to take into consideration the feelings and sentiments of all the citizens. He admitted that the nature of the country rendered a full representation impracticable. But he strongly urged that impractibility as a conclusive reason for granting no powers to the government but such as were absolutely indispensable, and these to be most cautiously guarded. He then recurred to the power of impeachment. On this subject he entertained great suspicions. He apologized for being suspicious. He entered into the world with as few suspicions as any man. Young men, he said, were apt to think well of every one, till time and experience taught them better. After a treaty manifestly repugnant to the interests of the country was made, he asked how they were to be punished. Suppose it had been made by the means of bribery and corruption. Suppose they had received one hundred thousand guineas, or louis d'ors, from a foreign nation, for consenting to a treaty, how was the truth to be come at ? Corruption and bribery of that kind had happened in other governments, and might in this. The House of Representatives were to impeach them. The senators were to try themselves. If a majority of them were guilty of the crime, would they pronounce themselves guilty? Yet, says he, this is called responsibility. He wished to know in what court the members of the government were to be tried for the commission of indictable offences, or injuries to individuals. He acknowledged himself to be no lawyer ; but he thought he could see that they could be tried neither in the State nor federal courts. The only means, therefore, of bringing them to punishment, must be by a court appointed by law ; and the law to punish them must also be made by themselves. By whom is it to be made ?—demanded he. By the very men who are interested in not inflicting punishment. Yet, says he, though they make the law, and fix the punishment to be inflicted on themselves, it is called responsibility. If the senators do not agree to the law, it will not be made, and thus they will escape altogether.

[Mr. Mason then animadverted on the ultimate control of Congress over the elections, and was proceeding to prove that it was dangerous, when he was called to order, by Mr. Nicholas, for departing from the clause under consideration. A desultory conversation ensued, and Mr. Mason was permitted to proceed. He was of opinion that the control over elections tended to destroy responsibility. He declared he had endeavored to discover whether this power was really necessary, or what was the necessity of vesting it in the government, but he could find no good reason for giving it ; that the reasons suggested were that, in case the States should refuse or neglect to make regulations, or in case they should be prevented from making regulations by rebellion or invasion, then the general government should interpose.]

Mr. Mason then proceeded thus : If there be any other cases, I should be glad to know them ; for I know them not.   If there be no other, why not confine them to these cases?   But the power here, as in a thousand other instances, is without reason.   I have no power which any other person can take from me.   I have no right of representation, if they can take it from me.   I say, therefore, that Congress may, by this claim, take away the right of representation, or render it nugatory, despicable, or oppressive. It is at least argumentative, that what may be done will be done, and that a favorite point will be . done by those who can. Suppose the State of Virginia should adopt such regulations as gentlemen say, (and in which I accord with all my heart,) and divide the State into ten districts.   Suppose then, that Congress should order, instead of this, that the elections should be held in the borough of Norfolk.   Will any man say that any man in Frederick or Berkeley county would have any share in this representation, if the members were chosen in Norfolk?   Nay, I might go farther, and say that the elections for all the States might be had in New York, and then we should have to go so far that the privilege would be lost altogether ; for but few gentlemen could afford to go thither.   Some of the best friends of the Constitution have advocated that the elections should be in one place.   This power is not necessary, and is capable of great abuse.   It ought to be confined to the particular cases in which they assert it to be necessary.   Whatever gentlemen may think of the opposition, I will never agree to give any power which I conceive to be dangerous.

I have doubts on another point.   The 5th section of the 1st article provides, " that each house shall keep a journal of its proceedings, and from time to time publish the same, excepting such parts as may, in their judgment, require secrecy."   This enables them to keep the negotiations about treaties secret.   Under this veil they may conceal anything and everything. Why not insert words that would exclude ambiguity and danger? The words of the Confederation, that defective system, are, in this respect, more eligible. What are they? In the last clause of the 9th article it is provided, "that Congress shall publish the journal of their proceedings monthly, except such parts thereof, relating to treaties, alliances, or military operations, as, in their judgment, require secrecy." The proceedings, by that system, are to be published monthly, with certain exceptions. These are proper guards. It is not so here. On the contrary, they may conceal what they please. Instead of giving information, they will produce suspicion. You cannot discover the advocates of their iniquitous acts. This is an additional defect of responsibility.

Neither house can adjourn, without the consent of the other, for more than three days. This is no parliamentary rule. It is untrodden ground, and it appears to me liable to much exception. The senators are chosen for six years. They are not recallable for those six years, and are reëligible at the end of the six years. It stands on a very different ground from the Confederation. By that system, they were only elected for one year, might be recalled, and were incapable of reëlection. But in the new Constitution, instead of being elected for one, they are chosen for six years. They cannot be recalled, in all that time, for any misconduct; and at the end of that long term may again be elected. What will be the operation of this? Is it not probable that those gentlemen, who will be elected senators, will fix themselves in the federal town, and become citizens of that town more than of our State? They will purchase a good seat in or near the town, and become inhabitants of that place. Will it not be, then, in the power of the Senate to worry the House of Representatives into anything? They will be a continually existing body. They will exercise those machinations and contrivances which the many have always to fear from the few. The House of Representatives is the only check on the Senate, with their enormous powers. But, by that clause, you give them the power of worrying the House of Representatives into a compliance with any measure. The senators living on the spot will feel no inconvenience from long sessions, as they will vote themselves handsome pay, without incurring any additional expenses. Your

representatives are on a different ground from their shorter continuance in office. The gentlemen from Georgia are six or seven
hundred miles from home, and wish to go home. The Senate,
taking advantage of this, by stopping the other house from
adjourning, may worry them into anything. These are my doubts,
and I think the provision not consistent with the usual parliamentary modes.

Monday, June 16.—[The 8th Section still under consideration.]
Mr. George Mason asked to what purpose the laws were read.
[Acts of the Va. Assembly—concerning the militia—read on
motion of Madison.] The objection was, that too much power
was given to Congress—power that would finally destroy the
State governments more effectually by insidious, underhanded
means, than such as could be openly practised. This, said he, is
the opinion of many worthy men, not only in this Convention,
but in all parts of America. These laws could only show that
the legislature of this State could pass such acts. He thought
they militated against the cession of this power to Congress,
because the State governments could call forth the militia when
necessary, so as to compel a submission to the laws ; and as they
were competent to it, Congress ought not to have the power.
The meeting of three or four persons might be called an insurrection, and the militia might be called out to disperse them. He
was not satisfied with the explanation of the word *organization*
by the gentleman in the military line. (Mr. Lee.) He thought
they were not confined to the technical explanation, but that
Congress could inflict severe and ignominious punishments on
the militia, as a necessary incident to the power of organizing
and disciplining them. The gentleman had said there was no
danger, because the laws respecting the militia were less rigid
in the other States than this. This was no conclusive argument. His fears, as he had before expressed, were, that grievous
punishments would be inflicted, in order to render the service
disagreeable to the militia themselves, and induce them to wish
its abolition, which would afford a pretence for establishing a
standing army. He was convinced the State governments ought
to have the control of the militia, except when they were absolutely necessary for general purposes. The gentleman had said
that they would be only subject to martial law when in actual

service. He demanded what was to hinder Congress from inflicting it always, and making a general law for the purpose. If so, said he, it must finally produce, most infallibly, the annihilation of the State governments. These were his apprehensions; but he prayed God they might be groundless.

[*Militia continued.*]

Mr. George Mason. Mr. Chairman, a worthy member has asked who are the militia, if they be not the *people* of this country, and if we are not to be protected from the fate of the Germans, Prussians, &c., by our representation? I ask, who are the militia? They consist now of the whole people, except a few public officers. But I cannot say who will be the militia of the future day. If that paper on the table gets no alteration, the militia of the future day may not consist of all classes, high and low, and rich and poor; but they may be confined to the lower and middle classes of the people, granting exclusion to the higher classes of the people. If we should ever see that day, the most ignominious punishments and heavy fines may be expected. Under the present government, all ranks of people are subject to militia duty. Under such a full and equal representation as ours, there can be no ignominious punishment inflicted. But under this national, or rather consolidated government, the case will be different. The representation being so small and inadequate, they will have no fellow-feeling for the people. They may discriminate people in their own predicament, and exempt from duty all the officers and lowest creatures of the national government. If there were a more particular definition of their powers, and a clause exempting the militia from martial law except when in actual service, and from fines and punishments of an unusual nature, then we might expect that the militia would be what they are. But, if this be not the case, we cannot say how long all classes of people will be included in the militia. There will not be the same reason to expect it, because the government will be administered by different people. We know what they are now, but know not how soon they may be altered.

[Mr. George Nicholas spoke next, and in reference to Mason and Grayson said : One objects because there will be select militia; another objects because there will be no select militia; and yet both oppose it on these contradictory principles, &c.]

Mr. Mason rose, and said that he was totally misunderstood. The contrast between his friend's objection and his was improper. His friend had mentioned the propriety of having select militia, like those of Great Britain, who should be more thoroughly exercised than the militia at large could possibly be. But *he*, himself, had not spoken of a selection of militia, but of the exemption of the highest classes of the people from militia service, which would justify apprehensions of severe and ignominious punishments.

[*Powers of Congress in District of Columbia.*]

Mr. George Mason thought that there were few clauses in the Constitution so dangerous as that which gave Congress exclusive power of legislation within ten miles square. Implication, he observed, was capable of any extension, and would probably be extended to augment the congressional powers. But here there was no need of implication. This clause gave them an unlimited authority in every possible case, within that district. This ten miles square, says Mr. Mason, may set at defiance the laws of the surrounding States, and may, like the custom of the superstitious days of our ancestors, become the sanctuary of the blackest crimes. Here the federal courts are to sit. We have heard a good deal said of justice. It has been doubted whether jury trial be secured in civil cases. But I will suppose that we shall have juries in civil cases. What sort of a jury shall we have within the ten miles square? The immediate creatures of the government. What chance will poor men get, where Congress have the power of legislating in all cases whatever, and where judges and juries may be under their influence, and bound to support their operations? Even with juries the chance of justice may here be very small, as Congress have unlimited authority, legislative, executive, and judicial. Lest this power should not be sufficient, they have it in every case. Now, sir, if an attempt should be made to establish tyranny over the people, here are ten miles square where the greatest offender may meet protection. If any of their officers, or creatures, should attempt to oppress the people, or should actually perpetrate the blackest deed, he has nothing to do but get into the ten miles square. Why was this dangerous power given. Felons may receive an asylum there and in their strongholds. Gentlemen have said that it was dangerous to argue against possible abuse, because there could be no power delegated but might be abused. It is an incontrovertible axiom, that, when the dangers that may arise from the *abuse* are greater than the benefits that may result from the use, the power ought to be withheld. I do not conceive that this power is at all necessary, though capable of being greatly abused.

We are told by the honorable gentleman [*E. Randolph*] that Holland has its Hague. I confess I am at a loss to know what inference he could draw from that observation. This is the place where the deputies of the United Provinces meet to transact the public business. But I do not recollect that they have any exclusive jurisdiction whatever in that place, but are subject to the laws of the province in which the Hague is. To what purpose the gentleman mentioned that Holland has its Hague, I cannot see.

Mr. Mason then observed that he would willingly give them exclusive power, as far as respected the police and good government of the place ; but he would give them no more, because he thought it unnecessary. He was very willing to give them, in this as well as in all other cases, those powers which he thought indispensably necessary.

[Art. I., Sect. 8, Clause 18.]

Mr. George Mason. Mr. Chairman, gentlemen say there is no new power given by this clause. Is there any thing in this Constitution which secures to the States the powers which are said to be retained ? Will powers remain to the States which are not expressly guarded and reserved ? I will suppose a case. Gentlemen may call it an impossible case, and suppose that Congress will act with wisdom and integrity. Among the enumerated powers, Congress are to lay and collect taxes, duties, imposts, and excises, and to pay the debts, and to provide for the general welfare and common defence ; and by that clause (so often called the *sweeping clause*) they are to make all laws necessary to execute those laws. Now, suppose oppressions should arise under this government, and any writer should dare to stand forth, and expose to the community at large the abuses of those powers ; could not Congress under the idea of providing for the general [Alien and welfare, and under their own construction, say that this Sedition was destroying the general peace, encouraging sedition, laws.] and poisoning the minds of the people ? And could they not, in order to provide against this, lay a dangerous restriction on the press? Might they not even bring the trial of this restriction within the ten miles square, when there is no prohibition against it? Might they not thus destroy the trial by jury? Would they not extend their implication? It appears to me that they may and will. And shall the support of our right depend on the bounty of men whose interest it may be to oppress us? That Congress should have power to provide for the general welfare of the Union, I grant. But I wish a clause in the Constitution, with respect to all powers which are not granted, that they are retained by the States. Otherwise, the power of providing for the general welfare may be perverted to its destruction.

Many gentlemen, whom I respect, take different sides of this question. We wish this amendment to be introduced, to remove our apprehensions. There was a clause in the Confederation reserving to the States respectively every power, jurisdiction, and right, not expressly delegated to the United States. This clause has never been complained of, but approved by all. Why not, then, have a similar clause in this Constitution, in which it is the more indispensably necessary than in the Confederation, because of the great augmentation of power vested in the former? In my humble apprehension, unless there be some such clear and definite expression, this clause now under consideration will go to any thing our rulers may think proper. Unless there be some express declaration that every thing not given is retained, it will be carried to any power Congress may please.

[Subject continued.]

Mr. George Mason still thought that there ought to be some express declaration in the Constitution, asserting that rights not given to the general government were retained by the States. He apprehended that, unless this was done, many valuable and important rights would be concluded to be given up by implication. All governments were drawn from the people, though many were perverted to their oppression. The government of Virginia, he remarked, was drawn from the people; yet there were certain great and important rights, which the people, by their bill of rights, declared to be paramount to the power of the legislature. He asked, Why should it not be so in this Constitution? Was it because we were more substantially represented in it than in the State government? If in the State government, where the people were substantially and fully represented, it was necessary that the great rights of human nature should be secure from the encroachments of the legislature, he asked if it was not more necessary in this government, where they were but inadequately represented? He declared that artful sophistry and evasions could not satisfy him. He could see no clear distinction between rights relinquished by a positive grant, and lost by implication. Unless there were a bill of rights, implication might swallow up all our rights.

[In answer to Mr. George Nicholas :]

Mr. George Mason replied that the worthy gentleman was mistaken in his assertion that the bill of rights did not prohibit torture ; for that one clause expressly provided that no man can give evidence against himself ; and that the worthy gentleman must know that, in those countries where torture is used, evidence was extorted from the criminal himself. Another clause of the bill of rights provided that no cruel and unusual punishments shall be inflicted ; therefore, torture was included in the prohibition.

Tuesday June 17.—[Art. I., Sect. 9.]

Mr. George Mason. Mr. Chairman, this is a fatal section, which has created more dangers than any other. The first clause allows the importation of slaves for twenty years. Under the royal government, this evil was looked upon as a great oppression, and many attempts were made to prevent it ; but the interest of the African merchants prevented its prohibition. No sooner did the revolution take place, than it was thought of. It was one of the great causes of our separation from Great Britain. Its exclusion has been a principal object of this State, and most of the States in the Union. The augmentation of slaves weakens the States ; and such a trade is diabolical in itself, and disgraceful to mankind ; yet, by this Constitution, it is continued for twenty years. As much as I value a union of all the States, I would not admit the Southern States into the Union unless they agree to the discontinuance of this disgraceful trade, because it would bring weakness and not strength to the Union. And, though this infamous traffic be continued, we have no security for the property of that kind which we have already. There is no clause in this Constitution to secure it ; for they may lay such a tax as will amount to manumission. And should the government be amended, still this detestable kind of commerce cannot be discontinued till after the expiration of twenty years; for the 5th article which provides for amendments, expressly excepts this clause. I have ever looked upon this as a most disgraceful thing to America. I cannot express my detestation of it. Yet they have not secured us the property of the slaves we have already. So that "they have done what they ought not to have done, and have left undone what they ought to have done."

[The 2d, 3d, and 4th clauses.]

Mr. George Mason said, that gentlemen might think themselves secured by the restriction, in the 4th clause, that no capitation or other direct tax should be laid but in proportion to the census before directed to be taken; but that, when maturely considered, it would be found to be no security whatsoever. It was nothing but a direct assertion, or mere confirmation of the clause which fixed the ratio of taxes and representation. It only meant that the quantum to be raised of each State should be in proportion to their numbers in the manner therein directed. But the general government was not precluded from laying the proportion of any particular State on any one species of property they might think proper.

For instance, if five hundred thousand dollars were to be raised, they might lay the whole of the proportion of the Southern States on the blacks, or any one species of property; so that by laying taxes too heavily on slaves, they might totally annihilate that kind of property. No real security could arise from the clause which provides that persons held to labor in one State, escaping into another, shall be delivered up. This only meant that runaway slaves should not be protected in other States. As to the exclusion of *ex post facto* laws, it could not be said to create any security in this case; for laying a tax on slaves would not be *ex post facto*.

[The 5th and 6th clauses.]

Mr. George Mason apprehended the loose expression of "publication from time to time" was applicable to any time. It was equally applicable to monthly and septennial periods. It might be extended ever so much. The reason urged in favor of this ambiguous expression was, that there might be some matters which require secrecy. In matters relative to military operations and foreign negotiations, secrecy was necessary sometimes; but he did not conceive that the receipts and expenditures of the public money ought ever to be concealed. The people, he affirmed, had a right to know the expenditures of their money; but that this expression was so loose, it might be concealed forever from them, and might afford opportunities of misapplying the public money, and sheltering those who did it. He concluded it to be as exceptionable as any clause, in so few words, could be.

Mr. Lee (of Westmoreland) thought such trivial arguments as that just used by the honorable gentleman would have no weight with the committee, &c.

Mr. Mason begged to be permitted to use that mode of arguing to which he had been accustomed. However desirous he was of pleasing that worthy gentleman, his duty would not give way to that pleasure.

[Mr. Nicholas, Mr. Corbin, Mr. Madison, approved of the clause.]

Mr. Mason replied, that, in the Confederation, the public proceedings were to be published monthly, which was infinitely better than depending on men's virtue to publish them or not, as they might please. If there was no such provision in the Constitution of Virginia, gentlemen ought to consider the difference between such a full representation, dispersed and mingled with every part of the community, as the State representation was, and such an inadequate representation as this was. One might be safely trusted, but not the other.

[The 1st clause of the 10th section.]

Mr. George Mason declared he had been informed that some States had speculated most enormously in this matter [Continental money]. Many individuals had speculated so as to make great fortunes on the ruin of their fellow-citizens. The clause which has been read [Art. VI., Clause 1], as a sufficient security, seemed to him to be satisfactory as far as it went; that is, that the Continental money ought to stand on the same ground as it did previously, or that the claim should not be impaired. Under the Confederation, there were means of settling the old paper money, either in Congress or in the State legislatures. The money had at last depreciated to a thousand for one. The intention of State speculation, as well as individual speculation, was to get as much as possible of that money, in order to recover its nominal value. The means, says he, of settling this money, were in the hands of the old Congress. They could discharge it at its depreciated value. Is there that means here? No, sir, we must pay it shilling for shilling or at least at the rate of one for forty. The amount will surpass the value of the property of the United States. Neither the State legislatures nor Congress can make an *ex post facto* law. The nominal value must therefore be paid. Where is the power in the new government to settle this money so as to prevent the country from being ruined? When they prohibit the making *ex post facto* laws, they will have no authority to prevent our being ruined by paying that money at its nominal value.

Without some security against it, we shall be compelled to pay it, to the last particle of our property. Shall we ruin our people by taxation, from generation to generation, to pay that money? Should any *ex post facto* law be made to relieve us from such payments, it would not be regarded, because *ex post facto* laws are interdicted in the Constitution. We may be taxed for centuries, to give advantage to a few particular States in the Union, and a number of rapacious speculators. If there be any real security against this misfortune, let gentlemen show it. I can see none. The clause under consideration does away the pretended security in the clause which was adduced by the honorable gentleman [*Mr. Madison*]. This enormous mass of worthless paper, which has been offered at a thousand for one, must be paid in actual gold and silver at the nominal value.

[The subject continued.]

Mr. George Mason. Mr. Chairman, the debt is transferred to Congress, but not the means of paying it. They cannot pay it in any other way than according to the nominal value; for they are prohibited from making *ex post facto* laws; and it would be *ex post facto*, to all intents and purposes, to pay off creditors with less than the nominal sum which they were originally promised. But the honorable gentleman [*E. Randolph*] has called to his aid technical definitions. He says, that *ex post facto* laws relate solely to criminal matters. I beg leave to differ from him. Whatever it may be at the bar, or in a professional line, I conceive that, according to the common acceptation of the words, *ex post facto* laws and retrospective laws are synonymous terms. Are we to trust business of this sort to technical definition ? The contrary is the plain meaning of the words. Congress has no power to scale this money. The States are equally precluded. The debt is transferred without the means of discharging it. Implication will not do. The means of paying it are expressly withheld. When this matter comes before the federal judiciary, they must determine according to this Constitution. It says expressly, that they shall not make *ex post facto* laws. Whatever may be the professional meaning, yet the general meaning of *ex post facto* law is an act having a retrospective operation. This construction is agreeable to its primary etymology. Will it not be the duty of the federal court to say, that such laws are prohibited ? This goes to the destruction and annihilation of all the citizens of the United States, to enrich a few. Are we to part with every shilling of our property, and be reduced to the lowest insignificancy, to aggrandize a few speculators? Let me mention a remarkable effect this Constitution will have. How stood our taxes before this Constitution was introduced? Requisitions were made on the State legislatures, and, if they were unjust, they could be refused. If we were called upon to pay twenty millions, shilling for shilling, or at the rate of one for forty, our legislature could refuse it, and remonstrate against the injustice of the demand. But now this could not be done ; for direct taxation is brought home to us. The federal officer collects immediately of the planters. When it withholds the only possible means of discharging those debts, and by direct taxation prevents any opposition to the most enormous and unjust demand, where are you ? Is there a ray of hope ? As the law has never been my profession, if I err, I hope to be excused. I spoke from the general sense of the words. The worthy gentleman has told you that the United States can be plaintiffs, but never defendants. If so, it stands on very unjust grounds. The United States cannot be come at for any thing they may owe, but may get what is due to them. There is therefore no reciprocity. The thing is so incomprehensible that it cannot be explained. As an express power is given to the federal court to take cognizance of such controversies, and to declare null all *ex post facto* laws, I think gentlemen must see there is danger, and that it ought to be guarded against.

[In answer to Mr. Madison :]

Mr. Mason was still convinced of the rectitude of his former opinion. He thought it might be put on a safer footing by three words. By continuing the restriction of *ex post facto* laws to crimes, it would then stand under the new government as it did under the old.

[2d clause, 10th section.]

Mr. George Mason. Mr. Chairman, if gentlemen attend to this clause, they will see we cannot make any inspection law but what is subject to the control and revision of Congress. Hence gentlemen who know nothing of the business will make rules concerning it which may be detrimental to our interests. For forty years we have laid duties on tobacco, to defray the expenses of the inspection, and to raise an incidental revenue for the State. Under this clause, that incidental *revenue* which is calculated to pay for the inspection, and to defray contingent charges, is to be put into the federal treasury. But if any tobacco-house is burnt, we cannot make up the loss. I conceive this to be unjust and unreasonable. When any profit arises from it, it goes into the federal treasury. But when there is any loss or deficiency from damage, it cannot be made up. Congress are to make regulations for our tobacco. Are men, in the States where no tobacco is made, proper judges of this business? They may perhaps judge as well, but surely no better than our own immediate legislature, who are accustomed and familiar with this business. This is one of the most wanton powers of the general government. I would concede any power that was essentially necessary for the interests of the Union; but this, instead of being necessary, will be extremely oppressive.

[In response to Mr. George Nicholas :]

Mr. George Mason replied, that the State legislatures could make no law but what would come within the general control given to Congress; and that the regulation of the inspection, and the imposition of duties, must be inseparably blended together.

[The 1st section of Article II.]

Mr. George Mason. Mr. Chairman, there is not a more important article in the Constitution than this. The great fundamental principle of responsibility in republicanism is here sapped. The President is elected without rotation. It may be said that a new election may remove him, and place another in his stead. If we

judge from the experience of all other countries, and even our own, we may conclude that, as the President of the United States may be reëlected, so he will. How is it in every government where rotation is not required? Is there a single instance of a great man not being reëlected? Our governor is obliged to return, after a given period, to a private station. It is so in most of the States. This President will be elected time after time : he will be continued in office for life. If we wish to change him, the great powers in Europe will not allow us. The honorable gentleman, my colleague in the late federal Convention [*E. Randolph*], mentions with applause, those parts of which he had expressed his disapprobation.[1] He says not a word. If I am mistaken, let me be put right. I shall not make use of his name ; but, in the course of this investigation I shall use the arguments of that gentleman against it.

Will not the great powers of Europe, as France and Great Britain, be interested in having a friend in the President of the United States? And will they not be more interested in his election than in that of the King of Poland? The people of Poland have a right to displace their King. But do they ever do it? No. Prussia and Russia, and other European powers, would not suffer it. This clause will open a door to the dangers and misfortunes which the people of Poland undergo. The powers of Europe will interpose, and we shall have a civil war in the bowels of our country, and be subject to all the horrors and calamities of an elective monarchy. This very executive officer may, by consent of Congress, receive a stated pension from European potentates. This is not an idea altogether new in America. It is not many years ago—since the revolution—that a foreign power offered emoluments to persons holding offices under our government. It will, moreover, be difficult to know whether he receives emoluments from foreign powers or not. The electors, who are to meet in each State to vote for him, may be easily influenced. To prevent the certain evils of attempting to elect a new President, it will be necessary to continue the old one. The only way to alter this would be to render him ineligible after a certain number of years, and then no foreign nation would interfere to keep in a

[1] The punctuation has been altered here, as otherwise the sentence is unintelligible.

man who was utterly ineligible. Nothing is so essential to the preservation of a republican government as a periodical rotation. Nothing so strongly impels a man to regard the interest of his constituents as the certainty of returning to the general mass of the people, from whence he was taken, where he must participate their burdens. It is a great defect in the Senate that they are not ineligible at the end of six years. The biennial exclusion of one third of them will have no effect, as they can be reëlected. Some stated time ought to be fixed when the President ought to be reduced to a private station. I should be contented that he might be elected for eight years ; but I would wish him to be capable of holding the office only eight years out of twelve or sixteen years. But, as it now stands, he may continue in office for life ; or, in other words, it will be an elective monarchy.

Mr. George Mason. Mr. Chairman, the Vice-President appears to me to be not only an unnecessary but dangerous officer. He is, contrary to the usual course of parliamentary proceedings, to be president of the Senate. The State from which he comes may have two votes, when the others will have but one. Besides the legislative and executive are hereby mixed and incorporated together. I cannot, at this distance of time, foresee the consequences ; but I think that, in the course of human affairs, he will be made a tool of in order to bring about his own interest, and aid in overturning the liberties of his country. There is another part which I disapprove of, but which perhaps I do not understand. "In case of removal of the President from office, or of his death, resignation, or inability to discharge the powers and duties of the said office, the same shall devolve on the Vice-President ; and the Congress may by law provide for the case of removal, death, resignation, or inability, both of the President and Vice-President, declaring what officer shall then act as President, and such officer shall act accordingly, until the disability be removed or a President shall be elected." The power of Congress is right and proper so far as it enables them to provide what officer shall act, in case both the President and Vice-President be dead or disabled. But gentlemen ought to take notice that the election of this officer is only for four years. There is no provision for a speedy election of another President, when the former is dead or removed. The influence of the Vice-President may prevent the election of the President. But perhaps I may be mistaken.

Wednesday, June 18.—[The 1st section of Article II. still under consideration.]

Mr. George Mason contended that this mode of election was a mere deception,—a mere *ignis fatuus* on the American people,—and thrown out to make them believe they were to choose him ; whereas it would not be once out of fifty times that he would be chosen by them in the first instance, because a majority of the whole number of votes was required. If the localities of the States were considered, and the probable diversity of the opinions of the people attended to, he thought it would be found that so many persons would be voted for, that there seldom or never could be a majority in favor of one, except one great name who, he believed, would be unanimously elected. He then continued thus :—A majority of the whole number of electors is necessary, to elect the President. It is not the greatest number of votes that is required, but a majority of the whole number of electors. If there be more than one having such majority, and an equal number, one of them is to be chosen by ballot of the House of Representatives. But if no one have a majority of the actual number of electors appointed, how is he to be chosen? From the five highest in the list, by ballot of the lower house, and the votes to be taken by States. I conceive he ought to be chosen from the two highest on the list. This would be simple and easy ; then, indeed, the people would have some agency in the election. But when it is extended to the five highest, a person having a very small number of votes may be elected. This will almost constantly happen. The States may choose the man in whom they have most confidence. This, in my opinion, is a very considerable defect. The people will, in reality, have no hand in the election. It has been wittily observed that the Constitution has *married* the President and Senate—has made them man and wife. I believe the consequence that generally results from marriage will happen here. They will be continually supporting and aiding each other : they will always consider their interest as united. We know the advantage the few have over the many. They can with facility act in concert and on a uniform system : they may join, scheme, and plot, against the people without any chance of detection. The Senate and President will form a combination that cannot be prevented by the representatives. The executive and legislative powers, thus connected, will destroy all balances : this would have been prevented by a constitutional council, to aid the President in the discharge of his office, vesting the Senate, at the same time, with the power of impeaching them. Then we should have real responsibility. In its present form, the guilty try themselves. The President is tried by his counsellors. He is not removed from office during his trial. When he is arraigned for treason, he has the command of the army and navy, and may surround the Senate with thirty thousand troops. It brings to my recollection the remarkable trial of Milo at Rome. We may expect to see similar instances here. But I suppose that the cure for all evils—the virtue and integrity of our representatives—will be thought a sufficient security. On this great and important subject, I am one of those (and ever shall be) who object to it.

[In reply to Mr. Madison :]

Mr. Mason arose, and insisted that the person having the greatest number of votes would not be elected unless such majority was one of the whole number of electors appointed ; that it would rarely happen that any one would have such a majority, and as he was then to be chosen from the five highest on the list, his election was entirely taken from the people.

[1st clause, section 2d, Article II.]

Mr. George Mason, animadverting on the magnitude of the powers of the President, was alarmed at the additional power of commanding the army in person. He admitted the propriety of his being commander-in-chief, so far as to give orders and have a general superintendency ; but he thought it would be dangerous to let him command in person, without any restraint, as he might make a bad use of it. He was, then, clearly of opinion that the consent of a majority of both houses of Congress should be required before he could take the command in person. If at any time it should be necessary that he should take the personal command, either on account of his superior abilities or other cause, then Congress would agree to it ; and all dangers would be obviated by requiring their consent. He called to gentlemen's recollection the extent of what the late commander-in-chief might have done, from his great abilities, and the strong attachment of both officers and soldiers towards him, if, instead of being disinterested, he had been an ambitious man. So disinterested and amiable a character as General Washington might never command again. The possibility of danger ought to be guarded against. Although he did not disapprove of the President's consultation with the principal executive officers, yet he objected to the want of an executive council, which he conceived to be necessary to any regular free government. There being none such, he apprehended a council would arise out of the Senate, which, for want of real responsibility, he thought dangerous. You will please, says he, to recollect that removal from office, and future disqualification to hold any office, are the only consequences of conviction on impeachment. Now, I conceive that the President ought not to have the power of pardoning, because he may frequently pardon crimes which were advised by himself. It may happen, at some future day, that he will establish a monarchy, and destroy the republic. If he has the power of granting pardons before indictment, or conviction, may he not stop inquiry and prevent detection? The case of treason ought, at least, to be excepted. This is a weighty objection with me.

[In answer to Mr. Lee :]

Mr. Mason replied, that he did not mean that the President was of necessity to command, but he might if he pleased ; and if he was an ambitious man, he might make a dangerous use of it.

[In reply to Mr. George Nicholas :]

Mr. Mason answered, that it did not resemble the State Constitution, because the governor did not possess such extensive powers as the President, and had no influence over the navy. The liberty of the people had been destroyed by those who were military commanders only. The danger here was greater by the junction of great civil powers to the command of the army and fleet. Although Congress are to raise the army, said he, no security arises from that ; for, in time of war, they must and ought to raise an army, which will be numerous, or otherwise, according to the nature of the war, and then the President is to command without any control.

[In reply to Mr. Madison :]

Mr. Mason vindicated the conduct of the assemblies [in Massachusetts] mentioned by the gentleman last up. He insisted they were both right ; for, in the first instance, when such ideas of severity prevailed, a rebellion was in existence : [Shay's rebellion] in such circumstance, it was right to be rigid. But after it was over, it would be wrong to exercise unnecessary severity.

[2d clause, 2d section, Article II.]

Mr. George Mason thought this a most dangerous clause, as thereby five States might make a treaty ; ten senators—the representatives of five States—being two thirds of a quorum. These ten might come from the five smallest States. By the Confederation, nine States were necessary to concur in a treaty. This secured justice and moderation. His principal fear, however, was not that five, but that seven, States—a bare majority—would make treaties to bind the Union.

[Mr. George Nicholas answered Mr. Mason.]

Mr. Mason differed widely from the gentleman. He conceived that the contiguity of some States, and remoteness of others, would prevent that reciprocity which he had mentioned. Some States were near the seat of government ; others far from it ; for instance, Georgia was eight or nine hundred miles from it. Suppose, says he, a partial treaty is made by the President, and is to be ratified by the Senate. They do not always sit. Who is to convene them ? The President. Is it presumable that he would call distant States to make the ratification, or those States whose interest he knew to be injured by the treaty he had proposed ? This, I conceive, will have a contrary effect from what the gentleman says.

Thursday, June 19.—[The subject of treaties continued.]

Mr. George Mason. Mr. Chairman, it is true that this is one of the greatest acts of sovereignty, and therefore ought to be most strongly guarded. The cession of such a power, without such checks and guards, cannot be justified ; yet I acknowledge such a power must rest somewhere. It is so in all governments. If, in the course of an unsuccessful war, we should be compelled to give up part of our territories, or undergo subjugation if the general government could not make a treaty to give up such a part for the preservation of the residue, the government itself, and consequently the rights of the people, must fall. Such a power must, therefore, rest somewhere. For my own part, I never heard it denied that such a power must be vested in the government.

Our complaint is, that it is not sufficiently guarded, and that it requires much more solemnity and caution than are delineated in that system. It is more guarded in England. Will any gentleman undertake to say that the King, by his prerogative, can dismember the British empire ? Could the King give Portsmouth to France ? He could not do this without an express act of Parliament—without the consent of the legislature in all its branches. There are other things which the King cannot do, which may be done by the President and Senate in this case. Could the King, by his prerogative, enable foreign subjects to purchase lands, and have an hereditary indefeasible title ? This would require an express act of Parliament. Though the King can make treaties, yet he cannot make a treaty contrary to the constitution of his country. Where did their constitution originate ? It is founded on a number of maxims, which, by long time, are rendered sacred and inviolable. Where are there such maxims in the American Constitution ? In that country, which we formerly called our mother country, they have had for many centuries, certain fundamental maxims, which have secured their persons and properties, and prevented a dismemberment of their country. The common law, sir, has prevented the power of the crown from destroying the immunities of the people. We are placed in a still better condition—in a more favorable situation than perhaps any people ever were before. We have it in our power to secure our liberties and happiness on the most unshaken, firm, and permanent basis. We can establish what government we please. But by that paper we are consolidating the United States into one great government, and trusting to constructive security. You will find no such thing in the English government. The common law of England is not the common law of these States. I conceive, therefore, that there is nothing in that Constitution to hinder a dismemberment of the empire.

Will any gentleman say that they may not make a treaty, whereby the subjects of France, England, and other powers, may buy what lands they please in this country ? This would violate those principles which we have received from the mother country. The indiscriminate admission of all foreigners to the first rights of citizenship, without any permanent security for their attachment to the country, is repugnant to every principle of prudence and good policy. The President and Senate can make any treaty whatsoever. We wish not to refuse, but to guard, this power, as it is done in England. The empire there cannot be dismembered without the consent of the national Parliament. We wish an express and explicit declaration, in that paper, that the power which can make other treaties cannot, without the consent of the national Parliament—the national legislature—dismember the empire. The Senate alone ought not to have this power; much less ought a few States to have it. No treaty to dismember the empire ought to be made without the consent of three fourths of the legislature in all its branches. Nor ought such a treaty to be made but in case of the most urgent and unavoidable necessity. When such necessity exists, there is no doubt but there will be a general and uniform vote of the Continental Parliament.

[1st and 2d sections of Article III. The Judiciary.]

Mr. George Mason. Mr. Chairman, I had some hopes that the candor and reason of the warmest friends of this Constitution would have led them to point out objections so important. They must occur, more or less, to the mind of every one. It is with great reluctance I speak of this department, as it lies out of my line. I should not tell my sentiments upon it, did I not conceive it to be so constructed as to destroy the dearest rights of the community. After having read the first section, Mr. Mason asked, what is there left to the State courts? Will any gentleman be pleased, candidly, fairly, and without sophistry, to show us what remains? There is no limitation. It goes to every thing. The inferior courts are to be as numerous as Congress may think proper. They are to be of whatever nature they please. Read the 2d section, and contemplate attentively the extent of the jurisdiction of these courts, and consider if there be any limits to it.

I am greatly mistaken if there be any limitation whatsoever, with respect to the nature or jurisdiction of these courts. If there be any limits, they must be contained in one of the clauses of this section; and I believe, on a dispassionate discussion, it will be found that there is none of any check. All the laws of the United States are paramount to the laws and Constitution of any single State. "The judicial power shall extend to all cases in law and equity arising under this Constitution." What objects will not this expression extend to ? Such laws may be formed as will go to every object of private property. When we consider the nature of these courts, we must conclude that their effect and operation will be utterly to destroy the State governments ; for they will be the judges how far their laws will operate. They are to modify their own courts, and you can make no State law to counteract them. The discrimination between their judicial power, and that of the States, exists, therefore, but in name. To what disgraceful and dangerous length does the principle of this go ! For if your State judiciaries are not to be trusted with the administration of common justice, and decision of disputes respecting property between man and man, much less ought the State governments to be trusted with power of legislation. The principle itself goes to the destruction of the legislation of the States, whether or not it was intended. As to my own opinion, I most religiously and conscientiously believe that it was intended, though I am not absolutely certain. But I think it will destroy the State governments, whatever may have been the intention. There are many gentlemen in the United States who think it right that we should have one great national, consolidated government, and that it was better to bring it about slowly and imperceptibly rather than all at once. This is no reflection on any man, for I mean none. To those who think that one national, consolidated government is best for America, this extensive judicial authority will be agreeable ; but I hope there are many in this Convention of a different opinion, and who see their political happiness resting on their State governments. I know, from my own knowledge, many worthy gentlemen of the former opinion.

[Here Mr. Madison interrupted Mr. Mason, and demanded an unequivocal explanation. As these insinuations might create a belief that every member of the late federal Convention was of that opinion, he wished him to tell who the gentlemen were to whom he alluded.]

Mr. Mason then replied, I shall never refuse to explain myself. It is notorious that this is a prevailing principle. It was at least the opinion of many gentlemen in Convention, and many in the United States. I do not know what explanation the honorable gentleman asks. I can say, with great truth, that the honorable gentleman, in private conversation with me, expressed himself against it ; neither did I ever hear any of the delegates from this State advocate it.

Mr. Madison declared himself satisfied with this, unless the committee thought themselves entitled to ask a further explanation.

After some desultory remarks, *Mr. Mason* continued : I have heard that opinion advocated by gentlemen for whose abilities, judgment, and knowledge, I have the highest reverence and respect. I say that the general description of the judiciary involves the most extensive jurisdiction. Its cognizance, in all cases arising under the system and the laws of Congress, may be said to be unlimited. In the next place, it extends to treaties made, or which shall be made, under their authority. This is one of the powers which ought to be given them. I also admit that they ought to have judicial cognizance in all cases affecting ambassadors, foreign ministers and consuls, as well as in cases of maritime jurisdiction. There is an additional reason now to give them this last power ; because Congress, besides the general powers, are about to get that of regulating commerce with foreign nations. This is a power which existed before, and is a proper subject of federal jurisdiction. The next power of the judiciary is also necessary under some restrictions. Though the decision of controversies to which the United States shall be a party may at first view seem proper, it may, without restraint, be extended to a dangerously oppressive length. The next with respect to disputes between two or more States, is right. I cannot see the propriety of the next power, in disputes between a State and the citizens of another State. As to controversies between citizens of different States, their power is improper and inadmissible. In disputes between citizens of the same State, claiming lands under the grants of different States, the power is proper. It is the only case in which the federal judiciary ought to have appellate cognizance of disputes between private citizens. Unless this was the case, the suit must be brought and decided in one or the other State, under whose grant the lands are claimed, which would be injurious, as the decision must be consistent with the grant.

The last clause is still more improper. To give them cognizance in disputes between a State and the citizens thereof, is utterly inconsistent with reason or good policy.

Here *Mr. Nicholas* arose, and informed Mr. Mason that his interpretation of this part was not warranted by the words.

Mr. Mason replied, that, if he recollected rightly, the propriety of the power, as explained by him, had been contended for; but that, as his memory had never been good, and was now impaired much from his age, he would not insist on that interpretation. He then proceeded : Give me leave to advert to the operation of this judicial power. Its jurisdiction in the first case will extend to all cases affecting revenue, excise, and custom-house officers. If I am mistaken, I will retract. "All cases in law and equity arising under this Constitution, and the laws of the United States," take in all the officers of the government. They comprehend all those who act as collectors of taxes, excisemen, &c. It will take in, of course, what others do to them, and what is done by them to others. In what predicament will our citizens then be ? We know the difficulty we are put in by our own courts, and how hard it is to bring officers to justice even in them. If any of the federal officers should be guilty of the greatest oppressions, or behave with the most insolent and wanton brutality to a man's wife or daughter, where is this man to get relief ? If you suppose in the inferior courts, they are not appointed by the States. They are not men in whom the community can place confidence. It will be decided by federal judges. Even suppose the poor man should be able to obtain judgment in the inferior court, for the greatest injury, what justice can he get on appeal ? Can he go four or five hundred miles ? Can he stand the expense attending it ? On this occasion they are to judge of fact as well as law. He must bring his witnesses where he is not known, where new evidence may be brought against him, of which he never heard before, and which he cannot contradict.

The honorable gentleman who presides here has told us that the Supreme Court of appeals must embrace every object of maritime, chancery, and common-law controversy. In the two first, the appellate jurisdiction as to fact must be generally granted ; because, otherwise, it could exclude appeals in those cases. But why not discriminate as to matters of fact with respect to common-law controversies ? The honorable gentleman has allowed that it was dangerous, but hopes regulations will be made to suit the convenience of the people. But mere hope is not a sufficient security. I have said that it appears to me (though I am no lawyer) to be very dangerous. Give me leave to lay before the committee an amendment, which I think convenient, easy, and proper.

[Here Mr. Mason proposed an alteration neariy the same as the first part of the fourteenth amendment recommended by the Convention.]

Thus, sir, said Mr. Mason, after limiting the cases in which the federal judiciary could interpose, I would confine the appellate jurisdiction to matters of law only, in common-law controversies. It appears to me that this will remove oppressions and answer every purpose of an appellate power. A discrimination arises between common-law trials and trials in courts of equity and admiralty. In these two last, depositions are committed to record, and therefore, on an appeal, the whole fact goes up ; the equity of the whole case, comprehending fact and law, is considered, and no new evidence requisite. Is it so in courts of common law? There evidence is only given *viva voce*. I know not a single case where there is an appeal of fact as to common law. But I may be mistaken. Where there is an appeal from an inferior to a superior court, with respect to matters of fact, a new witness may be introduced, who is perhaps suborned by the other party, a thousand miles from the place where the first trial was had. These are some of the inconveniences and insurmountable objections against this general power being given to the federal courts. Gentlemen will perhaps say there will be no occasion to carry up the evidence by *viva voce* testimony, because Congress may order it to be committed to writing, and trans- mitted in that manner with the rest of the record. It is true they may, but it is as true that they may not. But suppose they do ; little conversant as I am in this subject, I know there is a great difference between *viva voce* evidence given at the bar, and testi- mony given in writing. I leave it to gentlemen more conversant in these matters to discuss it. They are also to have cognizance in controversies to which the United States shall be a party. This power is superadded, that there might be no doubt, and that all cases arising under the government might be brought before the federal court. Gentlemen will not, I presume, deny that all revenue and excise controversies, and all proceedings relative to the duties of the officers of government, from the highest to the lowest, may and must be brought by these means to the federal courts; in the first instance, to the inferior federal court, and afterwards to the superior court. Every fact proved with respect to these, in the court below, may be revived in the superior court. But this appellate jurisdiction is to be under the regulations of Congress. What these regulations may be, God only knows.

Their *jurisdiction* further extends to controversies between citizens of different States. Can we not trust our State courts with the decision of these? If I have a controversy with a man in Maryland,—if a man in Maryland has my bond for a hundred pounds,—are not the State courts competent to try it? Is it suspected that they would enforce the payment if unjust, or refuse to enforce it if just? The very idea is ridiculous. What! carry me a thousand miles from home—from my family and business—to where, perhaps, it will be impossible for me to prove that I paid it? Perhaps I have a respectable witness who saw me pay the money; but I must carry him one thousand miles to prove it, or be compelled to pay it again. Is there any necessity for this power? It ought to have no unnecessary or dangerous power. Why should the federal courts have this cognizance? Is it because one lives on one side of the Potomac, and the other on the other? Suppose I have your bond for a thousand pounds: if I have any wish to harass you, or if I be of a litigious disposition, I have only to assign it to a gentleman in Maryland? This assignment will involve you in trouble and expense. What effect will this power have between British creditors and the citizens of this State? This is a ground on which I shall speak with confidence. Every one who heard me speak on the subject, knows that I always spoke for the payment of the British debts. I wish every honest debt to be paid. Though I would wish to pay the British creditor, yet I would not put it in his power to gratify private malice to our injury. Let me be put right if I be mistaken; but there is not, in my opinion, a single British creditor but can bring his debtors to the federal court.

There are a thousand instances where debts have been paid, and yet must, by this appellate cognizance, be paid again. Are these imaginary cases? Are they only possible cases, or are they certain and inevitable? "To controversies between a State and the citizens of another State." How will their jurisdiction in this case do? Let gentlemen look at the westward. Claims respecting those lands, every liquidated account, or other claim against this State, will be tried before the federal court. Is not this disgraceful? Is this State to be brought to the bar of justice like a delinquent individual? Is the sovereignty of the State to be arraigned like a culprit, or private offender? Will the States undergo this mortification? I think this power perfectly unnecessary. But let us pursue this subject farther. What is to be done if a judgment be obtained against a State? Will you issue a *fieri facias?* It would be ludicrous to say that you could put the State's body in jail. How is the judgment, then, to be enforced? A power which cannot be executed ought not to be granted.

Let us consider the operation of the last subject of its *cognizance.* "Controversies between a State, or the citizens thereof, and foreign States, citizens, or subjects." There is a confusion in this case. This much, however, may be raised out of it—that a suit will be brought against Virginia. She may be sued by a foreign State. What reciprocity is there in it? In a suit between Virginia and a foreign State, is the foreign State to be bound by the decision? Is there a similar privilege given to us in foreign States? Where will you find a parallel regulation? How will the decision be enforced? Only by the *ultima ratio regum.* A dispute between a foreign citizen or subject and a Virginian cannot be tried in our own courts, but must be decided in the federal court. Is this the case in any other country? Are not men obliged to stand by the laws of the country where the disputes are? This is an innovation which is utterly unprecedented and unheard-of. Cannot we trust the State courts with disputes between a Frenchman, or an Englishman, and a citizen; or with disputes between two Frenchmen? This is disgraceful; it will annihilate your State judiciary; it will prostrate your legislature.

Thus, sir, it appears to me that the greater part of these powers are unnecessary, and dangerous, as tending to impair, and ultimately destroy, the State judiciaries, and, by the same principle, the legislation of the State governments. To render it safe, there must be an amendment, such as I have pointed out. After mentioning the original jurisdiction of the Supreme Court, which **extends** to but three cases, it gives it appellate jurisdiction, in all other cases mentioned, both as to law and fact, indiscriminately and without limitation. Why not remove the cause of fear and danger? But it is said that the regulations of Congress will remove these. I say that, in my opinion, they will have a contrary effect, and will utterly annihilate your State courts. Who are the court? The judges. It is a familiar distinction. We frequently speak of a court in contradistinction from a jury. I think the court are to be judges of this. The judges on the bench are to be judges of fact and law, with such exceptions, &c., as Congress shall make. Now give me leave to ask, Is not a jury excluded absolutely? By way of illustration, were Congress to say that a jury, instead of a court, should judge the fact, will not the court be still judges of the fact consistently with this Constitution? Congress may make such a regulation, or may not. But suppose they do; what sort of a jury would they have in the ten miles square? I would rather a thousand times, be tried by a court than by such a jury. This great palladium of national safety, which is secured to us by our own government, will be taken from us in those courts; or, if it be reserved, it will be but in name, and not in substance. In the government of Virginia, we have secured an impartial jury of the vicinage. We can except to jurors, and peremptorily challenge them in criminal trials. If I be tried in the federal court for a crime which may affect my life, have I a right of challenging or excepting to the jury? Have not the best men suffered by weak and partial juries? This sacred right ought, therefore, to be secured.

I dread the ruin that will be brought on thirty thousand of our people, with respect to disputed lands. I am personally endangered as an inhabitant of the Northern Neck. The people of that part will be obliged, by the operation of this power, to pay the quitrents of their lands. Whatever other gentleman may think, I consider this as a most serious alarm. It will little avail a man to make a profession of his candor. It is to his character and reputation they will appeal. Let gentlemen consider my public and private character. To these I wish gentlemen to appeal for an interpretation of my motives and views. Lord Fairfax's title was clear and undisputed. After the revolution, we taxed his lands as private property. After his death, an act of Assembly was made, in 1782, to sequester the quitrents due, at his death, in the hands of his debtors. Next year an act was made restoring them to the executor of the proprietor. Subsequent to this, the treaty of peace was made, by which it was agreed that there should be no further confiscations. But, after this, an act of Assembly passed, confiscating his whole property. As Lord Fairfax's title was indisputably good, and as treaties are to be the supreme law of the land, will not his representatives be able to recover all in the federal court? How will gentlemen like to pay an additional tax on lands in the Northern Neck? This the operation of this system will compel them to do. They now are subject to the same tax that other citizens are; and if the quitrents be recovered in the federal court, they are doubly taxed. This may be called an assertion; but, were I going to my grave, I would appeal to Heaven that I think it true. How will a poor man, who is injured or dispossessed unjustly, get a remedy? Is he to go to the federal court, seven or eight hundred miles? He might as well give his claim up. He may grumble, but, finding no relief, he will be contented.

Again, all that tract of country between the Blue ridge and the Alleghany Mountains will be claimed, and probably recovered in the federal court, from the present possessors, by those companies who have a title to them. These *lands* have been sold to a great number of people. Many settled on them, on terms which were advertised. How will this be with respect to *ex post facto* laws? We have not only confirmed the title of those who made the contract, but those who did not, by a law, in 1779, on their paying the original price. Much was paid in a depreciated value, and much was not paid at all. Again, the great Indiana purchase, which was made to the westward, will, by this judicial power, be rendered a cause of dispute. The possessors may be ejected from those lands. That company paid a consideration of ten thousand pounds to the crown, before the lands were taken up. I have heard gentlemen of the law say (and I believe it is right) that, after the consideration was paid to the crown, the purchase was legally made, and ought to be valid. That company may come in, and show that they have paid the money, and have a full right to the land. Of the Indiana company I need not say much. It is well known that their claims will be brought before these courts. Three or four counties are settled on the land to which that company claims a title, and have long enjoyed it peaceably. All these claims before those courts, if they succeed, will introduce a scene of distress and confusion never heard of before. Our peasants will be, like those mentioned by Virgil, reduced to ruin and misery, driven from their farms, and obliged to leave their country :—" *Nos patriam fugimus—et dulcia linquimus arva.*"

Having mentioned these things, give me leave to submit an amendment, which I think would be proper and safe, and would render our citizens secure in their possessions justly held. I mean, sir, "that the judicial power shall extend to no case where the cause of action shall have originated before the ratification of this Constitution, except in suits for debts due to the United States, disputes between States about their territory, and disputes between persons claiming lands under the grants of different States." In these cases, there is an obvious necessity for giving it a retrospective power. I have laid before you my idea on the subject, and expressed my fears, which I most conscientiously believe to be well founded.

Friday, June 20.—[The 1st and 2d sections of Article III. still under consideration.]

Mr. George Mason. Mr. Chairman, the objection I made, respecting the assignment of a bond from a citizen of this State to a citizen of another State, remains still in force. The honorable gentleman [*E. Pendleton*] has said that there can be no danger, in the first instance, because it is not within the original jurisdiction of the Supreme Court ; but that the suit must be brought in the inferior federal court of Virginia. He supposes there can never be an appeal in this case, by the plaintiff, because he gets a judgment on his bond ; and that the defendant alone can appeal, who therefore, instead of being injured, obtains a privilege. Permit me to examine the force of this. By means of a suit, on a real or fictitious claim, the citizens of the most distant States may be brought to the supreme federal court. Suppose a man has my bond for a hundred pounds, and a great part of it has been paid, and, in order fraudulently to oppress me he assigns it to a gentleman in Carolina or Maryland. He then carries me to the inferior federal court. I produce my witness, and judgment is given in favor of the defendant. The plaintiff appeals, and carries me to the superior court, a thousand miles, and my expenses amount to

more than the bond.   The honorable gentleman recommends to
me to alter my proposed amendment.   I would as soon take the
advice of that gentleman as any other; but, though the regard
which I have for him be great, I cannot assent on this great
occasion.

There are not many instances of decisions by juries in the
admiralty or chancery ; because the facts are generally proved by
depositions.   When that is done, the fact, being ascertained, goes
up to the superior court, as part of the record ; so that there will
be no occasion to revise that part.

Monday, June 23.—[The 1st and 2d sections of Article III. still
under consideration.   The speeches of this day incompletely
reported.]

Mr. George Mason.   Mr. Chairman, I should not have troubled
the committee again on this subject, were there not some arguments
in support of that plan, sir, that appear to me totally unsatisfactory.
With respect to concurrent jurisdiction, sir, the honorable gentleman
[*Mr. Madison*] has observed, that county courts had exercised
this right without complaint.   Have Hanover and Henrico the
same objects?   Can an officer in either of those counties serve a
process in the other?   The federal judiciary has concurrent jurisdiction throughout the States, and therefore must interfere with
the State judiciaries.   Congress can pass a law constituting the
powers of the federal judiciary throughout the States : they may
also pass a law vesting the federal power in the State judiciaries,
These laws are *permanent*, and cannot be controverted by any law
of the State.

If we were forming a general government, and not States, I
think we should perfectly comply with the genius of the paper
before you ; but if we mean to form one great national government for thirteen States, the   arguments which   I have heard
hitherto in support of this part of the plan do not apply at all. We
are willing to give up all powers which are necessary to preserve
the peace of the Union, so far as respects foreign nations, or our
own preservation ; but we will not agree to a federal judiciary,
which is not necessary for this purpose, because the powers there
granted will tend to oppress the middling and lower class of people.
A poor man seized by the federal officers, and carried to the federal   court,—has he any chance under such a system as this?

Justice itself may be bought too dear ; yet this may be the case. It may cost a man five hundred pounds to recover one hundred pounds. These circumstances are too sacred to leave undefined ; and I wish to see things certain, positive, and clear. But, however, sir, these matters have been so fully investigated, that I beg pardon for having intruded so far, and I hope we shall go on in the business.

[The 1st section of Article IV. was then read.]

Mr. George Mason. Mr. Chairman : the latter part of this clause, sir, I confess I do not understand—*Full faith and credit shall be given to all acts ;* and how far it may be proper that Congress shall declare the effects, I cannot clearly see into.

[2d section, Article IV.]

Mr. George Mason. Mr. Chairman, on some former part of the investigation of this subject, gentlemen were pleased to make some observations on the security of *property* coming within this section. It was then said, and I now say, that *there is no security ;* nor have gentlemen convinced me of this.

[3d section, Article IV., was then read.]

Mr. George Mason took a retrospective view of several parts which had been before objected to. He endeavored to demonstrate the dangers that must inevitably arise from *the insecurity* of our rights and privileges, as they depended on vague, indefinite, and ambiguous implications. The adoption of a system so replete with defects, he appehended, could not but be productive of the most *alarming* consequences. He dreaded popular resistance to its operation. He expressed, in emphatic terms, the *dreadful effects* which must ensue, should the people resist ; and concluded by observing, that he trusted gentlemen would pause before they would decide a question which involved such awful consequences.

Tuesday, June 24.—[In answer to E. Randolph.]

Mr. George Mason. Mr. Chairman, with respect to commerce and navigation, he has given it as his opinion that their regulation, as it now stands, was a *sine qua non* of the Union, and that without it the States in Convention would never concur. I differ from him. It never was, nor in my opinion ever will be, a *sine qua non* of the Union.

I will give you, to the best of my recollection, the history of that affair. This business was discussed at Philadelphia for four months, during which time the subject of commerce and navigation was often under consideration ; and I assert that eight States out of twelve, for more than three months, voted for requiring two thirds of the members present in each house to pass commercial and navigation laws. True it is, that afterwards it was carried by a majority as it stands. If I am right, there was a great majority for requiring two thirds of the States in this business, till a compromise took place between the Northern and Southern States ; the Northern States agreeing to the temporary importation of slaves, and the Southern States conceding, in return, that navigation and commercial laws should be on the footing on which they now stand. If I am mistaken, let me be put right. Those are my reasons for saying that this was not a *sine qua non* of their concurrence. The Newfoundland fisheries will require that kind of security which we are now in want of. The Eastern States therefore agreed, at length, that treaties should require the consent of two thirds of the members present in the Senate.

IV.

AMENDMENTS TO THE CONSTITUTION.

The bill of rights here given is from the original manuscript in the handwriting of George Mason. The amendments, twelve in number, seem to be also penned by him. The other set of amendments, numbering nineteen, would seem to be in a clerk's hand. The latter is the completed draft, evidently used at a later stage in the work of the committee of opposition, and the first article or section has been altered in committee.

FORMS OF A RESOLVE TO ACCOMPANY THE DECLARATION OF RIGHTS AND AMENDMENTS.

Resolved, that the following Declaration of Rights and Amendments be referred to the committee of the whole Convention upon the new constitution of government recommended by the late federal convention ;

or

Resolved, that the following Declaration of Rights and Amendments to the new constitution of government recommended by the late federal convention, ought to be communicated and referred to the other States in the American Union for their consideration, previous to its final ratification ;

or

Resolved, that the following Amendments ought to be made to the new constitution of governmnt recommended by the late federal Convention previous to the ratification thereof, and that the said Amendments be by this Convention communicated and referred to the other States in the American Union for their consideration ;

or

Resolved, that the new constitution of government recommended by the late federal convention ought to be ratified when the following Declaration of Rights and Amendments shall be adopted ; and that the said Declaration of Rights and Amendments be by this Convention communicated and referred to the other States in the Union.

DECLARATION OF RIGHTS.

That there be a Declaration or Bill of Rights, asserting and securing from encroachment the essential and unalienable rights of the people, in some such manner as the following.

1. That all freemen have certain essential inherent rights, of which they cannot, by any compact, deprive or divest their posterity ; among which are the enjoyment of life and liberty, with the means of acquiring, possessing, and protecting property, and pursuing and obtaining happiness and safety.

2. That all power is naturally vested in, and consequently derived from, the people ; that magistrates therefore are their trustees and agents, and at all times amenable to them.

3. That government, is or ought to be, instituted for the common benefit, protection, and security of the people ; and that whenever any government shall be found inadequate, or contrary to these purposes, a majority of the community hath an indubitable, unalienable, and indefeasible right, to reform, alter, or abolish it, and to establish another, in such manner as shall be judged most con-

ducive to the public weal ; and that the doctrine of non-resistance against arbitrary power and oppression is absurd, slavish, and destructive of the good and happiness of mankind.

4. That no man, or set of men, are entitled to exclusive or separate public emoluments or privileges from the community, but in consideration of public services ; which not being descendible, neither ought the offices of magistrate, legislator, or judge, or any other public office, to be hereditary.

5. That legislative, executive, and judiciary powers of government should be separate and distinct, and that the members of the two first may be restrained from oppression, by feeling and participating the public burthens, they should, at fixed periods, be reduced to a private station, return into the mass of the people, and the vacancies be supplied by certain and regular elections ; in which all or any part of the former members to be eligible, or ineligible, as the rules of the constitution of government, and the laws shall direct.

6. That the right of the people to participate in the legislature is the best security of liberty, and the foundation of all free government ; for this purpose, elections ought to be free and frequent ; and all men having sufficient evidence of permanent common interest with, and attachment to the community, ought to have the right of suffrage ; and that no aid charge, tax or fee can be set, rated, or levied upon the people, without their own consent, or that of their representatives, so elected, nor can they be bound by any law to which they have not, in like manner, assented, for the public good.

7. That all power of suspending laws or the execution of laws, by any authority, without the consent of the representatives of the people in the legislature, is injurious to their rights, and ought not to be exercised.

8. That in all capital or criminal prosecutions, a man hath a right to demand the cause and nature of his accusation, to be confronted with the accusers and witnesses, to call for evidence, and be admitted counsel in his favor, and to a fair and speedy trial by an impartial jury of his vicinage, without whose unanimous consent he cannot be found guilty (except in the government of the land and naval forces in time of actual war, invasion, or rebellion) nor can he be compelled to give evidence against himself.

9. That no freeman ought to be taken, imprisoned, or disseized of his freehold, liberties, privileges, or franchises, or outlawed or exiled, or in any manner destroyed, or deprived of his life, liberty or property, but by the law of the land.

10. That every freeman restrained of his liberty, is entitled to a remedy to inquire into the lawfulness thereof, and to remove the same if unlawful, and that such remedy ought not to be denied or delayed.

13. That excessive bail ought not to be required, nor excessive fines imposed, nor cruel and unusual punishments inflicted.

14. That every freeman has a right to be secure from all unreasonable searches and seizures of his person, his papers, and his property, all warrants therefore to search suspected places, or to seize any freeman, his papers or property, without information upon oath (or affirmation of a person religiously scrupulous of taking an oath) of legal and sufficient cause, are grievous and oppressive ; and all general warrants to search suspected places, or to apprehend any suspected person, without specially naming or describing the place or person, are dangerous, and ought not to be granted.

11. That in controversies respecting property, and in suits between man and man, the ancient trial by jury of facts, where they arise, is one of the greatest securities to the rights of a free people, and ought to remain sacred and inviolable.

16. That the people have a right to freedom of speech, and of writing and publishing their sentiments ; that the freedom of the press is one of the great bulwarks of liberty, and ought not to be violated.

15. That the people have a right peaceably to assemble together to consult for their common good, or to instruct their representatives, and that every freeman has a right to petition, or apply to the legislature for redress of grievances.

12. That every freeman ought to find a certain remedy by recourse to the laws, for all injuries or wrongs he may receive in his person, property, or character ; He ought to obtain right and justice freely, without sale, completely and without denial, promptly and without delay ; and that all establishments or regulations, contravening these rights are oppressive and unjust.

17. That the people have a right to keep and to bear arms ; that

a well-regulated militia, composed of the body of the people, trained to arms, is the proper, natural and safe defence of a free State; that standing armies in time of peace are dangerous to liberty, and therefore ought to be avoided, as far as the circumstances and protection of the community will admit; and that in all cases, the military should be under strict subordination to and governed by the civil power.

18. That no soldier in time of peace ought to be quartered in any house without the consent of the owner; and in time of war, only by the civil magistrate in such manner as the laws direct.

19. That any person religiously scrupulous of bearing arms ought to be exempted upon payment of an equivalent, to employ another to bear arms in his stead.

20. That religion, or the duty which we owe to our Creator, and the manner of discharging it, can be directed only by reason and conviction, not by force or violence, and therefore all men have an equal, natural, and unalienable right to the free exercise of religion, according to the dictates of conscience; and that no particular religious sect, or society of Christians, ought to be favored or established by law, in preference to others.

AMENDMENTS PROPOSED TO THE NEW CONSTITUTION OF GOVERNMENT IN ADDITION TO THE DECLARATION OF RIGHTS.

1. That each State in the Union shall respectively retain every power, jurisdiction and right which is not by this Constitution expressly delegated to the Congress of the United States, or to the departments of the federal government.

2. That there shall be one representative for every thirty thousand, according to the enumeration or census mentioned in the Constitution, until the whole number of representatives amounts to two hundred; after which that number shall be continued or increased, as the Congress shall direct, upon the principles fixed in the Constitution, by apportioning the representatives of each State to some greater number of people from time to time as population increases.

3. That Congress, shall not exercise the powers respecting the regulation of elections, vested in them by the fourth section of the first article of the Constitution, but in cases when a State

neglects or refuses to make the regulations therein mentioned, or shall make regulations subversive of the rights of the people to a free and equal representation in Congress, agreeably to the Constitution, or shall be prevented from making elections by invasion, rebellion or insurrection ; and in any of these cases, such powers shall be exercised by the Congress only, until the cause be removed.

4. That the Congress do not lay direct taxes, but when the revenue arising from the duties on imports is insufficient for the public exigencies, nor then until Congress shall have first made a requisition upon the States, to assess, levy and pay their respective proportions of such requisitions, according to the enumeration or census fixed in the Constitution in such way and manner as the legislature of the State shall judge best ; and if any State shall neglect or refuse to pay its proportion pursuant to such requisition, the Congress may assess and levy such State's proportion together with interest thereon, at the rate of six per centum per annum from the time of payment prescribed in such requisition.

5. That the members of the Senate and House of Representatives shall be ineligible to and incapable of holding any civil office under the authority of the United States, during the time for which they shall respectively be elected.

6. That the journals of the proceedings of the Senate and House of Representatives shall be published at least once in every year except such parts thereof relating to treaties, alliances or military operations as in their judgment require secrecy.

7. That a regular statement and account of the receipts and expenditures of all public money shall be published at least once in every year.

8. That no commercial treaty shall be ratified, without the concurrence of two thirds of the whole number of the members of the Senate, and no treaty ceding, contracting, restraining or suspending the territorial rights or claims of the United States, or any of them, or their or any of their rights or claims to fishing in the American seas, or navigating the American rivers, shall be ratified without the concurrence of three fourths of the whole number of the members of both houses respectively.

9. That no navigation law or law regulating commerce shall be passed without the consent of two thirds of the members present in both houses.

10. That no standing army or regular troops shall be raised or kept up in time of peace without the consent of two thirds of the members present in both houses.

11. That no soldier shall be enlisted for a longer term than four years; except in time of war, and then for no longer term than the continuance of the war.

12. That each State respectively shall have the power to provide for organizing, arming and disciplining its own militia, whensoever the Congress shall omit or neglect to provide for the same.

13. That the militia shall not be subject to martial law except when in actual service, in time of war, invasion, or rebellion ; and when not in the actual service of the United States shall be subject only to such fines, penalties and punishments as shall be directed or inflicted by the laws of its own State.

14. That the exclusive power of legislation given to the Congress over the federal town and its adjacent district, shall extend only to such regulations as respect the police and good government thereof.

15. That no person shall be capable of being President of the United States for more than eight years in any term of sixteen years.

16. That the judicial power of the United States shall be vested in one supreme court, and in such courts of admiralty as the Congress may from time to time ordain and establish in any of the different States.

17. The judicial power shall extend to all cases in law and equity arising under treaties made or which shall be made under the authority of the United States ; to all cases affecting ambassadors, other foreign ministers and consuls ; to all cases of admiralty and maritime jurisdiction ; to controversies to which the United States shall be a party ; to controversies between two or more States, and between persons claiming lands under the grants of different States.

18. In all cases affecting ambassadors, other foreign ministers and consuls, and those in which a State shall be a party, the Supreme Court shall have original jurisdiction ; in all the other cases before mentioned the Supreme Court shall have appellate jurisdiction as to matters of law only, except in cases of equity, and of admiralty and maritime jurisdiction, in which the Supreme

Court shall have appellate jurisdiction, both as to law and fact, with such exceptions, and under such regulations as the Congress shall make. But the judicial power of the United States shall extend to no case where the cause of action shall have originated before the ratification of this Constitution, except in disputes between States about their territory, disputes between persons claiming lands under the grants of different States, and suits for debts due to the United States.

19. That in criminal prosecutions no man shall be restrained in the exercise of the usual and accustomed right of challenging or excepting to the jury.

AMENDMENTS PROPOSED TO THE NEW CONSTITUTION OF GOVERNMENT.

That there be a Declaration of Rights, asserting and securing from encroachment the essential and unalienable rights of the people, in some such manner as the following.

Here the Declaration of Rights to be inserted.

And that there be also the following amendments to the Constitution :

1. That each State in the Union shall retain its sovereignty, freedom and independence, and every power, jurisdiction and right, which is not by this Constitution expressly delegated to the Congress of the United States.

2. That there shall be one representative for every thirty thousand persons, according to the enumeration or census mentioned in the Constitution, until the whole number of the representatives amounts to two hundred.

3. That Congress shall not exercise the powers, respecting the regulation of elections, vested in them by the fourth section of the first article of the Constitution, but in cases when a State neglects or refuses to make the regulations therein mentioned, or shall make regulations subversive of the rights of the people to a free and equal representation in Congress agreeably to the Constitution, or shall be prevented from making elections by invasion or rebellion ; and in any of these cases, such powers shall be exercised by Congress only until the cause be removed.

4. That Congress do not lay direct taxes, nor excises upon any articles of the growth or manufactured from the growth of any of

the American States, but when the monies arising from the duties or imposts are insufficient for the public exigencies ; nor then until Congress shall have first made a requisition upon the States, to assess, levy and pay their respective proportions of such requisitions, according to the enumeration or census fixed in the Constitution, in such way and manner as the legislature of the State shall judge best ; and if any State shall neglect or refuse to pay its proportion, pursuant to such requisition, then Congress may assess and levy such State's proportion, together with interest thereon, at the rate of six cents per annum, from the time of payment prescribed in such requisition.

5. That the members of the Senate and House of Representatives shall be ineligible to and incapable of holding any office under the authority of the United States, during the time for which they shall respectively be elected.

6. That there shall be a constitutional responsible council, to assist in the administration of government, with the power of choosing out of their own body a president, who in case of the death, resignation or disability of the president of the United States, shall act, *pro tempore*, as vice-president, instead of a vice-president elected in the manner prescribed by the Constitution ; and that the power of making treaties, appointing ambassadors, other public ministers and consuls, judges of the Supreme Courts, and all other officers of the United States, whose appointments are not otherwise provided for by the Constitution, and which shall be established by law, be vested in the president of the United States with the assistance of the council so to be appointed. But all treaties so made or entered into, shall be subject to the revision of the Senate and House of Representatives for their ratification. And no commercial treaty shall be ratified without the consent of two thirds of the members present in both houses ; nor shall any treaty ceding, contracting, restraining or suspending the territorial rights or claims of the United States, or any of them, or their, or any of their rights or claims to fishing in the American seas, or navigating the American rivers, be ratified, without the consent of three fourths of the whole number of the members of both houses.

7. No navigation law or law for regulating commerce shall be passed without the consent of two thirds of the members present in both houses.

8. Neither the president nor vice-president of the United States, nor any member of the council shall command the army or navy of the United States in person without the consent of two thirds of the members of both houses.

9. No soldier shall be enlisted for a longer term than four years, except in time of war, and then for no longer term than the continuance of the war.

10. No mutiny act shall be passed for any longer term than two years.

11. The president of the United States, or any other officer acting under the authority of the United States, shall, upon impeachment, be suspended from the exercise of his office, during his trial.

12. The judges of the federal court shall be incapable of holding any other office, or of receiving the profits of any other office, or emolument under the United States or any of them.

V.

PAPER ON CONGRESSIONAL DISTRICTS.

The essential difference between the citizens of a free country, and the subjects of arbitrary or despotic governments, or in other words, between freemen and slaves, consists principally in this.— That the citizens of a free country choose the men who are to make laws for them, and are therefore governed by no laws, but such as are made by men of their own choosing, in whom they can confide, who are amenable to them ; and if they abuse their trust can be turned out at the next election. But the subjects of arbitrary governments having no such right of suffrage, in electing their own law-makers, are governed by laws made by men whom they do not choose, who therefore are not amenable to them, over whom they have no control, in whom they have no confidence, with whom they have no common interest or fellowship ; and whose interest and views may be, and frequently will be in direct contrast and opposition to the rights and interest of the bulk of the people. Hence proceed partial and unjust laws, oppression and every species of tyranny. From these premises it is evident that this right of suffrage, in the choice of their own lawmakers is the foundation and support of all the other rights and privileges of freemen. And whenever they shall be deprived of it, all their other rights and privileges must soon moulder away and tumble to the ground. Whenever it shall be impaired or weakened, all the other rights and privileges of a free people will be impaired or weakened, in the same proportion. And whenever, under any pretence whatever, the substance of this fundamental and precious right of suffrage shall be so far undermined or invalidated, as to leave the name or shadow of it only to the people, or to any particular part of the people, from thenceforward, such people will possess only the name and shadow of liberty, which without the substance, is not worth preserving.

It is surely therefore the duty of freemen—a duty which they owe to themselves, to their country, to their children, and to generations yet unborn—to watch over and guard this sacred and inestimable right of suffrage, and with manly firmness to resist the smallest attempt of invasion, or encroachment on it, for every encroachment will grow into a precedent for some other encroachment.

There is great cause to apprehend, that at the next session of the Virginia Assembly, an attempt will be made, to deprive the people of Fairfax County of their right of suffrage, in choosing members of Congress ; or which amounts to nearly the same thing, to take from them the substance, and leave them only the name and shadow of choosing. When the new Constitution for the general government of the United States of America was first formed, Virginia was entitled to send only ten members to the House of Representatives in Congress. The whole State of Virginia was therefore laid off into only ten districts, each of which chose one member. Kentucky being one of those ten districts, chose one of the said ten members. The six counties of King George, Stafford, Prince William, Fairfax, Loudoun, and Fauquier composed another of those ten districts, for choosing one of the said ten members. But by the census or enumeration of all the inhabitants of the United States, taken last year, the number of members in the House of Representatives, from almost every State in the Union, will be greatly increased. From Virginia the number will be more than doubled, and consequently the number of the former districts must be more than doubled also, and the size and extent of them lessened in the same proportion : for at the next election, sometime in the course of next winter, Virginia instead of sending nine members (exclusive of Kentucky) to the House of Representatives in Congress, will be entitled to send twenty-one members, exclusive of Kentucky. And for this purpose, when our Assembly meets next October, Virginia (exclusive of Kentucky) will be arranged, or laid off into twenty-one districts, each of which to choose one member. The five counties of Stafford, Prince William, Fairfax, Loudoun, and Fauquier (leaving out the county of King George, to be added to some of the lower counties) will now form two complete districts, and it will be attempted to make Fairfax and Loudoun compose one of these two districts ; and Stafford, Prince William and Fauquier compose the other district ; by which means the substance of the right of suffrage, in electing members of Congress will be taken from the people of Fairfax, and the name or shadow only left them. For the voters in Loudoun County being near three times the number of the voters in Fairfax ; while that local attachment and partiality continues to influence the bulk of mankind, which ever has influenced them, and ever will influence them, while human nature continues what it now is and always has been ; a candidate in Fairfax (let him be ever so good a man) will have no chance of succeeding against one in Loudoun ; the comparative merits of the candidates will be sacrificed to local attachment, and the people in Fairfax will, in reality, have little more hand in electing their *nominal* representatives in Congress than they have in electing the representatives of Maryland or Pennsylvania. And this act of injustice and oppression will be further aggravated, in eight or nine years ; for when the town of Alexandria and that part of the federal district of ten miles square which lies on this side of Potomack River, are taken out of the jurisdiction of Virginia, Loudoun County which now has three votes to our one, will then have near six votes to our one ; and the people of Fairfax will not find it worth their while to give their votes, or attend the elections of members of Congress. What the people of Fairfax County have done to deserve this injurious treatment, and forfeiture of their dearest rights and privileges, let the contrivers of this nefarious project declare.[1]

[1] Whatever may be the pretence, the real motive (here at least) for endeavoring to join Fairfax County in the district with Loudoun, is to secure the election of Mr. Richard Bland Lee, which his friends apprehend may be rendered precarious by placing Loudoun in the same district with Fauquier. This apprehen-

It is said (perhaps untruly) that some of the people in Alexandria, and within the federal district, are in favor of this scheme. Such of them as are men of liberal minds, can hardly be presumed to be so, but they stand on very different ground from the people of the county, for they will sacrifice only a temporary interest of short duration, as in eight or nine years (perhaps sooner) they will be taken out of the jurisdiction of Virginia ; but to the people in every other part of the county, the sacrifice will not be temporary but permanent. If the three small counties of Stafford, Prince William, and Fairfax compose one complete district, and the two large counties of Loudoun and Fauquier compose another complete district, as of right they ought to do, the counties in each respective district will have nearly an equal number of voters, and will be a fair match for each other. The people in each county will then have, not in name only, but in substance and reality, an equal right of suffrage in electing members of Congress : a candidate in either county will have a fair trial with a candidate in another county ; and the comparative merits of the candidates will generally prevail against local attachment and prejudice. It is notorious, that for these very reasons, when in the formation of the Virginia Government in the year 1776, the four and twenty districts were arranged for the election of senators, the counties of Prince William and Fairfax were formed into one district, and the counties of Loudoun and Fauquier into another district, and still continue so. And surely the same reasons hold at least equally strong, in the choice of members of Congress, whose powers, since the establishment of the new federal constitution, are much greater and more important, than those which now remain to the State Legislatures. And as there is just ground to believe that the arrangement of districts, which will be made next fall, will hardly ever be materially altered, it is of the utmost consequence, that they should be fairly and justly made, and not with a view of serving any temporary, local party-job whatever.[1]

sion seems to be ill founded, but if it was ever so well founded, and if Mr. Lee was the last man in the United States, nothing can be more absurd and wicked than to sacrifice the rights of the people to the views or interest of an individual. And a candidate for Fairfax County, by adopting this iniquitous scheme, will give the most indisputable proof of his being unworthy of public trust.

[1] An amendment to the Constitution of the federal government was, some time ago, recommended by Congress, since agreed to by more than two thirds

VI.

WILL OF GEORGE MASON OF " GUNSTON."

I, George Mason of Gunston Hall in the parish of Truro and county of Fairfax, being of perfect and sound mind and memory and in good health, but mindful of the uncertainty of human life and the imprudence of a man's leaving his affairs to be settled upon a death bed, do make and appoint this my last Will and Testament. My soul I resign into the hands of my Almighty Creator whose tender mercies are over all his works, who hateth nothing that he hath made, and to the Justice and Wisdom of whose dispensation I willingly and cheerfully submit ; humbly hoping from his unbounded mercy and benevolence thro' the merits of my blessed Saviour a remission of my sins. My body I desire may be decently buried at the discretion of my Executors hereinafter named, close by the side of my dear and ever lamented wife. And as for all the worldly Estate with which it has pleased God to bless me I dispose of it in manner and form following. Imprimis : It is my will and desire and I hereby direct and order that all my lands, slaves with their increase, stocks, rents, crops, tobacco and money and debts due to me with the yearly interest arising thereon, with all my other Estate of what nature soever, in Virginia, Maryland or elsewhere, be kept together and considered as one common stock for the payment of my debts and legacys and the maintenance and education of my children and the payment of their fortunes, until my said children respectively come of age or marry, when and not before, each of them is to receive his or her part of the same, as hereinafter respectively devised or bequeathed to each

of the States in the Union, and thereby become an article of the said Constitution ; by which (to the best of my recollection, for I have not a copy of the amendment by me) the ratio of thirty thousand is to be applied to the census of the inhabitants of the United States, to ascertain and apportion the representation, until the number of the House of Representatives shall amount to one hundred : after which Congress is empowered to alter and increase the ratio in such manner as they shall judge fit ; provided that the number of the House of Representatives shall never be less than one hundred. The late census will increase the House of Representatives to something more than one hundred members : and there is therefore cause to believe, that the arrangement of the districts to be made next fall, will never be materially increased or altered.

G. M.

of them, and when any one of my children shall come of age or marry and receive his or her part of the same accordingly, the residue still to continue and remain in the said common stock until another of my children shall come of age or marry, and so on in the same manner until the youngest of my children shall come of age or marry and receive his or her part of the same as aforesaid ; it being my intention that my Executors shall not have the trouble and perplexity of keeping different accounts with all my children, but only one general account for the whole.

Item : I give and bequeath unto each of my four daughters, Ann Mason, Sarah Mason, Mary Mason and Elizabeth Mason and each of their heirs forever when they respectively arrive at the age of twenty-one years, or marry, whichever shall first happen, the following slaves with their increase respectively from the date of this my will : to my eldest daughter Ann the four following slaves and their increase, to wit Bess (the daughter of Chloe) and her child, Frank, mulatto Priss (the daughter of Jenny) and Nell (the daughter of Occoquan Nell). To my daughter Sarah the three following slaves with their increase, to wit Hannah and Venus (the daughter of Becky) and mulatto Mima (the daughter of Jenny). To my daughter Mary the three following slaves with their increase to wit, Ann and Nell, the daughter of house Nell, and little Jenny (the daughter of Jenny). To my daughter Elizabeth the three following slaves with their increase, to wit Vicky (the daughter of Occoquan Nell), Sarah (the daughter of great Sue), and Rachel (the daughter of Beck). And I confirm unto my three eldest daughters Ann, Sarah, and Mary their right and title respectively to one negro girl given to each of them by their grandfather Mr. William Eilbeck deceased, to wit a negro girl named Penny to my daughter Ann, a negro girl named Priss to my daughter Sarah, and a negro girl named Nan to my daughter Mary. But in the meantime that is until my daughters respectively come of age or marry, the profits of all such of the above mentioned slaves as shall not be employed in waiting upon any of my said daughters, or for their use in the house, are to remain in and be considered as part of the common stock for the purposes hereinbefore mentioned, and if any one or more of my said daughters should happen to die under age or unmarried, then and in that case it is my will and desire and I hereby direct and order that all the slaves with their increase hereinbefore bequeathed to such daughter or daughters, shall go to and be equally divided between my other daughters or to the survivor of them, to be delivered them or her as hereinbefore directed. I also give to each of my said four daughters one bed and furniture to be delivered them at the time and in the manner aforesaid.

Item : I give and bequeath unto each of my said four daughters Ann, Sarah, Mary and Elizabeth, except such of them as may happen to marry and have actually received their fortune in my lifetime, the sum of six hundred pounds sterling out of my money debts due to me and the profits of the common stock of my Estate, the said sum of six hundred pounds sterling to be paid to each of them without defalcation or diminution, when they respectively arrive at the age of twenty-one years or marry, whichever shall first happen exclusive of any sum or sums given or to be given to any of them by their grandmother Mrs. Eilbeck, or for which I have taken or may take bonds for their use or in any of their respective names ; and if any one of my said daughters should die under age or unmarried, it is my will and desire and I hereby direct and order, that the money herein bequeathed to such daughter shall go to be equally divided between all my other surviving daughters, such of them as may happen to be of age or married at the time to receive their part of the same, and the residue to remain in the common stock until my other surviving daughters respectively come of age or marry, but if two or more of my daughters should happen to die under age or unmarried, then and in that case it is my will and desire and I hereby direct and order, that so much of their money only shall go to my surviving daughter or daughters as will increase the fortune of each or either of them to the sum of one thousand pounds sterling, exclusive of their slaves or of any money given them by their grandmother Mrs. Eilbeck as aforesaid, to be paid them or her in the manner above directed, and that the residue shall remain in the common stock for the benefit of my four youngest sons in the manner hereinafter directed.

Item : I give and devise unto my eldest son George Mason and his heirs forever when he arrives at the age of twenty-one years or marrys, whichever shall first happen, my mansion house and seat of Gunston Hall with all my lands thereunto belonging or adjoining, being between five and six thousand acres, also a small tract of land adjoining to the land of the Revd. Mr. Lee Massey purchased by my father of Giles and Benoni Tillett, and in general all my lands between Potomack river, Occoquan river and Pohick creek in Fairfax County, excepting and reserving unto my Executors the right and privilege of keeping three Quarters, upon the said land to be considered as part of the common stock of my Estate for the benefit of my younger children, and of working the same number of hands as are worked at the said three Quarters respectively at the time of my death, with the right and privilege of getting timber for the proper use of the said three Quarters or plantations on any part of the said lands, that is to say one Quarter in the bottom of Dogues Neck (commonly called the Occoquan Quarter), until all my sons come of age, with all the land which I have usually tended and made use of at the said Quarter, and such other convenient and adjoining land as is necessary for the use of the same, and the benefit of suffering all the stock properly belonging to the said Quarter to range and run at large in the said Neck, and the two other Quarters at Hallowing's Point and upon the land I bought of William Courts, until all my sons except the youngest come of age, with all the land between [the] upper line of the said tract bought of William Courts, the river and the great marsh, and the benefit of all the stock properly belonging to the said two Quarters, ranging and running at large within the new Neck fence, my Executors keeping the said Quarters and plantations in good order and repair and delivering up the same accordingly at the respective expiration of the times aforesaid, or when the crops then growing thereon are finished, unto my said son George Mason or his heirs. But if my said son George Mason should die under age and unmarried, it is my will and desire and I hereby direct and order that all the lands herein devised unto him shall go and descend unto his heirs at law and his heirs forever, in the same manner as if my said son George had been in the actual possession of the same before his death, and shall not be divided among my residuary Legatees hereinafter named.

Item : I give and bequeath unto my said son George Mason and his heirs forever when he arrives at the age of twenty-one years or marrys, whichever shall first happen, the seven following slaves to wit Alec, Bob, Dunk, yellow Dick, Bob (the son of Occoquan Nell), Peter (the son of great Sue), Judy and Lucy together with all the slaves which shall properly belong to and reside at my two upper Quarters in Dogues Neck adjoining to the great marsh at the time of my death, (except such of them as may happen to be any of the slaves by name specifically bequeathed to some of my other children,) also all my stock of horses, cattle, sheep and hogs which shall properly belong to and be wintered at my said two upper Quarters in Dogues Neck, at the time of my death, with all the plantation utensils and implements of husbandry thereto belonging, also one fifth part of all my Books and household furniture in and about my dwelling house, but if my said son George Mason should die before he comes of age and unmarried, then and in that case it is my will and desire and I hereby direct and order, that all the slaves as well as all the personal Estate hereinbefore bequeathed him, shall be equally divided between my other surviving sons, and for that purpose shall remain in the common stock until my other sons respectively come of age or marry. Item: I give and bequeath unto my said son George and his heirs forever, all my stock in the Ohio Company as a member thereof, together with my share and part of all the said Company's lands, but whatever ballance (if any at the time of my death) appears by my books of account to be due from me to the said Ohio Company is to be paid out of the common stock of my Estate in the same manner as any other debts.— I also give and bequeath unto my said son George Mason my Gold watch which I commonly wear, also a large silver salver which being an old piece of family plate I desire may remain unaltered. And I confirm unto him his right and title to a negro man named Dick given him by his grandfather Mr. Eilbeck, and likewise his right and title to two negro men named Tom and Liberty exchanged with him by me for two other negroes given him by his grandmother Mrs. Eilbeck, also to a large silver Bowl given him by my mother in which all my children have been christened, and which I desire may remain in the family unaltered for that purpose. And whereas my son George will soon be of age, and if I should happen to die during the minority of my other children they will probably live with him, and he may not chuse to charge his brothers and sisters with their board, altho' it must put him to considerable trouble and expence, then and in that case there-fore, I give unto my said son George whilst my children live with him as aforesaid the right and privilege of taking in any year from any of my Quarters whilst they remain in the common stock, such Quantity of provisions for his family's use, and also of employing such and so many of my house servants in his family as he and my other Executor shall judge reasonable and necessary for the above mentioned purpose and adequate to the expence and trouble thereby occasioned, without being accountable for the same.

Item : I give and devise unto my son William Mason and his heirs forever when he arrives at the age of twenty-one years or marrys, whichever shall first happen, all my lands upon Chickamuxon and Mattawoman Creeks in Charles County in the Province of Mary-land, that is to say all my lands in Christian Temple Manor and my tract of land called Stump Neck (formerly called Dogues Neck) with two hundred acres of land thereto adjoining and in-cluded in the same original patent, excepting and reserving to my Executors the right and privilege of retaining and keeping in their hands as part of the common stock of my Estate, for the benefit of my younger children, until all my sons come of age the last men-tioned tract of land called Stump Neck with the said two hundred acres of land thereto adjoining, and of keeping a Quarter thereon and working the same number of hands for the purpose aforesaid as worked on the same at the time of my death. I also give and devise unto my said son William Mason and his heirs forever, in like manner, a tract of one hundred and fifty acres of land (where-on George Adams now lives) near Port Tobacco in the said county and province, the same being one moiety of a tract of land called Partnership, and if my said son William should die before he comes of age and unmarried, then and in that case I give and devise all the above mentioned Lands upon Chickamuxon and Mattawoman Creeks unto my youngest son Thomas Mason and his heirs forever, and the above mentioned tract of land near Port Tobacco (upon which George Adams lives) I give and devise unto my son Thomson Mason and his heirs forever.—Item : I give and devise unto my said son William Mason and his heirs forever when he arrives at the age of twenty-one years or marrys, which-ever shall first happen, the two following slaves to wit Milly (the daughter of Kate) and Sampson (the son of Mr. Eilbeck's Bess), also one-fifth part of all my Books and household furniture in or about my dwelling house. I also give and bequeath unto my said son William Mason my silver Watch which I formerly used to wear, and I confirm his right and title to a negro lad named Cato given him by his grandfather, Mr. Eilbeck.

Item : I give and devise unto my son Thomson Mason and his heirs forever when he arrives at the age of twenty-one years or marrys, whichever shall first happen, all my land in Thompson's patent (repatented in my own name) between Dogues Run and the south Branch of little Hunting Creek, excepting and reserving to my Executors the right and privilege of settling two Quarters with eight working hands on each upon such parts thereof as they shall think fit unless the said Quarters shall be settled thereon by me in my lifetime, and retaining and keeping in their hands one of the said Quarters so settled by me or them, with land thereto adjoining sufficient to work the hands belonging to the same as part of the common stock until all my sons come of age. I also give and devise unto my said son Thomson Mason and his heirs forever, in like manner, all my lands upon both sides the north branch of Little Hunting Creek contained in Thomas Stafford's patent, Thomas Sandiford's patent (repatented in my own name), George Brent's sale to William Browne and part of Ball's patent which I bought of Mr. Sampson Darrell, also all my land in Mason's and Hereford's patent upon the branches of Dogues Run and Accotink, being one moiety of the land devised by my Grandfather, Col. George Mason decd. to his daughters Elizabeth and Rosanna, also a small tract of land contiguous thereto originally patented by one William Williams and purchased by my father of Winifred Ball, daughter and heir at law to the said Williams, it being the land whereon Edward Violet lived, also a tract of about four hundred acres of land patented by my father upon the upper side of Dogues Run adjoining to Matthew's patent, and in general I give and devise unto my said son Thomson Mason and his heirs forever when he arrives at the age of twenty-one years or marrys, whichever shall first happen (except as before excepted) all my lands upon the branches and waters of Dogues Run and little Hunting Creek in Fairfax county, being in the whole about three thousand, three hundred acres, and if my said son Thomson Mason should die under age and unmarried, then and in that case I give and devise all the above mentioned lands in Thompson's patent between Dogues Run and the south branch of little Hunting Creek (being about thirteen hundred acres), and also all the above mentioned lands in Stafford's and Sandiford's patents in George Brent's sale to William Brown, and part of Ball's patent which I bought of Mr. Sampson Darrell being about seven hundred acres upon both sides the North Branch of little Hunting Creek, unto my youngest son Thomas Mason and his heirs forever ; but it is my will and desire and I hereby direct and order that all the other land hereinbefore devised unto my son Thomson Mason shall if he die under age and unmarried, as aforesaid go and descend unto my eldest son and heir George Mason and his heirs forever, in the same manner as if my said son Thomson had been in the actual possession of the same before his death. Item : I give and Devise unto my said son Thomson Mason and his heirs forever, when he arrives at the age of twenty one years or marrys, whichever shall first happen, the two following slaves to wit Sall (the daughter of Lucy), and Joe (the son of Mr. Eilbeck's Bess), also one fifth part of all my Books and household furniture in and about my dwelling house, and I confirm unto my said son Thomson Mason his right and title to a negroe lad named Cupid given him by his grandfather Mr. Eilbeck.

Item : I give and devise unto my son John Mason and his heirs forever when he arrives at the age of twenty-one or marrys, whichever shall first happen, all my lands adjoining to and near Rock Creek ferry upon Potowmack River, that is to say the lands contained in Thomas Ousley's, Thomas Gowing's and my father's patents (all repatented in my own name), with the lands I purchased of Ellis and Bradie and of Daniel Jennings, and a small tract of land I took up as vacant land between my other tracts, and in general all my land between Four Mile Run and the Lower Falls of Potowmack River in the parish and county of Fairfax being about two thousand acres. I also give and devise unto my said son John Mason and his heirs forever, in like manner my Island in Potomack River opposite the mouth of Rock Creek which I hold under a patent from the Lord Proprietor of Maryland by the name of Barbadoes. I also give and devise unto my said son John Mason and his heirs forever, in like manner all my lands upon and between the main south run of Accotink and the branches of Difficult Run in the upper part of Truro parish in Fairfax county, patented by my father with a small tract of land thereto adjoining patented in my own name being together about two thousand Acres, and if my said son John Mason should die under age and unmarried then and in that case I give and devise all the above mentioned lands between Four Mile Run and the Lower Falls of the Potowmack river together with my before-mentioned Island of Barbadoes unto my youngest son Thomas Mason and his heirs forever. But it is my will and desire and I hereby direct and order that all the other lands hereinbefore devised unto my said son John Mason upon and between the main south run of Accotink and the branches of Difficult Run shall if he die under age and unmarried, as aforesaid go and descend unto my eldest son and heir George Mason and his heirs forever, in the same manner as if my said son John Mason had been in the actual possession of the same before his death.—Item : I give and bequeath unto my said son John Mason and his heirs forever, when he arrives at the age of twenty-one years or marrys, whichever shall first happen the two following slaves to wit Harry (the son of house Poll) and Peg (the daughter of Chloe), also one fifth part of all my Books and household furniture in and about my dwelling house.

Item : I give and devise unto my youngest son Thomas Mason and his heirs forever, when he arrives at the age of twenty-one years or marrys, whichever shall first happen, all my land upon the lower side of Occoquan River patented by my father and Col. Robinson, together with the right and benefit of keeping the ferry over Occoquan from both sides of the river, which has been vested in me and my ancestors from the first settlement of this part of the country and long before the land there was taken up or patented. Also all my land upon the branches of Neabecco [Neapsco ?] purchased by my father of Ann West, also all my land upon Potowmack river in Cockpit Point Neck, also all my land upon the upper side of Chappawamsick Creek and in general all my lands in the county of Prince William. I also give and devise unto my said son Thomas Mason and his heirs forever, when he arrives at the age of twenty one years or marrys, whichever shall first happen, all my lands adjoining to each other upon Goose Bay and Potowmack River in Charles County in the Province of Maryland, being four different tracts, the lowermost called

St: Benedict's originally granted to Bennett Marchgay, the next called Mason's Fields patented by my mother Mrs. Ann Mason, the next interfering with Mason's Fields, a tract of one hundred and fifty acres without any particular name whereon Henry Fletcher formerly lived who purchased the same of Henry Aspinall to whom it was originally granted, and the upper [part] called Fletcher's Addition originally granted to the said Henry Fletcher, and in general all my lands between Chickamuxon Creek and Goose Bay in the said county and province, and if my said son Thomas Mason should die under age and unmarried, then and in that case I give and devise all the above mentioned lands between Chickamuxon Creek and Goose Bay in Charles County in the province of Maryland, unto my son William Mason and his heirs forever. But it is my will and desire and I hereby direct and order, that all the other lands hereinbefore devised unto my said son Thomas Mason in the County of Prince William and Colony of Virginia, together with the right and benefit of keeping Occoquan ferry, shall if he die under age and unmarried, as aforesaid go and descend unto my eldest son and heir George Mason and his heirs forever in the same manner as if my said son Thomas had been in actual possession of the same before his death. Item : I give and bequeath unto my said son Thomas Mason and his heirs forever, when he arrives at the age of twenty-one years or marrys, whichever shall first happen, the two following slaves to wit Jack (the son of house Nell) and Daphne (the daughter of Dinah), also one fifth part of all my books and household furniture in and about my dwelling house. Item : I give and bequeath unto my said son Thomas Mason the sum of six hundred pounds sterling to be paid him when he arrives at the age of twenty-one years or marrys, whichever shall first happen, out of my money and debts due to me and the profits of my Estate if so much remain in the common stock after the payment of my debts and legacys, the maintenance and education of my children and the payment of my daughters' fortunes, and if there is not so much as the said sum of six hundred pounds sterling then whatever lesser sum there is remaining in the said common stock.

And least the manner in which I have limited and directed the descent of some of my land should occasion any dispute or induce an opinion that I intended to intail them, I hereby declare that it is not my intention to intail any part of my Estate upon any of my children, but to give all and each of my sons when they respectively come of age or marry, an absolute fee simple estate in all the lands respectively devised them and in all such lands also as any of them may happen to take by the death of any of their Brothers, the common legal descent of some of my lands being hereinbefore altered only in case any of my sons to whom such lands are respectively devised should die under age and unmarried while their lands remained in the common stock of my Estate and had not yet come into their actual possession.—And whereas I hold sundry tracts of land in the county of Hampshire in Virginia, and in the county of Frederick in the province of Maryland near Fort Cumberland, patented in my name in trust for the Ohio Company, I authorize and direct my Executors to convey the same by such deeds as council learned in the law shall advise (with special warranty only against my heirs and all claiming under me) unto the said Ohio Company upon their paying the ballance of my bond with the Interest thereon due to Mrs. Bladen or Mrs. Tasker's Executors, for the purchase of part of the said lands so that the said bond may be taken up and cancelled and my Estate indemnified therefrom excepting and reserving unto my eldest son George Mason and his heirs forever my part and share of and in the said lands as a member of the said Ohio Company.

Item : All the remaining part of my slaves with their increase, stocks of all kinds, and money and debts due to me, crops, profits and all other personal Estate whatsoever in the common stock not herein otherwise disposed of I give and bequeath unto my four youngest sons William, Thomson, John and Thomas (whom I make my residuary legatees) and their heirs forever to be equally divided between them when and as they respectively arrive at the age of twenty-one years or marry, whichever shall first happen, and if any one or more of my said youngest sons should die under age and unmarried, then and in that case it is my will and desire and I hereby direct and order, that all the slaves together with all the stocks, money or other personal Estate whatsoever bequeathed to such son or sons or which he or they would have been entitled to upon coming of age or marrying, shall be equally divided between the survivors of all my five sons George, William, Thomson, John and Thomas, such of them as may happen to be of age or married at the time to receive their part of the same and the residue to remain in the common stock until the others respectively come of age or marry or shall go to the survivor of my said five sons if only one of them should live to come of age or marry, and if any of my sons or daughters should happen to marry and die during the minority of their Brothers or Sisters leaving a child or children behind them, it is my Will and desire and I hereby direct and order that such child or children shall receive the same part or portion of the Estate which the parent or parents would have been entitled to upon the death of any of my sons or daughters respectively under age and unmarried as aforesaid.

And whereas there is in my hands as Executor of Mr. William Eilbeck decd. a considerable sum (as will appear by my account with his Estate) which by his Will is bequeathed to and divided among his Grandchildren, my children, which I am answerable to them for and have a power of laying out for their benefit, and as I have hereinbefore not only given much more to each of my said children than their respective shares of his Estate in my hands amounts to but have disposed both of that and my own Estate among them in order to make the best provision in my power for them all, and if any of my children were notwithstanding to claim after my death their parts of their said Grandfather's Estate in my hands over and above what I have given them, it would occasion much confusion and alter the disposition which I have hereinbefore made to the prejudice and injury of some of my children, I do therefore declare that what I have hereinbefore given unto all and each of my said children is inclusive of and in satisfaction for what was due to them from me as Mr. Eilbeck's Executor and that the several devises, bequests and legacys herein devised bequeathed or given to each of my said children are upon express condition of each of them respectively releasing and discharging my Estate and Executors from any claim or demand on account of the ballance due from me to the said Mr. Eilbeck's Estate per account already settled or to be settled with the commissary in Maryland, and if any one or more of my said children when they respectively come of age should refuse to release and discharge my Executors accordingly, then and in that case it is my Will and desire and I hereby direct and order that all the Estate herein by me given to such child or children shall be forfeited and shall go to

and be equally divided among my other children and their heirs
forever. And as there are debts due to me to a considerable
amount by bond the yearly interest of which will be a great advantage to the common stock of my Estate, I desire and direct my
Executors to continue the said debts upon interest either in such
hands as they shall be in at the time of my death, or in such other
hands and upon such other security as they in their discretion shall
judge best, until the money shall be wanting from time to time for
any of the purposes by me directed, and likewise to let out upon
interest such money as can at any time be spared out of the profits
of my Estate.—I also authorize and direct my Executors to settle
a Quarter or Quarters upon my land between Dogues Run and the
South Branch of little Hunting Creek, as hereinbefore mentioned
(unless the same shall have been settled by me before my death)
when they shall think it most for the interest of my Estate so
to do, as also upon any of the other lands herein devised to
either of my three youngest sons Thomson, John or Thomas,
either with any slaves that can be spared from my other Quarters or plantations or with slaves to be purchased by them for
that purpose with any money that can be spared out of the common stock of my Estate, without interfering with my daughters'
Fortunes or with the money bequeathed unto my youngest son
Thomas, all which Quarters and slaves are to be considered as part
of the common stock for the purposes before expressed.

I likewise impower and direct my Executors to erect marble
Tomb stones over the graves of my honored father and mother and
my dear wife if the same is not done by me in my life time. And
that no dispute or difficulty may arise to my Executors or my
children about the manner in which that part of my estate given
to my residuary Legatees is to be divided among them, I hereby
declare it to be my Will and intention that when each or either of
them comes of age or marrys, he is to receive his part or portion
thereof as it stands at such time respectively (always having regard
to and reserving a sufficient sum of my money and debts still in
the common stock to pay the money that may hereafter be due to
any of my daughters for their fortunes, as well as the money
bequeathed to my youngest son Thomas Mason) so that any of
them after having received and withdrawn their parts from the
common stock are not to be entitled to any share of the subse-

quent increase or profits thereof, and consequently not to any of the slaves that may afterwards be born or purchased, nor liable to any loss that may happen therein except such part of the common stock as may happen afterwards to fall to them by the death of some of their brothers or sisters, yet the fortunes herein given to my daughters in money are to be secured to them notwithstanding at all events, and in case of any deficiency in their said fortunes by failure of securitys or any other inevitable accident, the same is to be made good in equal proportion by all my residuary Legatees as well those who had before as those who had not received their parts out of the common stock. And I appoint my good friends the Revd. Mr. James Scott, the Revd. Mr. Lee Massey, Mr. John West jun., Colo. George Washington and Mr. Alexander Henderson (whenever it shall be necessary) to make such estimation, division and alotment to and among my several residuary legatees, and it is my Will and desire and I hereby direct and order that such estimation, division and alotment as they or any three of them shall from time to time make and give under their hands and seals, shall to all intents and purposes whatsoever be conclusive and binding upon my said residuary Legatees and their heirs. I hope they will be so charitable as not to refuse undertaking this trouble for the sake of a friend who when living would cheerfully have done them any good office in his power.

I recommend it to my sons from my own experience in life, to prefer the happiness of independance and a private station to the troubles and vexation of publick business, but if either their own inclinations or the necessity of the times should engage them in public affairs, I charge them on a father's blessing never to let the motives of private interest or ambition induce them to betray, nor the terrors of poverty and disgrace, or the fear of danger or of death, deter them from asserting the liberty of their country and endeavoring to transmit to their posterity those sacred rights to which themselves were born.

I release and remit unto my brother Thomson Mason and his heirs forever, a certain debt of three hundred and ten pounds, four shillings and five pence ⅜ sterling and nine pounds twelve shillings and four pence currency, due to me on account of money advanced for him many years ago while he was in England, for which it was never my intention to make him answerable as will appear by an entry to that purpose in my own handwriting annexed to the account in my book. And whereas my said brother is indebted to me a further considerable sum on account of a protested bill of exchange drawn by him and of a bond I paid for him to Mrs. Bronaugh's Estate, I desire and direct my Executors not to bring any suit against him for the recovery of the said debt but to wait until he can conveniently pay the same.—I give and bequeath unto Mrs. Heath the wife of Thomas Heath of Stafford County, the sum of forty shillings sterling in first cost of goods a year, to be laid out in necessarys for her own particular use during her life, and if ever her son Mr. Richard Hewit my old schoolfellow and acquaintance from my childhood, should unfortunately be reduced to necessitous circumstances I desire and direct my Executors to supply him with necessarys for his support and maintenance out of my Estate, and I particularly recommend this care to my children if it should be necessary after they come of age.

I give to Mr. John Moncure a mourning ring of three Guineas value which I desire him to wear in memory of my esteem for my much lamented friend his deceased father. I desire my old and long tryed friends the Rev. Mr. James Scott and Mr. John West junr. each of them to accept of a mourning ring of the same value. I leave to my friend and relation the Rev. Mr. Lee Massey a mourning ring of the same value, and I entreat the favour of him to advise and assist my Executors in the direction and management of my affairs. I am encouraged to request this of him from the experience I have had myself of his good offices that way, and I am satisfied that both he and my worthy friend Mr. Cockburn will excuse the trouble I now give them, when they reflect upon the necessity that dying men are under of thus employing the care and kindness of the living which must also one day be their own case, and as the most acceptable acknowledgement I can make them, I desire them to receive out of the common stock of my Estate, the sum of ten pounds a year to be laid out by them in private charitys upon such as they shall judge worthy objects. I also give to my cousin Mrs. Cockburn a mourning ring of the same value, and desire her and my cousin Miss Bronaugh and Mr. Cockburn to accept of a suit of mourning each. Lastly, I appoint my eldest son George Mason and my good friend Mr. Martin Cockburn, Executors of this my last Will and Testament and guardians to my children until they respectively come of age. And it is my Will and desire and I hereby direct and order that no securitys shall be required of them by the court but only their own bonds taken for the performance. In Witness whereof I have to this my said last Will and testament all in my own handwriting and contained in fifteen pages set my hand and affixed my seal this 20th day of March in the year of our Lord one Thousand seven hundred and seventy three.

GEORGE MASON.

[SEAL.]

Signed and sealed and published and declared to be the }
   last Will and Testament of Mr. George Mason in our }
   presence and subscribed by us in his presence. }

GUSTS. SCOTT,
ELIZABETH BRONAUGH,
ANN COCKBURN,
JOHN WEST, junr.,
ROBT. GRAHAM,
JOHN DAVIDSON.

At a court contd. and held for Fairfax County 16th October 1792 this will was presented in court by George Mason one of the Executors therein named who made oath thereto and the same being proved by the oath of Ann Cockburn and Robert Graham is admitted to record and the said Executor having performed what the law requires in such cases a certificate is granted him for obtaining a probate thereof in due form.

Teste   P. WAGENER, Cl. Cur.

LAND DESCRIBED IN GEORGE MASON'S WILL, AND NOW OWNED BY HIS DESCENDANTS.

It was incorrectly stated in one of the earlier chapters of these volumes that "Lexington" was the only one of the Mason places in Virginia now in the family. The writer had overlooked "Okeley," in Fairfax County, about six miles from Alexandria. The farms of "Okeley" and "Huntley" were both parts of the estate bequeathed by George Mason to his son, Thomson Mason, of

"Hollin Hall." A double ditch is still to be seen on the southern border of these two places, extending several miles from east to west, with a broad space about thirty feet wide separating the two ditches. These mark the line between the lands of George Mason and George Washington, as they were in the lives of those gentlemen. In General Washington's will, he refers "to the back line or outer boundary of the tract between Thompson Mason and myself . . . (now double ditching, with a post-and-rail fence thereon)," etc. And he mentions, in another place, "the new double ditch," in connection with the boundary line between "Mount Vernon" and the Mason property. In adding to his estate, he had purchased land at one time from George Mason. And among the Washington papers preserved in the Lewis and Washington families, and recently sold to autograph collectors, are three letters of George Mason, on the subject of the bounds between the Washington and Mason plantations, one written in 1768, the others in 1769. Washington adds a memorandum to the former, saying that "the lines to which this letter has reference were settled by and between Colonel Mason and myself the 19th of April, 1769 as will appear . . . by a survey thereof made on that day in his presence and with his approbation."

"Huntley," owned by Judge Thomson F. Mason, of "Colross," son of Thomson Mason, of "Hollin Hall," passed out of the family some years ago. "Okeley," which was the home of Dr. Richard Chichester Mason, another son of Thomson Mason, is still in possession of his descendants, and is the residence of Mr. Beverley Randolph Mason. The commodious dwelling-house, formerly to be seen there, however, was burned to the ground during the late war, and many valuable family papers perished in this wanton and unnecessary destruction of private property. The estate, of about seven thousand acres, is a beautiful and productive one.

A descendant of Thomas Mason, youngest son of George Mason, owns a farm in Charles County, Maryland, which may have been some of it, part of the Maryland land mentioned in the will of the second Col. George Mason. In this connection, the reader interested in the subject is referred to an article in *The Critic*, Richmond, Va., Oct. 22, 1888, entitled "Curious Wills in the Mason Family."

EXTRACT FROM A LETTER OF LUND WASHINGTON TO GENERAL
WASHINGTON.

The following extract from a letter of Lund Washington to
General Washington, dated " Mount Vernon," February 18, 1778,
kindly furnished the author by Dr. Joseph M. Toner, while these
volumes are going through the press, relates to "Conway's Cabal,"
which was supposed to have found supporters among members
of Congress. The conversation here related gives interesting
testimony to the admiration which was felt both by George
Mason and Richard Henry Lee, for the genius and patriotism of
the Commander-in-chief.

"Colonel Mason (who I showed your letter of the 16th of January) tells me he was informed of the cabal against you, before he
left Williamsburg, and some had hinted to him that R. H. Lee
was one suspected of having a hand in it, and as they knew the
intimacy existing between them, begged that he would talk to Lee
and discover whether anything of the sort was in agitation or not.
He did so. That Lee declares no such thing or even a hint has
ever been mentioned in Congress, and that he should look upon
it as one of the greatest misfortunes that could befall this continent, should you by any means whatever give up the command
of the army, for fully convinced he was in his own opinion no
other man upon this continent was equal to the task ; that he had
often lamented the heavy burden you bare, and the difficulties
you had to surmount more than any man ever had before. For
his part he looked upon it as one among the many favors we had
received from above, that the Supreme Being had been pleased to
save and protect in the most miraculous degree the only man in
whom every one could confide in. Mr. Mason is of opinion it is a
Tory manœuver for he thinks no friend to America can be an
enemy to you, for ' by ———,' which was his expression, there is
not nor ever was in the world a man who acted from a more laud-
able and disinterested motive than you do, and that he defied all
history to show a war, begun, and carried on, under more disad-
vantages than the present ; nor, he would venture to affirm one
that had been better conducted so far as it depended on the
Commander-in-Chief, for that he had observed you had foreseen
and pointed out what would be the event of all the blunders com-

mitted by the different legislatures, and that wherever you had given your opinion the event had proved you were right, then enumerated a number of instances to prove his assertion. Mr. Mason concluded by saying that he was convinced from the whole of his conversation with Lee, Harrison, and other members of Congress, that a faction in Congress against you had never existed. Our conversation passed in Alexandria before several gentlemen, among whom was Major Jennifer of Maryland."

ARMS OF MASON, FOWKE, AND THOMSON (OR THOMPSON) FAMILIES.

Masons of Stratford-upon-Avon, Warwickshire : Az. a point with three embattlements arg. charged with fleur-de-lis gu., on the middle battlement a dove with wings displayed standing thereon, proper. *Crest*—a talbot pass. regardant ar. eared sa. holding in his mouth a hart's horn or. *Motto*—Pro Patria Semper. (This was altered by George Mason of Gunston, after the Revolution to Pro Republica Semper.)

Fowkes of Gunston, Staffordshire : Vert., a fleur-de-lis ar., on a chief indented of the second a lion pass. gu. with a crescent difference sa. *Crest*—an Indian goat's head erased ar. *Motto*—Optimum Est Alienâ Frui Insaniâ.

Thompsons of Yorkshire : Per fesse ar. and sa. a fess counter-embattled betw. three falcons counterchanged, belled and jessed or. *Crest*—an arm embowed in armour, quarterly, or. and az. the gauntlet ppr. holding the truncheon of a broken lance of the first.

INDEX.

A

Aberdeen, Scotland, ii., 17

Accohick, Accokeek, Aquaceek, plantation of, i., 2, 16, 20, 22

Accotink Run. *See* Creeks.

Accotink turnpike, i., 112

Acoquane. *See* Occoquon.

Adam, Robert, i., 427

Adams, George, ii., 462 ; John, i., 180, 224, 257, 258, ii., 33, 39, 184, 237, 374, 377 ; John Quincy, i., vi.; Samuel, i., 168, 171, 180, 258, 336, ii., 217, 218, 283, 377 ; Thomas, i., 295

Adams' "Defence of the American Constitutions," ii., 237 ; "Thoughts on Government," i., 224, 257, 258

Adventurers for Virginia, i., 4, 156, 396-398, 401

Africa, i., 153

African, company, *see* Companies ; merchants, ii., 419 ; slavery, slave-trade, *see* Slaves.

Aix-la-Chapelle, peace of, i., 414

Alaska, ii., 289

Albany, N. Y., i., xiv., 36

Albemarle County, Va., i., 173, 176, 314

Albemarle, George, Duke of, i., 408

Albemarle Resolutions, i., 173, 174

Aldborough, England, i., 3

Alexander family, i., 92, 93 ; MSS. of, i., 38, 118.

Alexander, Charles, i., 118, 427 ; Gustavus B., i., 92 ; John, i., 93, 125, 392, ii., 39 ; Mr., i., 63, 87, 90, ii., 301, 337 ; Philip, i., 77, 93, 427 ; Philip of Chotank, ii., 36-39, 57

Alexandria, Va., i., xi.-xiv., 61, 63, 64, 75-77, 85, 87, 90, 93, 103, 112, 115, 120, 128, 154, 173, 177, 182,

185, 189, 191, 196, 198, 201, 217, 267, 269, 280, 281, 305, 315, 418, ii., 5, 9, 10, 12, 63, 64, 67, 79, 81, 82, 84, 92, 96, 97, 180-182, 209-211, 302, 310, 324, 335, 336, 348-351, 357-360, 455, 456, 472, 475

Alexandria Museum, i., 169

Alexandrians, ii., 336

Algerines, ii., 63, 328

Alien and Sedition laws, i., viii., ii., 417

Allerton, Maj. Isaac, i., 12, 15, 17, 19

Allison, William, ii., 47

Ambler, Jacqueline, ii., 338, 340 ; Richard, i., 55, ii., 340

America, i., ix., xiii., 1, 53, 59, 78, 87, 96, 97, 123, 125, 126, 129, 130, 142, 150, 152, 157, 175, 177, 195, 210, 216, 231, 237, 249, 263, 271, 293, 294, 299, 301, 317, 330, 333, 341, 343, 352, 360, 364, 366, 384-388, 390, 393-396, 398, 399, 411, 419, 421, 423, 426, 427, 432, 443, ii., 3, 4, 14, 16, 20, 24, 26, 28, 34, 40, 45-47, 49, 51, 59, 69, 114, 121, 130, 134, 135, 178, 211, 217, 230, 259, 277, 296, 301, 306, 317, 324, 327, 334, 368, 384, 386, 398, 404, 409, 414, 420, 425, 433, 454, 474

American, admirers, i., 153, 319 ; affairs, i., 319 ; army, i., 363, ii., 34, 50 ; cause, i., 296, 297, ii., 4, 9, 16, 18 ; charters, i., 399 ; coast, ii., 5 ; colonies, i., 175, 419, 421 ; ii., 25, 344 ; commerce, i., 389, 390 ; commissioners, ii., 48 ; Congress, i., 298 ; consignments, ii., 335 ; consul, i., 368 ; consul-general, ii., 305 ; council, ii., 29 ; discipline, i., 150 ; doctrines, i., 178 ; dominions, i., 154, 421 ; executive, ii., 111 ; forces, ii., 19 ; freedom, i., 138 ; gallons, ii., 314 ; government, i.,

mittee, 64 ; on commission to settle compact with Maryland, 72 ; mentioned in letter of G. Mason as absent from meeting of commissioners, 83 ; writes to Mason without referring to it, 84 ; his absence owing to a mistake in not receiving proper notification, 84 ; is in favor of religious assessment, 90 ; delegate to Annapolis Convention, 93 ; attends the Convention, 94 ; delegate to Federal Convention, 97 ; Governor of Virginia, 98 ; concurs with Mason on States-rights, 98 ; letters of George Mason to, in reference to expenses of delegates, 98, 99 ; in the Convention, 108 ; brings forward plan of government, 108 ; first resolution of his debated, 108 ; sixth resolution gave power to coerce a State, 109 ; failed to see the danger apparent to Mason, 109 ; sustains Mason's idea of a triple executive, 116 ; his plan considered in speech of Mason, 120 ; concurs with Mason as to treatment of new States, 133 ; moved that periodical census be taken to regulate representation, 135 ; his observations on the subject referred to by Sherman, 136 ; sustains Madison's motion for the appointment of the judiciary by the Executive, 142 ; one of the five members constituting Committee of Detail, 144 ; approved of section giving the House power to originate money bills, 150 ; concurs with Madison and Mason in holding a bare majority of a quorum insufficient to expel, 152 ; amends clause relating to money bills, 153 ; states his objections to the Constitution, 170 ; moves to submit it to Congress, State Legislatures, and Conventions, and finally to second General Convention, 171 ; supports Mason on veto question, 171 ; votes for bill of rights, 172 ; supports motion of Mason relating to standing armies in time of peace, 174 ; moves to except cases of treason from pardoning power of Executive, 175 ; considers powers given by the Constitution dangerous and indefinite, and moves for amendments to be offered by State Conventions to a Second Federal Convention, 176 ; refuses to sign the Constitution,

176 ; draft of a constitution in his handwriting among papers of Mason, 179 ; writes from Alexandria to Madison, as to sentiments of its inhabitants, 181 ; wrote to Mason, but his letter not extant, 181, 182 ; publishes his objections to the Constitution, 184 ; in the Assembly, 189 ; writes Madison in reference to Mason, 189 ; an academy called after him, 201 ; named one of the trustees, 201 ; personal characteristics as given by Cyrus Griffin, 210 ; his position on subject of Constitution considered wavering, 210 ; Washington apparently aware of his change of party, 210 ; in the Virginia Convention, 219 ; eulogy of his talents by Wirt, 219 ; comes out as a Federalist leader, 219, 225 ; speaks in reply to Henry, 225, 226, 392 ; Federalists elated by his accession to their ranks, 227 ; expediency his only plea for change of views, 228, 392 ; replies to Mason's argument as to impracticability of republican government in extensive territory, 229 ; his inconsistency of opinion, 230 ; reflects on Mason and Henry as law-makers, 230 ; Henry draws him out and then retorts upon him, 231 ; Randolph's angry reply, 232 ; exciting scene on the occasion, 232 ; insults Henry and refuses to explain his insinuations, 232 ; his pleas for accepting the Constitution answered by Mason, 239, 404–406 ; his illogical, indefensible position pointed out, 239, 406 ; dangers of rejection as given by Randolph ridiculed by Grayson, 241 ; speaks on subject of navigation of the Mississippi, 242 ; allusion to Randolph's course in letter of Col. Bland, 243, 244 ; danger of a duel between Randolph and Henry, 243 ; speaks on subject of the militia, 245 ; on the power of Congress over federal district, 248 ; his reference to the Hague answered by Mason, 248, 417 ; speaks in reply to Henry, 251 ; his definition of *ex post facto* law disputed by Mason, 252, 422 ; Mason proposes to make use of Randolph's former arguments against Constitution, 253, 254 ; Randolph speaks in reply, 254 ; declares that he still sees

THE END.

CPSIA information can be obtained
at www.ICGtesting.com
Printed in the USA
BVHW010209040619
549916BV00037B/330/P